FRANK AYDELOTTE OF SWARTHMORE

I: Frank Aydelotte. Portrait by Charles Hopkinson; courtesy W. O. Aydelotte.

Frank Aydelotte
of Swarthmore

BY

FRANCES BLANSHARD

Edited and with a Preface by

BRAND BLANSHARD

WESLEYAN UNIVERSITY PRESS

Middletown, Connecticut

Breaking the Academic Lockstep, by Frank Aydelotte, copyright © 1944 by Harper & Row, Publishers, Incorporated; quoted herein by permission of Harper & Row.

I Remember, by Abraham Flexner, copyright © 1940 by Abraham Flexner; quoted herein by permission of Simon & Schuster, Inc.

Universities: American, English, German, by Abraham Flexner, copyright © 1930 by Oxford University Press; quoted herein by permission of Oxford University Press.

The publishers gratefully acknowledge that publication of this work has been aided by grants from The Institute for Advanced Study and Swarthmore College.

ISBN: 0-8195-4023-4
Library of Congress Catalog Card Number: 70-108646
Manufactured in the United States of America
FIRST EDITION

CONTENTS

ILLUSTRATIONS

AUTHOR'S PREFACE

WHY a life of Frank Aydelotte? Because for thirty-five years he was a prolific source of ideas and a potent force for change in American higher education. His insistence was on quality—on higher academic standards and on the selection of persons with outstanding ability for special opportunities. His approach owed much to a Rhodes Scholarship at Oxford and the experience at first hand of a type of education differing widely both from that of the United States and from that of Germany, which America had been trying to emulate. Oxford stood in his eyes for humane and liberal values, fostered by small residential colleges where students were treated as individuals and as adults, where they were exposed to an athletic tradition remote from ours, and where, at the end of their course, they were expected to pass examinations at once exacting and comprehensive, set by scholars who were strangers to them.

Frank Aydelotte was much impressed by the Oxonian system and convinced that it had many features which Americans could study with profit. He was among the first to deplore the sacrifice of quality to quantity in our colleges and particularly the failure to stimulate gifted persons to do their best. When he began to teach English at Indiana University, he adopted what he conceived to be Oxford methods of making each of his courses a training in thought, notably the required course in writing. Then, with characteristic expansiveness, he put his experience at the service of other teachers through articles and books which gave new life to the teaching of English.

After World War I, when Germany's role had alienated American educators, Aydelotte drew on his Oxonian experience for a new system of honors courses designed to give the ablest students opportunities commensurate with their talents. He tried this out as President of Swarthmore College, where his program was a spur to similar efforts in many other institutions. Having begun to atone for the neglect of superior undergraduates, he went on to the aid of other gifted groups. As American Secretary to the Rhodes Trustees, he improved vastly the methods of detecting and selecting candidates for the Rhodes Scholarships. When Senator Guggenheim asked him to draft the program for the Guggenheim Foundation, he devised the famous fellowships, designed to set young scholars and artists free to fulfill their promise. And for older thinkers, already distinguished, he aided Abraham Flexner in planning the Institute for Advanced Study at Princeton, where he later became Director.

Frank Aydelotte's concept of excellence stressed freedom from provincialism. Gifted individuals should broaden their outlook by some residence abroad, and they would further international understanding in doing so. He echoed Cecil Rhodes's belief that "educational relations form the strongest tie." Ambitious to persuade "an American Cecil Rhodes" to bring British students to this country, he made detailed plans for such a scheme, which were largely taken over and applied by the Commonwealth Fund for its fellowships.

He won support for this cause by an enthusiasm that was infectious and all but irresistible, and when he discovered a good thing, he told the world about it joyfully, making his hearers feel that to join forces with him was a privilege. Though sometimes called "lucky Aydelotte," he succeeded because his programs were planned to the last detail.

His particular blend of energy, optimism, friendliness, and zest he owed partly to his middle-western boyhood in years when the qualities of a pioneer community were still cherished. His life is an American success story, unusual in that the hero's field is education. Starting in a small town on the prairie, as it then was, and in the face of such handicaps as a lame right arm, a stammer, and an abbreviated high-school course, he became a reformer and leader in American education and worked so effectively for educational ties between England and America that he was awarded an honorary knighthood by the Queen.

Frank Aydelotte's story should make instructive reading. But why should *I* undertake to tell it? Partly because of family connections. My husband was the first Rhodes Scholar he brought to Swarthmore to help develop his honors program. As wife of a Rhodes Scholar, I visited Oxford many times and came to see what the place might mean to an American college teacher. To picture Frank Aydelotte's boyhood in Sullivan was the easier because I had spent many summers in just such a middle-western town. My most important direct knowledge of his work I gained through serving as one of the Deans of Swarthmore during fourteen years of his administration. Most important of all, I have had the approval and sympathetic encouragement of the subject who sat for the portrait.

— FRANCES BLANSHARD

EDITOR'S PREFACE

FRANK AYDELOTTE hoped, and for a while intended, to write his own biography. Over the years he had carefully kept the records of his many activities and his immense correspondence, and when his retirement came, he had rows and rows of filing cabinets bulging with material. But he was always more concerned with the future than with the past. While in office, he was far too busy for retrospection, and when, in retirement and failing strength, he looked at those rows of cabinets, his resolution faltered. He no longer felt equal to the task of winnowing the mountainous material and extracting a story from it. At this point Frances Blanshard inquired diffidently whether he would care to have her undertake it. He said Yes at once and gratefully.

She was well qualified to do it. For fourteen years as a Dean at Swarthmore College she had worked in an office adjoining his, taking counsel with him constantly, studying his methods and ideas, helping to shape and execute his plans for the college, criticizing drafts of his speeches and letters, serving in countless ways as his apprentice, adjutant, and buffer against the world. If anyone knew his ideas and ideals regarding American education, she did. He placed all his files at her disposal, supplied her with early memories and general counsels, and bade her Godspeed. He died in 1956 when she was just getting under way.

The mountain of documents proved higher and the task far longer than she realized at the start. The care of her husband and her house always stood first in her mind, and she felt free to work at her biography only when these other claims had been met. And she found that a biography may call for much besides reading and writing. Repeated journeys were needed to the little town in the Midwest where Frank Aydelotte was born and where memories of him still lingered; to Swarthmore, where his reputation was made; to Princeton, where he spent his last years; and to his summer home in Waterford, Connecticut, where his archives are stored. She made a list, forever lengthening, of scholars and administrators who had known him, and like a bee collecting treasure she flew from one to another, storing the details she gathered in her many notebooks or in her retentive and accurate memory.

The book preoccupied her free time for many years. If it moved slowly, this was not only because of competing claims on her time but also because of her humility about her own writing. She would read over a chapter, pronounce it dull or not rightly organized, and do it over again from the beginning. There is hardly a page that follows which is not the product of many revisions. She had the researcher's care for correct detail, but she wanted to tell a readable story of a remarkable man, not to document him for storage on some remote shelf in a library. Characteristically, she wished her footnotes stowed away at the back of the book. Those who read her easy narrative without looking at this scholarly apparatus will hardly guess how much research went into the writing.

The momentum increased as the task neared its end. She was beginning to see light at the end of the tunnel and to feel the exhilaration of a goal attained and freedom near. Fifteen of the seventeen chapters she had planned were complete. During the day of December 9, 1966, she was busy as usual with her housework and her typewriter; that evening she was gone, cut off by a heart attack that was appallingly sudden and unexpected, though mercifully short. A sheet of her manuscript stood half filled in her typewriter.

When I went over what she had written, I was clear not only that it must be published but also that it should not be published in truncated form. So the last two chapters are mine. I have gone over the manuscript for the press and slightly compressed it, but the book never received the final revision that she would have given it. If errors of fact remain, they must be charged to me.

It is unlikely that anyone will read this book without wishing to know more about its author, though there is room here for only the essential facts. She was born in Fayette, Missouri, in 1895. Her father, Francis Bradshaw, and her mother, Margaret Rooker, were students together in the Yale Graduate School, he in Greek and she in English. The young man was appointed to an instructorship at Vanderbilt University, where he apparently had a distinguished career before him. But he was struck down almost at once by a fatal illness diagnosed as typhoid fever, leaving his wife and infant daughter desolate. The young mother returned with her child to her parents' home. Collecting herself after a year or so, she went back to a New Haven boardinghouse with her small daughter and was one of the first women to receive the doctorate from Yale. She became a professor of English at Smith College, where she taught for the remainder of her professional life.

She was resolved that her daughter should have a good education. Frances was entered as a student at the Capen School in Northampton and later at Smith College, where she was graduated near the head of her class in 1916, was elected to Phi Beta Kappa, and was awarded a graduate fellowship in philosophy. She chose to go to Columbia University, where there was a group of remarkable teachers of philosophy headed by Dewey, Woodbridge, and Montague. She took an M.A. and a Ph.D. at Columbia, the first after two years of study, the second many years later with a dissertation in aesthetics. Revised and enlarged, this dissertation was published in 1945 by the Columbia University Press under the title *The Retreat from Likeness in the Theory of Painting*, and it soon went into a second edition. It is the best account I know of the long, slow movement, beginning with Plato, that carried art from an attempt at copying its object to the nonobjective painting of today.

She met her future husband at Columbia, and their acquaintance ripened under circumstances unusual enough to be perhaps worth recalling. One of the most enthusiastic of John Dewey's disciples in those days was Albert C. Barnes, of Philadelphia, the discoverer and manufacturer of Argyrol, who later became famous as a collector of modern art. Having attended some of Dewey's seminars in social theory, he thought the professor should have a chance to test some of his theories against social facts. He reported to Dewey that there was a community of Polish immigrants in Philadelphia that was showing so high a resistance to the American ways of life as to have formed a kind of cyst within the city. Would Dewey be interested in examining this situation at first hand? Yes, answered Dewey; very much. Could he bring some of his graduate students with him? Barnes agreed and bought the group a house in the middle of the Polish district. The students Dewey invited were Frances Bradshaw, Brand Blanshard and his brother Paul, Irwin Edman, and the Polish novelist Anzia Yezierska. The group spent the summer of 1918 in Philadelphia inquiring into the ways of this Polish community and writing reports, some of which were printed by Mr. Barnes, on various aspects of the community life. Dewey wrote on the politics of the Poles. His inquiry quickly took him to the political movements of their homeland, and he ended by sending a long and warning report to the State Department about the nondemocratic tendencies of the Paderewski party. So far as I know, little ever came of this expedition except the friendships that developed among its younger members and among all these members for Dewey. But it was an exciting summer for Frances; she was the shepherdess and the household manager for the philosopher and his flock.

At the end of that summer she went to Hollins College, Virginia, as an instructor in philosophy, and her fiancé went into the Army. They were married shortly before he left for France and did not see each other for many interminable months. Her husband got his discharge in London in 1919; she rejoined him there, and they set off on a long-delayed honeymoon to the Isle of Wight. When it was over, they went on to Oxford. Her husband had been a Rhodes Scholar at Merton College, but had left Oxford in 1915 to serve as a British Army Y.M.C.A. secretary on the Tigris and in India. It was a rule that Rhodes Scholars could not marry while holding their scholarships. But the Rhodes Trustees suspended the rule to permit those who had married during the war to return with their wives and conclude their studies. So while her husband finished work for his degree, Frances became a noncollegiate student herself, listening to Schiller on philosophy, McDougall on psychology, the Master of Balliol, A. L. Smith, on Aristotle, and Ernest Barker on politics. She attended many club meetings where students with remarkable careers ahead—or in some cases already behind them—were likely to appear. She once remarked casually on returning from such a meeting that a shy young man sitting on the floor in the corner had spoken with exceptional point: he was Lawrence of Arabia.

That year in Oxford was a crucial one in her life, though it was not the most comfortable. The pair lived with the cheerful hardihood of youth in an icy flat in Marston Street. That seemed to matter little amid the incomparable beauty of the ancient city, where every quadrangle had its "immortal memories." She came to know at first hand the Oxford way of "reading" and teaching and to some extent its ways of thinking and discussion. She had a woman tutor of her own and used to chaperone another woman student to the rooms of a male tutor, where it was still considered improper for a woman to appear alone. She met a number of Rhodes Scholars who were later to achieve names in education: Stringfellow Barr and Scott Buchanan of St. John's, Felix Morley of Haverford, Charles Bagley of Dartmouth, Wilburt Davison of Duke, Wilder Penfield of McGill (who was to become a Canadian citizen and gain the Order of Merit). More important to her later writing, she became the firm friend of the Wylies (later Sir Francis and Lady Wylie), who administered the Rhodes Scholarships. Frank Aydelotte made one of his flying visits to Oxford in the spring of 1920, and she may have met him then for the first time. Aydelotte without Oxford would be unintelligible, and she did not know at the time how well her knowledge of Oxford would serve her when, many years later, she came to write his life.

The next year her husband went to Harvard in quest of a doctorate. The pair had little to go on in the way of money, and she was determined to find work of her own to help him through. For a week or two she answered ads and paced Boston streets without result. Then came the unexpected offer of an instructorship in English at Wellesley. She accepted joyously, and her husband saw her off daily on an early subway from Harvard Square, her pink cheeks and auburn hair making a bright spot among the grim-faced workingmen who were her fellow travelers at that hour. President M. Carey Thomas of Bryn Mawr descended on the Harvard Yard that spring and invited the pair to Bryn Mawr to replace the DeLagunas, who were about to go on sabbatical leave. The invitation was tempting, but it was for a year only, and when an offer came to her husband of a more permanent post at Michigan, they decided on a return to the Midwest.

They both expected Ann Arbor to be an enduring home, and they took a little house, with a mortgage on it, that was the first they could call their own. Frances preferred to go on teaching if she could, and for two years she did so, commuting to the State Normal College at Ypsilanti and continuing to teach English. Her interest in aesthetics was stimulated by much good talk with two friends, Dewitt H. Parker, who was then the best lecturer on philosophy at the University of Michigan, and E. F. Carritt, Oxford philosopher, who for the year 1924–1925 was a guest in the Blanshard home. He remained a warm friend till his death some thirty-five years later, and Frances and her husband always went to see him in his house on Boar's Hill when they returned to England.

In the spring of 1925 came an invitation to the pair from President Aydelotte to visit Swarthmore as his guest for a few days to see something of the college and to meet some members of the faculty. It was clear enough what he had in mind. He had just inaugurated the "honors system" at the college, which drew heavily on his Oxford experience, and in adding members to his staff he preferred persons who had been similarly exposed. The visit was made at Easter time, when the Swarthmore campus, always attractive, was breaking into bloom. The two young people were given a sharp but kindly scrutiny by senior faculty members. They attended the Friends' Meeting, where their future colleague Jesse Holmes gave the arresting Easter injunction that they should live intensely in the present, since they would be a long time dead. This, they concluded, must be a community in which there was a large liberty of brain and tongue. They went back to Ann Arbor with the conviction that important things for American education were brewing on the Swarthmore campus and that in Aydelotte the college had a leader of energy and vision. They promptly sent him word that they would come.

Frances Blanshard was appointed an instructor in philosophy. A year later, when Dean Ethel Brewster went on leave, she was made an acting Dean. Swarthmore had no Dean of Women in the ordinary sense; it had a man and a woman Dean, each of whom had academic as well as social responsibility. After a further year as Associate Dean, she succeeded Miss Brewster as a regular Dean of the college and except for brief leaves served in that office for the seventeen remaining years of her life at Swarthmore.

These were crucial years for the college, when it was breaking loose from its position as a respectable though not very well known Quaker institution to its present position as one of the foremost American liberal arts colleges. Frances Blanshard has told the story in vivid detail in the pages that follow. In a sense they are pages of autobiography. She characteristically says almost nothing of herself, but she was in the thick of all these struggles over the reform of the curriculum, alumni pressures, standards of admission, and particularly everything affecting the women students—their societies, sports, scholarship, morale, and—occasionally—morals. The administration prized her quiet responsibility and happily deposited at her uncomplaining door jobs that no one else wanted, such as editing the college catalogue. The women students were ready to make a confidante of her; some of them called her St. Frances because she was patient and sympathetic and would never betray a confidence. She constantly surprised them by how much she knew about them; she had studied their records in admitting them; she had admonished and advised and brooded over them along their way; and when she presented them at Commencement for their degrees, they were amused and amazed to see how seldom she had to refer to the list before her, even for their middle names.

For twenty years she and her husband lived on the Swarthmore campus or its borders. Their well-known red Chow, Pooh, first conducted her husband ceremonially to his eight-o'clock class, then returned and conducted her at nine to her office. This office was next door to the President's on the ground floor of Parrish Hall, where it was temptingly accessible to every student and staff member, though partially guarded by a series of able and devoted secretaries. Here Frances dictated her thousands of letters and interviewed countless students regarding their academic problems and personal upheavals. Happily she had a women's student government with whom she could talk things out and come to a joint agreement about the guidelines of student conduct; and the rules thus arrived at were notably well kept. She often spoke of how much she owed to the character of the women students, who were for the most part serious and self-respecting and felt "the generation gap" less keenly than their successors of today. She was also grateful for the Quaker tradition in which she found "sweet reasonableness" to be more than a name. She early joined the Society of Friends, regularly attended the First Day Meeting, and often contributed to its sincere and simple ministry.

When her husband was invited to Yale in 1945, he was naturally concerned about what an acceptance would mean for her; after all, she stood well above him in the academic hierarchy. But without hesitation she urged him to accept. She would no doubt have done so from devotion anyhow, but after her long and taxing years in the Dean's office, she was not averse to a quieter life. So the small child who had crowed over her mother in a Yale doctor's gown returned to New Haven, after forty-five years, as a faculty wife.

But it was not in her nature to be merely a faculty wife. Almost at once she was embroiled in the life of the city, doing those numberless unpaid and uncelebrated things that able women are called on to do. Mayor Lee, suspecting that here was a new municipal servant, appointed her to a commission to draw up a charter for the city, and she sat through dozens of protracted discussions in City Hall. Coming to New Haven just at the end of the war, she was asked by the Red Cross to visit the families of many Polish and Italian servicemen in the city, carrying messages and arranging relief. She served on the Civil Liberties Council. She was made president of the League of Women Voters. She was president of the Smith Club of New Haven and was elected a trustee of Smith College, which conferred on her in 1946 an honorary Doctorate of Laws. She was a trustee of the Day-Prospect Hill School for Girls. She was appointed by President Griswold to a committee on the position of women in the Yale Graduate School, and when the first residence for these women was built, Helen Hadley Hall, she was made chairman of its body of fellows. The impression she made on fellows and students alike was indicated by their response to the news of her death. They raised a Frances Blanshard Fund of ten thousand dollars to endow an annual visit by a distinguished woman to the Yale Graduate School.

Many intervals during these years she spent abroad with her husband. There was one memorable summer at the Seminar for American Studies at Salzburg, Austria, and another in France where she traveled about to Spanish refugee camps with Friends Service workers, her skill in languages making her a useful interpreter. She accompanied her husband to philosophical conferences in Brussels, Venice, Mexico, and Jerusalem. But most of all she enjoyed the longer visits to England and Scotland. During one leave of a year and a half, the two settled down in the historic little city of St. Andrews, within easy walking distance of its famous golf courses, and they often went out of an afternoon for a game played to the accompaniment of skylarks overhead and the rumble of the North Sea in the offing. When they were in London, they usually found lodgings near the British Museum, where they could pursue their researches together in the great library and at the day's end pick up a quick dinner in a local restaurant and go on to a London theatre. In one season they saw thirty plays.

Frances was not demanding about lodgings. Sometimes the pair stayed in a bed-and-breakfast hotel; for one fortunate season they had an apartment in Lincoln's Inn, in rooms that Sir Thomas More might have occupied; for another they lived a few doors from where Dickens wrote *Pickwick Papers;* and for a few months they inherited the house, library, and two servants of Sir Richard Livingstone in Oxford while he was away lecturing in their own country. Frances was equal to any exigency that arose. She enjoyed cooking and keeping her husband fit. And she needed all her arts in the days of postwar British rationing, when housewives had to stand patiently in a queue to buy their "ten-penny-worth of gristle."

Wives who accompany husbands on scholarly sabbaticals often have a thin time of it. Frances never did. She had her own projects of research, which kept her happily busy. One that especially interested her was proposed by her friend Helen Darbishire, Principal of Somerville College, Oxford, the editor of Wordsworth. Nobody knew how many likenesses of Wordsworth, in paint, etching, or marble, had been made or where they were. Frances undertook to find out. She found more than sixty of them, and in her book *The Portraits of Wordsworth* she has reproduced them and reported all that is known about them. This admirably scholarly and readable book (published in England by Allen and Unwin and in this country by the Cornell University Press) has had less notice than it deserves.

She once remarked that "a research worker may enjoy the excitement of living in an unusually pleasant detective story without a criminal or a corpse." A minor example will show what she meant. It was known that a drawing of Wordsworth had been made in his old age by a certain "L. Wyon." Frances ran down an obituary in *The Times* of August 29, 1891, reporting that a Leonard Charles Wyon, just deceased, had in his youth made "a remarkably fine portrait of Wordsworth." This was a good lead, but what had become of the portrait? She went to the English depository of wills in Somerset House and found the will of L. C. Wyon. She writes:

> The portrait itself was not mentioned, but the will listed one among Wyon's sons, William, as very young at the time. A boy in 1891 might still be alive in the fifties of the next century; he might even live in London. What better source here than the telephone book, and there I found the promising name, "W. Wyon." I wrote to him, asking him if he could help me trace L. C. Wyon's drawing, and he answered at once that he was the artist's son and had the portrait in his house.

He was, in fact, on his deathbed. She went to see him, and there was the portrait hanging in his room. At his death her suggestion was accepted that the portrait be sent to Dove Cottage in Grasmere, where it now hangs. While she was in Oxford in one of those years, an attractive French girl came to visit her. The girl was the direct descendant of Wordsworth and Annette Vallon, whom the poet had loved and lost in the early days of the Revolution.

Some might gather from this recital that Frances Blanshard was a rather formidable intellectual. That she was very able there was no doubt. That there was anything formidable about her would be grotesquely untrue. There are friends of hers who will read what has been said here with surprise, having gained no inkling from her own lips of what she was doing or could do. She never pushed herself forward; in company she was a good listener, always attentive and responsive, but taking her own part diffidently. She was far more interested in persons than in abstractions and sometimes thought that she should have made history rather than philosophy her special field. Deeply affectionate, and denied children of her own for no discoverable reason, her affection flowed out in all directions—to students, to nephews and nieces, to all four-footed things, and to a husband who, whatever his deserts, was always her first and last concern. Because she was serious and responsible, burdens were early thrown upon her that only a girl of character could have borne. She became Dean of an important college when just out of her twenties; and along with her official responsibility she carried for fifteen years the sorrow of a mother who, while a teacher of literature, suffered a stroke that canceled permanently her power to read or speak. This, too, one would never have guessed. Happily, beneath the official seriousness there was, besides courage, a well of gaiety that would easily bubble and overflow. Give her a ukelele and a little urging, and she could keep a company amused by the hour with songs retained in that extraordinary memory from a Missouri plantation or a London music hall. On long drives to their farmhouse in Vermont, her husband used to tap this fountain of song. It was unfailing, and he never reached the end.

One is tempted to think with sorrow of all the unrewarded labor she put into this book. In the time that it required of her, she could have read so many books she longed to read, given so many pleasant parties, paid so many carefree visits, done countless things that she would have enjoyed and now will never enjoy. She knew she was paying a price. She did not have to do it; she could have lived as most others in her position live, without the punishing self-discipline of a large and lonely task. But she chose the harder line. One may regret—regret beyond words—that she could not finish the course and hear some of the cheers that were so plainly her due. But one cannot regret the choice itself. To do that would be to regret the largeness of spirit that made her what she was. She had seen and taken part in a decisive experiment in American education, conducted by a leader of great force and unique personality, and she chose to absent herself for a while from the minor felicities of life to tell his story. It is an inspiriting story that needed telling. She has placed Frank Aydelotte, with his philosophy, his methods, and his character, on permanent record and has done it with such fidelity and fullness of detail that one may safely say she has done it once for all.

It would be out of order to say more of her here; this is a biography of Frank Aydelotte, not of his biographer; and the present writer must admit that he could not write impartially about her if he tried. Neither can he make the acknowledgments that she would certainly have wanted to make. Scores of persons helped her—friends and neighbors of the Aydelotte family still living in Sullivan, Indiana; the administration at Swarthmore, who gave her access to the minute books of the faculty and the Board of Managers and supplied her on call (and almost by the hundredweight) with catalogues and copies of the *Phoenix;* Swarthmore students of many vintages; Rhodes Scholars old and young; many members of the Institute at Princeton; and many persons in Britain and America whose paths had more or less casually crossed Frank Aydelotte's and who were willing to talk or write about him. Their names, where pertinent, appear in the notes at the end of the book. To all these persons she was thankful and would have wished to express her gratitude. They will understand if a few names only are mentioned here. Dr. William O. Aydelotte placed his father's files, and even occasionally the family house, in Waterford, Connecticut, at her disposal and supplied her with information and friendly comment at every stage of her study. Elsa Jenkins, who·was Frank Aydelotte's secretary for Rhodes affairs at both Swarthmore and Princeton, was often resorted to and never without helpful response. Mrs. Beatrice M. Stern, who knows the history of the Princeton Institute as probably no one else does, gave generously of her time and knowledge. The American Philosophical Society—Benjamin Franklin's distinguished old Society—of which Frank Aydelotte was a member, gave his biographer a timely grant which enabled her to visit his Indiana birthplace and follow with more security the path of his earlier years. To these and all others who helped her I would add my thanks to hers.

BRAND BLANSHARD

New Haven
February, 1970

FRANK AYDELOTTE OF SWARTHMORE

$\approx$ CHAPTER ONE $\approx$

INDIANA BOYHOOD

1880–1896

FRANK AYDELOTTE's ancestry was mixed French and English, with ad-venturous spirits and skilled tradesmen on both sides. His father's forebears were Frenchmen who came in the Huguenot migration to London, where the name was known by 1632.[1] Crossing the ocean half a century later, they founded an American line which began in Virginia, pushed north to Maryland and Delaware, west to Ohio, south to Kentucky, and finally to Indiana, Frank's birthplace in 1880.

The first of this American line, Benjamin Aydelott, made shoes in Snow Hill, Maryland, and set up a tanyard to produce the necessary leather; he also farmed on a scale large enough to yield the 1,920 pounds of tobacco he bequeathed to his heirs in 1703.[2] He left his shoemaker's "towls" to his son William, who added to them cooper's "tools"; for William operated a still with the aid of slaves and made the barrels for his whisky. Half his "big still" went to his son John, who always signed himself "Bricklayer." John was a man of some means, who helped build the Presbyterian church in Snow Hill, Maryland, and owned considerable property in Delaware. His grandson, William Leonidas Aydelott, was Frank's grandfather.

William Leonidas, born in Delaware toward the end of the eighteenth century, was soon taken by his parents to Ohio. There as a boy in his teens he saw service in the War of 1812, employed by the government to drive "supplies and munitions of war" from Cincinnati to St. Marys, Ohio. Once his wagon train was attacked by Indians, and he was wounded. On the basis of this war record, he put in a claim sixty-odd years later for a pension, which was denied because he had served as "a civilian and not as an enlisted man." For twenty years he lived in Kentucky, but when the clouds of a later war darkened over that state

3

and it was torn by conflicting sympathies, William Leonidas felt that he might be happier in a state committed to the Union and recrossed the Ohio River. But he did not go back to Ohio. He made his way farther west to the less developed Indiana, which offered greater opportunities to newcomers. After a year or two, he settled in Carlisle, Sullivan County, where he spent the rest of his life.

His son, William Ephraim, was destined to be Frank's father. He grew up in Carlisle, where he started his business career in a drugstore. When he was twenty-five (1875), he married Matilda Brunger.

Matilda's family also told its story of adventure. Her parents, Stephen and Sarah Brunger, had migrated to Indiana from England by way of Canada and Ohio. In Canada, according to family tradition, they took a hazardous interest in Papineau's Rebellion (1837), an attempt to transfer Canadian allegiance to the United States. When this failed, they escaped to American soil, where Matilda, their sixth child, was born. The Brungers, like the Aydelottes, had followed a skilled trade. Stephen came from a line of English weavers; his son Stephen was a weaver also. The two families met in Carlisle, where their children were married. Four years later, Matilda's brother and her husband decided to become partners in the woolen business with Stephen as the technical expert and William managing the "hands" and the sales. The mill they took over was in nearby Sullivan.

Sullivan, Indiana

When William and Matilda moved to Sullivan in 1879, it was still young—thirty-seven years old—with a population just over two thousand. Seven miles from the Wabash River, it had been placed at the mid-point of Sullivan County and planned as the county seat. It was laid out to center on the Court House, which stood in a large, grassy, tree-shaded square, framed by wide streets, with stores and office buildings on the outer side. By 1879 the town was beginning to take on a substantial look as the earliest frame buildings were replaced by brick, notably the Court House and a large school building, described as an "elegant three-story brick structure . . . said to be one of the finest in the State in architecture and furnishing" and costing the impressive sum of $25,000.[3] Three of the five churches were also brick: Methodist, Presbyterian, and "Reformed Christian" (the one attended later by William and the children). Baptists and Roman Catholics still worshiped in wooden structures. There was a railroad, the Evansville and Terre Haute, which ran six passenger and six regular freight trains a day. Lively interest in politics and local affairs supported three newspapers, the semiweekly *Democrat*, the weekly Republican *Sullivan County Union*, and the nonpartisan *Times*. The one manufacturing plant, conveniently near the railroad and a small stream, was the woolen mill of "Aydelotte and Brunger."

Life in Sullivan was not hard, thanks to the fertile land and the rich veins of soft coal lying close to the surface. Anyone willing to work could expect to be comfortable; nobody need worry about a livelihood. At the same time, those who had moved there from older, more settled places (and that meant many of the adult population) could not rest content with conditions that were still all too primitive: unpaved streets which blew away in clouds of dust or melted in rivers of mud; feeble street lights and wooden sidewalks, houses without any sort of plumbing; and, even more serious for young parents, a shorter school program than was commonly approved, and no public library. So much needed to be done that everyone's help was important, but nothing seemed impossible in a place that had already come so far so fast. And life had kept that delightful zest of pioneer America when one man's gain did not mean anyone else's loss.

In 1884 local pride produced a massive history of Sullivan (already quoted), including a kind of current *Who's Who* of seventy-nine leading citizens which begins, thanks to alphabetical order, with William E. Aydelotte. Newcomer that he was, and young in the bargain (at thirty-four), he would hardly have appeared on such a list in an older community. But most people in Sullivan were young. (A contemporary of Frank's in another new middle-western town remembers that as a child she never saw an old person until her parents took her to New England to visit grandparents, and she thought them so ugly she burst into tears.) Also, most other Sullivan citizens had recently arrived. Less than one-fourth of the subjects of the "Biographical Sketches" were native to the county; almost half had been born outside Indiana, and a large contingent came from southern states, notably Kentucky. Not a single man on the list came from New England, and only three from foreign countries— this at a time when Scandinavians, Germans, and central Europeans were pouring into other sections of the Middle West.

The seventy-nine success stories breathe pride in the town and the men who were making it—men who could turn their hands in any promising direction. Most of the businessmen had been farmers (or still were); many had taught school to earn money for more education. The historian gloats with special relish over those who "began with nothing": the barber who "now has a handsome property"; the owner of a hardware store and $20,000 whose first job on a six-week flatboat trip to New Orleans brought him $30, out of which "he bought a suit of clothes and paid his way home, and had left $16 which he loaned at 6 per cent interest." Appropriately in this county seat, the top profession was law: sixteen lawyers in a population of two thousand, a few prepared in law school, the majority in an office.

Father and Mother

The sketch of William notes that he is "one of the most successful business men of the county seat." There was a clear integrity in both William and his partner and brother-in-law, Stephen Brunger, that made their business succeed. Stephen, determined to use nothing but the purest wool, was twitted by his family with refusing to let anyone walk through the mill with cotton in his ears for fear it would fly into the looms. The firm took a strong line also against much combing of blankets, a process which makes them look thick and woolly at the expense of long wear. William, who bought the wool, hired the "hands," and managed sales, had a rare gift for judging people and getting along with them. The "hands" were his friends as well as his responsibility.

William and Matilda, though both the children of pioneering parents, were strikingly different persons: she a slight, high-strung intellectual, he sturdy, well-poised, and a "good mixer." William, Kentucky-born, had a southerner's sociability: he liked people, enjoyed their company, and was well liked in return, though he did little talking. He joined the Reformed Christian Church, which he attended regularly, taking the children with him. He was also a devoted Mason. While his schooling had been no more than average, he had a good mind and sound judgment. A steady, kindly person, he always attracted more than his share of responsibility and carried it well. Only two years after he came to Sullivan he was elected a trustee of the Town Board, and later when a dishonest mayor absconded with the public funds, William's fellow citizens asked him to fill out the term and restore order and confidence. His daughter remembered that Negro families in Sullivan made a practice of going to him for friendly advice: "No Negro ever bought a horse or a cow without consulting him. He was a Southerner who wanted

Negroes to get along." Perhaps more typically southern was his lively interest in politics and his loyalty to the Democratic party. Yet he kept an unusually open mind, greatly admiring the Socialist Eugene Debs, though not to the extent of voting for him. For some years William held the office of Postmaster, appointed first by a Democratic administration and reappointed by the Republicans, thanks to Will Hays, Sullivan-born Postmaster-General.

Matilda, slender and tense, was inclined to avoid people. She never felt at home in Sullivan or anywhere else, partly as a result of too much uprooting in her childhood. The Brungers had not stayed in any one place long enough to be completely accepted; they were always "that queer English family," and she an outsider. This feeling may have been deepened by her girlhood education as a Protestant in a Roman Catholic convent in Canada. Her eldest brother sent her there, following a practice not unusual in privileged circles at a time when many of the best schools for girls in the United States as well as Canada were managed by cultured European nuns.[4] Unfortunately for Matilda, in the small towns where she lived she was the only girl with convent training—another oddity. And though she had profited enormously by exposure to books and ideas, she had acquired what would have distressed her teachers: an uncompromising distaste for some of the usual feminine activities. She could not bear housework, hating even to see it done. She felt superior to clothes or trying to make a good appearance. So far as we know, she never sat for a photograph. To her children she seemed to want to be "different." She was British in minor ways, saying "wear" for were, "bean" for been, and drinking strong cups of tea at all hours. It was no secret in the family that she regarded middle-western customs unfavorably and took no interest in the social elite who become important even in a small, new town. At that time in Sullivan, as in most of the Middle West, men and women went to church as a matter of course; Matilda, never. Her neighbors explained her absence by her poor health. When anything happened to upset her, she had a "sick headache" and took to her bed, leaving her husband to cope with the children, as he always managed to do. Eventually her face hardened in a discontented expression, according to her son-in-law, who attributed it to her awareness of a "brilliant, wasted mind."[5] Brilliant or not, she had a good mind, and it was not wasted on her children. They were constantly stimulated by her ideas and love of reading. And her husband, genial and tolerant, always produced a "hired girl" to do the work, who ate her meals with the family, according to local custom, and was treated almost like a daughter.

In a small frame house beside the mill, Frank, the eldest child, was born on October 16, 1880, followed three years later by a brother, Will, and in 1886 by their sister Nell. In spite of the parents' differences in temperament, the tone of Aydelotte family life was affectionate and pleasant. William gave it warmth and stability and a firm connection with the outside community through his liking for people and his business success. Matilda, almost always at home reading, provided an atmosphere both lively and secure. She saw to the children's welfare with a certain detachment that gave them a feeling of independence. They were not "interfered with" and consequently escaped many irksome frustrations. Thanks partly to this, partly to their inheritance from their father, they grew up a remarkably sweet-tempered trio. At the same time, their mother's aloofness from neighbors' opinions, and her insistence on standards she thought superior, made two of her children, Frank and Nell, unusually self-sufficient and ready to go their own way. Will, though he looked like the others, never had their force.

It was Frank, for three years her only child, who grew to be Matilda's particularly good companion. She taught him to read before he could remember and to share her joy in books. He grew into a slender, tow-haired boy with bright blue eyes like his father's, a precocious intensity, and a shy but friendly smile. If he had an oddity in appearance it was his large and protruding ears. Perhaps they prevented his becoming vain.

In an uneventful, healthy childhood, a single incident which threatened serious consequences stood out in his memory. His father discovered that the boy could hardly bend his right arm, and the doctor said it must have been broken without their knowing it and badly knit. The only cure was to break it again and set it properly. This happened when Frank was seven, he thought, though he might have been younger. What he recalled most vividly was the long-drawn-out exercising of the elbow; he kept at it himself for years, determined not to give up until he could play games like other boys. Perhaps his passion for sports was the result of this handicap. Eventually he overcame it so well that he played baseball for Sullivan, football for Indiana University, and rugby for his Oxford College, Brasenose, where he also rowed in the eight. But his elbow was never completely normal. As he grew older, he shook hands with his left hand, saying with a chuckle that he saved his right arm for golf. The chuckle hid a discomfort he chose to ignore.

A Hoosier Boyhood

Like most small middle-western towns, Sullivan was a place where a boy was free to find his own amusements. Frank always had a dog, usually a stray, which made itself at home and slept on his bed. The dog would sit beside him on the front steps and watch the trains go by: wonderful trains, especially at night with a mysterious sleeping car showing slits of light below the shades. Sometimes boy and dog wandered through the woods, down to a little creek where tiny fish flashed, pretty, but no good to catch. Frank had a pony, too, a stubborn little creature which let him ride only where it chose to go. If the pony decided it had been out long enough, it would wheel and gallop home, no matter how hard Frank pulled. The best he could do was to hang on desperately, tears of vexation running down his cheeks. But he always managed to stick. When he was ten or twelve he rode a larger and gentler beast, the family horse, Kibus. He took full care of Kibus, feeding, watering, and grooming him and cleaning his stall. The horse responded by living to a great age. Kibus contributed to family life on pleasant evenings when, hitched to a fringed-top surrey, he took all the Aydelottes rolling along quiet country roads. Frank looked forward to these drives as a chance to talk over with his parents anything he happened to have on his mind.

When "safety bicycles" were the rage and still expensive, Frank had one, thanks to a generous father, and entered a race for boys at the county fair. He prepared seriously, dashing out day after day to ride a fast three or four miles on country roads. When he won second prize, he was sure it was thanks to the training.

As far back as he could remember, he had loved the mill next door. He liked to watch the machines weaving flannels, jeans, and blankets. When the mill was closed in winter for want of heat except in his father's little office, he liked to go there to see him balance accounts and hear his talk with customers. To Frank the "hands" were part of his family, and when they had their picture taken, of course he and his brother and sister planted themselves in the front row. Later he worked there in the summer. The hours were long—from half-past six in the morning until six at night—but in the dyehouse where he worked, the hands were allowed to leave at five if the wool they had put out was dry. Frank liked to make speed on sunny days. He enjoyed beating his own record, and all the more when he could use the time for something he wanted to do, like swimming or playing tennis. Once in the summer he was given a free day or two to drive his mother behind old Kibus into a wild section of Indiana, Brown County, where she loved to sit on a hilltop and watch the sun set and the moon rise.

When Frank was a grown man he came on a picture of the mill in Theodore Dreiser's book *A Hoosier Holiday*, with the title, "My Father's Mill." It seemed that Dreiser's father had, indeed, once owned a mill on that site; it had burned down before Theodore was born. The Dreisers had moved away, but when Theodore was seven, Mrs. Dreiser came back with the younger children, hoping to support them by running a boardinghouse. They stayed in Sullivan three years, which Dreiser remembers as the happiest of his boyhood. Almost forty years later he described Sullivan as "of all places that I ever lived in my youth the most pleasing to me and full of the most colorful and poetic memories." He loved the woods and fields, and the birds—blue jays and scarlet tanagers—flashing color everywhere. Like Frank, he loved the trains: "Over half the glory of Sullivan for me was due to the visible arrival and departure of these trains."[6] Mrs. Dreiser's boardinghouse failed, and she moved away with her children when Theodore was ten. In the little house by the mill Frank had been born the year before.

Another Sullivan boy to become well known was Frank's classmate Will Hays, who went from politics into the President's Cabinet as Postmaster-General and thence to Hollywood as "Czar of the Movies." The son of a Republican lawyer, Will was particularly alive to the activities of the Court House and to the politicians who came to see his father: the Presidential candidates James G. Blaine and Benjamin Harrison, and Robert Todd Lincoln, awesome figure to a boy brought up on stories of the Civil War President.[7] Frank must have seen them, too, but they meant less to the son of a strong Democrat. Will and Frank differed too much in personality as well as background to be close friends. Will was small for his age, no athlete, and sometimes lazy about his homework. Then, to avoid being found out, he would get the teacher to talk about something not in the lesson. A waste of time, Frank thought, who liked to get on with his studies.

In the summer, boys had plenty of time for fun, in spite of extra chores in the garden. Every Friday night the Sullivan Band played in the Court House Square where Frank and his friends would listen to the music, munch popcorn, and saunter to the drugstore for the newly invented luxury of an ice cream soda. Sometimes a party of boys and girls in a hay wagon jolted over seven miles of rough dirt road to the

banks of the Wabash River for a picnic on the bluffs at Merom. They
would build a fire, cook their supper, and sing to Frank's accompaniment
on his guitar. One of their favorite songs was by Theodore Dreiser's
brother—who called himself Paul "Dresser"—"On the Banks of the
Wabash Far Way."

A Sullivan boy in those days was not likely to travel much, even in
his own state. Nevertheless he learned a good deal about Indiana and took
pride in being a "Hoosier." No one seemed sure where the name came
from, though many explanations were current.[8] Boys of Frank's age had
not heard the early use of the word as a reproach for roughness and
ignorance.[9] The famous novel which made the name well known, Eggle-
ston's *Hoosier Schoolmaster*, described a boisterous life that seemed remote
history. To Frank and his friends the state nickname stood for traits they
admired: a Hoosier could turn his hand to anything, toss off the hardest
physical work, and go his own independent way, though always ready
to help a neighbor. He would have the kindly humor of characters in
James Whitcomb Riley's poems. Riley was a sentimental Hoosier Poet
Laureate, writing in a dialect which was beginning to seem primitive
even to his contemporaries.

Frank liked Riley's poems well enough, but was more interested in
what his father told him of a learned strain in Indiana history coming
from the little town of New Harmony. William Ephraim himself had
once lived near there and heard tales of the colony established by the
Glasgow Socialist Robert Owen. Though it had quickly come to grief as
a socialist Utopia, it had succeeded as a center of scientific inquiry,
thanks to some of the men imported by Owen in his "boatload of
knowledge." This boat had sailed from Pittsburgh down the Ohio in
December, 1825, when Indiana as a state was not quite ten years old. The
passengers included several adventurous scientists attracted by country
unexplored and unspoiled, two with special interest for a boy: William
Maclure, wealthy Scottish merchant turned geographer, who made maps
of the new state and a vast territory besides, and Charles A. Lesueur,
originally from the West Indies, who had already studied primitive tribes
in Australia and was one of the first to examine the Indian mounds of
Indiana, such as those quite close to Sullivan. Frank was impressed also
with the story of Robert Owen's three sons and what they did for
Indiana.[10]

The eldest, Robert Dale Owen, served three terms in the state
legislature, where he helped put through a bill to support free public

schools. He also took an important part in the Convention of 1850 which revised the Indiana Constitution. Meanwhile he had been sent to Washington as a Democratic Congressman (1843–1847), where he helped found a great museum, the Smithsonian. Always an advocate of freedom, he worked for Negro emancipation and wrote *The Policy of Emancipation*, which was said to have had a decisive influence on the policy adopted by Lincoln. The two younger Owens made their names in science. David Dale, a geologist, was employed by the government in Washington "to examine Western mineral lands." This required him to make long and difficult journeys through little-known parts of Illinois, Iowa, Wisconsin, Minnesota, and Arkansas. Later he was a pioneering state geologist, first of Kentucky and then of Indiana. The youngest Owen, Richard, showed unusual versatility. He helped David make surveys, earned a degree in medicine (though he never practiced), and eventually had a distinguished career as professor of natural sciences at Indiana University, where he was said to have occupied "not a chair but a settee" and in addition to several sciences taught also "a way of life."[11] A native southerner like William Ephraim Aydelotte felt warmly toward Richard Owen as a humane Civil War Colonel in charge of Confederate prisoners at Camp Morton, Indianapolis. (He looked after them so well that years later, in 1913, the surviving prisoners put up a monument in his honor.) To Frank the Owen brothers seemed very near, partly because his own father knew so much about them, partly because he was ten years old when Richard died and was greatly mourned.

Indiana writers of popular romantic novels also appealed to Frank: Lew Wallace who published *Ben Hur* in the year Frank was born, Charles Major of *When Knighthood Was in Flower*, George Barr Mc-Cutcheon, creator of *The Prince of Graustark*. More than most Sullivan boys, Frank loved to read, and he devoured every book he could lay hands on—no great number, since Sullivan had no public library and the books in the old County Library, established in the 1820's, had long since been worn out. But there was a small collection in the Christian Church Sunday School, and he made the most of it. There was also the weekly *Youth's Companion* which he and a multitude of other young Americans read eagerly without missing a word.

The *Youth's Companion* was an excellent family paper, not written down to children, but in a style anyone might enjoy, and on a fascinating variety of subjects. In 1891, when Frank was eleven, there was a series on "The Latest Discoveries in Science" by experts in geology, astronomy, navigation, and other fields. There were brief biographies, such as "Birthday of Two Great Men," on Lincoln and Darwin, and "Another Child Monarch" on Queen Wilhelmina, who was just Frank's age. In political science, there was an account of "the Senate" by no less an authority than the Hon. Hannibal Hamlin, former Speaker of that distinguished body as Vice-President of the United States (1861–1865). It was from the *Youth's Companion* that Frank probably first heard of Oxford and Brasenose, which was to be his college, in a little article, "The Nose of Brass," published January 15, 1891. The article begins, "One of the most famous of the colleges which, taken together, form the great University of Oxford, is named Brasenose," and goes on to tell the story of the odd brass knocker which gives the college its name: a face of brass with a ring through its nose. This was fixed to the outer door of Brasenose until 1334, when the students rebelled against college authority and seceded to set up a new college at Stamford in Lincolnshire, taking the knocker with them. In a year or two the students were coaxed back to Oxford, but returned without their knocker, which stayed at Stamford for 556 years. Then in 1890 it was restored to its rightful owners and placed again on the Brasenose College door, making a headline in the *Youth's Companion*. To the boy in Sullivan, the tale must have seemed as remote and romantic as a Scott novel.

The Great Fair

In the fall of Frank's last year in grammar school the *Companion* was concerned with an exciting event of national importance, the first celebration of Columbus day on October 12, 1892,[12] the four-hundredth anniversary of the discovery of America. To make sure that the government's program for use in the schools should be circulated widely, it was published in the popular *Youth's Companion* (September 8, 1892), clear evidence of the paper's status. The program included the now familiar oath of allegiance to the flag, used then for the first time, and recited by thirteen million children.

The World's Columbian Exposition at Chicago in honor of this same anniversary should have been held in 1892, but the elaborate preparations were not completed until the year following. Then Frank, not yet thirteen, made his first great venture away from Sullivan, a trip to the Chicago World's Fair. The Aydelottes had cousins in Chicago who invited them to stay for two weeks in August. But as early as February

Frank began to read about the marvels to come. Every week the *Youth's Companion* carried notes on the fair, and in April it announced a special World's Fair Number, to be distributed "with the regular paper of the first week in May." This urged parents to take their children: "To studious and observant young people a visit to the World's Fair will be equivalent to a liberal education." The Sullivan *Democrat* also whetted appetites by a weekly "World's Fair Letter." The writer sometimes lumped together a strange assortment of attractions, as on March 3: an exhibition of ancient and modern musical instruments, "one of the most complete collections in the world," sent by Mr. Steinert of New Haven, Connecticut; Imperial Infantry and Cavalry Bands of Germany, to play for six months in the "German Village" (replica of a village where the players might live at home). There was a reproduction of Solomon's Temple, and a Syrian exhibit transported from Beirut in a steamboat large enough for four hundred people: horsemen and dancing girls, forty Arabian horses, and twelve dromedaries. After the fair opened in May, the art treasures were specially praised: "In everything that pertains to art, in painting, in sculpture, in architecture, in decorative work and in industrial art, no such collections have ever been gathered together in any part of the World at any time" (May 26, 1893). And again (June 2), "Of all the buildings that hold the visitor enthralled, and there are many that do, the Art Gallery leads." Young Frank had never seen an oil painting or any piece of sculpture better than a Civil War monument. He could hardly wait to go.

Once arrived in Chicago, Frank was allowed to plan the family program, and how he loved to plan! Every night he studied the guide-book eagerly and outlined what they should see next day. Consequently nothing surprised him (he never liked to be surprised). Always afterward those two weeks stood out as the first high point in his education—a wonderful panorama of subjects, people, and countries which he hoped to see again near at hand. It was true for him, as for millions of Americans, that the fair revealed "the splendid possibilities of art, and the compelling power of the beautiful," in the words of Harry Thurston Peck.[13] More sophisticated critics may have been right to deplore the effect on American architecture of magnificent buildings which were all imitations of wonders of antiquity, or at the latest of the eighteenth century, all "fakes and frauds," according to Henry Adams. The exception among architects, Louis Sullivan, whose Transportation Building at the fair was like a voice crying in the wilderness that "form follows function," spoke truly when he predicted that what he called "the damage" caused by the World's Fair "will last for half a century from its date, if not longer."[14] It is true that American academic Gothic dominated the scene until World War II and still has its conservative admirers. But though American architecture might have found its own line more quickly if the buildings at the fair had not been "plagiarisms," it is true also that the total effect for many young Americans from frontier towns was "a shimmering dream of loveliness," a blend of "form and colour in a symmetrical and radiant purity such as modern eyes, at least, had never looked upon before."[15] Frank was one of those open-mouthed young gapers.

In "Sullivan High"

The following month Frank entered high school, still keyed up with excitement at the marvels he had seen and the new vistas that had opened up. Latin he had regarded as an alluring gateway to glories of the past, but what he found was dull and plodding exercises in grammar, spooned out in such small doses as to be neither hard nor interesting. He was disappointed and bored. Outside the classroom, too, there was nothing stimulating—no athletics and hardly any other school activities. In his second year Frank decided to leave school altogether. His parents must have felt concerned, but let him work things out for himself. They told him he could stop on two conditions: he must keep up with class assignments, and he must not leave his own yard during school hours. These he accepted readily and was absent six weeks at one stretch; there were no attendance laws in those days in Indiana. He did his lessons quickly and had plenty of time for reading and practicing target shooting with his pistol; in six weeks he became a good shot. Memories of this pleasant chance to go at his own speed may have later fortified his enthusiasm for similar opportunities in his honors plan for Swarthmore.

At last so much solitude began to pall, and Frank decided to put up with high school; after all, it would help him go to college. In his third year he took to geometry because of the originals; he had a gift for working out the problems. His geometry teacher liked to tell that once when she gave a particularly difficult original which baffled the whole class, Frank urged her not to explain it. "Please let us try again," he asked; "please give us another week." She agreed, and he solved it. "Just like him," she said later; "he never gave up anything he had made up his mind to do."

The chief weakness in the Sullivan High School program was its length: three years instead of the usual four. This meant that Frank could study Latin for only three years, a handicap he felt for a long time. It was a slight disadvantage that the school was small, not more than seventy-five altogether, nineteen in his class when he was graduated in 1896, with less variety and less stimulus, probably, than in a larger group. But the school was "commissioned"; that is to say, its diploma was accepted for admission to Indiana University, and the course of study followed the usual "classical" lines: "common Branches [the 3 Rs], English Composition and Literature, Algebra, Plane and Solid Geometry, three years of Latin, General History and Physics." These required subjects are listed in the University catalogue of his last year in high school (1895–1896) with titles of required books, some for "general reading," others for "minute and careful study." In the first group, *A Midsummer Night's Dream*, Defoe's *A Journal of the Plague Year*, Irving's *Tales of a Traveler*, Scott's *Woodstock*, Macaulay's *Essay on Milton*, Long-fellow's *Evangeline*, George Eliot's *Silas Marner*. For "careful study," *The Merchant of Venice*, *L'Allegro*, *Il Penseroso*, *Comus*, and *Lycidas*, and Web-ster's *First Bunker Hill Oration*. Only three American titles among the thirteen—the usual emphasis on British background. Frank enjoyed them all.

He took part also in a popular activity organized by Sullivan boys outside school: a debating society sponsored by the Lyceum League of America. Those were the years of formal debates with careful scoring of points, appealing to a boy's competitive instinct as well as his ambition to explore subjects of public importance and to learn to talk on his feet. Frank had the clear head and the good temper needed for argument, but was beginning to be troubled by a stammer. His mother said it came from impatience; he never could speak fast enough to keep up with his thought. He determined to slow down and eventually got the stammer under full control, but not soon enough for success on the Lyceum platform. Most of the prizes were won by his classmate Will Hays, already looking forward to law and politics.

As the Aydelotte children grew older, their parents left them increasingly free to do what they liked, provided they could show it was practicable. Their father might make them think twice by asking, "You're *sure* that's what you want to do?", but if the answer was Yes, he accepted it. At the same time both parents held their children to firm standards of responsibility. Once they undertook something, they must put it through. When Frank was working in the mill and broke his jaw playing baseball, his father expected him to stay on the job. And though Matilda was no churchgoer, she had strict ideas of Sunday observance and of refraining from gossip which she called "talk." Sunday must be a day of rest for everyone, including the hired girl, with a minimum of cooking, no other housework, and rarely any guests. As to "talk," Frank's sister Nell remembers her shocked surprise when she first heard any in their house: a caller criticized a girl visiting in Sullivan for wearing scandalously short skirts; they showed her ankles above her shoes.

A member of the Brunger family who often visited the Aydelottes in the winter was Matilda's eldest brother Jim. Uncle Jim would appear after Christmas and was given the best room and the privilege of a late breakfast—at half-past eight. He liked to talk and to smoke a pipe in the warm little office in the mill. Frank would go over in the evenings to hear his ideas, "always very conservative." Uncle Jim was thought to be rich and known to be generous. Not only had he paid for Matilda's convent schooling years before but now, great smoker that he was, he made Frank an offer to give him $500 when he was twenty-one if he would not smoke in the meantime. Frank earned the money and used it for graduate work at Harvard, where he formed his undying attachment to a pipe.

Frank's Sullivan school days came to an end in the spring of 1896; the Sullivan *Democrat* of May 22 carried a notice of his high-school Commencement the next week. This was the fifteenth class to be graduated, the largest so far, "six young women and 13 young men," "unprecedented" in having "more men than ladies." A new departure in programs was to omit the reading of the nineteen senior essays; they would simply be listed by title. Frank's essay showed his concern about recent Turkish atrocities: Armenians had been massacred by the Turkish soldiers supposed to guard them. Frank stated his subject as the affirmative side of a debate: "Resolved, that the United State Government immediately tender its support to the interference by Russia in the Armenian Affair." He was already concerned with Near East problems in which, a half-century later, he would play an adviser's part. The *Democrat's* next issue gave pleasant details of commencement: the girls had worn white, the boys were "handsome in suits of black with white ties." At the banquet the table was trimmed with class colors, "old gold and white"; the waiters in white suits wore these colors and served "cake, ice cream, and several kinds of fruit." "A witty after dinner talk" was given by "the newly elected superintendent of schools."

In this summer before a Presidential election, Frank, like other young Democrats, hung on reports of the National Convention which met early in July in Chicago. The party was in a turmoil over the "free silver" issue, one faction urging the innovation of unrestricted coinage of silver in the belief that an increased supply of money would lead to greater prosperity; the more conservative claiming that strict adherence to the gold standard was essential to healthy international trade. After violent discussions culminating in the overwhelming oratory of a young man from Nebraska, William Jennings Bryan, with his famous "Cross of Gold" speech, the party was swept into a crusade for free silver, choosing Bryan as their leader and candidate for President. What was the excitement in Sullivan when Bryan carried his campaign to this Democratic stronghold, drawing the largest crowd in the town's history, forty thousand people! They marched in from eight surrounding townships, each contingent led by its own glee club and band. "When all joined together in parading the streets of Sullivan, the occasion was one that will never be equaled."[16]

Under the spell of Bryan's mellow voice and fervent speech, Frank chafed at being too young to vote. But political concerns faded quickly before the personal adventure of leaving the one place he knew well for the strange, alluring world of Indiana University.

What kind of person had he become by the time he entered college? In some ways older than his less than sixteen years, an effect partly of his parents' personalities. The unusual differences between them had given him an early interest in understanding people. And from accepting his mother's oddities, he had learned to regard other eccentrics without alarm, even with a tolerant affection—an asset in later academic life. Again, his parents' practice of respecting their children's plans and preferences gave him a quiet self-confidence and saved him from a common adolescent revolt against authority. He had already become a responsible citizen with an attitude toward his younger brother and sister that was almost paternal. He took care of them, discussing their problems with his mother in the tone of one adult to another. He had matured also through coping with difficulties: the broken arm, badly knit, which he exercised with a persistent self-discipline rare at any age; the stammer he was managing to control. He would never suffer the disadvantages of too easy early success, of underestimating the effort necessary to do anything really well. But he was still obviously youthful in his relations with girls. A boy of fifteen can hardly seem more than a gauche youngster to blooming young women classmates two or three years older.

Frank was fortunate in the traits he inherited—or adopted—from his parents; his father's geniality and liking for people, his mother's intellectual gifts and independence. He profited also from growing up in an environment strong in friendliness, optimism, and courage and in its Calvinistic zest for strenuous work.

CHAPTER TWO

STUDENT AT BLOOMINGTON

1896–1900

WHEN Frank Aydelotte entered college in 1896, there was no certainty that an ambitious Indiana boy would choose the state university for his higher education. DePauw at Greencastle offered a more varied program. The collection of books in the Wabash College library at Crawfordsville was more extensive. Butler in Indianapolis had a larger endowment, and Earlham in Richmond offered pleasanter living arrangements. And for sound teaching of a classical curriculum, no college surpassed Notre Dame. These were all denominational, supported by religious sects: Methodist, Presbyterian, Christian, Quaker, and Catholic. The Baptists had Franklin College and the Presbyterians a second institution at Hanover. Originally these colleges represented missionary efforts to keep young frontiersmen in the true faith and to prepare promising recruits for the ministry. They represented also a firm belief that education, to be effective, must be religious, the belief expressed in Froebel's dictum that "all education not founded in religion" is "vain."[1] In contrast, the University as part of the public school system was strictly secular and consequently condemned in some quarters as "godless."

Such strictures did not frighten Frank and his family. Perhaps as a result of Matilda's convent schooling, they preferred education without church influence. They would have supported the University's move away from a common custom of choosing a retired clergyman for president, the appointment going instead to a promising young scientist, David Starr Jordan. How sharp was the break with academic precedent in having a biologist for President, Jordan himself noted in his first month in office: "More than a hundred years ago, Karl von Linné, whom we call Linnaeus, was at the head of the great Swedish University of Uphsala, but from that day to this, no naturalist has been called to be a College President."[2] Jordan's appointment in the year when Frank began his education in the Sullivan public schools may have first attracted his parents' interest to the man who would become one of the best Presidents in American academic history and put Indiana University on a footing that made them think it worthy of their son.

Jordan had already become well known to the University and state as a lively professor of biology, specializing in ichthyology, who involved his students in energetic extracurricular projects.[3] He had led strenuous field trips to study fish on the Pacific Coast, the Florida Keys, and the Gulf of Mexico. He had conducted inexpensive student tours to Europe, adding to the usual sight-seeing a difficult peak to climb and out-of-the-way fjords to scan for rare specimens. When he took office as the nation's youngest university President, he was not yet thirty-five. Both his youth and his scientific interests were assets, bringing openness of mind and a fresh outlook to university problems. As a scientist, he was critical of the neglect of science in the traditional "fixed curriculum," with its rigidly prescribed subjects of Greek, Latin, and mathematics. As a teacher, he knew the stimulus to students of a chance to strike out their own lines. So he planned a new curriculum with greater range of choice and more opportunity to specialize. This was not the free elective system, made famous by Eliot at Harvard (though tried out much earlier by Thomas Jefferson at the University of Virginia).[4] Already the Harvard plan had shown the danger of superficiality; a student left to himself might choose chiefly elementary courses and never learn to go deeply into a subject. As a corrective, Jordan proposed to control electives by requiring a "major subject" in which a student specialized in a program chosen with the advice of a "major professor." "Major subject," "major professor," long since part of the academic stock in trade, represented new ideas in education when Jordan developed them at Indiana.

Jordan became known also for insisting on the first importance of good teaching. He made the point in every county of Indiana in a lecture on "The Value of a College Education."

> There is but one thing that can make a college strong and useful, and that is a strong and earnest faculty. All other matters are of little importance. Buildings, departments, museums, courses, libraries, catalogues, names, rules and regulations, students even, do not make a university. It is the men who teach. Go where the masters are in whatever department you

wish to study . . . to the men who can lead you beyond the primary details to the deeper thought and researches which form the work of the scholar.

Jordan went on to quote Ezra Cornell in a statement that could not apply to Indiana, and to offer a better one. Cornell had said, "I would found an institution in which any person can find instruction in any study." This would obviously require larger funds than Indiana could command, but Jordan believed there was another aim, more desirable and also possible to attain: "It is possible, I believe, to have a college in which each study in the list, be they few or many, shall be taught by a master."[5] This was so much the line dear to Frank's heart when he became a college president that it would be tempting to trace a direct "influence." This is not possible, since Jordan left Indiana a few years before Frank appeared on the campus. But his influence did touch Frank indirectly through his resolute policy of building up the Indiana faculty. Nothing persuades a student of the value of teachers like having good ones.

Jordan had observed that appointees from the East, despite their prestige in some quarters, did not always work out well. Sometimes the older ones went west to escape difficulties which proved to be rooted in their personalities. The younger often felt exiled, more eager to go home than to do their best for Indiana. Jordan decided to recruit new men close at hand by singling out the ablest of his young graduates and encouraging them to study in the East or in Europe, promising positions at Indiana when they returned. This plan pleased both the University and the state by recognizing home talent, and it strengthened the faculty with teachers who had taken a step toward freedom from academic provincialism and also devoted themselves happily to their alma mater.

Jordan made such a name for himself that after six years he was invited to launch the new Leland Stanford Junior Memorial University in California. What man with his concern for the best in higher education could resist the chance to build a university from the ground up? Jordan accepted, leaving behind him a revitalized institution with a curriculum and faculty to be proud of.

The University Frank entered could maintain its quality because its aims were simple and its numbers small. Indiana was chiefly an undergraduate college of liberal arts, its professional training limited to courses in education and a department of law. Its enrollment in 1896–1897 was 944, of whom only 65 were not undergraduates.[6] The University's responsibility was almost exclusively intellectual: to provide teachers, curriculum, and the buildings needed for instruction—classrooms, libraries, and laboratories—but no dormitories or dining halls. The only concession to the physical man was a new gymnasium, used also for university lectures, plays, concerts, and convocations. Athletics were still undeveloped and unimportant, baseball, which had been played for thirty years, being the one well-established sport. Football, after ten years' struggle under volunteer coaches, was just beginning to gain student support. Frank knew no more of the game than he had read in the papers, but hoped to learn to play.

The lack of dormitories and dining halls was taken for granted in a state university in contrast to private institutions like Harvard or Yale. A state university belonged to the system of tax-supported public day schools. For such a one to go into boardinghouse-keeping would have seemed unsuitable to legislature and taxpayers and even more to citizens with similar businesses in Bloomington who would have resented such competition. Fraternities, originally purely social groups, had begun to build houses, but their capacity was small. Most students shifted for themselves, finding rooms where they could and taking their meals at "boarding clubs." This was what Frank set out to do as a matter of course.

A Freshman in the Nineties

Independent as he was, he was not sorry to have his father go with him to Bloomington to help make his "simple arrangements." They discovered "a cheap room in an out of the way corner of a house ten or twelve blocks from the university."[7] The cost of $1.40 a week did not include heat, but the room had a wood stove. Frank would buy his own fuel from farmers who drove their loads to town on Saturday afternoons. They sold it by cubic measure, the cord, and Frank soon saw that the amount he got depended on the way the wood was piled; so he learned to pile it himself. He found one of the least expensive boarding clubs where he could get his meals for $2.25 a week. Including the annual fees of $18, his total outlay would fall well below the catalogue estimate of $250 to $300. This was a relief to a boy who was incurring his first large debt; he was borrowing the money for his education from his father.

Such borrowing was approved practice in many American families, partly because the father of several children, unless he was rich, could hardly manage to pay outright for each one's education. If he gave the eldest a loan, the money would come back for use by the younger ones. But there was another reason; even in well-to-do midwestern households, it was considered a virtue for a young man to earn his own way. If he could not manage to accumulate enough before or during his college course, he could make up the balance by borrowing and earn it later. This financial responsibility was supposed to "teach a young man the value of money." Frank borrowed now, and he would borrow and pay back on many later occasions, always with cheerful confidence. But he may have felt the burden of debt more than he would admit. Much of his work later had to do with providing students and scholars with grants that were not to be repaid.

Frank's freshman program included English composition, Shakespeare, and novels, German, solid geometry and trigonometry, and physical training.[8] Not difficult on the face of it for one of his ability, but he found the work all he could manage. Every day's assignments put him on his mettle, leaving little time for anything but study, though he did make a point of keeping fit by playing handball regularly. Many years later, after a lifetime of changes, he admitted that the transition from Sullivan to Bloomington was by all odds the hardest he ever faced. He explained it in terms of intellectual standards: from a three-year high school where he could miss six weeks without falling behind to a university where more work was suggested than anyone could do. But there were other differences. For a boy not yet sixteen, it was a shock to leave a protected life among neighbors he had always known and plunge into a community where everyone was a stranger. Most of his classmates were two years older, and many had seen far more of the world. To Frank, whose experience scarcely went beyond Sullivan and the Chicago World's Fair, Bloomington was formidably sophisticated.

This was, indeed, the impression his fellow students hoped to create. According to one of them, "At that time in the history of the mid-west, we were trying so hard to shed all the marks of the pioneer, that the preferred type in young manhood was one who wore tight (striped) trousers, fitted coats, heavy cravats, slickly smoothed hair, and derby, or even top hat."[9] In contrast, Frank "was an overgrown youngster, and untrained in social graces. He was not ungainly—he had to have good muscular coordination to be the athlete he was and the good football player he became—but he had a kind of "exuberance" which "produced

an awkwardness in face and body," and his face was overexpressive, "the
emotions flashing through with great rapidity and change."[10] His intensity
in any line he pursued was "almost too keen for comfort."

Frank passed his freshman courses; how well no one knows, as the
only grades given at the time were "passed" and "not passed." This
undiscriminating system had been introduced two years earlier and
warmly praised by the undergraduate paper, the *Daily Student:* it is
"eminently fair to all . . . and a recognition of the constantly increasing
democratic tendencies that prevail throughout the whole country in
industrial as well as other circles."[11] This unfortunate idea of democracy
as obliterating distinctions in quality was later to become one of Frank's
chief targets of attack.

When he went home for the summer, he was glad to take his old job in
the mill, working hard as always, but managing to find time to play
baseball with the Sullivan team which challenged nearby towns. As all
players had jobs, they must schedule games on Sunday. Frank's parents
disapproved, though admitting that no other day seemed possible. One
Sunday at a critical moment in a game with their dearest rival, the
town of Robinson, Illinois, a swift ball hit Frank's jaw and broke the
bone. It felt strange, but he played out the game, and Sullivan won. (To
this day every Sullivan boy knows that story.) The victory made him a
hero to the town, but not to his father, who thought he was excessively
devoted to sports and was troubled by a shortage of hands at the mill. A
job was a job, and broken jaw or not, somebody had to do Frank's
work. So Frank kept at it himself and lost ten pounds in a week.

Still shorthanded in September, his father needed Frank in the mill
until after the term at Bloomington was well begun. This was a blow, as
the boy had set his heart on learning football and feared his lateness
would count against him. But once arrived, his eagerness appealed to the
coach, who needed all the support he could muster for a still underprivileged game, and he allowed Frank to begin. His first appearance on
the field, as remembered by a classmate, was not impressive: "He was a
green, awkward country boy with no natural ability as an athlete." But
then as always he proved good at learning—a "plugger," one of those
men who "are always watched carefully for if they stand the test of
working through the first year or two, with little or no encouragement,
they usually prove to be the best of all athletes. While there are stars on
all teams, these steady, persistent fellows win the games."[12] Frank was

indeed a "plugger," but one with a rare gift: he could "plug" with enthusiasm all along the way. By the end of the season he had the fun of an occasional chance to play with the substitute Varsity.

Bloomington Characters

On the social side, as a sophomore he began to blossom out. His roommate this year, a gay young man with a horse and buggy, took him for pleasant drives in the country. He accepted an invitation to join a fraternity, Sigma Nu, and enjoyed living in the house, though both accommodations and food were "very simple." Most important, he began what was to be a lifelong friendship with a young instructor in fine arts, Alfred Mansfield Brooks, who had come to Indiana in 1896 to introduce the study of art history. A graduate of Harvard in the Class of 1894, he had worked under Charles Eliot Norton (first Harvard professor of the history of art and teacher of a famous course in Dante) and shared his teacher's enthusiasm for Ruskin, who was Norton's personal friend. Frank never took a course with Alfred Brooks, but declared there was no one to whom he owed so much, then and later.

Alfred must always have been a "character," odd in appearance and unusual in personality. He was a slight, wiry, quick-moving man of medium height, with a beaked nose and a birdlike way of jerking his head as he surveyed a scene or person. Though he lacked the build for athletics, he was a tireless walker and also used his hands with marvelous skill—an excellent draftsman and a gardener with a green thumb. He seemed to have read everything, been everywhere, seen what other people would have missed, forming unshakable judgments on what was shoddy and what was first-rate. He was saved from pedantry by a crisp blend of zest and wit. How keenly he enjoyed the surfaces of things—textures, colors, and shapes! How he relished the foibles of human beings, chortling over them with Puckish glee, and what odd adventures he described in his brilliant, racy monologues! When he ended, one felt like begging him to "do it again."

Though born in Michigan, Brooks was a New Englander at heart, from a family deeply-rooted in Gloucester, Massachusetts. He stayed there often in a household of great-aunts, "wonderful old ladies" who lived surrounded by treasures brought from China by their seafaring ancestors. Naturally he went to Harvard. After graduating, he stayed in

Boston to study architecture at M.I.T. and before coming to Bloomington had spent some time in Europe.

Such a man of the world might have made some Sullivan boys self-conscious, but not young Frank. With a gift for appreciating distinction, he saw in A. M. Brooks a creature from a marvelous world. It was true that Brooks could be formidably sharp with people who were dull or pretentious, but Frank was neither; no less than Brooks himself, Frank was unbendingly honest and intolerant of bores. This was one bond between them; another was their unfailing gusto. And while Brooks shared his enthusiasm for Ruskin and Turner, for good wine, good food, and rooms furnished with comfort and charm, he incidentally introduced his young friend to the ways of a larger world, preparing him to feel at ease anywhere. Frank was blessed with a complete lack of vanity that made him quick to learn.

He was making another friend who would be important to him through years to come, the new President, Joseph Swain. Swain was an Indiana Quaker with a warm, personal interest in students, to whom he used the plain language: "thee" and "thee's" for "you" and "yours." A towering giant of a man, born on a farm in Pendleton, he had done much hard, physical labor between bouts of teaching in the district school. Coming late to the University, he was twenty-six when he got his degree and then stayed on to teach mathematics. He was one of the promising young men, so Frank heard, whom Jordan encouraged to study abroad. Swain had gone to the University of Edinburgh, returning to Bloomington as a professor, but was soon lured by Jordan to Stanford. After a short stay, he came back to be President of Indiana.

One of Swain's recognized strong points was his success with the legislature. Among other truimphs, he persuaded them to pass a University Tax Bill, almost doubling the annual appropriations.[13] People said he succeeded partly through sound judgment on business matters, partly through good public relations. He knew how to win the confidence of legislators and to stir an interest and pride in the University in voters all over the state. Eventually he became president of a Quaker college, Swarthmore, and made his mark again with finances and public relations to such an extent that when he retired, he could use the soundness of college affairs to persuade the man he wanted to succeed him. This, in the distant future, would be Frank Aydelotte.

Frank as a sophomore began to come into his own on the academic side. In German he had reached the point of reading well enough to enjoy the literature. For the science requirement he took chemistry and amused himself with an ingenious scheme for doing the experiments in record time. He tells how he and his roommate worked together:

> We purchased a large supply of beakers and other items of laboratory equipment and started a large number of experiments simultaneously. As an experiment came through we made our joint notes on it and turned these in as our report for the term. The result was that we completed what was to be three months work in about one month. The supervisor of the laboratory saw no objection to this and the result was that we had practically one-third of our time free for the remainder of the term.

With this luxury of leisure to spend, Frank went to his English professor, Martin Wright Sampson, for advice on what to read. His reply was, "Begin with Matthew Arnold and go where he leads you."[14]

By this time Frank had decided to major in English literature, thanks partly to Sampson's power as a teacher. Sampson, in his early thirties, was already head of his department and a man of striking personal force as well as "a rare genius in teaching." One of his students describes him as "a tall, lithe man, with blue-black hair, large eyes, dark complexion, and a long, narrow, most expressive face. . . . He never wore the conservative professorial black suit, was one of the first in town to wear a tweed jacket in the class room, and I still can see his bright ties."[15] Another of Frank's contemporaries writes of Sampson as a teacher:

> His house was full of books. . . . He had read every one of them, and the joy he got out of them he seemed to have a passion for trying to impart to his students—to all of them if they would attend, if not, to those among them whose interest he could capture. From Old English drama, through the lyrics, through the poetry of the 16th, 17th, and 18th centuries, he browsed, with vigor, with determination, with charm, . . . and his students, some of them lagging, some of them waking up, some of them eager for the chase, followed. For well they knew that whatever his brilliant quips, his sincere pity for those who seemed to be falling behind, the day of reckoning would come with finals—they must know the field.[16]

Indeed, to some of his students Professor Sampson seemed "too stern, too aesthetic" to be a "popular " teacher. Even a very able one remembers chiefly" his severity in class." But Frank responded to his skillful leading with wholehearted joy and found him "a great inspiration." The two men were drawn together partly by likeness in temperament—both sensitive and intense—partly by an uncommon combination of enthusiasms, for athletics and English literature. Football, just coming into its own, was Sampson's special love, and Frank was learning the game. They met often on the players' bench, where Frank gained from criticism and encouragement as much as in the classroom. Sampson involved Frank later in another of his enthusiasms, dramatics. Undertaking to produce *As You Like It*, he chose for the romantic Orlando none other than the gawky young man from Sullivan. There was a stir of horror among "the other students and faculty interested. [They] thought he had lost his mind. [But] later they admitted they were all wrong, as Professor Sampson developed in the seemingly awkward boy the attractive lover Orlando."[17]

What Sampson thought of Frank as a student he tells in his recommendation to the Indiana Rhodes Scholarship Committee:

> In scholarship, Aydelotte has ability of unusually high order. He has a keen, quick mind, which seems at first at odds with his athletic, boyish appearance. This keen quality of mind I have tested again and again in the classroom, for it seemed too good to be true that I should have in the same person a young fellow of searching mind, of indefatigable diligence, of hearty sanity, of attractive manner. And he never failed at any point. I could always count on him when all the rest of the class had come to their limit. But he was never pedantic; his answers were whole-souled and genial: he seemed to master a subject so well that it did not worry him when he came to talk about it.[18]

Other teachers at Indiana whom Frank recalled gratefully were Professor Samuel Bannister Harding, for his "hard course" in history, and Professors William Lowe Bryan and Ernest H. Lindley, who jointly gave a course in ethics, "remembered to this day by all students who were lucky enough to take it." Professor Harding, distinguished for his writings, went later to a professorship of history at the University of Minnesota. Both teachers of ethics became Presidents of state universities, Bryan of Indiana and Lindley of Idaho and Kansas. But though the University community was not large, the relation between faculty and students was hardly personal, according to Frank's later account.

> I remember once that Dr. Bryan stopped me on the campus to say something complimentary about my playing in one of the football games. Naturally his remark gave me great pleasure, but over and above

the pleasure was the surprise that any member of the faculty should have noticed what we did on the football field.[19]

Free Hours

In his junior year, Frank's work in English took on a professional cast, adding the study of Old English to literature. History and philosophy he took as supporting subjects, a combination he thoroughly enjoyed. Also, football was gaining ground at Indiana; for the first time there was an excellent coach, James H. Horne. Frank by now had earned a firm place among the Varsity substitutes, with the wonderful luck of being called out to play on Thanksgiving when Indiana tied with Cincinnati. The team's record for 1898 was the most successful in Indiana history: victory in a majority of games. But student support was not even halfhearted; less than one-third of the 1,050 took the trouble to attend what promised and proved to be a most exciting game.[20] The team was at least getting good publicity in the college newspaper, which carried an article after the season with items about members of the squad, including Frank Aydelotte, "substitute end."[21] "This is his first year on the 'Varsity team. . . . He is 18 years old, weighs 152 pounds, and is 5 feet 8 inches in height." What he lacked in size and weight he made up in drive.

Next to football, Frank's favorite activity was reporting for the college paper, the *Daily Student*. His name first appeared on the masthead in December, 1898, before he was sent to Indianapolis to cover a state oratorical contest. What he wrote of the winner reflects his own good sense: "Mr. Farrar was entirely at ease on the platform and spoke in an earnest convincing tone which showed that he was full of his subject. His speech was neither bombastic nor stiff—it was full of warmth and feeling which were genuine.[22]

With all his hard work and serious interests, Frank was considered a good sort. He had a schoolboy sense of fun which made him the goat in an interclass scrap between juniors and seniors. He describes the incident with relish:

> It was the custom . . . for the senior class to appear at chapel in caps and gowns on a certain day in the spring. . . . [When we were juniors] we stole the . . . caps and gowns the day before . . . and collected them in our Sigma Nu fraternity house. Naturally the seniors came in a body to retrieve their property and nobody went to chapel. David Starr Jordan

II: Sullivan, Indiana. Above, Frank Aydelotte, age fifteen, as a high school senior. Below, the Aydelotte home; the boy in the foreground is W. E. Aydelotte, Jr.

III: Indiana University. Above, Frank Aydelotte's senior class photo. Below left, as Orlando in *As You Like It*. Below right, the All-State end.

happened to be the speaker that day and I can remember Dr. Swain standing on the top of the hill urging us all to come to chapel which of course nobody did. The seniors defied us to wear the caps and gowns out of the house and I was finally chosen to wear one of them supported by the rest of the juniors in ordinary clothes. Needless to say I was rolled in the dirt, the cap and gown torn to ribbons. I can still remember the man who owned it complaining to me that he was the real loser.[23]

The summers of 1898 and 1899 Frank spent at home in Sullivan, working to earn money and enjoying his friends. He hired himself to a carpenter who was building a new house for the Aydelottes and took on the job of dipping shingles in creosote, a process both messy and malodorous. The family admired his courage from a distance, but urged him to eat his lunch outdoors and to keep from the windward side until he had cleaned up at the end of the day. Another job he did for love was installing a system of speaking tubes from room to room—unnecessary gadgets in a house of that size, of course, but to figure out how to put them in had the charm of an original in geometry. And to Frank's triumph, they worked. (This house, to the man who owned it sixty years later, seemed a monument to the elder Aydelottes' sense of values. Built in a "good but not pretentious part of town," by the best workman in the region, its "beautiful fireplaces" and "handsome oak staircase" show the effort "to construct a house that was of the finest in material and craftsmanship." The Aydelottes were people "of character and substance, entirely devoid of ostentation."[24])

In one of these summers at home Frank began to notice girls. Neighbors, observant of these things, thought he had good taste; his two favorites were the prettiest girl in town and the brightest. There was a rumor that he was briefly engaged to the prettier one, but "his mother put a stop to that!" The brighter one remained his friend for many years. She and he read Stevenson together and played tennis. She admired him, but not without reservations: he went in too much for "strenuousness," and he could walk through beautiful country and hardly see the view. She was right about these shortcomings, as he would have agreed. He knew he could not resist trying to beat his own record, and it was true that he sometimes almost forgot where he was. But how could he attend to landscapes when people were so much more fascinating?

When Frank returned to Bloomington for his senior year he was one of the best-known members of his class as an athlete, a student, and a friendly fellow of sunny disposition. His first triumph was to earn a place on the Varsity football team; he was chosen right end. This season of '99 proved by all odds the best so far for Indiana. Under its first professional coach, "Jimmy" Horne, Indiana won its first victory over Purdue's formidable farmers and engineers. With five other wins and only two defeats, I.U. at last was champion of the state. Frank played all through these eight games with increasing speed and skill. From a "green, awkward country boy" he had developed into a well-coordinated, aggressive end, admired in football circles not only in Bloomington but throughout the state. When the All-Indiana Team was chosen for 1899, it included Frank Aydelotte.

No sooner had the football season ended than Frank was cast by Professor Sampson in the part of Orlando which he played with astonishing success, as has already been told. The Senior Class Book, *The Arbutus*, lists his name in many activities: he had served as a director of the *Daily Student* and an editor of *The Arbutus*; in lighter moments he had strummed a guitar in the University orchestra. He appears in several group pictures: a sensitive young face, chin resting on high stiff collar, hair parted in the middle according to the prevailing style. Photographed with the football team, he wears a turtle-necked sweater with the coveted big "I." And as Orlando he is a poetic personality in Elizabethan dress. *The Arbutus* also publishes a story of his, "A College Case," runner-up in a competition for "the best story of college life."[25]

The story suggests that Frank was still shy with girls and troubled about it. The characters are two men, Huffman and Williams, and a pretty blue-eyed, fair-haired freshman, Alice Lanford. Huffman was a "fake," but good-looking and "not a fool." He dressed well, had a way with the ladies, and saw no reason to play fair. Williams, "big, strong, boyish," was on the football team, inarticulate and inclined to be over-serious. Both men wanted to take Alice to a dance, Williams because he adored her, Huffman because he wanted to show her off. Huffman used a trick to get her; he bribed a messenger boy to deliver his invitation ahead of the one Williams had given him several hours earlier. When Alice told Williams she had agreed to go with Huffman, the clumsy, earnest boy tried to force her to "choose between them," obviously feeling there was much more at stake than a Pan-Hellenic dance. Alice, thinking she would be gayer with the lighthearted Huffman, turned Williams down cold. The story ends here, with the conflict not yet resolved. It is clear enough that Frank identifies himself with Williams and condemns Alice for preferring a smoothie to a rough diamond; any nice girl should have known better. But he is dissatisfied with Williams, too, who needs to learn how to get along with girls.

Frank's spate of senior activities did not interfere with study; indeed, on the academic side he ran ahead of the field. By the end of the middle term he had taken enough extra courses to meet the requirements for graduation, with the third term to spare. Just then he heard that South-Western Normal School at California, Pennsylvania, needed a teacher of English to fill out the year. He took the job, partly because he was impatient to begin to pay back his father for his education. In June he went back to Bloomington to graduate with the class of 1900. At the time he had no particular honors, but in 1911 when a chapter of Phi Beta Kappa was formed at Indiana, he was among the first graduates elected. And in 1914 he received another retroactive honor: the Varsity *I*, recognizing a combination of athletic skill, character, and service to the University.

CHAPTER THREE

TIME OF TESTING

1900–1905

As an undergraduate, Frank Aydelotte hoped to be a writer and consequently got all possible practice by working on University periodicals and reporting in the summer for the Sullivan *Democrat*. Teaching did not attract him. All the same, he was not sorry to earn some money as a substitute for one term at the normal school in California, Pennsylvania. He went with the highest recommendations from Professor William Lowe Bryan, later President of Indiana, who described him as "an exceptionally gifted young man . . . with teaching ability, strong scholarship, athletic skill, a forceful personality, upright character, and leadership."[1]

In spite of these impressive qualifications, Frank found the work hard. His youth was one hazard; he was only nineteen, and many of his men students were as old or older. Also, he not only taught them but lived in a dormitory, perpetually on call. Teaching alone would have been difficult enough because of the disparity in students' preparation: some were graduates of high school, some had finished only two years, and others, none at all, these last still meeting the bare entrance requirement of graduation from elementary school. To add to the confusion were differences in students' aims. These in a normal school might have been expected to bear on teaching; but some students were using the institution simply as a convenient preparatory school for a four-year college, others for terminal education before going to work in some other line. Frank deplored the overgenerous admissions policy which was explained by the strange status of Pennsylvania normal schools: they were not state-owned, but belonged to a private corporation whose investments were supplemented by state appropriations for students' tuition. Since the amount allotted depended on enrollment, there was pressure to keep numbers high.[2] In 1900 the graduating class included 120, appreciably larger than Frank's own class of 91 at Indiana. If he needed to be convinced that education should be adjusted to meet individual preparation, talents, and aims, he surely learned this lesson at California. He remembered that term as something of a nightmare when his mother wrote years later that his young sister Nell was finding her first teaching hard. Frank replied with brotherly sympathy and good sense: "I suppose Nellie is having a repetition of my California experiences. Tell her to keep cheerful, not think much about herself, and above all keep her troubles to herself or in the family" (October 15, 1906, from Oxford).

But, whatever the difficulties, Frank taught with characteristic verve. One class in English grammar, a subject he had to prepare from the ground up and would have said he hated, brought forth a student comment which surprised him: "Professor, I wish I could be as enthusiastic about grammar as you are."[3]

Thankful when the term had dragged to an end, Frank went back to Bloomington for his diploma, delighted that an opportunity in journalism was coming his way. One of his fraternity brothers had started a newspaper in Vincennes, Indiana, and offered him a job. He accepted eagerly, got his degree on June 20, 1900, and was soon en route to Kansas City to report the Democratic Convention, which began its cavortings on the Fourth of July. In spite of clamor and oratory, the excitement was only superficial. Most people believed that the Republican incumbent, McKinley, would be re-elected, partly because he had a good record in office, partly because his party profited from two bits of luck: the Spanish War which had recently been won in less than four months (April–July, 1898), had given the United States a new position as a world power and, as a result, unprecedented prosperity; also, the issue of bimetallism, so important in the last election when gold was scarce, had lost its meaning after the discovery of rich deposits in Alaska and South Africa. Abundant gold took away the Democrats' strongest talking point, free silver. But Bryan was nominated again, this time by acclaim. Frank listened a second time to the "golden voice," reported events carefully, and returned to his paper in Vincennes.

He liked this small city on the Wabash with its charm of an antiquity uncommon in the Middle West. Its history went back almost two hundred years to a French fort on the "Ouabache" established to protect communications between Quebec and Louisiana. The town was named in memory of the fort's builder, a young French officer, François Margane Sieur de Vincennes, who met his death in 1736 after a battle with the Chickasaw Indians. He could have escaped, but refused to desert wounded soldiers in his command and was burned at the stake on Easter Sunday.[4]

The name of Frank's newspaper, the Vincennes *Capital*, reflected a brief period of glory at the beginning of the nineteenth century when Vincennes was capital of the vast Indiana Territory extending over areas destined to become the States of Illinois, Michigan, Wisconsin, and a part of Minnesota. Though the *Capital* was relatively new, it was acknowledged "the peer of any paper" in the city, "ably edited," and "strongly in the interest of Republican principles and men.[5] Here was Frank, son of an ardent Democrat, on the staff of a Republican paper.

Perhaps this uncongeniality helps explain his early loss of enthusiasm for a reporter's life. Also even Vincennes' historic glamour could hardly give zest to the usual round of organizations and weddings and first families' goings and comings. In September Frank felt a pang of wistfulness for the academic life when he heard that friends in Bloomington, notably President Swain, were trying to help him come back for graduate work, but on sober thought he decided he must remain where he could earn. "By staying here," he wrote President Swain, "I can pay off a pretty good part of my college debt and my father would like that."[6] Even so, he was not wholly out of touch with college life. During the autumn he coached the football team at Vincennes University to such good effect that it had by all odds its best season so far. As a reporter he covered a speech by the President of Cornell, Jacob Gould Schurman, who was supporting McKinley's campaign. After the meeting, Frank wanted to clear up some points and went with the speaker to a restaurant for talk and a glass of beer. Dr. Schurman warmed to the young reporter and, finding that he had taught, began to enlarge on the attractions of an academic career. Frank was in a mood to listen, with the result that he took the slight first step of writing to California for a recommendation. The President replied that he would recommend Frank gladly or better still, welcome him back to the faculty for the winter and spring terms. At this distance past trials seemed less irksome than present boredom, and Frank decided to accept. Once he was in the classroom again, he began to feel the pull of teaching, which never lost its hold.

In these months from January to June, 1901, Frank undertook the new task of tutoring a boy for an examination in Latin. He had not studied Latin since his three years in high school, but his interest was only sharpened by this handicap. He coached the boy as he would a football player: methodically, tirelessly, and in the best of spirits, with the result that the boy passed well and Frank advanced his own command of the language.

By June he was sure that teaching was his line, but at the same time, he hankered to see more of the world. Hearing that a professor of pedagogy at Bloomington, Elmer B. Bryan, had charge of new teaching appointments in the Philippines, Frank wrote to apply, and he might have gone if Professor Bryan's plans had not been stopped by illness. Frank mentions his interest in this job in a letter to his mother, adding a word about his work at Califorina: the students were sunk in examinations and the end of term was in sight, with Commencement and the "annual bawl" only a week away. His dormitory duties, though confining, he had well in hand: "I will have to stay until the last one leaves and help hold them down at which business I am gaining some skill" (June 11, 1901).

This term ended Frank's teaching at California, to the regret of the President, who declared he had more than earned Professor William Bryan's praise. A fellow teacher wrote warmly of his success: "Frank displayed a skill in dealing with new conditions which is very rare indeed. The boys saw in him a scholar who was not a prig, and a comrade they both liked and respected" (March 18, 1905; Anna Buckbee).[7] Frank thought well enough of the school to recommend it to his brother Will, who was graduated in 1903 as president of his class. His mother kept a teacher's letter praising Will's speech "to a very large audience" and himself as a "fine kind of boy."

In September Frank returned to Bloomington to take a substitute's position in English at a salary of $600 from which he squeezed out $200 to help Will with his expenses at California. Frank was happy to belong to a department he admired, with a program of courses he found attractive: Scott, Shakespeare, and "Novels" in addition to the inevitable composition which he accepted willingly enough. The year at Bloomington more than met his hopes. He enjoyed the peculiarly pleasant dignity of teaching where he had once been taught; he enjoyed the warm response from active-minded young people; and thanks to his lively friend Alfred Brooks, he had plenty of fun.

First News of Cecil Rhodes

In April something happened to open amazing new possibilities to able young men of Frank's age throughout the English-speaking world: Cecil Rhodes's will was published, with its provisions for a wholly original system of scholarships. Rhodes proposed to devote much of his great fortune to bringing men from the colonies and the United States to study at Oxford, in the hope that they would be convinced of the value of British civilization (which he considered the finest in existence) and go home to spread British influences throughout the world, thus building a kind of spiritual commonwealth.

In a codicil, written after Rhodes had observed the rising power of Germany, he added fifteen scholarships for German students, with the explanation that "a good understanding between England, Germany and the United States will secure the peace of the world, and educational relations form the strongest tie."

The German Scholars were to be nominated by the "Emperor." Rhodes left the method of selecting the others to his Trustees, contenting himself with describing the combination of qualities he thought essential.

Rhodes wanted his Scholars to be not "merely bookworms": in addition to excellence in "literary and scholastic attainments" they should show interest and proficiency in "manly outdoor sports" and distinction in character—"manhood, truth, courage, devotion to duty, sympathy for and protection of the weak, kindliness, unselfishness and fellowship." And finally, he wanted them to be public-spirited men who "will be likely in afterlife to esteem the performance of public duties as . . . their highest aim."[8] In other words, they should give promise of such intelligence, physical stamina, and idealism as would command respect and support for their efforts toward a better world order.

Such men should not live meanly. Rhodes proposed stipends large enough for comfort at Oxford and vacations of travel on the Continent: 300 pounds (then $1,500) a year for three years. He may have wanted also to let his Scholars live on something of an equality with undergraduates from well-to-do and distinguished British families who would be their co-workers in "afterlife."

Rhodes's intentions had been known to only a few close friends before his will electrified the English-speaking world. In its large-minded generosity it was compared to Caesar's: "Since the will of Julius Caesar was delivered to the people of Rome, no man has bequeathed his fortune to the public benefit in so grandiose a manner as Cecil Rhodes."[9] Indeed, the startling novelty of Rhodes's action can hardly be imagined in these later years when the academic scene seems crowded with generous scholarships, some of them inspired by his, and many men of wealth have established foundations for devoting their fortunes to the public good. But to Rhodes's contemporaries he seemed daringly original. Hear an Oxford teacher of philosophy, F. C. S. Schiller: "The endowment of *international* scholarships is a totally new idea," as is also the "recognition of the political significance of a common academic life, and of the power of ideas in drawing together and alienating nations."[10] The size of Rhodes's Scholarships, according to *The Times*, represented "a scale of unprecedented munificence." "Considering that 300 pounds a year is the *maximum* value of a fellowship [salary of a teacher] and that scholarships nowadays rarely reach the value of 100 pounds, this provision seems almost lavish."[11] The combination of qualities Rhodes wanted—athletic and moral distinction added to intellectual—seemed so unusual, not to say impossible, that an undergraduate reaction was to cry, "Absurd!"[12]

In the United States, comments were on the whole enthusiastic: the will was described as "magnificent in its enlightened statesmanship and catholic philanthropy" and the assignment of scholarships to students from the United States as "one of the noblest legacies ever left to a people by a citizen of another country." Of course, at least one anti-British critic must ask "why an American youth should go to England for education when he could get a better one at home,"[13] but apparently no one raised the objection which would have been inevitable sixty years later: that Rhodes was advocating "indoctrination of imperialism." His belief in the superiority of British civilization apparently seemed too natural (and perhaps too convincing) to be challenged.

On the morning when the will appeared in Indiana papers, Frank devoured every word in it and about it, reveling in the tribute to qualities he admired and would possess if he could and in the glamour of study and travel abroad. Later in the day he met President Swain, who greeted him with a gratifying remark: "Frank, has thee heard of these Rhodes Scholarships? Thee ought to get one of them." To which Frank replied; "Dr. Swain, I had already thought of it."

At the moment no date was set for the first awards; obviously plans of selection would involve weighty problems which might take a long time. Of what age should the Scholars be, schoolboys or men of maturity with experience in universities in their own countries? What examinations would be required? Until Frank heard the answers, he would not know whether he would be eligible.

Harvard Yard

Already for more than a year he had thought longingly of graduate work at Harvard. While on the staff of the Vincennes *Capital* he had written to President Swain about the possibility of a Harvard scholarship and later from California had again appealed to him for a recommendation to the Harvard Graduate School. Nothing came of this; no scholarship, no other funds. But now, having reached his twenty-first birthday without smoking, he had earned the reward of five hundred dollars promised him long ago by his Uncle Jim. Supplementing this with a loan from the Sullivan Bank, he could manage a year without a job. So he decided to go to Cambridge in September.

Frank was one of many ambitious students attracted to Harvard in 1902 from every part of the country, though not in numbers so large that an individual need feel submerged. There were less than two thousand in the college and slightly more than three hundred in the Graduate School of Arts and Sciences. As a graduate student in English, Frank could hope to know his teachers.

And what teachers there were to know! Later these years would be called Harvard's Golden Age, glowing with faculty stars. Frank had heard that the most brilliant department was probably philosophy with its famous five, never matched at any time or place: William James and Josiah Royce, George Herbert Palmer, George Santayana and Hugo Münsterberg. Recently Royce and James had been the first Americans honored by invitations from Scotland to serve as Gifford Lecturers: Royce at Aberdeen (1899) and James at Edinburgh (1902). James's classic series on the *Varieties of Religious Experience* had just been published (June, 1902).

More important to Frank was the English department's share of luminaries, distinguished both as teachers and personalities and at the peak of their powers. There was Barrett Wendell, already widely known at forty-seven for his writings, including the recent *Literary History of America*. This very year he was away in England giving the Clark Lectures at Trinity College, Cambridge. This was very disappointing. Frank had read Wendell's *English Composition* and would have enjoyed his lectures and the sight of this Harvard character—man of the world, elegant in dress and bearing, with his European pointed beard, his Anglicized way of talking, his passion for Britain at a time when academic enthusiasm still ran to Germany; his mannerisms in the lecture room where he paced the platform twirling his watch chain, uttering devastatingly honest judgments, with occasional bursts of eloquent enthusiasm. But the three men on the scene were a host in themselves: George Lyman Kittredge, Charles Townsend Copeland, and Le Baron Russell Briggs.[14] Frank was to know them all well.

Kittredge, five years younger than Wendell, had published less, but enough to establish his reputation as a leading scholar in the field of English language. Personally he was a regal figure, tall and graceful, with a statesman's square gray beard. He dressed impeccably in gray and struck awe by his commanding glance and astringent comments on undergraduate ineptitude and mediocrity. Surely the very pattern of the full professor and department chairman he had become at thirty-three. In the classroom his gift was to wake students to the rigors and satisfactions of pure scholarship, showing them how to examine a tale of Chaucer's or a play of Shakespeare's, line by line, until it took on the life they could feel the author intended. Though aloof from undergraduates, with graduate students he became another person, treating them with the courtesy and kindness due to gentlemen who hoped one day to become scholars.

"Copey," Kittredge's classmate, could hardly have been less like him. Copey was a little man in a checked suit and a derby hat who might have looked more at home at a race track than in Harvard Yard. Academically he was far less advanced than Kittredge, partly because he had come later into teaching, joining the department as an instructor in the same year when Kittredge became chairman. Previously Copey had been a journalist, especially apt at literary and dramatic criticism—not a bad preparation for teaching composition. But in 1902 he was still an instructor and would remain so until President Eliot, who did not like him, was succeeded by President Lowell. It was true that Copey was not a professorial type and not in the class with Wendell as a writer of belles-lettres or with Kittredge as a scholar. But as a teacher, he was incomparable, as Frank heartily agreed. No man ever made a greater impact on students, and in two very different ways, each hard to master. He was good with individuals, seeing their gifts and weaknesses and helping to develop or nip them, sometimes with ferocious zeal. And with groups he had an unusual power of communicating almost by magic the meaning and spirit of a work by reading it aloud. He read to the boys in Stoughton, the hall where he lived in Harvard Yard when Frank first knew him. Later, during his many years in Hollis, he went on reading to an ever widening group of students and devoted alumni until he became a "legend in his lifetime," a "cult."

Frank's first friend was Le Baron Russell Briggs, who in 1902 had completed a decade as Dean of Harvard College and was taking on the deanship of the faculty of arts and sciences, while continuing his effective teaching. For almost twenty years he and Wendell had been experimenting with courses in composition and were responsible for "Freshman English," with "daily themes" designed to help students write simply and directly about what they saw and thought from day to day. These Harvard courses served as models all over the country, turning the fashion in student writing from florid rhetoric to the natural phrasing of a diary or a good newspaper, a revolutionary change and one that appealed to Frank. To pupils and colleagues Briggs brought the same selfless benevolence, the same warm sympathy, perceptiveness, and humor that made him so pre-eminently successful a Dean, beloved by generations at Harvard and later at Radcliffe, where he served as President. One of his admirers may have exaggerated when he said that Briggs "could fire a boy from college and make it seem like a benediction," but if an overstatement, it was still in character. Of course, he had personal oddities: a disarmingly shy manner, a pink-cheeked look of being younger than he was, an oddly uncertain voice "wrinkling with kindness," as a freshman described it; but these only added to his charm.

Cambridge Ups and Downs

In arranging his personal life, Frank was guided by his resourceful friend Alfred Brooks, who found him a place to stay at 54 Garden Street, the house of the Parsons sisters, Sabra, Carrie, and Kitty. They were daughters of a professor in the Harvard Law School, Theophilus Parsons, who had died many years before (1882). Their grandfather, also Theophilus Parsons, an even more distinguished jurist, had been Chief Justice of the Supreme Court of Massachusetts (1806–1813). His portrait, painted by Stuart, hung in the Parsons house and was always called to a visitor's attention. With a touch of the Irish in their manners and wit (though none in their blood), the ladies were as lively as they were kind, their talk full of unexpected sallies. When Charles Eliot Norton once said that the outline of the White Mountains was vulgar, one of them retorted, "Wicked old man, don't you know who made those mountains?"[15] While arranging casually for his comfort, they saw to it that Frank had entertaining glimpses of Cambridge society.

On the academic side Frank's reception at Harvard was disappointing; he was accepted only as a candidate for an A.B., the degree he had already taken at Indiana. This was partly explained by lack of clear-cut interuniversity practices: the graduate of another university could not *ipso facto* qualify as a candidate for a Harvard A.M. Also, his deficiency in Latin rose up to plague him. Three years in the Sullivan High School fell one year short. On this last point, Frank offered an ingenious claim for extra credit, based on his success in tutoring a boy at California Normal School, a claim supported by a strong letter from President Noss of California. But not until late in March was Frank told that his Latin was clear.

Meanwhile he was admitted to graduate courses with Professor Kittredge and Dean Briggs. For recreation he joined the football squad, although in his first year not eligible for the team. An unexpected addition to his program was heralded one night by the sound of stamping up the stairs to his third-floor room, the noise of Dean Briggs with his dog coming to say that Copey needed an assistant to read daily themes and hold conferences with students. Would Frank like to be recommended? Would he! Eventually he was given full charge of a section of the famous English A.[16] Another duty, purely social, entrusted to him by Copey was to bring student parties to a timely end. It was Copey's custom to entertain students in his rooms every Saturday night at eleven o'clock. He asked Frank to come and to rise promptly at midnight, saying in a loud voice, "I'm afraid it's time to go home." Frank enjoyed the sociability and the readings and was glad of an excuse to attend regularly.

Even for a young man of Frank's vitality, the demands of teaching added to full-time graduate work were heavy, but he attacked it all with gusto, and at the end of the semester he wrote his mother in the best of spirits, proud of his plan for taking examinations in his stride and allowing time for exercise and fun.

> I have the art of getting ready for exams down fine. I reviewed all week but the afternoon before the exam I stopped and went into the gymnasium to exercise an hour or so and then ate an extra big dinner and went to the symphony concert (with Miss Parsons who had invited me) and then

came home and went to bed rather early and had about nine hours sleep so that I felt bully for my exam and the things coming after, . . . conferences with my Freshmen all afternoon and then the play that night. I felt equal to it all however [and] am going to do the same with my exam this week, going to a reception at the home of one of my Professors [Kittredge] the night before.

The play was a performance of *Julius Caesar* with Mansfield as Brutus. Frank was deeply impressed by the interpretation:

It showed a knowledge of Shakespeare far beyond that of the ordinary actor. Mansfield acted with a simplicity of gesture that was simply fine. In the last scene he did not change his position once. The curtain went up with him sitting on a rock and he made his farewell speeches to his friends and after they left him, killed himself . . . simply dropped his head forward on his breast—no melodramatic throwing up his arms and falling and spouting of red ink for blood.

Frank was happy also in his social life, finding New Englanders more friendly than he had expected.

Contrary to the usual experience of Westerners—so they say—I find the people of Cambridge very cordial. I had gone pretty slowly at first, but am gradually being invited to one place or another and am getting to know some very nice people.

A week later he still wrote cheerfully, though reporting a disappointing grade in Kittredge's course, only B plus, which he hoped to raise to A by the end of the year. The grade was given by a reader who had difficulty with Frank's penmanship, which was always bad. "The instructor told me he couldn't read my exam paper very well." (Frank practiced a kind of personal speed writing, beginning words and letting them go as his thinking flew ahead.) This letter ends with a message to his sister that Kate Douglas Wiggin's novel is a best seller: "Tell Nellie that *Mrs. Wiggs of the Cabbage Patch* is becoming all the rage in Boston. It is on sale at the Harvard Co-op and everybody is reading it."

Writing again at the end of February, Frank was cast down by reports of his grades—no A's—and also by hearing that his Latin shortage was still under scrutiny. But he could view the situation objectively. If he should have to make up Latin, he would enjoy coming back to Harvard for another year. He would like to know the place and people better and would surely profit from what he had learned about using his time.

In many ways I haven't been at my best this year, I don't think you can be until you get acquainted and know what to do and what not to. I feel that it would be a very good thing for me to come back next year and take my A.M. I think I could pay my own expenses. I could get more out of my work and I could be better acquainted with the men in the English Department all of whom have been very kind to me. I have got such a good start toward knowing absolutely the biggest men in English teaching that if I am going to be a teacher I ought to come back next year and absorb more of the Harvard ideas. . . . This year I have had too much to do and have been unwise in getting into football and too much English etc. I hate to leave without showing them what I can do. They may make some allowances for my extra work but I can't expect them to. The way to do is to plan things out yourself rightly and then be judged in comparison with other men. Harvard is too big a place for the authorities to know all about everybody's private affairs.

My mid-year grades were all B's and B pluses (so far as I've heard). Two of these B's I hope to raise to A's in the finals and one of them, B in English Composition, is as good as I can expect—rather better than I did expect. So you see my work is by no means poor. But on the other hand, it is not at all what I can do.

Frank had consistently tried to do too much, and the strain began to tell. When he fell ill, Copey came to the rescue with characteristic kindness and good cheer. He asked Frank's doctor to drive him past Stoughton where, as Frank told it, "Copey came down carrying a bottle of whiskey and ordered me to stay away for two weeks. I said, 'Mr. Copeland, how will you manage with your students?' 'Oh,' he said, 'the old man can always manage.' I went off and took a holiday as he ordered and returned to Cambridge entirely cured."

The teacher from whom Frank felt he gained most intellectually was Kittredge, especially from "his famous course on Shakespeare." And Frank thought it was to Kittredge that he owed the A.M. he finally got in June.

One day I was working in the stacks of the Harvard Library when Kittredge came along and asked to see what book I was taking out of the stacks. I showed it to him. He apparently was impressed. He talked to me a little about it and then asked me what degree I was applying for. I said I had been required to put in an application for the A.B. He said: "Go to the office and change that to the A.M." I accordingly did this, but I never knew until Commencement whether I was going to get the A.B. or the A.M.[17]

Other teachers besides Kittredge were well disposed. When Frank was being considered for a position at the University of Colorado, Copey wrote:

> 7 Stoughton Hall
> 27 April 1904

Dear Mr. Briggs:

As a teacher, Aydelotte was one of the few best out of the many young men that have helped me teach English Composition during the past ten years.

Besides doing his work faithfully and well, he was a friend to his pupils, and made it pleasant for them to go to see him at his lodgings. In this human, highly important, generally neglected department of a teacher's duty, Aydelotte did far more than any other assistant of mine has even tried to do. I wish he might live in the Harvard "Yard," teach Harvard undergraduates, and be their genial yet highly respected associate. Happy the college that adds him to its staff, and is wise enough to let him take his own kind, hearty way.

> Yours truly,
> (Signed) C. T. Copeland

To Professor L. B. R. Briggs

And Dean Briggs wrote:

I saw a good deal of him [Aydelotte], because he was in a small class of mine, and I liked him very much. He is able, earnest and thoroughly human. His love of football and his ability to play football put him into touch with the young life of the students, and make his intellectual enthusiasm the more telling with them. All of us liked him personally; and those of us who knew his work recognized his ability.[18]

Frank's interest in a Rhodes Scholarship continued strong; he had written twice in the past year to the newly elected President of Indiana, his old friend William Lowe Bryan, to ask when the terms of eligibility would be announced. "It is only my very great interest in the matter which makes me trouble you."[19] But so far no one could answer.

Louisville

Fortunately Frank was offered a position in Louisville which he was glad to accept. His work combined teaching English and coaching football in the Louisville Male High School at what was then the respectable salary of $1,000. But with debts to pay, Frank decided to take also a resident's job in a social settlement, Neighborhood House. Aside from the financial help, the idea of a settlement appealed to him as a kind of adventure in friendliness.

The spiritual roots of Neighborhood House went back to Toynbee Hall in the East End of London, established in 1884 with the idea that "little can be done *for*, which is not done *with* people." In 1886 the first American Settlement House was founded in New York by Stanton Coit in a Forsythe Street tenement; soon afterward in Chicago Jane Addams opened Hull-House and Graham Taylor began his work in the Chicago Commons. It was Graham Taylor who stood godfather for the Louisville enterprise: a group of concerned citizens asked his help in 1895 and the next year put his suggestions to use by converting an old saloon into a two-room clubhouse. Soon a generous gift of buildings made a real Neighborhood House possible. It was well started when Frank went there to live, joined by a cousin from Indiana, Carl Sproat.

As a resident, Frank was expected to give some time to social work, and he chose to conduct a gymnasium class for boys, most of them of foreign birth or parentage: Italians, Russian and Polish Jews, and Syrians. Some came from families where the parents had lost control and the boys were at loose ends—a sharp contrast to the relatively protected and homogeneous group Frank had known in the Sullivan High School. But with his passion for athletics, Frank saw them above all as underprivileged physically; and having been similarly handicapped himself when kept out of games by his stiff right arm, he had a special urge to help them. "I had a wonderful time with this class," he remembered later, and according to the Head Resident, Eleanor Tarrant, with rare results.

> He made them into "law-abiding American citizens" . . . by means of athletics. His splendid body commanded the respect of every boy the very first night they met. Later, in the gymnasium or on the baseball field they felt his muscle and asked many personal questions and he met them with such friendliness and sympathy that they were drawn closer to him. He put ambition into the weak, thin boys who had no muscle and they worked hard to get what Mr. Aydelotte had.[20]

Some of Frank's own recollections centered humorously on problems of discipline which he handled by surprise attack:

> The boys were always eager to do something which was not allowed. I evolved the technique of spotting a boy just before he made some motions to break over the rules and punishing him before he had time to carry out his intention. I found this had a wonderful effect on discipline.[21]

He was fortunate to have his cousin Carl's help with the class and "the manifold details" for which Frank's high-school duties left no time.

As usual, Frank was attempting more than was humanly possible. In the high school he taught five classes in English a day and read 125 themes a week. The atmosphere of the school "was an uncompromising search for excellence" on the part of both teachers and taught. Frank believed that there were "few secondary schools in the United States with the same standards," thanks largely to the principal, Reuben Post Halleck, "a great man in secondary education in the middle west." Frank liked Halleck at first sight because "one of the pigeon holes in his desk was stuffed with a pipe and tobacco," though he later discovered that the smoking equipment had been "confiscated from some unlucky student." Frank learned a vast amount about teaching from his work under Halleck and was grateful to be allowed to try out ideas of his own. One was to encourage the boys to read by letting them use the period set aside for required chapel; he excused "any boy from chapel who spent the time reading in [his] classroom." Frank got together a collection of books and was convinced that "the boys profited as much from their reading as from 'chapel.' "

On the gridiron Frank made history as the school's first "professional" coach: "The years 1903 and 1904 saw the beginning of professional coaching at Male High, with the advent of Frank Aydelotte, Indiana University star, as head coach."[22] His work made history again in its results: the team of his second year not only won all its games except one scoreless tie, but was never scored on. Frank tells the story:

> The first year the team was fair but not too good. For some reason I felt deeply mortified and after the Thanksgiving game I got all the boys together. I exacted a promise from each that they would not smoke for a year and undertook to keep the same rule. [His attitude here was ambivalent; he enjoyed smoking socially, but disbelieved in it athletically.] I required them also to take certain exercises to keep them in good condition. In the fall of 1904 I got these boys together full of enthusiasm and certainly they produced the best team Louisville had ever had.

Playing for High Stakes

Between his two football seasons the rules for choosing Rhodes Scholars were finally announced. To Frank's joy, the decision had gone against awards to schoolboys. Candidates must have completed at least two years of college work and should be not younger than nineteen or older than twenty-five. But he was taken aback by another requirement: a qualifying examination (Oxford "Responsions") which included both Latin and Greek in addition to mathematics. In mathematics his preparation was adequate; in Latin, only fair; and Greek he had never studied at all. In the years that followed, many men in his situation abandoned the idea of competing. Not Frank. Conceding that he could not be ready to compete in the first group, 1904, he determined to learn enough to try the second year, the last before he reached the age limit.

Knowing that Abraham Flexner, then head of an excellent college preparatory school for boys in Louisville, was an expert at teaching languages, Frank appealed to him for advice. It happened that Flexner himself had been in a similar quandary when he entered Johns Hopkins with almost no Greek and had been shown by Professor Charles Morris how to teach himself successfully. Obviously he was just the one to encourage Frank and to suggest methods of study.[23] Now and often later Frank had cause to be grateful to Abraham Flexner as their association grew into a friendship of first importance to both.

Frank added work on the two languages to an already full program. Even though a horse for energy, he felt the strain: "I used to be so sleepy after I had read my themes and done my exercises in Latin and Greek that I would keel over at my table." His only chance to be coached and to give full time to study came during the Christmas vacation. Then he stayed in Bloomington, tutored every day by Harold Whetstone Johnstone and Miss Lillian Berry in Latin and by Frank William Tilden in Greek. Miss Berry remembers she had no wish to spend her vacation teaching anybody, but Frank argued so persuasively that she finally agreed. When he came for his lessons he always dashed up in a cab; just then money meant less than time. Such cramming was not to Frank's taste—he disliked "smatterings" and admired thoroughness—but he had no choice: it was this or nothing. When the examinations were given in January at Indianapolis, Professor Johnstone went up with him for last-minute advice and moral support. Fortunately Frank passed. But he declared that he "probably knew less Greek than anyone who was ever admitted to the University of Oxford."

Responsions were only the first hurdle. Since nominations were made by states, Frank must now be compared with other young Hoosiers eager to represent Indiana. There were no set rules about testimonials. Candidates submitted one or many and collected them personally; no notion then that recommendations should be confidential. Frank had Alfred Brooks's help in planning his little campaign and hired a secretary to do the mechanical work. Always thorough, he drew up a list of thirty-three referees who represented every place where he had lived and worked and many fields of interest: ministers, businessmen, neighbors, teachers, fellow students, employers. Alfred had the idea of adapting one of Rhodes's early suggestions (not followed by the Trustees): that a candidate's leadership should be tested by his schoolmates' vote; and accordingly he encouraged undergraduate friends to send in a petition in Frank's favor. They produced an enthusiastic tribute, signed by 163 supporters. It was also Alfred's idea to have this document and the thirty-three letters duplicated and mounted in a scrapbook for each member of the selection committee. Fortunately one of these books survives as an invaluable composite portrait of a promising young man.

The tone of the letters is naturally friendly; anyone who took the trouble to write probably liked Frank and wanted to help him. And it is natural, too, that they stress the qualities stipulated by Cecil Rhodes; indeed, several writers point out that Frank is precisely the kind of man Rhodes had in mind. There is also a special warmth for a typically American success story of a boy who had to work hard for what he got, always played fair, and helped his friends. A frequent spark of pleasure, too, in what was unusual in Frank—his energy and enthusiasm, his knack for making a hard job seem like fun. One letter from a fellow athlete catches qualities so characteristic that it might have been paralleled twenty years later by colleagues at Swarthmore.

> In athletics his good spirit, energy, dash, nerve, and enthusiasm were always admirable and inspiring. His playing was always persistent, capable, and reliable; his energy ceaseless. His best quality, however, is what is commonly called "good sportsmanship"; he always recognized the rights of his opponent, was more than fair toward him, and was ready to yield a disputed point and then outplay his man. He seemed always at his best and yet was trying to outdo his previous work. His presence put confidence and life in his own side and convinced his opponents at once of his fairness and his ability.
>
> (John A. Foster, Quarter-back Foot-ball Team for 1899.
> Captain for 1900)
> Faribault, Minn. March 25, 1905[24]

The Indiana committee, composed of Presidents of all the colleges and universities in the state, was inexperienced in the kind of selection involved and hesitated to cause hard feelings by comparing "favorite sons." Like similarly embarrassed committees in some other states, they hit upon the expedient of "passing the scholarship around." If a graduate of Indiana had been appointed in 1904, some other college would have taken its turn in 1905, and Frank would have lost out. Luckily for him, the 1904 man had come from Earlham; this year could be the University's. And so it proved. Frank had a powerful friend in President William Lowe Bryan as well as unusual papers: he had accomplished a great deal for a man of twenty-four. When the committee met and chose him, President Bryan gave Alfred Brooks the privilege of reporting the good news. Frank celebrated his success by a grand dinner in Bloomington for everyone who had helped him compete. He could spend with a flourish when occasion justified, even in the years of making every penny count.

In the excitement of competing for his scholarship, Frank did not forget his young brother and sister and discussed their affairs with his mother. "Willie" had been at Bloomington for the first two terms of 1904–1905, but his work had been so poor that there was a question whether he should leave at once. Frank urged his mother to let Willie stay, arguing that he could live with Alfred Brooks, who would give him all kinds of help. "Nellie" was at boarding school—Monticello Seminary in Illinois—homesick and unhappy. In May Frank paid her a visit to see how things were and passed on a reassuring opinion to his mother. Even if Nellie wasn't happy, he said, "few people are their first year away from home," and she had learned a good deal. He agreed that "those old maid teachers and some of the foolish, snobbish girls would make anybody weary," but "some of the teachers (one anyway) and some of the girls are all right." He ended with firm, brotherly pride: "Nellie is easily the pick of the school I think and they'd think so too if she stayed long enough but I doubt if convincing them is worth while." However he was certain that she should not come home at once, as she had wanted to do, but should finish the term.[25]

Frank's two years in Louisville had been remarkably successful. He had taught his English classes well, created a fine spirit toward physical fitness among the boys at Neighborhood House, and coached football to such good effect that he was a popular figure in the city. An editor of the Louisville *Courier Journal*, A. Y. Ford, pays his tribute:

Mr. Frank Aydelotte has established himself in a most enviable position in this community, not only by his fine qualifications as a scholar and teacher, but by his manliness of character and his exemplification of a very high type of citizenship, . . . his readiness for unselfish labor in behalf of others, his devotion to the community . . . and good fellowship.

A student tribute appeared in the Male High School monthly magazine, the *Spectator*, in October, 1905 (p. 14), when he was already in Oxford:

> The fact that we knew last June that Male High School was to lose Professor Aydelotte does not make us miss him any the less. In the class room and on the athletic field, Professor Aydelotte was immensely popular. He coached the immortal team of 1905—the champions of Kentucky and Indiana by the score of 188 to 0.
>
> We are hoping to hear from Professor Aydelotte soon, as everyone in school would appreciate his notes from Oxford. We will say for the benefit of Freshmen that Professor Aydelotte won a Cecil Rhodes scholarship to Oxford, awarded by the State of Indiana.[26]

CHAPTER FOUR

RHODES SCHOLAR: FIRST YEAR

1905–1906

EVEN before he had won a Scholarship, Frank Aydelotte read everything he could find about Cecil Rhodes and became convinced that the bequest was hardly more remarkable than the man himself. Rhodes was a pioneer in a favorite nineteenth-century tradition: he had subdued a wilderness and made a fortune under peculiarly difficult circumstances and with spectacular success. Born in an English parsonage in 1853, and so delicate as a boy that he was sent to a brother in South Africa to try to improve his health, he died there at forty-nine. But in his short life he had become famous as a fearless explorer, a mine owner of fabulous wealth in diamonds and gold, Prime Minister of Cape Colony, developer of Rhodesia, one of the great builders of the British empire. He had also found time to give himself an education at Oxford, matriculating when he was twenty, keeping terms as business permitted, and finally taking a Pass degree at twenty-eight. It was important that his years at Oxford fell at the time when Ruskin's influence was strong. Ruskin's teachings echoed in Rhodes's "Confessions of Faith" (1877), as Frank himself pointed out later in his essay "The Vision of Cecil Rhodes."[1] Both Ruskin and Rhodes, like many of their contemporaries, believed quite simply that the English were "the finest race in the world," with "firmness to govern," "grace to obey," and a noble inheritance of a religion of "pure mercy" and "honour." To give these traits their broadest scope, Ruskin urged the expansion of the empire through new colonies. This idea was seized by the practical Rhodes and put into action, often ruthlessly; eventually he brought large sections of southern Africa under British rule.

But for Rhodes the dreamer this was not enough. Looking for a way to use his fortune both to extend British influence and to further the cause of peace, he had finally decided, as has been told, to trust to the slow power of education. When Frank became a Rhodes Scholar, he shared with other similarly fortunate young men a sense of "public duties," though the award in itself was wholly without conditions.

To help prepare for his new venture, Frank devoured a book by John Corbin, *An American at Oxford*, opportunely published some five weeks after Rhodes's will was announced.[2] The book gave the first full account of the Oxford system at a time when it was little known in the United States. The dominant European influence on American education then and until after World War I was still the German university. Corbin, a graduate of Harvard, had taken the unusual step of going for a year to Balliol College, Oxford, returning to spread the gospel of English education. Americans, he urged, should learn to supplement Teutonic respect for advanced, scholarly research with the Oxford concern for a kind of undergraduate community life which developed common sense and flexibility of mind—character as well as intellect.

This Oxford life he described as centering in the Colleges—each a corporate body of undergraduates and teachers (called indiscriminately "fellows" or "dons"), each with its ancient quadrangles which include living quarters, dining hall, chapel, and library; each with its clubs and athletic teams, its ferment of student parties at breakfast, lunch, and tea, put on by a corps of college servants ("scouts"), and providing unceasing opportunities for good talk. When a stranger asks to see "the University" he is mystified to learn that it hardly exists except as a federation of Colleges, an organization chiefly responsible for setting examinations ("Schools") and granting degrees. The College takes the responsibility for helping a man prepare for examinations, assigning him to one of the dons, who serves as his tutor. The tutor guides his work not only during the three terms of the academic year—about six months—but also during the vacations: six weeks at Christmas, six at Easter, three months in the summer. Indeed, it is in the vacation that an undergraduate settles down to his most concentrated study. During term he does some reading, of course, and writes a weekly essay for his tutor; he may attend a few lectures if his tutor recommends them. But none of this must interfere with his full enjoyment of the "life": sports, clubs, hours of quick-witted exchange of ideas which contribute notably to his education.

To Frank, remembering months of lonely plodding at Bloomington and summers of hard physical work to earn money for college bills, this picture of Oxford had the glamour of a fairy tale. He got Corbin so nearly by heart, and studied maps and photographs in other books to such good effect, that three years later when he finally arrived at the Oxford station, he felt he could have conducted a tour at once.

While still at home in Sullivan he faced the crucial choice of a college and decided to put Brasenose first. Perhaps he was guided by a buried memory of something he had read as a boy in the *Youth's Companion*. The attraction he recognized as an adult was the Brasenose record in sports (particularly rowing) and the distinction in literature of one of its past fellows, Walter Pater. Another point was its relatively small size—one of the eight Colleges with fewer than one hundred undergraduates—the largest being Christ Church and New College, each with more than two hundred.[3] In such a group as Brasenose, Frank might hope to make acquaintances easily and have a chance to play on a team. If he read John Buchan's book on Brasenose (published in 1898), he must have liked the middle-of-the-road position described there: Brasenose "has never fallen into a clumsy conventional orthodoxy; nor, on the other hand, has it gone after strange fashions and crude enthusiasms."[4]

By 1905 Oxford had time to digest the idea of the Rhodes Scholarships and was ready to take their holders almost for granted. This stage of acceptance followed a turmoil of earlier reactions: on the part of conservatives, fear of the "barbarian invasion" (meaning the Americans); on the part of reformers, fervent hope that the needs of the newcomers might show points at which even Oxford could be improved. Conservatives included groups of undergraduates: the minority of the Union who supported a motion that the Rhodes scheme was "impracticable and incompatible with the best interests of Oxford," the motion "defeated by 133 votes to 30";[5] also editors of a short-lived little magazine, the *Oxford Point of View* (including young Compton Mackenzie) which approved scholarships for colonials and Germans, but not for Americans: "There can be no doubt that America has ideals which are not those of England, and which are in some respects opposed to those ideals," especially on the subject of the Boer War, then in progress. "Germans will prove to have more points in common with Englishmen."[6] On the other hand, would-be reformers, disturbed by the lack at Oxford of research and graduate work, were prepared to rejoice if the Scholars should prove to be older men who would need precisely these opportunities. Might not such a need carry conviction at last that England had fallen behind France and Germany in the intellectual vigor which produces research for its own sake? This question was urged by the distinguished professor of archaeology Percy Gardner in his *Oxford at the Cross Roads*;[7] also by a young philosophy don, F. C. S. Schiller, recently returned from America, where he had been impressed by the quality of "graduate students."[8]

Excitement had died down by the time the first official group arrived in 1904. An undergraduate periodical, the *'Varsity*, welcomed them in what seemed the prevailing spirit of good will: "We can only wish those who have come to us from our colonies and foreign countries a happy three or four years in Oxford, and that they will learn some of the lessons which Cecil Rhodes believed Oxford had to teach, and at the same time impart some of the things which even the most churlish will agree that Oxford has yet to learn."[9]

Face to face, the Scholars seemed not at all alarming, indeed, not particularly noticeable except for their age. Among the Americans the average was twenty-two, and four were twenty-five. One of their boyish contemporaries at Balliol, L. E. Jones, describes "these rather elderly young men" with some liking.

> It was rumored that they had come to teach as much as to learn. If this were so, those we were lucky enough to have at Balliol were entirely successful in disguising their mission. . . . They were all gentle, modest men who, mature as they were among other freshmen, made no overt attempt to invigorate us with clean winds from great open spaces. They appeared, rather, to be even more sensible than ourselves to the enchantments of Oxford, and on the physical side, to be impressed, tough athletes as they were, by the hardiness of a race who could sleep in unheated bedrooms and keep clean without hot baths.[10]

The newcomers endeared themselves to Oxford as a source of amusing stories; for example, of one American with a practicality "not common among undergraduates" who was given a choice of college rooms and proceeded "to light one fire after another to see whether 'these old chimneys had a proper draught.'"[11] Or of another who asked a policeman for directions, which he gave politely, then added in some concern, "You do *understand* English, don't you?"

All in all, the first group had cleared the air of alarm. As the *Oxford Magazine* put it before the advent of the second group: "There was a time when we dreaded the invasion of Rhodes Scholars. But those who have joined us . . . have proved such admirable additions to our community that each annual batch is now assured of a hearty welcome."[12] The ice had been broken for men of the second "batch," which included Frank Aydelotte.

In late September, 1905, he embarked at Philadelphia on the little *Haverford* and found himself surrounded by Rhodes Scholars, some returning for their second year, others new like himself. They impressed him as likable but not intimidating. Before the ship sailed he wrote his mother: "They are just ordinary college boys—no better or worse," adding that he had "more experience and training than most of them being rather older" (September 30, 1905). He may have looked older than his age because already he was noticeably bald. A letter at the end of the crossing goes into more detail: some of them are brilliant, notably his cabin mate from Yale, Albert Stevens, but on the whole below what he imagines "the average Rhodes man will be in a few years." He is grateful to the second-year men for good advice about money: $1,500 does not provide lavishly for a year's expenses. The sum had seemed such a fortune at first that many had bought too much too soon, joined all sorts of costly clubs, and found themselves hard up by the end of the year. Frank was glad to learn ahead of time what "not to join and not to buy." He felt fortunate that he had already found his line and taken a Harvard degree.

> I see very clearly that if a man knows what he wants to do and how to do it he can get along very well at Oxford anywhere. Some of the old men who did not are still at sea because the English ideas are so different from ours that it's hard to get advice as they could in colleges at home. Most of the men are younger than I, especially in experience. I'm glad I have my degree from Harvard for I guess that is about the only American University the Englishmen know anything about (October 8, 1905).

As to the trip itself, he had enjoyed the rest and the sociability, the latter particularly pleasant when based on reading aloud: "We have tea parties every afternoon in our room with Swinburne and Emerson and Poe's tales and Browning's poems to stimulate conversation." Probably "Copey's" influence here.

The most exciting event on shipboard he did not mention until much later: he had met a young woman from Boston, Marie Osgood, whom he liked at once. She was going to France to join a cousin, the wife of the sculptor George Grey Barnard, in the little village of Moret outside Paris. Fortunately she had another cousin and an uncle then living in Oxford whom she might naturally want to visit. Fortunately also Frank had always meant to spend his Christmas vacation in Paris. From the beginning their acquaintance was blessed with a possible future.

Oxford: The First View

Frank left the train at the Oxford station with two other new Rhodes men bound for Brasenose: Carol Foster, of Idaho, and Talbot Papineau, of Quebec, who was to become his greatest friend. They rode with dignity in a cab to the old door with its famous brass knocker, a ring through a lion's nose. Asking whether they should report to someone, they were told they might see the vice-principal, Dr. Bussell. Climbing his staircase, they found "a man with a red and white schoolboy complexion and a monocle, wearing a very high choker collar." When Frank as spokesman announced, "We are the new Rhodes Scholars," Dr. Bussell, fixing them with his monocle, exclaimed in a squeaky falsetto voice, "How quaint!" Surprised, slightly abashed, but more amused, they retreated, realizing that they had encountered a "character" with a flair for the unexpected—a flair they saw later to be at the root of his unusual success with college discipline. Later they realized also that it was, indeed, quaint for newcomers to make an "occasion" of their arrival in a place where to be casual was the thing. They could now make a minor addition of their own to the large collection about Dr. Bussell, begun years before when he was first appointed to a Brasenose fellowship. He had applied at the same time to his own undergraduate college, Magdalen, which had turned him down; whereupon he remarked, "Either Magdalen or Brasenose has made a great mistake." Another rumor held him responsible for the Oxford mannerism of using "rather" to qualify the most unlikely words, as in a Brasenose version of Descartes' central principle, "I am rather thinking, therefore I rather am."[13] For Frank, Dr. Bussell, as a one-time close friend of Pater's, wore a special aura to which further acquaintance added friendliness and respect. The principal of Brasenose, Charles Heberden, Frank rarely saw, but regarded as a kindly, remote man, well-disposed toward undergraduates.

The location of Brasenose, Frank found to his satisfaction, was close to much that was important in Oxford: the Bodleian Library, St. Mary's Church where University Sermons were preached on Sundays, the Sheldonian Theatre, scene of impressive lectures, convocations, and ceremonies for granting degrees. One side of the College lay along "the High," in 1905 still a quiet street. Most of the time nothing passed the windows; every half-hour there was a clop-clopping as the one-horse tram jogged by. A threat of noisier and more frequent busses was quashed during Frank's first week in Oxford when a syndicate's request to run sixteen "motor omnibuses" was refused by the City Council.[14] Only two Brasenose men owned automobiles. The future Lord Nuffield was still William Morris who kept a cycle shop in Long Wall, but—sinister note—he had added a small garage for motors. The number of undergraduates in the whole university was 2,858; in Brasenose, less than 100. Surprisingly, the Brasenose record of victories on the river was more distinguished than that of some larger colleges, though in 1905 it was going through a slump. There was also a tradition of friendliness which Frank was glad to recognize. As one of his English contemporaries put it, "Everyone knew everyone, and even Etonians spoke to the merest scholars."

"Mere" was the word for scholars in this atmosphere where academic prowess was commonly played down. Holders of scholarships were in a sense outsiders; the fact of their having stipends commonly meant they were poor and looked to their university standing to advance their careers. In contrast, the ordinary Brasenose man, financed by his family and almost certainly with "something to go on to" after Oxford, was there principally for "the life" and incidentally to have his rough edges rubbed off. Rhodes Scholars formed an intermediate group, to be "accepted on athleticism and sociability." Having met these tests, they could be forgiven more serious interests.

Frank told the story of day-to-day events in frequent letters to his mother, careful usually to explain what she might not understand, occasionally telling her to look up something in Corbin's *An American at Oxford*. (Frank knew it well enough to leave it in Sullivan.) He wrote in the best possible mood for a student abroad: delight in local color and customs, the less like home the better. Incidentally, his letters as a "fresher" serve as a pleasant document in the history of Oxford, 1905–1906.

His first full account was written on his twenty-fifth birthday, October 16, 1905, when he had been in Oxford only four days. Already he had plunged into the life, begun to plan his work, play "rugger," and row.

> I came up Thursday and have got settled, bought my dishes and so on for my room, seen my tutors and arranged my work roughly, started rowing and "rugger"—as they call English Rugby—Oxford slang puts an "er" on everything—ordered some English clothes, been out to a dozen or so breakfasts, teas, luncheons and after dinner coffees and altogether got quite into the life of Oxford.

His "English clothes" included a "navy tweed Norfolk Jacket and gray flannel 'bags' and by virtue of getting the best thing in town (which will probably wear forever) [he] paid the sum of $19.00—5% discount for cash." He had heard that clothes were still cheaper in London and might go down soon "to order an evening suit," then as important as tweeds to an undergraduate.

His rooms at first sight struck him as quaint and cold.

> My rooms are in the old quad of our college—a very old building indeed. We have open fires, walls finished in panelled wood, somewhat dingy in effect, large round shallow bath tubs in which we stand and splash cold water on ourselves in the morning. There are drafts every-where, and the only way not to feel them is to wear warm clothes, especially warm outside coats. My Norfolk jacket is like an overcoat in weight. I've been feeling bully so far, not even a bad cold on the voyage over here. Cold baths and exercise are the things in Oxford I can see.

From his windows he looked out on the Brasenose tower and the Radcliffe Camera, one of the finest views in Oxford and the subject of an engraving by Turner which Frank sent home later for Christmas.

Strange New World

He described the oddity of the daily routine, especially the service by his "scout."

> It seems awfully queer to get up in the morning and have breakfast in your own room—you tell your scout what you want when he wakes you and it's ready by the time you have your bath. Lunch is the same way. No one eats much unless he has people in, for everybody goes out for athletics immediately after it. You get back for tea between four and five and have dinner in hall at 7:30 (October 16, 1905).

The Brasenose don assigned to help him plan his work, his "moral tutor," was G. H. Wakeling, whose subject was history, Brasenose not yet having a tutor in the recently established English literature "School." Wakeling made arrangements for Frank with Ernest de Selincourt of University College (later professor of English literature at Birmingham, professor of poetry at Oxford, and distinguished editor of Wordsworth). Frank's first question had to do with his prospective degree. At home or in Germany this would have been the Ph.D., but no such degree existed at Oxford until 1918 when the equivalent D.Phil. was established. In 1905 the characteristic Oxford degree was the B.A., followed by the M.A., granted not on the basis of further work, but as a privilege to a holder of a B.A. who had "kept his name on the books," that is, paid certain small fees to his College, for a specified number of terms. An M.A. was prized for carrying the privilege of membership in one of Oxford's governing bodies, Convocation. At first glimpse an American college graduate might resent advice to work for a second B.A., but Frank, like many Rhodes Scholars, realized that different teaching methods would make the experience worth while. At the same time he knew the professional value of a research degree, such as the recently established B.Litt. Always eager to grasp every possible good, he decided to work for both (eventually contenting himself with the second). But before beginning either, he must know whether he would have to spend months preparing for an intermediate examination in Latin and Greek called "Moderations." This he emphatically did not want to do. A later letter would carry the good news that he was exempt. Now, concluding his first long letter to his mother, Frank felt a twinge of homesickness.

> I enjoy the life here very much—you couldn't help it—but that has not kept me from looking forward rather (I fear I'm already learning to use that word oftener than I used to) eagerly to coming home Easter.

The pang is only momentary. He ends cheerfully: "I'm twenty-five today. I'm not doing anything to celebrate but consider the chance to live in Oxford a pretty fair birthday present."

After his first week:

> My English work is looking up, since yesterday. Professor Walter Raleigh from the University of Edinburgh—a new man here—is organizing the work in a way that is going to be fine, better than the German University methods and better than Harvard for original work anyway because the classes are smaller and you get more individual attention and because of the libraries here. He is a kindly sympathetic fellow and I like him very much (October 19, 1905).

On the social side, an event of first importance was a tea he had given the day before for some young ladies he had met on the *Haverford*, including Marie Osgood, whom he did not name: "it went off very well indeed." In Brasenose he was making acquaintances. He quoted a Rhodes man of the year before as saying that he "was getting on famously with the Englishmen." Naturally Frank was pleased, though not unduly: "I've been doing as I liked, acting like any other Fresher and not saying much." But he took an amused satisfaction in not letting upperclassmen put him through an English equivalent of hazing:

> All the Rhodes men here are laughing at a thing that happened at our Freshman "bonner" [bonfire] Tuesday night. An upperclassman ordered me to go and get more faggots. I was doing something else and told him I couldn't go. He looked at me and said: "Well you're a cool hand. If you weren't an M.A. from Harvard University I'd give you a good licking." I simply said "would you?" He was a little shorter than I and not as well built. If he had tried to lick me I think I might have made life interesting for him for a while (October 19, 1905).

Within the month he was increasingly happy. He had been granted the coveted "senior standing" which freed him from "Mods." He could begin at once on research in Professor Raleigh's Elizabethan seminar. What luck that Raleigh had admitted him! His college tutor had invited him to dinner, the Rhodes Secretary to lunch; he had not yet been "chucked out" of rowing and was still playing rugger, though "it's not the game that American football is." He found his classmates at Brasenose "thoroughly nice fellows." And he was anticipating eagerly going the next day with "an American lady living in Oxford" to meet "an old man who knew Browning very well personally" (Dr. G. U. Pope, Chaplain of Balliol, born in 1820). It was worth cutting both rowing and a rugger match, as he would have to do.

Frank felt at home in Oxford more quickly than many Rhodes Scholars, a fact he would have explained by saying that unlike some of them, he knew what he wanted to do; also he enjoyed sports as much as any English undergraduate. But there were other reasons. His mother's "British ways" had prepared him for trivial differences, and a background free from Blue Laws made him tolerant of practices which shocked some other Americans. His family had regarded card playing, smoking, and whisky and soda as acceptable in moderation; consequently he was not distressed by them in Oxford. This was not true of Rhodes Scholars from more Puritanical homes, and there were many in the early years. His friend at Brasenose, for example, R. P. Brooks of Georgia, son of a Methodist minister, was horrified to find such practices, not only among undergraduates but in the household of a clergyman.[15]

Frank was free also from the handicap of what some English critics took to be American besetting sins: the tendency to talk at length in pompous paragraphs and to be drearily in earnest. When Max Beerbohm creates a Rhodes Scholar in *Zuleika Dobson*, he makes the unfortunate young man hold forth in pages of solemn platitudes. The Oxford *'Varsity*, known for sprightliness, observed that while most undergraduates talked about musical comedy, "the Rhodes Scholar disserts on some abstruse subject." The *'Varsity* also published an outburst from one of the few openly unreconciled opponents of the American invasion, who objects to the Rhodes Scholar as "a great blot on Oxford life," partly owing to his "earnestness."[16] Frank was too impatient with dullness to be long-winded, and though intensely serious about what he thought important, was reserved about exploiting it socially.

Another advantage was his unusual experience in adapting himself to very different environments: to the university town of Bloomington, so much more sophisticated than Sullivan's community of farmers and miners; to the slightly austere New England cultivation of Harvard and Cambridge; to the southern aristocratic tradition of Louisville. He had met handicaps and coped with them by self-discipline and hard work. In spite of a crippling stiff elbow, he had made himself adept at baseball and tennis and plugged away so untiringly at football that the awkward beginner had become an All-Indiana end. Meagerly prepared by a three-year high school, he had thrown himself into study at Indiana to such good effect that he had surpassed most of his classmates. Again at Harvard, with his status as a graduate student uncertain, he read and discussed with enough energy and intelligence to prompt the critical Kittredge to intervene in his behalf and assure him an M.A. When his greatest ambition was to pass examinations for a Rhodes Scholarship, he managed to crawl over the almost insuperable obstacle of his little Latin and no Greek. At every turn he had made his way by cheerful prodigies of effort. The result: when he went to Oxford, and indeed throughout his life, he believed profoundly that if he worked with all his might, he could do anything, even what might seem impossible.

Dons

When Frank wrote home exultantly about his research in English literature, he hardly realized his luck in arriving soon after both the teaching of English and the giving of advanced degrees had been added to the Oxford program. It was as recently as his last year in high school that examinations for an Honours B.A. in English had been offered for the first time and two new degrees announced: the B.Litt. and the B.Sc., both requiring research. (Frank's B.Litt., conferred in 1908, was only the seventh in English literature in Oxford history.) It is true that much earlier (in 1795) a chair in Anglo-Saxon had been established and earlier still (1708) the famous professorship of poetry. But as a student's major subject (to borrow an American term), English literature was slow in winning acceptance in this stronghold of Latin and Greek. And even after it was approved by statute, no adequate provision for teaching had been made until 1904, when the professorship of English literature was established and Walter Raleigh appointed.[17]

Raleigh's strength lay in appreciation of great literature and in communicating to his hearers and readers something of his own perceptiveness and gusto. As described by a younger colleague, H. W. Garrod:

> He brought to letters the same catholicity of taste which he carried into society, and a temperament extraordinarily responsive to the note of magnanimity. Other professors have been men of greater learning (though it was possible to catch Raleigh possessing much more learning than he owned to). But Raleigh was a first-class lecturer and a first-class writer, for the reason that his authors were men to him. He took fire from them exactly as he took fire from talking to you. They were just splendid people, and what they said excited him, and their manner of saying it; and he poured out, in books and lectures, a running commentary of inspired or ingenious annotation. It was all natural to him—both that they should be great, and that he should see wherein it lay, and that he should say notable things about them and find life in doing so.[18]

Frank admired Raleigh enormously as a man of learning without a touch of pedantry and with an Elizabethan sense of adventure in both literature and life. It is significant that Raleigh thought his own best book the study of Elizabethan adventurers—Drake, Frobisher, and Grenville—*English Voyagers*, which came out shortly before he began to teach at Oxford. With this fresh in mind, and already at work on his *Shakespeare* (to be published in 1907), what more natural than to give a seminar in Elizabethan literature? And how fortunate for Frank that in this seminar he could begin the lively research which culminated in his book *Elizabethan Rogues and Vagabonds!* It was characteristic of Raleigh that in World War I he was captivated by the young explorers of a new frontier in aviation. Gladly agreeing to write the history of the Royal Air Force, he flew for facts to the Near East, where he met the accident and subsequent illness which caused his death—an end somehow in keeping with his temperament and his life.

Wholly different from Raleigh in background and personality—

indeed, unique among Oxford professors—was Frank's teacher of Gothic, the man who had succeeded Max Müller as professor of comparative philology, Joseph Wright, illiterate until he was fifteen years old. Professor Wright's learning, great though it was, impressed Frank less than the intellectual, moral, and physical drive which made him the hero of an unprecedented success story.[19] Born in a poor Yorkshire village, the son of a mother deserted by an indolent husband when Joseph was six, he had earned his living from that age, first driving a donkey cart for a blacksmith, at seven going to work in a woolen mill where he began to help his mother support two younger brothers. Whatever he did—changing bobbins, making himself an expert wool sorter—he stood out for persistence, thoroughness, accuracy, and simple friendliness. When he was fifteen he learned to read and write in evening courses after a long day's work, adding, as he could, mathematics, French, and German. Without a penny of help for his education, and always sharing responsibility for his family's support, he took himself eventually to German universities, where he gained a Ph.D. in philology at the age of thirty. Meanwhile he had discovered a gift for teaching. He performed miracles by expecting them, demanding of his students an untiring dedication like his own, firing them with his rare vitality. At Oxford he was first employed to teach women students, whose position in the University was only peripheral (they were not granted degrees for many years). One of his pupils, Elizabeth Mary Lea, he made central to his life and happiness by marrying her. For research he turned to the little-known field of English dialects, especially attracted, perhaps, because he had spoken one as a boy in Yorkshire. His greatest work was the incomparable *English Dialect Dictionary*, begun in 1889 and completed some months before Frank became his student. Frank, admiring him as a scholar and as a man "self-made" in a pattern more warmly approved in Indiana than in Oxford, described him with special sympathy.

> This Gothic Professor . . . has done what is a wonderful thing in England—risen from the rank of a common laborer or servant to the position of a professor at Oxford: he has the position formerly held by Max Müller. He lives in a house the building of which he superintended just as we did ours at home. I think things are still a bit hard for him and his wife socially here but intellectually he is one of the big men of Oxford. He is the editor of the *English Dialect Dictionary*, and known all over the world. His wife belonged to a very aristocratic family and had to break off all relations with her folks when she married him.

The older man at Oxford who meant most to Frank in personal ways was the Rhodes Secretary, Francis Wylie. A wiry, vigorous, sandy-haired Scot, eyes wrinkling with humor and kindness, he brought to bear on Rhodes Scholars' difficulties not only a native warmth and shrewdness but knowledge of Oxford gained during twelve years as philosophy don and fellow of Brasenose. Earlier he had tutored the two small sons of Lord Rosebery, an influential Rhodes Trustee, who recommended him for the new position at Oxford. Wylie accepted it, not without hesitation—it was no promotion for a fellow of Brasenose—but he decided that the chance to take part in an unusual new venture was too good to miss. Before the first full contingent of overseas students arrived in October, 1904, he had married a distinguished and beautiful young American, Kathleen Kelly, a student of history at Lady Margaret Hall. Together they welcomed the first of many generations of Rhodesians at their house in South Parks Road, helping the sometimes bewildered young men to accept Oxford's oddities along with its soundness and charm.[20] As a mediator between Scholars and Colleges, the Secretary showed an inspired combination of tact and good sense which won him the confidence, respect, and affection not only of his charges but of the whole community. When he retired in 1931, he had created a position for which his successor gave up an Oxford professorship.

Frank came to know more slowly another representative of the Rhodes Trustees, the Organizing Secretary, Dr. George Parkin, appointed immediately after the will was published to draw up the plan for "translating . . . [Rhodes's] great idea into a working system." Parkin had devoted two years to the undertaking, traveling 140,000 miles to consult men in education and public affairs in all parts of the world where Scholars would be chosen. He was "a Canadian cast in the prophetic mould," an Oxonian who had matriculated in the same year with Rhodes, shared his devotion to the empire, and was precisely the person to interpret his ideals. In addition to a talent for oratory and persuasive writing, Parkin had the practical sense about education of a teacher with seven years' successful experience as headmaster of an excellent school for boys, Upper Canada College in Toronto. Add to all this a minor but indispensable point of strength—unlimited relish for conferring; he could talk eagerly far into the night about the infinite details necessary to set up a wholly new scheme on a scale without precedent. Fortunately his talk had the leaven of humor. At a solemn meeting of American university and college Presidents, he told them that if the selection committees would choose from each state "the candidate most likely to become President of the United States, Chief Justice of the Supreme Court or American Ambassador to Great Britain, then Oxford and the Rhodes Trustees would probably be satisfied." And fortunately again, he was not pompously correct; he had an engaging touch of what a friend called "dishevelled gaiety."[21] Frank found him likable, kind, and easy to work with. Eventually it was largely to Parkin that Frank owed his appointment as American Secretary to the Rhodes Trustees.

New Friends

At Brasenose Frank quickly made friends with two Rhodes Scholars— Robert Preston Brooks from Georgia and Talbot Papineau from Canada—and almost as quickly with an English fresher, S. E. Trotter. Frank and Papineau had much in common. They both rowed and played rugger and never tired of discussing plans for the future cooperation between Rhodes Scholars of their two countries. (Unhappily for these plans and much besides, Papineau was killed in action in World War I.) R. P. Brooks, a year senior to Frank at Oxford, never felt so much at home there, partly because he was less of an athlete, though in his one sport, tennis, he played on the Brasenose team. He has already been mentioned as brought up to disapprove of card playing, smoking, and any strong drink—all common enough at Oxford—and he found frustration, too, on the intellectual side. He had no contact with his teachers except his tutor, whom he heartily disliked.[22] Small wonder that he depended on his American friends for cheer and comfort. He and Frank were attracted to each other by discovering that they both enjoyed good literature. Brooks noted in his diary going to Aydelotte's rooms to hear him read aloud Browning's *Saul* and *Grammarian's Funeral*, Tennyson's *Idylls*, and Shakespeare's *Henry III*, adding, "his understanding and interpretation fine."[23] In lighter moments they entertained young ladies at tea. When the time came for them to move out of College to leave room for younger students, the two went into "digs" together. In later life both rose to important positions in the same field, education, Brooks at the University of Georgia, where for many years he was a Dean. Always Frank's loyal friend and admirer, Brooks in his memoirs records his judgment that Frank was "perhaps the greatest Rhodes Scholar the United States has sent to England."[24]

Frank's English friend Trotter was in some ways a typical Brasenose fresher: he belonged to a well-to-do family, came to Oxford from one of the great public schools, Harrow, and read law, preparing to join his father in the family firm of barristers. It was his devotion to rugger that drew him first to Frank and Papineau; later he and Papineau studied law together. The three often had lunch with three other Englishmen, making an informal little club. The Trotters' house in London was probably the first where Frank stayed overnight. He wrote his mother that the family was "rather well off" and lived "in some style." "You dress for dinner and have coffee and bread and butter before you get out of bed in the morning. This latter is French, I think" (December 10, 1905).

Outside Brasenose two of Frank's closest Rhodes Scholar friends, Paul Kieffer and Leonard Cronkhite, were to remain his friends for life. Paul Kieffer, jovial, and wonderful teller of funny stories, had come from Maryland to Oriel to read law. In spite of seeming to be always the popular center of a lounging group, he worked well enough to get a First Class in the B.C.L., preparing for a distinguished career as a Wall Street lawyer (and Frank's legal adviser). Leonard Cronkhite, son of missionary parents, serious and able, won his appointment from Rhode Island and went to Worcester College, where, like Frank, he worked for a research degree, in his case the B.Sc. He shared Frank's interest in poetry and admired his friendly, good-humored self-confidence. More sensitive and less at ease, he envied Frank his imperturbable acceptance of English behavior that in an American would have been deliberately rude: an English undergraduate would invite a Rhodes Scholar to break-fast, meet him an hour later on the street, and look at him with the blankness of a complete stranger—the cut direct. Most Americans shriv-eled under their first such encounter, thinking they must have done something dreadful without knowing it. Not Frank. He saw that this was nothing more than an Oxford preference for not being sociable on street corners. Gradually Cronkhite realized that Frank's understanding of people came partly from a kind of independence; he could view them clearly because he was never deeply involved. Though Cronkhite himself had the temperament and tastes of a scholar or an artist, he turned instead to business, devoting himself with conspicuous success to the new field of electronics.

Extracurricular Oxford

By November Frank felt at home. He had joined the Union, which he described to his mother as the model for the one at Harvard. He expected to profit from its "fine library of 40,000 volumes" and its famous debates on political questions. "To speak at a Union debate is about the biggest honor in Oxford." Already he was struck by undergraduate interest in politics. "I notice that these English fellows, however little they study—always read the newspapers and are well up in English politics." He had helped celebrate Guy Fawkes Day, November 5—in 1905 "the 300th anniversary of Guy Fawkes' attempt to blow up the House of Commons (The Gunpowder Plot). Our college celebrated it with fireworks and a bonfire and dinner." When the Bishop of London spoke at St. Mary's against drunkenness at Oxford, a sermon that "made quite a stir in Oxford and all over England," Frank heard him and reported his own experience.

> There is a good deal of drinking here but I have never had any trouble in doing as I liked. We have a very good class in that respect in B.N.C. and are planning to manage things more decently (that is to make it perfectly comfortable for every man to drink or not as he likes) next year when it comes our turn to run things. I am not posing as a reformer or anything of the sort, myself, of course, but the English fellows occasionally come in to talk to me about such things and I let them know that I'm willing to do my part (November 19, 1905).

The *Oxford Magazine* reacted more strongly to the sermon, urging the need of improving undergraduate standards of taste:

> Oxford is no hell of delirious drunkards: we all know that; but its standard of decency in this respect is lower than that of the London clubs. . . . Public opinion in most colleges approves, and in rare cases endeavours to enforce, a state of intermittent drunkenness. . . . It is important, then, that public opinion should be improved in this respect, that drunkenness should not confer a glamour of distinction, but earn the reprobation of the general sentiment as an ungentlemanly social solecism.[25]

A literary event which must have attracted Frank was A. C. Bradley's lecture on "Aspects of Modern Poetry," the last of two series in his five-year tenure as professor of poetry (1901–1906). Frank did not mention hearing him, but the next month he bought a copy of Bradley's published first series. The item appears on a receipted bill from Blackwell's book store, other purchases including two books on rowing and one on football. The lecture was reported in the *Oxford Magazine* with appreciation of the speaker and a touch of complacency at "Oxford self-repression" which refused to recognize an occasion:

> Probably even Professor Bradley has never had a larger or more representative audience . . . (his) treatment of the five aspects of modern poetry was philosophical and impersonal; . . . Oxford self-repression prevented any word of public notice that this was a final lecture; but there are hundreds at Oxford who feel grateful to the late Professor for his tenure of the Chair.[26]

To a young American, how odd this unwillingness to praise! Of special interest to Rhodes Scholars that fall term was a dinner for the whole group, given by the Rhodes Trust, with Rudyard Kipling as guest speaker.

> Mr. Rudyard Kipling, whose presence as a guest was enthusiastically welcomed, dealt, in a speech of characteristic suggestion and humour, with the shrinking of the earth's crust.
> Well! Behind the exuberance of a festive evening there lie—veiled, but not obscured—high purposes and great possibilities. Time is with the Rhodes scheme.[27]

In Frank's letters the celebration which stood out was the American Thanksgiving Dinner, at which he was one of the speakers: he represented the men of his year. The dinner was one of a spate of activities: rowing, rugger, and a track meet.

> This letter marks the conclusion of a few days of real American strenuous life which I have come through with some ups and some downs not unsuccessfully on the whole and now I'm just ready to be off for a day of pleasure in London. I had our B.N.C. Track meet on Thursday, speech at Thanksgiving dinner Thursday night, Knights' Eights race Friday, dinner with the American Consul immediately after, and a football game with St. Paul's school here [London] yesterday. How is that for three days? I came off with first in one sprint and a second in another (two silver cups for my mantel-piece in prizes), our eight won in the boat race, the American consul is going to ask me to Liverpool to stay over Sunday with him next term, and what pleased me most of all—the people thought I made a good speech at the Thanksgiving dinner and I received congratulations on all sides. I talked about the difficulties besetting an American at Oxford and said that I thought the man who was naturally a

fool or a slacker or not well poised in any way was much more likely to
show it here—removed from the conventional restraints and incentives to
work which he had at home. . . . I'm getting ready to do quite a lot in
the next six weeks vacation in Paris (December 3, 1905).

Frank kept reassuring his mother about his health, apparently in
answer to worried questions.

There is no danger of my getting cold or rheumatism rowing. The
weather here is never really cold—practically no snow or skating ever—and
our barge has an open fire in it and is nice and warm inside. We stay in
it going out in "tubs" or fours two or three times for about twenty
minutes at a time rowing all the time. Read the chapter on rowing in the
American at Oxford and you'll understand it. . . . I have felt perfectly
well, gained seven or eight pounds and been free from cold so far. The
one thing that will do you up here is lack of exercise.

As particularly good evidence of vitality he mentioned that his baldness was decreasing: "I think my hair is growing more than for two or
three years. Perhaps it's being out without my cap" (November 11,
1905).

Paris

The week after term ended Frank went first to London, where he
stayed with the Trotters and saw Shaw's new play, *Man and Superman*.
Then he and his friend Papineau crossed to Paris for six weeks of study,
sight-seeing and renewed acquaintance with Marie Osgood, who still
figured in his letters as "an American girl." The young men stayed in the
household of a Protestant minister where none of the family or servants
spoke any English. Papineau, as a Canadian, spoke French fluently, but
Frank was determined that this should not prevent his learning and exacted
a promise to let him do his share of the talking. Papineau kept the promise
faithfully, even when Frank was almost lost in the adventure of giving
the cabby their address, "Cent dix-sept, Rue Notre Dame des Champs."
He wrote his mother that he had to work his "small stock of French words
overtime," though he was fast adding to his capital; his accent and pro-
nunciation were unmistakably American.

His first reaction to the French people was not enthusiastic.

I can't say that I am especially impressed with the French people so far as
I have seen them. They are pleasant and kind and polite but I don't think
I should ever like them as I do the English and in a way, imagine I shall

the Germans. Of course it's pretty early to be venturing an opinion (December 14, 1905).

A fortnight later he celebrated New Year's Day by giving his mother a gay account of his "frivolity" and the work which he had enjoyed even more.

> For Christmas I went down to Moret (about an hour's ride from Paris) with some American girls I met on the steamer. They have a cousin there, a rather well known American sculptor [George Grey Barnard]—that they were visiting and invited me down for Christmas tree etc. with the family. It was mighty nice and pleasant—and interesting to see the old town.
>
> The night before Christmas I went to Midnight Mass at St. Eustache. The music—which they say is probably the best in Paris—was wonderful rolling along the aisles of the church. They have famous singers for this service and make it really a sort of sacred concert. After the mass we came along the Boulevard in the Latin Quarter watching the people celebrate. Old and young, they enter into their good times in a way that makes you think they never did anything else, as I guess some of them don't. I can't say I like the people of France especially—certainly not as I do Englishmen and they don't compare at all with Americans—but they are great fun when they are out for a good time. I am continually struck with the tremendous respect which the people in France and in England both have for Americans.

Frank remained unimpressed by the French until the next summer when he went to Germany and suddenly by contrast with Teutonic heaviness saw Gallic traits in a more agreeable light.

Now he writes in high spirits of playing a successful practical joke.

> Last night—New Year's Eve—I went to the theatre with Behr (a Harvard man . . . who is in Paris for Christmas. . . . He is studying in Heidelberg, Germany, this winter). He and I took the two American girls to the theatre and afterwards along the boulevards and to one of the Cafés. We had a great "rag" all around. Among other things, I had got lost from Behr who had all the money and when they wanted to know how I would have got anything to eat if we had not found them, I said I would have induced some café to let me have it on credit. Everybody hooted and said "impossible" so just for a joke I said I'd do it and so I said to the boy "Où est Monsieur le Propriétaire?" hunted him up and with the aid of a waiter who knew a little English and using all my French, told him who I was and what I wanted, and referred him to the American Consul

and actually got him to trust me for the supper which we paid for today. He seemed a little surprised at my request and still more that we were not going to have any wine (indeed I suppose we were the only people in the place who didn't) but was very handsome about it.

Don't think I am entirely given over to frivolity in Paris. I have been getting in from eight to twelve hours a day of the hardest kind of work on Oxford studies and on French. It is the first real work of the kind I used to do in America that I've had a chance at since I left home (you can never work all day solid at Oxford) and I like it. It's as much fun for me to work all day solid as it is to play bridge whist or do any of the other things which take up your time at Oxford. I am going to try to cut out some social life from now on though of course I can't cut loose from all of it.

Here is Frank on French meals and the beauties of Paris:

The French live much as we do at home in regard to meals. You have café-au-lait any time you want to get up in the morning—sometimes in bed but here we go down to the dining room, which I like much better. Then we have lunch, or déjeuner as they call it, at 12:30 and dinner at 7:00. They don't have afternoon tea, and I often feel as if I'd like some.

I never saw such broad and beautiful Boulevards and squares in my life as they have here: there's a whole string beginning at the Louvre (the big picture gallery)—the Garden of the Tuilleries, Place de la Concorde, and running down through the Champs Elyseés, under Napoleon's Arch of Triumph into the Bois de Boulogne which gives you a holiday feeling, simply to walk through (Paris, January 1, 1906).

Frank observes his own reactions to paintings and finds them slow.

I have been going to the great Paris picture gallery—The Louvre—lately but have not been often enough nor seen enough of the pictures to get over the first confused impression which miles of paintings always give me. I have to see a good deal of a painting—see it many times before I know whether I like it or not. I don't believe I am as sensitive to color effects as most people for I care about as much for engravings as I do for paintings (Paris, January 7, 1906).

His last letter from Paris, and more about odd French ways of living:

One thing the French people do rather seldom is to change the sheets and pillowcases—never oftener than once in two or three weeks, and they see no reason why you shouldn't use the same towel at least one week. Luckily I have another bath towel along with me and here we get (what is rather unusual) an ordinary towel and a bath towel each week, so I get on very well.

The people who have real French table manners carefully sop up their plates with a piece of bread (and eat it) after each course, so that they leave their plates as clean as if they'd just been washed. I think however they do wash them after the meal just the same. The food is awfully good, well cooked and deliciously seasoned. However they have an affection for game that is "high" (that has been left a long time) and strong cheese which I cannot go. Some of their cheeses are about the consistency of thick molasses in the winter time and you smell them as soon as they are brought into the room. On the other hand they have Roquefort and Swiss cheese that is better than anything of the like I have ever tasted (Paris, January 14, 1906).

Marie

The most thrilling event of his stay in Paris Frank did not mention to his mother: he became engaged to the "American girl on the steamer." As he was going home fairly soon for his Easter vacation, he postponed giving his news until he could tell it face to face.

Marie Osgood's growing excitement during these weeks radiates from a little diary which records only items having to do with Frank: the first in October when they had left the steamer and met again in Chester; the chief entries in January. Marie could not keep her feelings wholly to herself; a diary seemed a safe outlet. Twice she called him "Mr. Aydelotte," then used a series of verbs without a subject—too shy still for the intimacy of a first name. They took a walk in the rain which was "perfect" although she "arrived home late to dinner—thoroughly soaked." The next day she moved into Paris, fortunately for further excursions. They walked home from the Bois on a "glorious moonlight evening." "Came to dinner and read Browning." "More Browning and The Golden Treasury (marked) which he gave me," this last on a wonderful evening. "We talked after the lights went out by candle light, and I felt as if Heaven had opened its arms to me, but I did not dare to enter."[28]

Was this only a modest girl's natural surprise at finding herself beloved, or the lack of confidence that in Marie went deep? Although she was pretty, with the added charm of sweetness and breeding, she had never fully regained assurance after the shock of her mother's death when she was eleven and her father's marriage two years later to a woman

IV: Marie Osgood Aydelotte. Portrait by Charles Hopkinson; courtesy W. O. Aydelotte.

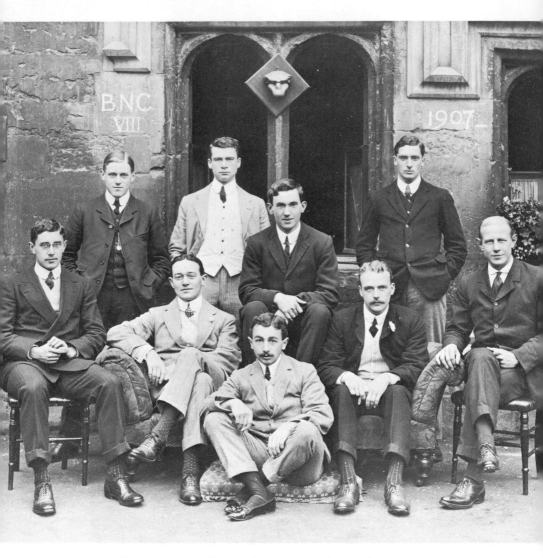

V: The Brasenose College eight, 1907; Frank Aydelotte seated at extreme right. Photo: J. W. Thomas.

she found wholly uncongenial. One of the Osgood cousins remembers that Marie fainted at the wedding and describes the stepmother as seeming to wish "every trace of the first wife's life obliterated." After trying unsuccessfully to find a place in her father's new household, Marie had lived since she was fifteen with her father's elder sister, Mrs. Monroe, whose daughter, Edna, was now Mrs. George Grey Barnard. Though the Monroes and the Barnards were devoted to her, Marie grew up uncertain about herself and her future. She had not gone to college. Her chief job had been as dietitian of a summer camp. Already twenty-eight when she and Frank first met, she may have begun to doubt whether she would marry. Then to be sought out by an exciting young man for evenings of poetry and walks in the moonlight—no wonder she could hardly believe this was happening to her!

Though Frank was as confident as Marie was shy, he may have had moments of doubt whether an exquisitely lovely girl could be drawn to a man with oversized ears and scarcely any hair. But such moments would fade quickly before his usual drive to win the best of everything. Before he left for Oxford, they were engaged.

Marie Osgood's background and upbringing had been very different from Frank's. It is true that both were descended from ancestors who had emigrated from England in the seventeenth century, but John Osgood had gone to Boston and helped settle nearby Andover,[29] starting a line which remained established in eastern Massachusetts, for many years the hub of cultivated America. Frank's ancestors, liking to be on the move, had struck out from Delaware and Virginia south or west in almost every generation. Marie's father, George Laurie Osgood, a Harvard graduate, was an exceptionally competent musician: a singer, composer, conductor, and teacher. Having spent six years studying in Germany and Italy, he returned to Massachusetts to play a leading part in Boston's musical life for three decades, doing an "invaluable service" in forming high standards by his "inflexible demand for perfection."[30] His brother, Hamilton Osgood, had become a doctor distinguished for new ideas in medicine. After study in Germany, that Mecca of doctors, he had gone to Paris to learn about Pasteur's recently discovered antitoxin for rabies, then to Nancy for Bernheim's use of "psychotherapeutics," and he took an important part in introducing both into the United States.[31] In contrast, Frank's father, though intelligent and able, had little formal schooling. The debit side for Marie was her disturbed adolescence, unsheltered by settled family life, and an abbreviated education. Frank, fortunate in the steady moral support of devoted parents, had profited by a wealth of opportunities to study. During their engagement and always, Frank and Marie at first sight seemed oddly unlike: she, with a touch of Back Bay hauteur and a quick, almost English way of talking; he a friendly, downright Hoosier, with speech that placed him unmistakably in the Middle West. But on further acquaintance no one could doubt that they supplemented each other well. Frank had the strength and assurance to lend Marie confidence, heightened by his obvious reliance on her social experience and skill in appraising people. She knew he thought her indispensable. A serious young man, he owed much to her natural gaiety. And if she was high-strung, his own mother was more so; he was not afraid of "nerves."

Whatever their differences, they saw eye to eye in personal standards. Both had a firm integrity and intolerance of pettiness and pretense. Both treated human beings with warm courtesy. Wherever they created an atmosphere together, it was one in which other people enjoyed being at their best and were often surprised at how good that best could be.

All this was far in the future in January, 1906, when Frank returned to Oxford. In his first letter home, the only point that might have indicated a change to a suspicious mother was his sudden interest in having his life insured.

On the River

During the eight-week winter term, Frank's letters centered chiefly on the boat races—"Torpids," "Toggers" in Oxford slang—his paper for Professor Raleigh's seminar, and plans for going home for the six weeks of Easter vacation. Torpids, winter races of relatively inexperienced crews, excluded any man who rowed in the eight the year before. In the usual Oxford style, they were "bump" races, that is, shells lined up a specified distance apart, the object being to touch the boat ahead and avoid being touched by the one behind. When a boat makes a "bump," it goes up one place in the line for the next race. During the six days of the races, a boat can move six places up or six down, hold its own—neither bumping nor being bumped—or zigzag.

Frank's training for Toggers began almost three weeks before the races and consisted of enormous meals, extra sleep, and much exercise, running as well as rowing.

We get up at 7:30, trot out in flannels for a walk of a mile or so and a short sprint, then back for a cold bath and an enormous Togger breakfast at 8:30,—five courses always, oatmeal porridge, fish, some meat, chops, steak or chicken as it happens,—eggs and toast and marmalade. The whole College entertains the Toggers in turn. We have a very light lunch at one, row from two till about 4:00 or 4:30, have very light tea (I have none usually) and another enormous meat-dinner in Hall at 7:30. This is even worse than breakfast for amount. Then we have fruit and so on after it and get to bed at 10:30. I have been cutting out one or two courses of both breakfast and dinner for I can't possibly eat so much and study any. I feel bully, as you may imagine. Yesterday we rowed up from Iffley in a high wind with a lot of rain and hail, and then trotted home, and in twenty minutes I had had my bath and dressed and felt warm and fresh as could be (February 11, 1906).

Brasenose had two eights in the Torpids, Frank in the second, his friend Papineau in the first. Neither boat was lucky; Frank reported wryly that on the fourth day he and Stroke "caught a crab," with disastrous results.

Today is the Fourth day. Our first Togger started out in second place and has been bumped every day so far making them now sixth. The second which I am in started out second in the third division and has been bumped every day but one. Our coaches this year were poor and didn't know how to select the best men. They never could get a first Togger that could beat the second. On Monday before the races they changed them all around again and then changed on Saturday morning after two days racing with the result that they have spoiled both boats. Had they left the second alone we should have probably gone up six places and had our oars for souvenirs. As it is we have made a better showing each day then the first—rowing through yesterday with Worcester chasing us all the way but never catching us and doing the same today except that, when we were only a boat length from the finish, Stroke and I each "caught a crab"—got our oars twisted and swung the boat around into the bank and Worcester who had been two or three lengths behind rowed up and bumped us. I don't suppose we'll be able to bump them back tomorrow.... The races are fun even though we don't win and the Englishmen don't take losing so seriously as Americans (February 26, 1906).

The climax of the crab catching came when the Worcester coach ran up, shouting inappropriately, "Well-rowed, Worcester!" whereupon the

Brasenose coach seized him and threw him into the river (both coaches being undergraduates).

The day after the last race Frank presented his paper in Raleigh's class, on "Elizabethan Rogues and Vagabonds." He wrote his mother that it was "very successful"; Raleigh had said "it is a good start toward my B.Litt." With both Toggers and paper out of the way, even a lover of hard work might feel let down and inclined for once to be lazy. Frank made what was for him a surprising admission: "It's awfully easy to let a week or a month go by here without doing anything. It's the only place I ever found where I really enjoy loafing and 'slacking'" (March 10, 1906).

Home Again

On March 17 he sailed for New York by the American Line steamer *New York*, not simply going home eagerly, as he had expected, but representing the Rhodes Trust in the grim duty of conveying the body of a Rhodes Scholar who had died of "acute meningitis," A. K. Read of Louisiana. Frank wrote his mother from the boat that he would have to go with the coffin to Louisiana unless he was met in New York by a member of the family.

> Mr. Wylie, the Oxford sec'y to the Rhodes Trustees and the man who looks after us in every way, is very anxious to have me do it, both to explain to the family that Read's death was pronounced by all three of the Doctors (one of them Dr. Osler and the others among the best in England) to be due in no sense to over work or worry, and that the nursing and treatment and hospital care were the best that was to be procured. It is a sad affair and will be a sad trip to New Orleans but I know how much it might mean to his mother to hear all about it from some one who was in Oxford (March 20, 1906).

When he wrote next, he was on board the train from New York to New Orleans, having "got through all the Customs and Health Board of New York City today (and an awful job it was too). . . . I'm awfully homesick and have already arranged my return by a later boat to make up for this time lost. I can hardly wait to get home" (March 26, 1906). Since he went home directly from Baton Rouge, there is no letter about what happened there.

While Frank was at home he told his mother about his engagement, and she took it hard, as was to be expected. Any fiancée of the son who had been her close companion was likely to seem an interloper; add to this the fear that a girl "with an aristocratic Boston background" might infect a Sullivan boy with a superior attitude toward his home. This fear, indeed, did both Frank and Marie less than justice, but when was justice to be expected of a prospective mother-in-law, and especially one who was an odd recluse, given to sick headaches? When Frank wrote her from the train on his way to sail for England, his letter was a model of kindness and good sense:

> If you feel like it after a while I should appreciate it very much if you would write to Marie. I think you would feel better when you do meet her if you had. You need not say much except that you take a great interest in her on my account and from what I have told you and that you hope she will really become one of us. Put the whole thing just as you like and just as you feel and perhaps indicate that you are speaking for Papa as well. I know she would appreciate the letter and think you both would be awfully glad you wrote it (April 20, 1906).

In spite of the reasonableness of Frank's request, his mother did not write Marie, either then or until long after their marriage. Meanwhile Frank mentioned Marie in almost every letter: she came to Oxford to visit her cousin, she made plans for the summer camp she helped direct, she mended his clothes.

> I enjoyed Marie's visit immensely. She is a fine girl. She says she understands perfectly your not writing and thinks it decidedly better to wait until you meet each other, since you could hardly know what to write before. She was delighted when I told her you said you were glad she was not rich. She said she dreamed about you once and thought you immediately wanted to know about her dowry and were rather put out when you found she hasn't any. I am quite sure you will like her. [He wrote in the margin] She sewed on all my buttons, mended my gloves and fixed me up in great style (May 18, 1906).

The cousin whom Marie visited in Oxford, Dr. Hamilton Osgood's daughter Gretchen, Mrs. Fiske Warren, was a beautiful woman with artistic talents and a brilliant mind. Her portrait with her small daughter Rachel, painted by John Singer Sargent two or three years before Frank met her, shows no more than a conventional "great lady," but in fact she was much more. Thanks to living abroad in her childhood while her father inquired into medical advances, she had escaped the kind of formal education which might have blunted her taste and restrained her enthusiasms. Instead she had heard and seen the best in music and art and studied with gifted teachers: singing with Fauré of the Paris Conservatoire, French diction and acting with Coquelin Aîné of the Comédie Française. Thanks to her marriage at twenty to Fiske Warren, son of the founder of a paper company which stood out as much for its unusually humane labor policy as for its financial success, she enjoyed years of cordial support from a husband with both a fortune and ideas on important public questions. When Frank first met him, Fiske Warren was particularly concerned with reconstruction in the Philippines, traveling back and forth to the Far East from Oxford, where his wife had taken a house for three years. She had come there to study philosophy, persuading two distinguished dons to tutor her: the idealist J. A. Smith and the pragmatist F. C. S. Schiller. At the end of her stay they gave her unofficial final examinations, reporting that she did well enough to get First Class Honours if she had been regularly enrolled.[32] When Marie visited her in the spring of 1906, she had been in Oxford almost two years, her household including her father and mother as well as three little children: two daughters and a son.

It was during this visit that Frank met Marie's relatives at a family dinner arranged to let them look him over. This purpose was so obvious and the assembled Osgoods and Monroes so formidable as to shake Frank's usual self-confidence. He was nervous and knew he showed it. Afterward Dr. Osgood gave him a "semimedical" lecture on nervousness and proffered the more effective cure of cordial friendship.

At this time Dr. Osgood was suffering from a bad heart, could take no exercise, and was not expected to live long, but his mind and kindliness were unimpaired. Finding that Frank needed to improve his German, Dr. Osgood offered to read with him twice a week. Frank gladly accepted and came to look forward to these sessions for more than German. He welcomed particularly the chance to talk about Marie, who had gone to America for the summer to help manage a summer camp, leaving him "blue and homesick." Some of the uncle's wise observations are preserved in a sketch Frank wrote after Dr. Osgood's death.

> He commented on [Marie's] faults, worries, especially her habit of thinking of the injustice she had received [through her father's remarriage] and of her own shortcomings. He did not make light of the first nor take seriously the second: he said little about the fact in either case but spent his time convincing me that her own thinking about them did the harm—the truth of which we have both learned.

Frank had first planned to spend most of the long summer vacation in France, but was persuaded by Professor Joseph Wright to divide his time in favor of Germany and philology. He advised Frank to go to Baden-Baden, where he could live in the family of a philologist, "Herr Doktor Professor Lenz." Frank arranged to do this, but allowed himself the luxury of two weeks in France on the way. There he stayed at Senlis in a small hotel recommended by Alfred Brooks, where the people were friendly and the food the best he had tasted in France. Even in so short a time he hoped to make progress in the language and hunted up a priest in the local Collége St. Vincent who would exchange French lessons for English. This gave him, incidentally, a chance to see the point of view of devout French Catholics at a moment when they were greatly disturbed by recent events: the disestablishment of the church and the release of Dreyfus.

The Catholic Church has just been disestablished in France and their schools are doomed because the present Republican Government is afraid of them and sooner or later will close them up. It is right too for they are behind the times and while it seems pathetic now that they are going out, if they were in power they would be just as merciless and unscrupulous as the other side could be. Witness the case of Dreyfus whom the Government has just declared innocent and who is going to be publicly reinstated. I have been reading some of the comments of the Catholic newspapers (Of course the Catholics, siding with the aristocrats, as they always do, were against Dreyfus and even preached against him from their pulpits); the things they say now are awful ... to quote one from memory "If we do not comment more upon this disgraceful liberation it is because he will add but one more to the many traitors (meaning, practically, all the new Republican Government, the people who disestablished the church) who are at large and in official positions in France" (July 13, 1906).

As to the priests at St. Vincent, they are "second rate thinkers, but faithful and much grieved at the turn things are taking—the lack of religion in France—meaning the desertion of the Catholic Church."

When Frank moved to Baden-Baden, he looked forward to admiring the German scholar Herr Doktor Professor Lenz and to liking German people more than the French. To his shocked disappointment, he found his host dull, not in the same class with Professor Wright, and his new acquaintances so unattractive as to put him off their language.

My host is a product of the German University system. He took his Ph.D. on "The meaning and use of the verbal prefix ge- in Anglo-Saxon" and is what you might expect. No man could remain educated through such a thing if an educated man could be got to undertake it. It's pretty well the opposite of all that Oxford stands for (July 19, 1906).

In the last sentence Frank repudiated the customary American reverence for German education. Professor Raleigh and his perceptive methods had done their work. As to the study of German versus French and his liking for the two peoples, he had made an about-face since his first days in Paris: "I don't care ever to speak German well: I simply want to read it easily without a Dictionary, and when I get to that point I'm going to desert Germany for good and keep on with French, where the people interest me more" (July 19, 1906).

Nevertheless he settled down to work hard, taking only one day's holiday every two weeks for tennis and sight-seeing. "For the first time this year I feel as if I was really accomplishing something and I shall go back to Oxford in good shape for next year's work." He had to admit being "a little lonely," not finding the professor's family congenial and "so far having met no one else in the town." The Germans strike him as unsociable people; they "have less to do with their neighbors than anyone I ever saw." But he does enjoy an occasional band concert in a "big open Garden. Some of these German military bands would be hard to beat."

Just when he had begun to make the best of his situation, he got the bad news that Marie's father had said No to her returning to France at the end of the summer. There was a strong probability that the Barnards would not have room for her, and he refused to give her permission to live alone nearby. A sign of the times, when a father thought fit to take this line with a woman of twenty-eight! It is true that he might have exerted pressure by withholding her allowance, but his real power lay in the commonly accepted opinion of a dutiful daughter's role.

Fortunately for Frank, Mr. Osgood and his wife were living in Switzerland, at no great distance from Baden-Baden. Frank decided to take a week's vacation, plead his case in person, and get a glimpse of the Alps on the way. When he told the Frau Professor that he was going to see the father of his fiancée, she and her husband at once took a great interest and asked about the girl's dowry. "I told them she hadn't any and that I didn't want any, at which they were rather surprised. They wanted to know if, with us, the girl brings all the furniture to start housekeeping. I told them not that I knew of. It seems they do here and a girl who hasn't that much money practically can't get married." This exchange of views made the host and hostess noticeably more friendly, and Frank could add, "I've enjoyed myself rather better here since."

Happily the trip to Switzerland accomplished all that he had hoped. He got on well with the Osgoods after "a couple of days of friendly sparring," and Mr. Osgood finally gave "his permission for [Marie] to come back this winter and we're all looking up a place for her to stay." Doubtless Frank impressed them as an honest, able young man, wholly devoted to their daughter. Fortunately also he had Dr. Osgood as a powerful ally who had already said a good word to his brother.

From Baden-Baden Frank reported exciting news from Alfred Brooks: President Bryan had asked Alfred if he thought Frank would be interested in a position in the English department at Indiana. Frank's jubilant answer, "Wouldn't I, though. I'm writing Alfred a long reply about how to open the matter. I hope it can be arranged soon." The thought of being near home appealed to him, though he warned his mother that sooner or later he would want to see more of the world. "I feel as if I could be contented to revolve between Sullivan and Bloomington and Brown Co. for quite a while, summer and winter, but I realize that every so often the travel fever seizes me" (August 15, 1906).

Wanting more variety in his experience of Germany, Frank decided to move to Heidelberg. He arranged room and board in the family of the University librarian, Herr Professor Doktor Hintzelmann, cheaper by $15.00 a month than the Lenz's in Baden, with the added attraction of a young son who played tennis and would talk German with him. The librarian himself proved hardly less dull than the philologist.

> I have concluded that my place in Baden wasn't so bad after all, all things considered. The Germans are all a bit dull and one must expect that if he stays in Germany. The Librarian of a great University like this one would expect to find an extraordinary man, but he is quite homely and rather dull though not so bad as Herr Prof. Dr. Lenz. He reads to us often after supper out of an awfully good funny book—one I want Nellie to read if she can—and that is pleasant and good for one's German too (September 9, 1906).

In spite of the number of English and American visitors who distracted him from speaking German, Frank found Heidelberg an attractive place.

It is a pretty town stretched out along the river Neckar, with a mountain range and castle behind. . . . They had the castle illuminated the other night in honor of something or other with . . . quantities of red fire making it look as if it were burning. It was a tremendous sight (September 9, 1906).

Frank enjoyed also his success in tennis. He and another Rhodes Scholar won the Handicap Doubles.

Early in September, the month when Americans begin to think of school or college, Frank wrote his father one of his solicitous letters about his brother Will. Frank mentions "influences" in Sullivan which do Will no good and the possibility of his going back to Bloomington, where he can live with Alfred Brooks again. "Living with Alfred has done more to straighten him out than anything else ever has." Frank had made a loan of $300 for Nell's education, and his father had promised to pay it back when he could. Knowing that his father was "hard pressed for money," Frank suggests that no repayment be made. Relieved of this, perhaps he can help Will now. As for borrowing more himself, Frank says apologetically that it would not be safe.

Then and always Frank hoped that something would spark Will's ambition and develop his sense of responsibility. But Will remained a person of whom people said, "No harm in him, but weak." As a boy he was one of a crowd, inclined to loaf and drink too much. He had his good points: a pleasant disposition, fine physical coordination (much better than Frank's) which made him a "natural athlete," good in almost any sport, a "beautiful dancer." But he lacked drive and self-discipline. Perhaps he had been discouraged early by Frank's intensity and success. Perhaps Frank's very readiness to help, in season and out, may have kept him dependent. Will became an engineer of sorts, served overseas in World War I, and died suddenly in middle life—a sad ending which Frank found hard to accept.

Through Frank's weeks in Germany his letters referred again and again to announcing his engagement; he built up a long list of friends and relatives to whom he would like to write the good news. Finally he decided sensibly to limit the letters to one or two. In September he waited impatiently for Marie to come back to France. She was to sail on the twelfth, landing two weeks later. The day when he and George Barnard went to meet her in Boulogne marked the happy end of months of worry. And after all the agitation about where Marie could stay, the

Barnards had room for her again in their house in Moret, where Frank returned with her for "two wonderful weeks."

He wrote his mother that Marie was not well, but was "looking better every day," even though she found the Barnard household far from restful. They lived in a stir of excitement about "their financial troubles," which were "of almost daily occurrence."

The Barnards

This was, indeed, a time when the Barnards had cause for worry about money. They had been living in Moret with almost no income, while the sculptor worked at great expense on an important commission.[33] He had been engaged by the State of Pennsylvania to provide statues for the façade of the new capitol at Harrisburg, the plan calling for a startling number of figures—sixty-seven—(Barnard pointing out that "Michael Angelo did only nineteen figures in all his life"). The work required a huge studio, where Barnard employed fifteen men to help him and used materials that were far from cheap. Owing to political pressures, the fee promised him by the legislature, $700,000, had been cut to $150,000 (for work which would cost the artist $200,000), and the payment of even the smaller amount was indefinitely postponed. Whatever he lost financially, Barnard was confident that this sculpture would make him famous. Meanwhile he had to pay his workmen and support his family. This he at last contrived to do by a kind of antique business in which he became involved almost by accident.

As he rode his bicycle along country roads near ancient Gothic ruins, he had often noticed pieces of sculpture put to practical use by a farmer—a wooden torso of Christ set up in a field as a scarecrow, two madonnas in a chicken yard to encourage the hens to lay. These and other remains not classed by the French government as "national monuments" could still be legally bought and exported by a private collector. Barnard got many at the farmers' low prices, selling them to advantage to dealers and museums. Frank explained this to his mother, adding that Barnard could make much more if he were a better businessman. He could not resist telling how little "he can buy them for himself and so never gets much profit." Also he was too much attached to his best pieces to part with them at any price. (He did manage to make ends meet rather scrappily until his difficulties came to the ears of public-spirited men in New York, including Professors Seligman and Carpenter of Columbia, who admired him and formed a committee to help him. His own collections, transported years later to New York, constituted "The Cloisters," which were acquired in 1925 through a gift from Rockefeller for the Metropolitan Museum of Art.)

Barnard gave Frank his first near view of an artistic genius. With the sculptor's intensity, energy, and dedication to his work Frank could sympathize; these were traits he shared. He did not doubt Barnard's genius nor frown on his oddities; Frank liked "characters." At the same time he could not avoid concern about the impact of Barnard's personality on the high-strung Marie. A man described as a "human dynamo," a "mystic" who followed "a flaming ideal . . . [with] unswerving contempt for compromise," could hardly be an easy person to live with. And he was given to "scenes"—about money, sometimes about young men who called on the ladies of his family. Even after Frank and Marie were engaged, George insisted that Frank never stay later than ten o'clock, and when Frank met Marie's boat at Boulogne, George went along as a formidable preserver of proprieties. But he could also be thoughtful and generous. Realizing the young people's need of funds before they could be married, he offered Frank a chance to invest in his antique business or to earn commissions by arranging sales. Later their positions were reversed. When Barnard got into difficulties, and that was often, Frank did what he could to help.

During Frank's two weeks in Moret, he reported in boyish triumph an exploit with a little car someone had given the Barnards: "I went out in it yesterday and learned to run it. But it stopped three times and we had to stop at a garage and have a new battery put in before we could get home. I learned to run it entirely in French from their hired man" (October 2, 1906).

When Frank crossed the channel for his second year at Oxford, he felt a new confidence in himself and his future. He had won the girl of his choice and succeeded in bringing her back to France for another year. His long hours of hard study during the summer had added cubits to his intellectual stature. And his chance to compare England with France and Germany had convinced him that the English were, indeed, "the finest race" in Europe; that Oxford, not a German university, was without doubt the model for Americans to adapt to their own needs. He could look forward in wholehearted enthusiasm to crusades in education as his share of the "public duties" Rhodes hoped his Scholars would carry through.

CHAPTER FIVE

RHODES SCHOLAR: SECOND YEAR

1906–1907

FRANK AYDELOTTE returned to his second year at Oxford in a glow of ambition. Not content merely to take the two informal examinations (Collections) given by his tutor on his summer's work, he asked for two more and did well in all four. Confident of enjoying his program— "literature of the pleasant sort, with only Middle English Grammar" for drudgery—he was soon engrossed and happy in his work. "It takes every moment of my time but it is pleasant and makes me enjoy Oxford much more than last year." This remark ends in surprise. Surely his last year's letters describing "the life" could hardly have been more appreciative. But the fact was that nothing ever satisfied him so much as hard, absorbing work. "I am so keen and enthusiastic about my studies this year that the whole place seems different.... I have almost cut out society and am jealous of every moment away from work. I'm not overworking—five or six hours a day and one or two lectures only: but that's more than I did last year. There are so many outside things."

Some outside things he could not miss, such as rugger and rowing. Also, as a would-be writer, he was glad to have a chance to join the B.N.C. essay club, the "Ingoldsby," limited to eleven members: "a rather select thing but not over profound. . . . Only one other man from my year got 'on' it—as they say—and only one other Rhodes Scholar." The first paper he contributed grew out of his research, "Life in the Sixteenth Century."[1]

To show his mother where his time went, he described "a typical Oxford day":

> I went out to breakfast with the four I was to start in the Junior Fours race in the afternoon. Then back home to do a philology paper for my tutor which I finished just in time to go to him at 12:00. I had the lunch

club in to lunch at one, was dressed at the barge ready to row at 2:00.
(Our four won in the first heat and came 2nd in the final, Papineau's four
winning.) I got dressed and away from the final race just in time to
bicycle to Dr. Pope's (the man who knew Browning) to tea and from
there to the other end of Oxford, $2\frac{1}{2}$ miles away, to a special Practical
Philology class at 5:30. Thence back home by ten minutes to seven to
dress and go out to dinner with my Univ. tutor at 7:30, and back to my
room about 10:30 when I had visitors and notes to write and a call on
Papineau to make which took till after midnight. You get used to it so
that you don't get nervous or excited about things and if you are late or
forget something nobody minds, but it doesn't leave much time to think
(November 4, 1906).

With all his enjoyment of Oxford life he was not free from personal
worries: his lingering debts and Marie's uncertain health. As to his
finances, not even his cheerful philosophy that to borrow for his education
was sound investment could prevent his feeling depressed by paying
interest and putting off clearing the loans. "I am tired of being behind
and am going to economize desperately now till I get square."

Partly to save money, partly to cut down interruptions of his work,
Frank asked to be allowed to move out of College into lodgings after
Christmas, a permission not usually granted until a student's third year.
Fortunately both the Rhodes Trustees and the Brasenose authorities
approved. He played with the idea of earning a little money by writing
articles for an American magazine on George Barnard and took seriously
the possibility of investing in Barnard's antique business, even urging his
father to come in on it. Apparently his father could not be tempted, but
Frank himself eventually succeeded in negotiating some sales and made
fifteen hundred dollars.

Marie Across the Channel

Marie's health he mentioned in almost every letter: Marie was not so
well; she was slightly better; she still suffered from the summer's nervous
strain—noisy children at camp, worry about possibly having to spend
the winter an ocean away from him. Now back in France, she was upset
by the perpetual turmoil of the Barnard household. Early in November
he made a "sudden trip to France to see Marie who was worse." (This
channel crossing was the first of nineteen for Frank that year. Each time
during term he had to get permission to be away over night from the
vice-principal, Dr. Bussell, who fortunately was friendly.) One letter

home reported that Marie had a sick headache, brought on by an invitation from her stepmother to come to Switzerland for a month's visit. Add to this annoyance at a new "fad," taken on by her father at his wife's insistence, for "spiritualism," Frank's name for Christian Science. Marie's father had sent her "Mrs. Eddy's book" and wanted her to give up medicine that was doing her good: "she is quietly keeping on with it." Years later Marie was to discover that Christian Science could help her.

Convinced that Marie would hardly be well until they had a home of their own, and impatient himself, at twenty-six, to begin married life, Frank considered shortening their time of waiting. He knew, of course, the Trustees' rule that a Rhodes Scholar who married must resign his scholarship, though with the consent of his College he might stay on as a student. Suppose Brasenose did consent: could he earn enough to support them in Oxford by commissions from George Barnard, or would he have to take on more debts? What if he gave up his third year altogether: how much could he finish in two? Could he hope to get both a B.A. and a B.Litt.? An important practical question: might his position at Bloomington be open in 1907 instead of 1908? On this last point he had already asked Alfred Brooks to sound out Dr. Bryan.

By the end of the first term, his tutor had encouraged him to think he had a "promising chance" for a First Class in the B.A. Honours Schools. "I feel that everything here is getting me used to an intellectual pace much above anything I've ever had." Professor Raleigh suggested that his research should "take the form of a book" and gave him sound advice about style: "I ought to write my research with one eye on the general public—not make it too dry and learned in the wrong sense. He says I can make it read like a novel and be none the less sound." And—a rare generosity in a professor who is commonly free from tutorials—Raleigh offered to be his tutor for the next term: "He told me I might 'chuck' (the word he used) my tutor and read essays to him next term, which I consider a great chance." Still, an opportunity to teach at Bloomington in the fall would be too good to miss. Before he could hear what his mother thought, he set off for six weeks in Moret, eager for a stretch of concentrated work combined with seeing Marie every day.

A gay letter to his sister Nell described in readable if inelegant French his life in a peasant household. His room, formerly a kitchen, had a stone floor and was so cold that he studied wrapped in a heavy coat, his feet on a warm stone; he expected to need wooden "sabots" as well. Madame, his hostess, like all Frenchwomen, was a good cook. Her husband's table manners were odd but efficient, his only utensil a large pocket knife which he managed with great skill.

Every day Frank studied from eight until four, then took Marie for a walk and perhaps had dinner at the Barnards'. Often in the evening he would get her opinion of something he had written during the day. He left early enough to be in bed at ten o'clock. After three weeks of this regime he wrote: "I have never worked so well since I've been in Oxford or enjoyed it as much as this vacation. . . . I have so much more interest in all my studies since I'm not worried about Marie and can see her every day."

The Lure of Alma Mater

Meanwhile Alfred reported the good news that Dr. Bryan would be glad to have Frank begin at Indiana the next September, and at a higher rank than was first proposed, *Associate* instead of *Assistant* Professor.[2] The salary of $1,500 Frank estimated would let him pay his debts at the rate of $500 a year—$1,000 being ample for the simple life he and Marie would lead. Confident of his mother's approval, he did not wait for a letter before cabling his acceptance. What was his chagrin next day to get three letters, from Will and Nell as well as his mother, all not only opposed to his plan but scandalized at the idea of his leaving Oxford until he had finished his three years. They wrote with a sharpness unusual among the Aydelottes, blaming Marie as a bad influence; his eagerness to be married had destroyed his ambition and would ruin his career. These letters do not survive, but their line of attack is clear in his answer. His tone did not echo their bitterness, but showed affectionate concern to clear their misunderstanding of his situation and of Marie.

> I am awfully sorry you are all so worried; I am sure you will not be when you understand the situation.
>
> My idea of getting married next year began on account of Marie's health but I had not decided definitely to do it nor had she consented nor would she unless we could scrape together money enough . . . to live married in Oxford next winter, where I could go on with my work and courses exactly as if I had not been married. The marriage rule applies only to holding Rhodes Scholarships—not to membership in University or College: they are absolutely separate things. . . .
>
> Now as I was casting about to make this money [buying and selling two Gothic cloisters with E. A. Abbey and Marie's cousin—George

Barnard] this word comes from Dr. Bryan and Alfred. . . . The Eng. Dept. there is in bad shape, the worst in the University, I believe. Sampson began it by neglecting things. The man they are trying in Sampson's place now does not seem to be making a success. The only other first rate man in the Dept.—Sembower—is going away for two years and Dr. Bryan and the University Trustees are very eager to have me come out at once as Associate Professor and, if I do well, I have the finest kind of chance of coming out Head of the Dept. soon instead of having the years and years of working up to it that I should have ordinarily. I should certainly consider the opportunity too good a one to refuse if Marie were out of the question entirely.

I insisted and Dr. Bryan and the Trustees agreed that the moment I have things going well enough to be left a year and am able myself, I shall have a year's leave of absence when I intend to come back to Oxford and work out my D.Litt.—which is the one degree I want after the B.Litt. . . . I shall be eligible for the D.Litt. when my name has been on the books four years or more.

I don't think you will feel that there is any disgrace in my leaving now. The very men who got me the place are the ones who want me. It isn't as if I were creeping back to a two-penny High School job or Instructorship merely for the sake of getting married—a thing which Marie would no more consent to than I would do. But a chance like this is rare. It means position and honor at home in Indiana where I'd like to have them. And it means a speedy chance to try my own ideas . . . about what could be made of a University English Department (December 29, 1906).

Frank added that he would wait to hear from his mother before mentioning his plan to the Rhodes Trustees. "I hate to have you worried and opposed to what I'm doing." As to his ambition, she could rest assured that it has never been stronger: to become Head of the Department at Bloomington and to get an Oxford doctorate, the D.Litt., as soon as regulations allowed. (Neither ambition would, in fact, be realized.)

Touched by Frank's concern and reassured by his array of facts, his mother wrote in a more sympathetic tone which brought great relief to the young people. "Your letter written Xmas Eve has just come and cheers us both up tremendously—especially me for I did not like you to think I had lost my ambition or that Marie was a bad influence. As a matter of fact she will not let me think of anything except what is best for my work and advancement in the long run."

Before Frank's weeks in Moret ended, his finances had begun to improve. With the money earned from sales for George Barnard, he had the satisfaction of sending $1,000 to Sullivan to repay a loan from the bank.

Back in Oxford for the winter term, Frank and his Brasenose friend R. P. Brooks moved into lodgings at 20 Manor Place, where Marie and her aunt had once stayed. Frank liked the landlady and the house: "It is quiet and comfortable and home like." He reported much work ahead, preparing to take his B.A. in June and trying also to complete research for his B.Litt. Even so, he was no recluse. In February he went to London twice, once to a dinner where he made a speech that was "well spoken of," again to see Parliament open. Training for Toggers began this month; "we have an excellent boat . . . and ought to make some bumps." It was late in February before arrangements in Bloomington became definite enough to permit his presenting to Wylie Dr. Bryan's proposal.

To Frank's relief, Wylie "was heartily pleased" at the offer and volunteered an opinion which Frank delighted to report: it was "worth giving up my scholarship . . . unless I was sure my year of advanced work here would help me more in the long run. . . . He was awfully nice about it and I feel good at the prospect of leaving with no strained relations." Also Wylie had paid him a compliment, repeated by Gretchen Warren. Mentioning Frank to her, Wylie remarked, "I hear you know my favorite Rhodes Scholar." Dr. Parkin's humor seems to echo in a comment Frank attributed to the Trustees: "The sooner I'm a great man, the better for them and for me too." Tucked away in a postscript Frank told of a victory to which he would once have given first place. "Torpids are on. We rowed through yesterday and bumped New College II today— the first bump made by a B.N.C. boat for two years. We are rather heroes in College tonight." But he added: "My own affairs absorb me too much to be very excited just now."

In these months of important decisions, the one longest in the air concerned his degree. He hated to give up the B.A. because it was characteristic of Oxford and could be taken with a First Class—he would prize a chance at this distinction. On the other hand, now while he had access to some of the best libraries in the world, he would like also to carry through the research for his B.Litt. But at last even Frank's invincible optimism could see no way to do both. As late as March he decided to let the B.A. go and concentrate on work for the B.Litt., assuming that he would have to complete it in Bloomington. Then, depressed by the thought of going home without any degree to show for all his efforts, in July after his marriage he had a new idea: to stay in Oxford until he had finished not only his research but the thesis itself. If it should be accepted, he would be on hand for the required oral examination and could go home with the diploma all but in his pocket. It would be mailed to him after formalities, from which he could be excused. This new plan would postpone his return to Bloomington until the end of December, but fortunately Dr. Bryan and the English department saw the advantage and generously agreed to wait.

Raleigh, Firth, and Research

Already in Professor Raleigh's seminar Frank had made substantial progress on his thesis, "Elizabethan Rogues and Vagabonds." These classes of displaced persons increased alarmingly in the sixteenth century with the eviction of tenant farmers from their livelihood by enclosures for sheep raising and with the cutting adrift of retainers and serfs as the feudal system disappeared. Frank hoped to discover how far Robert Greene's account of the particular rogues who specialized in cheating at cards (conycatching) and other forms of swindling could be taken as historical fact.[3] Since the thesis would lie as much in history as in literature, he was given a second supervisor, the distinguished professor of history C. H. Firth (in addition, of course, to Professor Raleigh). Raleigh Frank described as "gay and rollicking," Firth as a "sound and thorough scholar," an ideal combination. Both told him to work on his own, but stood ready to give advice.

Frank remembered one occasion when he consulted Firth in his library about some historical problem. Firth went to a shelf, pulled out one book, then another, until, in Frank's words, "I had around me on the floor a little mound of historical works. I carefully put down the title and author of each and said to him, 'Which ones do you consider the most important for me to read,' 'All of them,' he said, 'read them all, read them all.' "

Frank was fortunate in having additional help from two scholars in London: Sir Frederick Pollock, "one of the greatest legal authorities in England," and Dr. Furnivall, "the most famous Elizabethan scholar in the world." Frank met Sir Frederick through Erskine Childers—son of a Lord Chancellor and husband of Marie's cousin Molly Osgood—then at work on a history of the Boer War.[4] Sir Frederick's connection with the

Record Office opened Frank's eyes to its treasures of documents. Dr. Furnivall he encountered "in a little tea room where he goes every afternoon" and people go to find him "after the manner of the Elizabethans of the Mermaid Tavern. Except that this tea room is rather a barren place, not very like my idea of the Mermaid Tavern." Dr. Furnivall gave him "access to some very fine M.S.S. records of the City of London in the Guildhall Library."

When Frank needed rest from study, he amused himself with a favorite game of planning details long in advance. As early as January he wrote about the announcements of their June wedding. Would his mother send names of relatives and neighbors who whould get them? "Don't miss anybody." At the same time he discussed arrangements for living in Bloomington. "We want a small five-room house if we can afford it. $15.00 a month is our limit. We're going to have a kitchen, a dining room and sitting room all in one, my study and two bed rooms so we can have a place to put a visitor," (Eventually their kind friend Alfred Brooks found a four-room apartment, with no guest room, for $19.00 a month.) In January also Frank began to ask about furnishings he might borrow from home. He and Marie hoped to eke out wedding presents with loans and makeshifts, such as "rugs over trunks for seats," a "pine table for the study." An awkward result of his forehanded planning: when he postponed the date of his return to late December, he found himself with an apartment firmly engaged from September 1. He would have to pay rent for it, unoccupied, for almost four months. But he made the best of the situation by offering it to his sister Nell, who expected to enter the University in the fall, suggesting how it could be made habitable with some of his possessions, scattered in Bloomington, which the indefatigable Alfred Brooks would help assemble. Like so many of his plans, this one worked.

The urgent question early in 1907 was where Frank and Marie should be married. Marie's first idea, so she wrote an American friend, was a "lovely quiet English wedding" with a wedding dress and guests, but this plan had to be "nipped in the bud" because her stepmother was "inopportunely to have a baby. . . . Thus it happens that I am to have no celebration but shall be married in my traveling suit with probably only Papa present." Whether the wedding should be in England or France "depends largely upon which country has the less red tape for foreigners."[5]

Their first inclination was for France. Frank began at once to unravel the red tape, drawing up in French the kind of "consent" his parents would have to sign. "One must have 'consents' like this from the parents of each party, age certificates of each, a certificate from the consul that we are both single and of capacity to be married, and proof of the banns having been published here [in Oxford] as well as in France, where one of the parties must have resided continuously for six months." Frank found it all amusing: "It's fine practice in French." But when Marie and her father came to England for the spring vacation, they decided that she should stay there and have a very small June wedding in Abingdon, close to Oxford. After the vacation, which she would spend in London, she would go for a rest to a sanitarium near Reading, later to Abingdon to establish residence. In both places she and Frank could meet every Sunday.

The spring vacation was full of excitement for Frank, partly from wedding plans and the chance to see Marie, but almost more from progress in his work. "I simply revel in the British Museum Library, which is a wonderful place. It seems as if they have every book in the world and I'm getting some corking things for my research." Not liking to be away from Marie all day, he got admission to the library for her, too, so that she could help him: "She's copying quotations which I want to use in my B.Litt. book."

The summer term at Oxford went well for them both. Frank's research went on apace.

> I never felt so ambitious in my life and never felt before that I really knew what scholarship meant. I used to be in such a fix because I couldn't think of a subject for research—simply because I didn't know enough about English Literature. I come across dozens now and should like nothing better than to spend years working them out and writing books—indeed that's what I intend to do. . . . I am so eager to make a success of my book and of my lectures next year I can hardly wait to begin (May 31, 1907).

In sports he "made the College Eight" and rowed in the races late in May. "Our Eight finished one place higher than we started, having made two bumps and got bumped once." Marie had come over twice to see him row, chaperoned once by her aunt and once by Mrs. Wylie. Christ Church became head of the river and went wild: "The undergrads tried to burn the Oxford pageant grandstand for a celebration (having figured up in the law-abiding English fashion that they could pay for it by every man in the college paying $10.00) but were prevented by the police and firemen."

As to Marie's health, she was "better every week. . . . She was in something of the fix you are sometimes but not so bad—perhaps just as bad but easier to cure because it hadn't been going long. Remembering what is good for you helps me looking after her." He was trying to win his mother's sympathy for Marie, and there were, indeed, likenesses between the two, both suffering from the effects of youthful insecurity and loneliness.

The climax of the year for the Rhodes Scholars came on June 12 when a tablet to Cecil Rhodes was unveiled and a dinner given them by the Trustees, the speaker on both occasions the Senior Trustee, Lord Rosebery. Frank's comment, "He is a splendid speaker," was elaborated in the *Oxford Magazine:* "[His speech] was the most genuine, generous, and discriminating tribute which has yet been paid to the memory of a man who in his life was never rightly appreciated, and whose achievements, even since his death, have been darkened and obscured by the dust of conflict and controversy." The tablet, erected in the new Examination Schools, was designed by T. Graham Jackson, R.A., with the simple inscription: "This Tablet commemorates the Foundation, A.D. 1902, of the Rhodes Scholarships by the Munificence of Cecil John Rhodes, M.A., Hon D.C.L., sometime of Oriel College." There seemed a special fitness in a memorial at this time when the first group of Scholars had reached their final term. Frank still thought it would be his own last term also and heard Lord Rosebery's closing words as a parting charge: "I do not know what other methods may be taken to perpetuate the memory of Mr. Rhodes in this country, or in South Africa, but sure I am of this, that in this ancient University his surest and noblest monument will be the career, the merits and the reputation of the scholars whom he has summoned within these walls."

The *Magazine* mentioned the Rhodes Trustees' dinner as a kind of "farewell banquet" for the seventy men who were going down, and it paid them a graceful trubute: "To those seventy the *Magazine* would wish most heartily God Speed! They came to Oxford strangers not unwelcomed; they leave us friends whom we would not willingly forget."[6]

Marriage

On June 23, 1907, Frank and Marie were married in Abingdon, in a ceremony performed by Dr. Pope, "the man who knew Browning," whom Frank had come to know as a wise and kindly friend.

There was nobody there except Marie's father and aunt and married cousins and two of my friends—Papineau and Brooks. We wore just the things we were going to travel in—had it at 12:00 and left at 1:30. Dr. Pope was wonderful. We were glad we had Papineau and Brooks—they made the little lunch Marie's father gave us go off better. Some of the people from the sanatorium drove over (20 miles) to strew flowers in front of us as we left and congratulate us. . . . We had your nice letter just the day before and were awfully pleased to have it (July 6, 1907; Grosthwaite near Windermere).

Among Frank's treasured papers is the bill for Marie's flowers: "1 Shower Bouquet with Ribbon, 1/2/6 [one pound, two shillings, sixpence]." Marie's father had given them their wedding silver, a beautiful, plain design. There were "pieces of silver and a clock and kit bag . . . books from the Principal of the College," and a tea cloth from Mrs. Wright, wife of Professor Joseph Wright, whom Frank so much respected.

The first days after the wedding the young pair spent in London so that Frank could "invigilate" Harvard entrance examinations for a welcome fee which would pay the cost of their week's honeymoon near Windermere. Then back to London for research in the Record Office, with Marie helping to copy the sixteenth-century manuscripts which Frank had taught her to read. At Dr. Furnivall's suggestion, Frank looked up some unpublished records in the Guild Hall—accounts of trials and punishments of rogues and vagabonds in the sixteenth century—and was delighted to discover a book

> describing a great pageant and torchlight procession which they used to hold once a year in Henry VIII's reign. . . . It was written in 1585 by a man who wanted the procession revived and it describes exactly the number of men, route of the march, dress, music, etc. necessary. Dr. Furnivall was much interested in it and I may have the chance to edit it for the Early English Text Society if they decide to reprint it.[7]

He says proudly that Marie is copying it for him.

Toward the end of July, a month after their wedding, they left London for more research in the Bodleian Library at Oxford, staying in Frank's old lodgings. Such a beginning of married life, given to proctoring examinations and copying sixteenth-century documents, would have been a dull business with some husbands, but not with Frank Aydelotte. He radiated a happy excitement about his work that was infectious, and Marie reflected his enjoyment, proud of having a share in his undertakings.

Through the year and a half since Frank's engagement, his mother had not written to Marie, contenting herself with messages. Now Marie felt the silence must be broken and sent her mother-in-law a letter that is a model of tact:

20 Manor Place
Oxford
August 18, 1907

Dear Mrs. Aydelotte:

I am afraid you are beginning to despair of our ever getting home. To me it seems such a long time before I shall meet you that I hope you will forgive me and not think me presuming in writing you first. I want to thank you for the sweet messages that have come from you through Frank. Frank is so devoted to his family that you all feel very near me and I long to know you.

In many ways it was hard to make up our minds to remain here until Christmas. But it was so much the best thing for Frank's work that we were thankful when Dr. Bryan's permission came. I am sure you must worry about Frank and think he works too hard, for it used to trouble me before we were married. But it is really a marvel how much he can do and yet keep well and strong. Since he has heard he must hand his thesis in in October (a month earlier than he had expected) he has been working in The Bodleian from nine until four and every evening until twelve at home. He takes three hours in the afternoon for rest and exercise and sleeps eight hours and feels fine. He finds ways in which I can help him in his work and I generally spend the mornings with him in the Bodleian.

These are delightful lodgings we are in and I haven't a single household care. We are very happy here. But we long for our own little home in Bloomington no matter how simple it is. I do hope Nellie is going to be able to make use of our rooms this fall. I only wish we could furnish and make them look homelike for her.

I wonder if Frank wrote you that after the 4th of October we are going to visit some cousins of mine who will have a house in Oxford. It is going to be a great help to us and altogether delightful.

Please don't feel you must answer this for I know you are far too busy.

With love,
Marie

Whether Frank's mother answered this letter or ever wrote to her daughter-in-law is uncertain. No such communication survives. But the older woman's attitude was always odd. When Marie sent presents at Christmas, her mother-in-law would open them, make some comment, wrap them up again, and put them away. She never used them. Marie for her part persisted in keeping relations pleasant when they met. Frank doubtless saw the situation and accepted it, as he had always accepted his mother's eccentricities.

The "cousins" whom Marie mentions were the Fiske Warrens. During the previous summer Dr. Hamilton Osgood, Gretchen Warren's father and Frank's good friend, had died after a long illness. With her family sadly diminished, Gretchen had room for Frank and Marie and invited them to be her guests from early October until they left for Indiana. Frank also reported this happily; the Warrens had a large house and the means to be hospitable.

As the first married Rhodes Scholar and his wife in residence at Oxford, Frank and Marie "were entertained most cordially by all sorts of college and university friends." Frank recalled especially "a dinner given in our honor by the Principal of Brasenose," Mr. Heberden, at which "Bussell, the Vice Principal, appeared in knee breeches and silk stockings, much to Marie's astonishment."[8] If she realized that this was the dress he would wear to be received by Royalty, she must have been touched by the compliment.

Whatever the occasional distraction, Frank applied himself steadily to his thesis, keeping in shape by playing tennis every good day. Marie copied notes and manuscripts, discussing them with him, challenging anything obscure. Her cousin, Molly Osgood Childers, remembers overhearing them at Gretchen Warren's house, "Marie like a gifted tutor questioning Frank, making suggestions, listening and discussing points he wished to think out. He needed training in phrasing, in increasing his powers of expression, preparing for his oral Examinations."

That Marie had this kind of skill might surprise those who knew her only in later years. Then she seemed little interested in ideas and discussion, though immensely able in practical matters and an astute judge of people. But she seldom talked in a group. If Frank was present, she felt he was the one to be heard; if absent, she guarded against saying something which might be misinterpreted at his expense. She "made Frank possible," no doubt of it, and any cost to herself seemed unimportant.

Bachelor of Letters

At last the thesis was ready to show to Professor Raleigh. He advised handing it in, though Frank was not well satisified with it. He had it typed in London and submitted it to his three examiners, Raleigh, Firth, and the Shakespearean scholar Sidney Lee. In due course they announced through the *Oxford University Gazette* that his public examination would be held "on Saturday, November 30, at 5 p.m. in the Schools." A week later came official notice of his success, which he reported to his mother, enclosing a clipping from the *Gazette* giving the examiners' gratifying statement:

> The investigations of Mr. Aydelotte elucidate several obscure points in the history of those classes Elizabethan Rogues and Vagabonds, and illustrate the development of the literature describing them. He proved satisfactorily an aptitude for literary research, and a wide acquaintance with published and unpublished materials.
>
> We therefore recommend that so far as proficiency in the subject of his special research is concerned he has attained a high standard of merit.
>
> C. H. Firth
Sidney Lee   Examiners
W. A. Raleigh

December 7, 1907

On March 17, 1908, the *Gazette* notes, "In a Congregation holden on Thursday, March 12," the Degree of Bachelor of Letters was conferred on "Aydelotte, Frank, Brasenose College (in absentia)."[9]

After Frank had heard from his examiners, he called on Dr. Parkin, who told him that the Trustees were pleased with his success. and wanted to give him a present. Then, Frank wrote,

> We got to talking about my plans and I said that as soon as I could get leave of absence from Indiana University I wanted to go back to Oxford to finish the Rogues and Vagabonds and get them into print. Dr. Parkin inquired whether I would rather have the third year of my Scholarship if and when that happened . . . than any present. . . . Of course, I jumped at the chance. He made it clear that it was no promise on the part of the Trustees, but when five years later I was able to say that I did have a year's leave of absence from Indiana, the Rhodes Trustees gave me the third year of my Scholarship.[10]

The possibility that this might happen was enough of a present to take home.

Before Christmas, 1907, Frank and Marie sailed on the *Baltic* from Liverpool, momentarily cast down by an accident in the harbor: one of their trunks had been dropped into the water, the one "containing absolutely all of Marie's good dresses." It was fished out, unfortunately, because on that ground the company refused to accept responsibility for more than minimal damages, even though all the contents were ruined beyond repair. This was the verdict when the Aydelottes made their claim in New York, represented for the first time by their Oxford friend Paul Kieffer, who would be their lifelong legal adviser. But no loss of merely material things could daunt them for more than the moment. Without money to buy replacements, Marie made a joke of wearing her traveling suit to parties in her honor in Sullivan and Bloomington.

Happily the sodden trunk did not contain Frank's handsome new B.Litt. gown of heavy black silk with braided trimming on yoke and sleeves. He prized it as a symbol of all that Oxford had meant to him. He came home with his mind in a ferment of new ideas about means and ends in education, about student life, about attitudes toward sports— ideas he would need time to brood over and to test. Eventually he would make them into a set of essays, "the educational creed of a Rhodes Scholar," published in 1917 with the title, *The Oxford Stamp*. But now in January, 1908, his first thought was of the classrooms he was about to enter as professor of English at Indiana.

＊

CHAPTER SIX

TEACHING ENGLISH AT INDIANA

1908–1915

"Acting Associate Professor" Frank Aydelotte joined the English department at Indiana University in January, 1908, determined to make his mark quickly and confident of a bright future. He had heard from no less an authority than President Bryan that the department needed building up and felt prepared by what he had learned at Oxford to make his contribution. The students welcomed him as a famous member of the first I.U. football team to become state champions and, even more admiringly, the first alumnus to win one of the remarkable new Rhodes Scholarships. Members of the faculty who had known and liked him as an undergraduate were glad to have him back.

The University was still as he had known it—primarily a college of liberal arts with a clientele largely from the state. Of approximately 2,000 students in 1908, 1,689 constituted the undergraduate college and 125 the Graduate School, with the rest divided between Law and Medicine. Indiana residents numbered 1,893; 56 came from the neighboring states of Illinois, Ohio, and Kentucky, with a scattering from other parts of the country. Nine students represented the rest of the world.[1]

Taking for granted that the University was predominantly Hoosier, and liking it as it was, Frank Aydelotte had no idea that he might seem suspect as a man who had left his native state to study abroad and might come back putting on airs. Some of his colleagues remembered him as a green freshman from Sullivan, "none greener." Some were suspicious of a Bostonian wife who might look down on Bloomington ladies. In fact, those who came to know Marie were quickly won by her shy, New England charm. When President Bryan met her, he told Frank he had more luck than he'd any right to. The wife of a colleague recalls her "candor and simplicity" and a "sophistication not so evident as to cause alarm." Others who hardly knew the young pair continued to regard Marie as an alien and misinterpreted as "criticism" Frank's eagerness to do his best for Indiana without delay. But it was three or four years before a storm threatened to break.

The program of his first term included two advanced electives, Chaucer and Elizabethan literature, and the required freshman composition.[2] It was in this last that he saw his opportunity. At Indiana, as at most American colleges and universities, "composition" was a course in rhetoric, with frequent, often daily themes on no matter what subject, judged mainly for correctness.

Harvard had given birth to this kind of course, and Frank as a graduate student had taken a section for the famous Professor Copeland. At that time he had not questioned the method or the separation of composition from literature. He had accepted also the usual American introductory survey of English literature, presenting facts about books which students commonly did not know at first hand. But at Oxford he had been struck by the absence of "courses in writing" and "surveys." In English literature, instead of listening to lectures "from Chaucer to Tennyson," a student was expected to digest thoroughly one masterpiece after another. On the basis of this study he wrote essays for his tutor which were expected to show both an understanding of a book and a sense of its importance. He wrote, not "for practice," but because he presumably had something to say. This was the usual approach to writing, not only in English literature. Tutors in most subjects set frequent essays, to be criticized both for content and for effective expression. The result, so far as Frank could judge, was that Oxonians on the whole wrote far better than most Americans and read more widely and intelligently. Apparently survey courses developed little taste for reading, and daily themes resulted in a perfunctory style.

What Frank proposed in effect was to adapt the English method, combining work in composition and literature so that a student would be stimulated by a good writer to form and express his own opinions. The new kind of course would be, above all, training in thought. And the writers Frank wished to stress as peculiarly thought-provoking were Newman, Arnold, Huxley, Ruskin, and Carlyle in prose, followed by four poets: Wordsworth, Pope, Milton, and Shakespeare. The five essayists could be expected to make a student think by their discussions of a subject which concerned him personally: the subject of education. Also they differed from each other sufficiently to prod him into drawing comparisons and deciding what he could accept. And when the student was confronted by the four great poets, with their strikingly individual views of nature and human life, how could he resist weighing one against another and trying to formulate a view of his own?

Though in charge of the course at Indiana, Frank was only one of several teachers. He must persuade the others to see the need for improvement and to agree to experiment with his plan. On the first point, there was little difficulty; many teachers, after years of drudgery on daily themes, most of them hopelessly dreary, were ready to look for a better and brighter way. One of the department, Cecilia Hennel Hendricks, remembers the method by which his plan was adopted: "Everything was done in a democratic manner, with staff meetings to consider every suggestion,"[3] but there was little question that Frank's enthusiasm would carry the day.

Frank could win quick support because he was recognized as a lively, effective teacher. He had profited by the example of men he had worked with: Kittredge, Briggs, and Copeland at Harvard, Raleigh at Oxford, not to forget the man at Indiana who first attracted him to English literature, Martin Wright Sampson. Each in his way knew how to strike fire.

Frank liked to stir students by surprising them, by a kind of shock tactics. A man who later became a professor of English at Indiana, Frank Davidson, describes assignments which startled him into dogged and rewarding work. One was to contrast two concepts of nature, Wordsworth's and Darwin's, on the basis of key quotations: "Knowing that Nature never did betray / The heart that loved her," and "Nature is a great battlefield, where everything fights for its position of advantage." In Davidson's words: "For the theme that week we were to express our views, from our experience and our reading, on this poetic and this scientific approach to nature. Were they entirely at odds? Was one wholly right and the other wholly wrong? I cannot remember whether, before that hour, I had ever attempted to pursue an idea." Aydelotte's plan seemed to be, "not to answer questions, but to raise them as a guide might deer, and to station us like inexperienced hunters where the deer might run." The first assignment for a paper on Browning was "Caliban on Setebos."

> He didn't tell us who Caliban was or who Setebos was, and I doubt that a single one of us knew. Could we find out? I read the poem for the

twelfth time, I believe, before I knew who was talking. Then the episode began to be clear, and I felt a great respect for Browning. Later, when I came to my senses, I was to have a great respect for the man who left me to carve a path through the wilderness.[4]

When Frank met a class, he became so absorbed in teaching that he sometimes forgot himself to a degree that made him an almost comic figure, one of those "characters" with a special place in undergraduate affection. His colleague Professor Hendricks, who had been his student, describes his way of twisting his body into strange contortions.

> I can still see him sitting on one corner of the desk, leaning as far as possible toward the class, his legs twisted one about the other (and sometimes around the leg of the desk), one arm braced to keep him from sliding, the other used in gestures to emphasize what he was saying. Students used to be ready to wager on how many times he could twist his legs about each other, and whether or not he would some day fall off the corner of the desk. He never did!

To teach well himself and to revolutionize freshman English at Indiana was not enough. Frank wanted to carry the good word to English departments everywhere. First he wrote a letter to the *Nation* with the heading, "The Freshman English Course," describing the experiment at Indiana; two years later, articles reaching a wider audience of teachers, "English as Training in Thought," in the *Educational Review*, and an attack on a mistaken way of teaching, "Robert Louis Stevenson Darkening Counsel," in the *English Journal*. Here he takes Stevenson to task for his famous "sedulous ape" theory of composition which has influenced teachers to encourage imitation of a favorite style. The result is self-consciousness, bad writing, and failure to get the valuable point implied in Stevenson's account, that in fact he learned to write not by imitating what he read but by reading eagerly, widely, thoughtfully, to satisfy a restless curiosity about ideas and experience. A student should learn from Stevenson how a man reads in order to quicken his mind and have something to say.

When a teacher of composition writes about writing, his words are bound to be subjected to special scrutiny. Here Frank had nothing to fear. His style was admirably suited to the content: clear, direct, concrete, and with a rhythm and emphasis easy and pleasant to follow. But his ambition went beyond essays on teaching English; he hoped to produce scholarly works which should be "as interesting as a novel" (Raleigh's requirement). He even tried his hand at planning a play or two; there are notes among his papers, but no evidence that the plays were completed.

There is also an unpublished essay, "On Not Doing One's Duty," dated May 31, 1910, which gives an unexpected, touching glimpse of a hard-working young man reacting against his usual strenuous efforts. He takes the line that a man sometimes does his duty "a little too thoroughly for a little too long a time" and becomes "discontented and depressed." The remedy: "to commit some little sin such as giving out that he is ill and lying about all day with a good novel and a pipe, or chucking a pile of essays into the wastebasket unread, or spending time and money that he cannot afford on a drive or a dinner downtown." The result will be wonderful refreshment. He will go back to work with "any amount of earnest, cheerful endeavor, spending any amount of time and trouble on the task immediately before him, and not content with that, dreaming dreams of a thousand more to be accomplished in the future, wishing for nothing more in this world than a long life of hard work."[5] Is there an echo here of Stevenson's "Apology for Idlers" and of William James's advice to take a "moral holiday" once in a while? Whatever the blend in Frank's essay of irony, fantasy, and fact, he shows that his prodigies of effort required self-discipline; also, that he recognized his own seriousness and was determined not to be solemn or dull.

Personal Life

Marie and Frank lived simply in an apartment furnished with their wedding presents, book shelves made of orange crates, and for seats, a trunk or two covered with rugs. They enjoyed their friends, among whom Alfred Brooks was easily first.

They entertained students by inviting them to tea on Sunday afternoons, but knowing that they were likely to stay too long, asked Alfred Brooks to help break up a party as Frank had once helped Copey. Alfred "would get up at the proper time and excuse himself, ask a student near him if he was walking the same way, say something to another student, and get the whole crowd on their feet and moving. . . . Alfred would then walk around the block and come back again" for supper.

Frank coached a play occasionally, kept in touch with his fraternity, Sigma Nu, and was gratified by election in 1911 to the newly formed chapter of Phi Beta Kappa, though, for economy's sake, he waited six years to buy a key. One of his close friends was a crotchety teacher of philosophy, Warner Fite, as clever as he was often difficult in personal relations. With Frank he showed his difficult side only in expecting a great deal of practical help, on one occasion asking him to ship an oil heater and a sewing machine from Bloomington to Cambridge. Another friend of those years, Mrs. Hedwig Leser, widow of a professor of German, remembers gratefully Frank's kindness when her husband was desperately ill and had to be taken to the hospital in Indianapolis on a cot in the baggage car. Frank and Alfred Brooks rode with him, doing what they could to make him comfortable, and when the doctors knew he could not recover, stayed within call until the end. At home in Bloomington the Leser children were with Marie.

The financial difficulties of a young associate professor burdened with debts for his education were lightened occasionally by Marie's generous cousin, Gretchen Warren, who had entertained them so hospitably in Oxford. For the summer after their first semester in Bloomington she wrote from England offering them her house in Harvard, Massachusetts, complete with someone to do the hard work and all their expenses for food and travel. Her affectionate, effervescent letter persuaded them to accept:

> We shall consider you our guests from *yr* door to *yr* door again. You must order enough food to *burst.* . . . You can take your meals into the woods every day & can sleep out every night, there is a huge balcony outside my bedroom with two beds on it & awnings against storm—oh it is all too wonderful, I *cd weep* with pure joy—I am only terrified for fear you will say no—won't like the climate or something. I want you to cable at my *expense* . . . "Yes"—and then I shall shriek with joy!! . . . *I go on my knees to you both to say yes.*
>
> Your loving sister
> Gretchen

Frank and Marie had not yet seen the place at Harvard where Fiske Warren, in his enthusiasm for Henry George, was setting up a Single Tax colony. While the Aydelottes felt no great concern for the Single Tax, they liked the place so much that Frank eventually built a cottage on land owned by Gretchen's mother. He planned it and did all the work and in return was allowed to occupy it free of rent as long as he liked. According to Gretchen's daughter Rachel, Frank threw himself into the project of building it "with all his ingenuity. The rooms were to be of a size to correspond with a standard length of boards, thus

eliminating a tremendous amount of sawing. . . . The living room ceiling
went up into the peak of the roof and had a big field-stone fireplace built
by Cousin Frank himself"; it drew well. The Warrens ransacked attics
for furniture to be reconditioned, and the whole house was built and
furnished for well under—$2,000. Ash Tree Camp, as it was called, was a
favorite place for Aydelotte vacations, especially easy of access when
they lived in Cambridge.

Gretchen's kindness took another practical turn when their first and
only child, William, was born in Bloomington in 1910. She sent out the
excellent nurse who had helped at the birth of her own children to take
care of Marie and the new baby. Then when Marie's poor health made a
serious operation necessary, Gretchen brought her to a Boston hospital
and looked after her during her convalescence.

Meanwhile Frank cared for the baby himself with help from a young
Negro girl, Ethel Lewis, who came in while he was teaching. He was
glad to know his child better than most fathers, but sobered by finding
how much a mother has to do. After Marie's return he was confident
that she could not manage alone, and they kept Ethel as a nursemaid.

Year's Leave in Oxford

From the time when Frank left Oxford in 1908 he had determined to
go back to revise his thesis for publication, hoping also to use it in
applying for a D.Litt. degree. Both the D.Litt., and the D.Sc. degrees had
acquired a double status in 1901. Hitherto always honorary, awarded to
men of outstanding distinction, now they could also be earned on the
basis of "published papers or books containing an original contribution
to the advancement of learning or science,"[6] submitted by a scholar who
already had an Oxford Bachelor's degree. Frank became eligible to
submit his papers or books, that is, to "supplicate" for the degree, after
twenty-six terms during which he had "kept his name on the books" of
his college. This meant that he had maintained an official connection
with his college by paying a small fee each term (a practice for which
there is no American equivalent). Frank would reach this point of
seniority by March, 1912. So he arranged to get leave of absence from
the first of August. Convinced that Marie would not profit from her
stay in Oxford if she had the whole care of William, he persuaded Ethel
Lewis to go with them. They could afford her because Frank had earned

full salary for his leave by teaching in summer school for three years, and added to this they had a gift from the generous Rhodes Trustees of the stipend he had forfeited when he married.

About this important stay in England we know little. Apparently Frank's mother had stopped saving his letters. His principal work was revising his *Elizabethan Rogues and Vagabonds*. To his great satisfaction, it was published by the Oxford University Press as the first volume (1913) of a series, *Oxford Historical and Literary Studies*, directed by his supervisors, Professors Firth and Raleigh. The book is slender but impressive, scholarly in content, and beautifully printed and illustrated. Of its 187 pages, 37 form an appendix of documents relating to vagabonds, beggars, and rogues for the years 1517–1612, when their numbers climbed to a dangerous level. Written in a concise, natural style, it was a good first step toward Professor Raleigh's ideal of humane scholarship.

But regardless of the book's merits, Frank apparently did not submit it for the coveted D.Litt.; indeed, he did not supplicate for the degree then or ever. Once back in Oxford, he must have seen that he had underestimated the maturity and productiveness expected for this doctorate. At the ceremonies where he had hoped to receive it, in June, 1913, the only man who got a D.Litt. by supplicating, the orientalist Lionel Giles, had been for twelve years a member of the British Museum staff, with seven notable publications to his credit. The recipients in the first two groups to supplicate (1901 and 1902) included such established scholars as L. R. Farnell, E. G. Hardy, and G. B. Grundy in ancient history, the philosopher Hastings Rashdall, and the Arabic scholar D. S. Margoliouth. Because the degree had first been exclusively honorary, there may have been a feeling that to earn it, a man must approach the distinction of those who would receive it *honoris causa*. When Oxford conferred an honorary degree on Frank himself in 1937, it was not the D.Litt., but a Doctorate of Civil Laws for success in administration.

In 1913 Frank must have been cast down for the moment at not trying for a D.Litt., but he had an effective way of dealing with a disappointment by first trying to understand its cause and then dismissing it from his mind. This particular one he forgot so completely that when he wrote later of this year at Oxford, it was in a tone of unqualified satisfaction: "It practically doubled the value of my Rhodes Scholarship and it gave my wife a chance to become acquainted with Oxford and the Rhodes Scholars which has been a great asset to me ever since."

His experience of freedom to write, thanks to adequate funds then rarely obtained by a young teacher, may have given him the idea he put to good effect in planning the Guggenheim Fellowships.

The Oxford University Press published a second book by Frank Aydelotte in 1913, *College English*, designed to help teachers organize the kind of course combining literature and composition which he had introduced at Indiana. By the time he returned to Bloomington in the autumn of that year, this course had been removed by the English department from the list of options for fulfilling the freshman requirement. A strong member of the department had been away on leave during Frank's first two years, and having missed the planning stage, he may not have been convinced that the change he found on his return was desirable. Or the department as a whole, once Frank's forceful presence was removed, may have felt that he had swept them off their feet, and recovered their orginal stance. But he could hardly fail to see also an element of personal antagonism. There was a curious "clerical error" in the catalogue for 1913–1914. All his courses which had been bracketed during his leave of absence, to show they were omitted, appeared again in brackets as though he had not come back. Did someone wish he would stay away?

That year he gave four courses in literature, but no composition then or later at Indiana. And henceforth all his work was limited to juniors, seniors, and graduates—a "kicking upstairs" for a man who had taught freshmen with special pleasure and apparent success. William Aydelotte remembers that his father once mentioned "difficulties" at Indiana, without details. He would probably have been equally reticent if he had written his autobiography. He rarely recalled mishaps unless they were funny. But to his biographer the incident is important because it seems to have taught him that he must find conciliatory methods to gain and keep support. He began to see the truth of the maxim he sometimes quoted at Swarthmore: "It is not enough to be right; you must also be persuasive." By the time he came to Swarthmore he was said to have a "genius" for working with people. But it was a genius developed by experience and by infinite pains.

In the long run his colleagues at Indiana might have been won over by the growing response of teachers of English elsewhere to his articles and his book *College English* but there was no "long run." The years 1913–1915 proved to be his last in Bloomington. He enjoyed those two years, first of all, for the wealth of testimony from outsiders that he was reforming freshman English in the right direction. His article, "English as Training in Thought," was praised by Norman Foerster of the University of Wisconsin for being "entirely sound as well as extremely refreshing." Some months later Foerster reported its influence on the Wisconsin department and mentioned a similar, perhaps independent, movement at Columbia:

> Your name and your convictions are by this time familiar to our entire teaching staff in freshman English, and our plans for next year have been made in such wise that we shall devote the whole second semester to exposition, using one or more complete books—Carlyle and Hazlitt or Newman and Thoreau—as a basis for class discussion and theme writing. You may also be interested to hear, if no one has told you, that two Columbia instructors, Steeves and another, are publishing a 500-page book of long and solid selections with the title "Representative Essays in Modern Thought," and that their prospectus lays great emphasis on "Cultivation of Ideas." And various things point to the fact that throughout the country substance is to be stressed, rather than "artistic" fluency or accuracy of detail.[7]

Harrison Ross Steeves of Columbia, whom Foerster mentions, had contributed an article to the *Educational Review* on "The Cultivation of Ideas in the College Writing Course," published two months after Frank's in the same periodical. Another bit of evidence that "substance is to be stressed" was a plea for deferring attention to expression until students had ideas to express, this in an essay by Thomas Lounsbury, emeritus professor at Yale, "Compulsory Composition in Colleges," which appeared in *Harper's* almost a year later than Frank's letter to the *Nation*. It is possible that Steeves and Lounsbury had not noticed the opinions of a young teacher in Indiana, that all three were reacting independently against the common weakness of writing without ideas. Whether or not Frank had influenced the other two, here, as often, he was a step ahead of his time, one of the first to speak to the condition of many teachers.

One teacher who appealed for help, Roosevelt P. Walker of the University of Arkansas, gave the gratifying news that he wrote on the advice of the famous William Lyon Phelps: "Professor Phelps of Yale has referred me to you as a person who can render valuable help in an attempt we are making at the University of Arkansas to make the work of our English department more effective."[8] Frank could refer Walker to his *College English* as showing at least his methods of teaching poetry and the greater Victorian essayists.

For readers interested in Frank Aydelotte's personal development, this book serves as his intellectual portrait at thirty-three: excited about ideas, acute in analysis, independent in his conclusions on the place of literature and science in education. This was a question, incidentally, which troubled Plato, is fiercely debated in the mid-twentieth century, and can never be settled by a computer. The portrait might be described as genetic, showing his growing response to some great Victorians who had a powerful influence on many thoughtful and "advanced" teachers of his generation.

Frank owed to Cardinal Newman his conception of "liberal knowledge" as the end of education. Knowledge was "liberal" when it extended beyond a single specialized discipline to a grasp of others sufficient for an understanding of their relations to one another. Liberal knowledge is knowledge in perspective, whose objects are grasped ideally in relation to the whole of things. This idea contributes to Frank's conception of literature and science in education. To be liberally educated in either literature or science, a man must know something of both and of the connections between them. Later Frank extended the idea to engineering. An engineer may be liberally educated if he learns to see his technical subjects in relation to broader ones such as sociology and economics and, through attention to such humane thinkers as Newman and Arnold, comes to see the bearing of his studies on the ends of education.

Arnold's notion of culture as the assimilation of the best thought of the present and past fortified Frank's devotion to masterpieces and his impatience with the spending of time on mediocrity. He concurred with Arnold again in valuing literature for its interpretation of life, great literature giving the interpretation of a great mind able "to see life steadily and see it whole." He accepted also Arnold's religious purpose: to make "reason and the will of God prevail," understanding God in Arnold's sense of a "power not ourselves making for righteousness." Arnold at that time was suspect in fundamentalist circles as a humanist. In adopting his position, Frank Aydelotte showed that he had become a liberal in religion.

College English, though primarily intended to help teachers stimulate students to think so that they will have something to say, includes also direct advice on writing and style which again throws light on the author. The first quality of acceptable writing he takes to be sincerity: a student must "express freely and spontaneously what he thinks himself." The value of what he writes to anyone else depends on two other qualities, truth and style. The need for truth is obvious. As for style, it is the reflection of the writer's personality:

> Style cannot be borrowed or learned or stolen; it can only be developed by thinking and expressing one's thoughts. . . . No man's style is better than his matter. To write clearly one must think clearly, to write nobly one must think nobly, to have a great style one must think great thoughts. . . . As a man thinketh in his heart, so is he. The problem of improving a man's writing is usually the problem of improving his character.

Writing in 1913, Frank Aydelotte spoke to the condition of a host of college students who were seeking what would later be called their own identity. For them he had a "moral authority" which was still recognized at Swarthmore in the thirties. As a student of those years remarked, "He was certain of his values, and those values and his very simple presentation of them were singularly appealing to young people."

In his last years at Indiana he was encouraged by the very cordial reception of *College English* to edit a companion volume of essays for students' use—essays by Newman, Arnold, Huxley, Ruskin, and Carlyle. Published in September, 1914, his *Materials for the Study of English Literature and Composition* differed from other current books of readings in the uniformly high quality of the selections, all of them first-rate, and in the substantial block of essays representing each writer, giving enough to show his development of thought. No "smatterings" here. Also the group of essays were related to each other "closely enough to form progressive steps in the solution of one great question: What is the place and value of the study of English literature in a liberal education?"[9]

This last question Frank undertook to answer directly in an essay, "English as Humane Letters," published in the *Atlantic Monthly*. Here he reaffirmed his belief that English literature should be a study of English thought, adding the controversial point that this could be comparable in intellectual seriousness to the study of Greek and Roman thought in the famous "Greats" course at Oxford. To this end he urged renouncing concern for "appreciation," philology, or literary history and focusing attention instead on the interpretation of life by writers of intellectual power.

So ends Frank's first crusade in education. Its spirit and course of events followed a pattern he would use again.

Football and English Literature

Though Frank was becoming more and more absorbed in intellectual interests, he still played outdoor games and liked to be remembered as a football player. He was pleased in 1914 to be awarded retroactively the "Varsity I." The notice came from the chairman of the Faculty Athletic Committee, C. S. Sembower, who was also chairman of the English department.

> The men of your day had no opportunity to earn the letter, but history and tradition have kept fresh the memory of your youthful prowess. Quite as much as the later sons of Alma Mater, you gave her notable service in the field. More than they, you have shown what an athlete can accomplish in the game of life. The University, therefore, awards you thus formally, through its Athletic Committee, your "Varsity."[10]

Was it after or before this award that Frank took a leading part in a controversy in the English office? A young assistant of the time recalls: "The quarterback of the football team had failed an English course and needed the credit to play. Pressure was strong for a make-up examination. . . . Professor Aydelotte was the only man on the English staff . . . who had played varsity football. And it was he who stood out vehemently" against coddling an athlete by breaking a university rule.

Launching the American Oxonian

A new outside interest of Frank's had to do with the Rhodes Scholarships: how to make them better known and more prized by able young Americans. Already he had expressed himself on the point in a letter to the *Nation*, deploring the "slight interest in the Rhodes Scholarships." The interest was slight, he argued, because teachers and students failed to recognize the values of an Oxford education and to see that these were precisely the values needing to be strengthened in American institutions: thoroughness of study, as opposed to breadth of information; opportunities for students to live together in residential colleges and to educate each other through the give and take of good talk; sports for everyone instead of concentrated coaching of the few on teams; the correlation of literature and composition (ideas which developed eventually into his book *The Oxford Stamp*).

Recently in Oxford he had gathered facts which justified his concern.

For example, in every year to date a number of scholarships had gone begging, sometimes for want of qualified candidates, sometimes for want of any candidates at all. In his own year of 1905, ten states had not made appointments. This could be explained partly by the Greek requirement: relatively few Americans knew Greek, and many would have been reluctant to do as Frank had done: to learn it from the beginning on the mere chance of being selected. A minor concession, granted in 1910, allowed a candidate to postpone the Greek examination until he had been elected provisionally on other grounds, but this caused little or no increase in numbers. Another obstacle to better competition, according to Frank and his Rhodes Scholar friends, was the make-up of the committee of selection. Most of the members knew little or nothing about Oxford and could not answer candidates' questions about it. Frank was in no position to affect the status of Greek or the composition of committees, but he could and did take steps at once to make the scholarships better known.

The men best equipped to rouse interest were old Rhodesians who knew Oxford at first hand. But how to get in touch with them? An *Alumni Magazine*, published in 1907 by the first returning Rhodes men, who organized an Alumni Association, had collapsed in 1912 for lack of funds. Frank felt so strongly the need of such a means of communication that he set to work, almost on his own, to start a new periodical, the *American Oxonian*. To finance it he asked help from groups of Rhodes Scholars in various centers, and he was delighted by their response. In New York "some could and did give as much as $25.00, a handsome sum in those days." He and his wife contributed the work of editing and mailing. Triumphantly they produced the first issue in April, 1914, announcing that the second would appear in October and that the *Oxonian* had the blessing of the Alumni Association as its official magazine.

The aim of the *Oxonian* was a broad one: "To interest members of Committees of Selection and prospective Rhodes Scholars as well as men who have been at Oxford or are there at present."[11] Rhodes Scholars were urged not only to subscribe themselves but "to see that their own college and high school libraries subscribe also." Some way of reaching high-school boys was "imperative." Believing that the best advertisements were free copies, Frank sent them broadcast to Oxonians; committees of selection; high-school, college, and public libraries; a thousand in all—this at a time when the whole number of American Rhodes

Scholars, returned and still at Oxford, was no more than three hundred. The response in subscriptions and enthusiasm was so gratifying that even before the second issue, one group of Rhodes men in Boston and another in New York had decided that the magazine should be published four times a year. Two men offered to underwrite any loss. The groups at both the Boston and the New York meetings include the same three names: W. W. Thayer, L. W. Cronkhite, and F. Aydelotte (respectively President of the Alumni Association, Business Manager, and Editor of the *Oxonian*).[12] The idea that they should all be present on the two occasions was probably Frank's. He liked to work in a team. Also he was adept at enlisting help on the broadest possible base: he saw to it that old Oxonians who were not Rhodes Scholars were represented in New York by A. G. Evans, who agreed to serve on Leonard Cronkhite's Board of Business Managers. For Frank himself, nothing was too much trouble in such a cause; he was quite ready to travel from Bloomington to New York and Boston at his own expense if he might hope to increase the prospect of his magazine's success.

As an editor he had a flair for seeing what would appeal to a variety of readers and for persuading writers to contribute. The leading article in the first number, "Oxford's Opinion of the Rhodes Scholars," would be scanned eagerly and anxiously by the men discussed, the more because many had known and liked its author, Sidney Ball, fellow and senior tutor of St. John's College and moving spirit of the social service center in Oxford, Barnett House.[13] In the process of describing Oxford reactions to the overseas invasion, Sidney Ball incidentally helped Americans at home to understand some Oxford scales of values. Americans could also recognize in him the traits of a popular don—friendliness and modesty, intellectual keenness and genial humor—far removed from the German "Herr Professor" sometimes imitated in the United States.

In the second issue, Frank came straight to the crucial point, "the lack of competition for the Rhodes Scholarships," with a lively symposium of opinions from nine members of committees of selection and thirteen former Rhodes Scholars; among the former, Dean W. H. Carpenter of Columbia, President A. Lawrence Lowell of Harvard, and President Benjamin Ide Wheeler of California. The Oxonians included Frank's old friend R. P. Brooks, professor of history at the University of Georgia; J. J. Tigert, professor of philosophy at the State University of Kentucky, later United States Commissioner of Education; Stanley Hornbeck, political scientist at Wisconsin, one day to become a power in the State

Department; John Crowe Ransom, teacher of English at Vanderbilt, eventually to make his name as critic and poet. The favorite explanation for the lack of competition was ignorance: ignorance of the requirements, including an exaggerated notion of the emphasis on Greek; ignorance of the subjects stressed in the Oxford program; ignorance of the tutorial method and of the character of life in the Colleges. Another explanation had to do with the relative impracticality of an Oxford education: nothing learned at Oxford would help an American professionally except in teaching or law; in other lines, three years at Oxford would be a serious interruption of a career. This to Frank was only another admission of ignorance of what made an Oxford education important.

The same *Oxonian* of October, 1914, carried the first news of Rhodes men at the beginning of the war, chiefly the difficulties of those on the Continent as they tried to return to England. Since nobody had needed passports before the war, a man might well find it hard to prove suddenly that he was an American. In Nuremberg one Rhodes Scholar from the Middle West with a German name, who spoke the language "unnecessarily well," was seized by the Army and "had to march all the way to Russia" before he could find an American consulate and prove his identity. Another problem was transportation: such trains as still ran were overcrowded; a trip that ordinarily took twenty-four hours might last "five days and four nights." This was the experience of W. C. Davison (future Dean of the Duke University Medical School), when he traveled from Switzerland by way of Paris to Oxford. In Paris he saw a new and startling sight: a German airplane. It was "the German bomb-thrower, and . . . a wonderful picture in spite of its deadly and treacherous purpose, for bomb throwing in an open sky is not quite fair. . . . It dropped a bomb a few blocks from me . . . aimed at the Gare St. Lazare. Fortunately it did no harm. . . . [The plane] then coolly sailed off, in spite of the firing of the sentries and troops and even the maxims mounted on the Eiffel Tower."[14]

In the *Oxonian's* second volume, for 1915, the editor established a pattern of combining articles of information about Oxford with news of returned Rhodes Scholars and their own accounts of their work. Among those engaged in college teaching he was glad to find witnesses to the influence of English methods on American education, and he planned to launch a series of reports beginning with the October issue. Before this was published, Frank had left Indiana and gone to teach English at Massachusetts Institute of Technology.

Proposed Move to Cambridge

President Maclaurin of M.I.T. had become interested in Frank through his article in the *Atlantic Monthly* on "English as Humane Letters." The point there, that English literature should be valued as a record "of the meaning of our civilization," appealed to the head of an institution for engineers where English might be the only liberalizing subject. What an advantage if it could be taught with the depth and sweep of a teacher convinced, as Frank was, that "the poets and novelists and essayists are men who are trying to unify and explain life to us, and to give us their own zest for it." Also, Maclaurin's own British background disposed him to confidence in a Rhodes Scholar's education. He asked Frank to come to Boston for an interview, and the two men took to each other. Both had grown up as second-generation pioneers, Maclaurin in New Zealand and Frank in Indiana. Both had profited greatly by study in England. Frank could not fail to be struck by Maclaurin's unusual intellectual range and power—distinction in law as well as mathematical physics—and by the honor of his election to a fellowship at St. John's, his Cambridge college. Add to this the phenomenal record of his six years at M.I.T. Having taken office at a time when the college was obliged to seek larger quarters, he had found an excellent new site of fifty acres in Cambridge on the Charles and raised money for the land and for impressive new buildings which would be ready for use within a year. Soon he hoped to devote himself to what he and Frank would agree was of far greater importance than buildings: organizing the kind of education he had touched on in his inaugural address: "science and culture must be combined"; "the root of culture . . . is the possession of an ideal broad enough to form the basis of a sane criticism of life."[15] Education for mere technical competence would no longer suffice, now that engineering was growing into a profession of public importance. Maclaurin was the man to kindle Frank's imagination and convince him that here was a place to work out something new and significant in the teaching of English. Shortly after the interview Frank accepted a full professorship at a salary of $2,700, a substantial increase as well as a promotion.

There was much to say in support of Frank's decision. A promotion was attractive to an ambitious young man whose only advance in rank had come at the end of his first semester when "Acting" disappeared before his title of "Associate Professor." The larger salary would be a godsend; he was still repaying debts for his education and sometimes had to borrow again to meet heavy family expenses. There were also incidental advantages: Frank could use the Harvard library for the research he had begun on Robert Greene, Marie would be nearer her relatives and old friends, and William, five in September, could go to better schools. It is true that on a crucial point, the status of the department, the prestige and scope of English at Indiana was far greater than in a stronghold of science and engineering where there were no English majors or graduate students. But the Indiana department's action on his freshman course left Frank dubious about his future and all the readier to respond to the attraction of a new problem in a new place, especially under a President who seemed his kind of man.

Frank's interest in the move to the East was strengthened by a timely letter from Riborg Mann, an old friend and able physicist. Mann mentioned that he was engaged in a study of engineering education sponsored jointly by the Carnegie Foundation for the Advancement of Teaching and the National Engineering Association, and he had the subject of English for engineers very much on his mind; indeed, he found it "one of the most difficult and distressing problems in engineering education."[16] For Frank, the chance to tackle a problem judged by an expert to be "difficult and distressing" made the opening at M.I.T. all the more attractive. His official connection with the new venture began before he left Indiana, when he agreed to serve on the Committee on Fundamental Subjects of the Society for the Promotion of Engineering Education to help make a study of aims and methods of teaching English.

Frank had a chance to discuss these and less serious topics with Riborg Mann during the summer of the move to Cambridge when the two men met in holiday mood on Bailey's Island off the coast of Maine. Marie's aunt, Mrs. Monroe, and several of Riborg's family had cottages there, where the Manns and the Aydelottes became lifelong friends.

Riborg, his brother, and three sisters, children of Danish parents, were all unusually vigorous and able. Riborg, though a physicist, was best known for later administrative work as Director of the American Council on Education (1922–1934). His brother Horace, an eminent architect, formed a partnership with his brother-in-law, Perry MacNeille. One sister practiced medicine. The two others had studied with Jung, Kristine becoming a psychoanalyst, and Clausine MacNeille, a semiprofessional consultant for parents of disturbed children. Riborg admired Frank and, after his move to M.I.T., recommended him for some interesting assignments, the first to write a history of the teaching of English for the Carnegie Foundation. This gave Frank a new perspective and a welcome fee of four hundred dollars. Riborg also put him in the way of two other part-time jobs, attractive for their novelty, one with the Bell Telephone Company in New York, the second under the War Department's Committee on Education and Special Services. Fortunately by the time he accepted these responsibilities he was well on his way to becoming established as a teacher of English to engineers.

CHAPTER SEVEN

TEACHING AT M.I.T. (Part One)

New Lines to Explore: 1915–1918

FRANK AYDELOTTE went to the Massachusetts Institute of Technology with two strong ambitions: to teach English as an important liberal element in engineering education; to do research on the Elizabethan dramatist Robert Greene. He would continue to edit the *American Oxonian*, expecting to enjoy the practice in writing and the chance to keep in touch with Oxford. Except for his work on the *Oxonian*, he had little experience in administration, though an observer might have detected signs that he would be good at it: he loved to plan a program or course of action in minute detail; he had a knack for bringing in other people to work with him as a team. During his first three years at M.I.T., he would be called on by the War Department to organize the War Issues Course on a national scale and would discover the exhilaration of achieving results quickly. He would begin to wonder whether he might be most useful not by teaching himself, but by helping many teachers do a better job.

Cambridge and M.I.T.

Before the Aydelottes left Bloomington they knew that Tech was soon to move from Boston to its new Cambridge site, and consequently they settled in Cambridge at once. They rented one floor of a three-family house at 36 Hawthorn Street, not far from the Harvard library where Frank in his spare time would work on Robert Greene, expecting to send William to the nearest public school.

William at the age of five was a "character," precocious in some ways, though childishness "would keep breaking through." His cousin Rachel, Gretchen Warren's daughter, describes him as a boy who didn't act like anyone else of his age. . . . He was at times a very solemn seeker for truth, and then suddenly impish. . . . He was also a planner to a distressing degree. Everything he did was planned—even some of the impishness—to see how people would react. Finally one day Mother said, "Bill, you really do too much planning. We find it rather hard to bear. Couldn't you cut down on it a little?" . . . Bill took this criticism very seriously and after a few moments' thought replied: "Cousin Gretchen I think you are right, so *today I will plan not to plan!*"[1]

A resolution his father might have made reluctantly.

Was it planned impishness or a reversion to infancy that was responsible for an incident described by a friend of Marie's to illustrate her "gift of understanding . . . and rare sense of humor"? She was giving a formal dinner and had set the table with great care before hurrying out to get some flowers. When she came back "she found William busily engaged . . . in the dining room." He had brought in the earth he used for mud pies, "then made a mud pie bird's nest at every place. 'Oh look, Mother,' he said, with the air of having placed works of art on the beautiful table cloth." As Marie told it: "I just sat down and laughed till I nearly cried. I said, 'Oh William dear, did you think this was *helping* Mother?"[2]

Teachers in the large classes of a public school might have found William disconcerting. His parents had not yet entered him when they heard of a little private school just started by a new Harvard professor of philosophy and his wife, William Ernest and Agnes Hocking. The Hockings had thought the public school unsatisfactory for their son and proposed to hold experimental groups in their own house, with Agnes in charge. Later this would become famous as "Shady Hill," beloved of students and parents alike; but when the Aydelottes chose it for William, they acted on faith in Agnes Hocking, whom they recognized to be a remarkable person. Frank liked to base important decisions on a person's quality, confident that someone really first-rate could not let him down. And in Agnes Hocking's case, he was surely right. Daughter of an Irish poet, John Boyle O'Reilly, and wife of a wise philosopher, she combined virtues of both. Agnes Hocking *was* poetry to the children and at the same time astute in selecting teachers with talents that supplemented her own, notably with inspired passion for accuracy to the last date and decimal point. Bill the imaginative imp, and Bill the solemn seeker for truth, could both be satisfied. There was a magic about Agnes Hocking, celebrated later by one of William's contemporaries, May Sarton, in a *New Yorker* sketch: "I Knew a Phoenix in My Youth . . . "[3]

The Aydelottes and the Hockings grew to be good friends, Marie closer than Frank because she taught an occasional class and served on the Board. Ernest Hocking recalled forty years later the warmth of her nature and her special interest, unusual at that time, in the Vedanta movement in India.[4]

The English Department

Frank's coming had a memorable impact on the English department at M.I.T., according to the recollections of a genial colleague, Henry Latimer Seaver, who describes English then as a "service department . . . its function mainly to scrub up illiterates": the many boys who had shone in high-school mathematics and physics but entered the institute with a condition in English. Such "scrubbing" took more than half the department's time, the rest going to a course "acquainting the undergraduates with the names in English Literature . . . which was to be entertaining for three-fourths of the class and a wee bit inspiring for the other fourth." Henry Pearson, recently made head of the department, had taught for many years as right-hand man to the colorful and dictatorial Arlo Bates, known to generations of undergraduates as "the last of the Concord group"—younger friend of Emerson and Thoreau— and to teachers of English as author of two useful little books: *Talks on Teaching Literature* and *Talks on Writing English*. Pearson and Seaver gave the newcomer a generous welcome; indeed, it was Seaver's impression that Frank had been " 'wished' on the department by the president" and that he was "too good a man for the job," "a star out of our sphere."[5]

Before Frank agreed to join the department, he had recognized that its program repeated the pattern he had found and challenged at Indiana: composition separated from literature; the required course in literature, a survey; in composition, a dull grind of writing for correctness. When told he could offer an elective for juniors, he seized the chance for the sort of reform he had tried out at Indiana, basing composition on his favorite nineteenth-century essayists, his aim (according to the course announcement) "to give training in the careful reading of thoughtful English prose, and practice in oral and written discussion of ideas suggested by the reading." His students' response impressed his colleagues so favorably that they adopted a similar plan for the freshman requirement the next year, putting Frank in charge. Again, he carried the department with him in a completely new catalogue statement of purpose: "to enlarge the student's acquaintance with general ideas and to broaden his interests by showing how scientific conceptions are related to other fields of thought." The old survey of literary history was replaced by the reading of a few important authors, each considered "at sufficient length so that the students may get a fairly comprehensive view of his interpretation of life."

These new aims were pure Aydelotte, and he seems to have carried the department with him. But he did not do so at all points. In his zeal for full attention to a great work, he proposed that sophomores should concentrate on Wordsworth's *Prelude* for an entire term. This struck the department as preposterous, and they "jeered him down."[6]

English and Engineering

Frank's main contribution to engineering education was a course supported by his book of readings: *English and Engineering*. He declined to admit any such subject as "engineering English." At bottom English study should be the same for all: a training in thought and expression stimulated by reading what first-rate minds have written about important human problems. To be sure, the first step is to interest the student in ideas related to his own education. Fortunately in those years engineering was coming to be seen in a new light, "not as a trade but as one of the liberal professions," and Frank saw it as leading out into "many of the gravest problems of our civilization, human problems as well as mechanical, problems in finance, in government, in education, and in social life." His readings dealt with "The Engineering Profession," "Aims of Engineering Education," "Pure Science and Applied," "Science and Literature," "Literature and Life"—obvious topics, perhaps, but never before brought together. The writers were all thinkers of note—famous engineers such as George S. Morison and A. C. Christie; the scientists Huxley and Tyndall; the philosopher John Stuart Mill; and such reflective men of letters as Arnold and Emerson, Carlyle and Ruskin, Stevenson, Macaulay, and Wordsworth.

For the first time Frank here describes his ideal teacher. He is one who will think with the class, who will "drop the role of master and assume that of the seeker after truth," who will play the Socratic part of presiding "over the birth of ideas," exposing false opinions, and "appealing not to authority . . . but to reason."

Published in January, 1917, *English and Engineering*[7] was in use the following September in fourteen institutions and two years later acquired an international reputation, imported by McGill to Canada, by the Chinese Government's Institute of Technology, and by Waseda University to Japan. The first of its kind, the book owed its popularity partly to virtual monopoly of the field, partly, no doubt, to the prestige of M.I.T., but also in great measure to its own vitality, communicating enthusiasm for a rising profession, introducing its readers to a wealth of new ideas. It held its place on the publisher's list for twenty-two years.

Inventive Teacher

Frank's growing reputation as a teacher brought him many requests for help. When the Bell Telephone Company of New York decided on the novel experiment of offering their employees a course in English for their personal development, they considered Frank the best man to undertake it, and he accepted their invitation. He prepared with his usual care, getting permission to spend some time in the Telephone Company's Boston headquarters, studying procedures and absorbing atmosphere. For reading, he assigned his old favorites, Arnold and Newman, again. He gave one lecture a week to the whole group of two hundred, dividing it into small units to discuss weekly papers with thirty-five tutors chosen from well-educated members of the staff. It was agreed that students should attend lectures on company time, use half an hour of their lunch period once a week for discussion, and write their papers outside.

The response was all he could wish. The course had succeeded in interesting the students in "real literature." One of them recalls that he was "impressed and not a little bit awed by Frank Aydelotte," having never before met anyone who moved with freedom on this level of education. But with all his learning, he "possessed a warmth and understanding which communicated itself quickly to the students." After the last lecture Frank wrote enthusiastically to Riborg Mann:

> We finished in New York yesterday with a grand love feast. I don't know when I have had more fun out of giving a course of lectures. The only difficulty was the beastly trip down and back each week. I shouldn't mind if it were twice as long and I could get a little sleep.[8]

The "love feast" was probably the occasion when the President of the Company, T. N. Vail, "personally presented each of the students with a diploma certifying to his satisfactory completion of the studies."[9] An official who wrote a memorandum on the course for the company reported that it taught not merely English but a philosophy of work as in itself potentially a source of education and "one of the durable satisfactions of life."[10] The memorandum bears witness to Frank's gift for doing far more than a job required, for bringing to vigorous life what for many would have been a routine assignment.

War Issues Course

Another opportunity to which Frank gave educational importance was to organize and direct the War Issues Course for the Students' Army Training Corps. He owed this to Riborg Mann, then adviser to the War Department's Committee on Education and Special Training, who asked him to move to an office in Washington with the rank of Major.[11] On June 1, 1918, Frank set to work with two able assistants, Leland Olds and E. D. McDonald, preparing a plan for use in the fall in the S.A.T.C.'s first term.

The S.A.T.C., one of the earliest government attempts to combine college education with military training, had hardly begun work before the Armistice brought it to a premature end. Even in so short a time the War Issues Course had taken effect through the numbers involved: it had introduced attractive content and methods of teaching to 125,000 students and 25,000 instructors in 540 colleges and universities.[12] Such widespread attention, when most of it was favorable, was likely to influence postwar curricula. This was, indeed, the expectation of one Army officer, Colonel John H. Wigmore, when he wrote to congratulate Frank: "Certainly that course is the one brightest spot in the history of the S.A.T.C., and will remain the one permanent contribution. Let us hope that the course has put new life into the study of history."[13] What sort of enterprise was this?

The stated aim was to build soldiers' morale by helping them learn "what the war was about" and why the United States had joined the Allies. Such a course might have been little more than propaganda, but Frank saw it as an element in a liberal education—the thoughtful study of the history and culture of countries involved in the conflict. He had reason to hope that young soldiers would respond, having tried out a lecture along this line on a soldier audience taking vocational training at

Wentworth Institute in Boston. He had talked about "our relations with England, and Anglo-Saxon ideals of democracy," and "was perfectly amazed at the way they took it. . . . They made one of the finest audiences" he had known. And as to the wider implications: "We can never have open diplomacy unless we train the whole nation to some knowledge of the international situation, and I think we might as well begin with the army in order to prepare them to get the most out of their experience abroad."[14]

In content the course was a modest and modern application of the theory that lay behind the "Greats" course at Oxford. Where a student in Greats specializes in Greek history, philosophy, and literature in order to understand Greek civilization (and through this, his own), in the War Issues Course he would explore these fields in the life and thought of the present day. To carry out this aim, the colleges were asked to combine "the points of view of history, government, economics, philosophy, and modern literature," which meant bringing in instructors from these departments to teach together. Such teamwork in a college faculty was virtually unheard of, but proved to be stimulating for both teachers and students. As Frank's friend Ernest Hocking wrote him, this "co-operation across departmental boundaries" was likely to form a precedent for "further enterprises of the same kind." Hocking was one of twelve directors who had charge of the twelve geographical districts in which the 540 participating institutions were grouped. Each director traveled a circuit, ready to give help when asked, reporting impressions to Frank in Washington. For his directors he chose men of academic distinction whose visits to colleges would not only assist local instructors but give the course prestige: men such as Hocking himself and two others in philosophy, James H. Tufts and George Herbert Mead from the University of Chicago, W. E. Lingelbach in history from the University of Pennsylvania, John S. P. Tatlock in English literature from Stanford.[15]

The recommended method of teaching must have been warmly approved by followers of John Dewey. As a first step, students formulated questions for which they would hope to find answers. Two hours a week were given to discussion, with only one lecture. Instructors were urged to rely on facts rather than emotional appeal, to emphasize "the positive side, the ideals of democracy and freedom," not "hatred of the German," not tales of atrocities. Leaving the students free to draw their own conclusions was "the most effective of all methods for producing conviction."[16]

When the course opened on the first of October, its success was threatened by the influenza epidemic already gathering strength, and again in November after the Armistice by a slackening of purpose, the greater since its end was set officially for late December. But in spite of illness, change of pace, and premature close, the course won staunch friends. Between two and three hundred institutions decided to carry it through the rest of the year on their own. It was praised by Dean Woodbridge of the Columbia Graduate School as constituting "the elements of a liberal education for the youth of today." Woodbridge was shortly to be influential in starting what Frank described as the "outstanding result" of the War Issues Course, the famous Contemporary Civilization course at Columbia.[17]

The Oxonian

In Frank's move from Bloomington to Cambridge, he took with him a small sheaf of papers constituting the "editorial files" of the *American Oxonian* which he had recently started almost singlehanded and continued to edit throughout his years at Tech. A series of articles showing Oxford influences on American college education began in the issue of January, 1916, with Robert Scoon's account of the preceptorial system at Princeton. It was followed in April by Leigh Alexander's "Pass and Honors Courses at Oberlin College" and "Liberalizing the Curriculum" by two professors of English at the University of Washington, A. C. Benham and J. M. Johanson. The latter article noted an Oxford influence on requirements for graduation: where they had once been purely quantitative—adding up hours and credits—they now included emphasis on superior quality. In July "The System of Honors at Yale" was discussed by C. A. A. Bennett, an old Oxonian but not a Rhodes Scholar, and in October, "The Honors Degree at Columbia," by two members of the faculty without Oxford connections, Dean Keppel and J. J. Coss.[18] All these contributors urged greater opportunities for the abler students and recognition of their success by degrees with honors.

Before Frank had received a commission and an office in Washington, he had tried to enlist in the R.O.T.C., but had been turned down. He was an all-out supporter of the allied cause. His impressions of Germany had left him convinced that not the Germans but the British were our natural and best allies. He wrote Theodore Roosevelt to ask whether he might need Rhodes men as officers and interpreters, "if as we all hope you are put in charge of a force to carry our flag to France." He wrote also to Herbert Hoover, expressing the wish that "the 400 ex-Rhodes Scholars now living in the United States" could help in the work "of organizing our national food supply."[19] No answer from Roosevelt, but Hoover replied with appreciation of the offer; his plan for using volunteers, worked out with Frank's assistance, was spread on the front page of the *Oxonian* for July.

The Oxford Stamp

In that same spring of 1917 Frank's lively mind was particularly concerned with Oxford because he was revising a collection of his essays which he described as the "fruits of a Rhodes Scholarship." A year earlier he had offered his first version of the book to the Oxford University Press with an unfortunate title, *The First Distemper of Learning*. This he had borrowed from Francis Bacon, who invented the term for a phase of learning which paid more attention to words than to ideas. As such misplaced emphasis was precisely what Frank took to be wrong with much American teaching of composition, he liked the title, forgetting for the moment that it would mean nothing to the general reader. The Press had promptly returned the manuscript, pointing out that it would appeal to a very limited market. Fortunately Frank could learn. He revised not only the title but much of the book as well and sent back what he now called *The Oxford Stamp* with a persuasive covering letter. He met the criticism of "limited appeal" by urging that this was the first book showing the "kind of value Oxford training may have for a man who is going into education in this country," adding that there was sure to be a new interest in the Rhodes Scholarships, since Oxford was instituting the degree of Doctor of Philosophy, hitherto obtainable only in Germany. "I think we are now ripe in this country for the doing away with many of our German University methods and for the substitution of humaner English ones."[20] The Oxford University Press accepted the new version and brought it out late in 1917.

The years since the end of Frank's terms as a Rhodes Scholar had allowed him to digest and appraise his experiences and to test much that he had learned there in his own teaching. Appropriately *The Oxford Stamp* bears the subtitle: *Articles from the Educational Creed of an American Oxonian*. A modest volume of 225 small pages, it attracted gratifying attention. Most Americans knew little about Oxford—indeed, about England as a whole—having learned in school scarcely anything beyond the Revolu-

tionary grievances against George III. But our recent entry into the war
had wiped out lingering resentments and quickened interest in our ally.
One reviewer praised the book for its "earnest desire to draw America
closer in comprehension and sympathy to England, from whom she has
so much to learn, but of whom she is so ignorant." He went on to note
how "novel" were the ideals of education set forth.[21] Since the book is
indispensable to an understanding of Frank's crusades in education, it will
be well to look at it a little more closely.

The first three essays in *The Oxford Stamp* form a confession of faith
in values distinctive of Oxford. The title essay pictures the social charm
and intellectual ferment of life in an Oxford college and offers three
Articles of the promised "Creed": (1) belief that such a residential
college gives invaluable education through good conversation; (2) belief
in athletics for all as indispensable training in sportsmanship; (3) belief in
a system of teaching which stresses thoroughness, independence, and the
individual student's responsibility for educating himself. The second essay,
"Spectators and Sport," reaffirms the belief in athletics for all by pointing
to the resulting benefit to those who will be future spectators: having
learned sportsmanship through playing themselves, they will recognize
and demand it when they watch competing teams. The result: elimination
of the chief source of corruption in American sports—spectators intent
on victory at any price.

"The Religion of Punch" gives us another all-important article of
belief: in intellectual honesty and thoroughness as good in themselves
and necessary to save American education from corruption by business
methods. The point of departure is a middle-western educator's criticism
of a Rhodes Scholar applicant for a position: "*Oxford has tamed him . . . he
has lost his punch!*" The remark provokes Frank to such an unusual
outburst of irritation as to suggest it has been said of himself. He
becomes caustic at the expense of American devotion to "punch," which
is "the ability to achieve the end without the means," "educational
institutions without educated men," "*bluff* raised to a higher power."
Conceding that it may have a place in business, he warns against its
intrusion into education, especially at a time when values are already
confused. The classics have lost prestige; no one is certain what should
replace them; consequently "practical methods, . . . efficiency, scientific
management," are taking over. "Flashiness, show, advertising" in the
colleges mean "charlatanism in the intellectual world."

Americans who already recognize and attack these evils, he thinks, should welcome the support of returned Rhodes Scholars whom Oxford has freed from the cult of "punch." Under Oxonian demands, they could hardly help seeing the "necessity for thoroughness in intellectual work, the difference between knowledge and smatterings." The effect is "to sober them," to make them unpretentious, ready to work "without organization or machinery, but quietly by individual thought and effort . . . against the operation in our intellectual life of the American ideal of punch."

In defense of the middle-western educator, it might be said that his comment does note a fact which Frank fails to acknowledge fully. If "punch" means, as surely it often does, nothing more sinister than drive, energy, self-confidence—American pioneer virtues—admittedly these tend to become less obvious under Oxford influence. To be aggressively self-confident in that climate of understatement is bad manners. And going deeper, when an American who has been easily first at home finds himself struggling to meet new standards, however well he may succeed eventually, his self-confidence when it returns will certainly carry with it a more chastened sophistication. That such loss of aggressiveness brings a gain in maturity the middle-western educator might on further thought agree.

The remaining seven essays are chiefly concerned with the teaching of English, developing convictions on which we have already touched.

Frank had the pleasure of finding that his book appealed not only to men who wanted to learn about Oxford but to those who knew it well. The Rhodes Scholar reviewer in the *American Oxonian*,[22] for example, while he might naturally be polite to the editor, surely exceeded the call of duty when he rated the book as "one of the most satisfying evidences yet available of the solid utility of the training which Oxford can give an American graduate." The writer, Tucker Brooke, professor of English at Yale, was a man Frank greatly admired, whose favorable opinion he would treasure. But the most welcome of all comments came in a personal letter from an English Oxonian whom Frank had not yet met, John St. Loe Strachey, editor of the *Spectator:*

> May I venture to congratulate you and all Oxford men, myself among them, on your perfectly admirable book "The Oxford Stamp." I have a boy of sixteen and a half who will be going to Oxford in another two years, unless he has to enter the sterner college of War, and I mean to give him your book at once, in order that he may understand what Oxford is and what it does for men's minds. . . .

But though I think all this sympathetic criticism and defence of Oxford so sound and so good, what I perhaps like about it best of all is that you write so thoroughly in the spirit of "a good American," of the man, I mean, who wants to make his own country the best in the world, and not of one who is pining for something different. Honestly, I am one of the people who think that we Englishmen have got, in many senses, a great fortune before us. But for all that, the biggest future is of course yours. Our duty is to keep the sacred home fire burning, as it were, like a nation of Vestal Virgins. If it were only for ourselves, and for these little islands in the Atlantic, it might not be worth while. But if it is for the whole English-speaking community, then it is worth while. I see that if you have your way, as may Providence decree that you shall have it, you will hearten us in our task.[23]

Strachey was enthusiastic also about Frank's essays on English as humane letters: "every sentence and almost every word struck sparks out of me as I read." He agreed heartily that there is "only one way by which people could learn to write, and that way by making them think," having reached this conclusion by observing that when a man has thought about something until he has something to say, he writes well, even with little or no training. Witness Cobden, a "young and very badly educated commercial traveller," but on the subject of "our foreign policy as it affected Russia," as eloquent as Burke.

How heartening such a letter to a little-known crusader! For a man like Strachey to read his book so carefully was in itself a compliment. But to find that Strachey agreed with his suggestions gave Frank a priceless reassurance that he was on the right track. When he answered, he wrote what was true then and always, "The ideas in that book underlie almost everything I am doing."

CHAPTER EIGHT

TEACHING AT M.I.T. (Part Two)

Bent toward Administration: 1918–1921

American Secretary for the Rhodes Trustees

IN directing the War Issues Course, Frank Aydelotte had his first experience of important administrative work and enjoyed it so much that when he was asked to become the first American Secretary for the Rhodes Trustees, he did not hesitate to accept, on condition that he should not give up teaching. He expected to be a full-time teacher and part-time secretary, carrying both in his stride. President Maclaurin was glad to approve the arrangement and to give the Rhodes Trust an office at M.I.T.

If there was to be an American Secretary, Frank seemed the inevitably right choice. As Secretary of the Alumni Association and editor of the *American Oxonian*, he was known at least by name to every American Rhodes Scholar. As editor he had developed a magazine of unusual range: it not only kept old Oxonians in touch with each other and with Oxford but also supplied useful information to possible candidates for Rhodes Scholarships and fulfilled the function of a journal of higher education, giving lively accounts of important developments in colleges and universities at home and in Britain. His editorial policy strongly supported the unity of the English-speaking world which Rhodes had labored to promote. Moreover, in his teaching he was adapting what he had learned at Oxford to create new opportunities for American college students. No one was better prepared to make the position of Secretary respected.

His work on the *Oxonian* had the further advantage of keeping him in touch with Rhodes officials in England. The summer before his appointment he had been asked by the Organizing Secretary, George

Parkin, to travel with him in this country on Rhodes Scholarship business. The two men had been friends since Frank's years at Brasenose. Now, as they toured the states by train, Parkin used to look out of the window and think aloud. One of his questions addressed to the passing scene Frank liked to quote: "Is the civilization of the United States going to be as broad as the prairies, or as uninteresting?" Parkin prepared for any important move by taking endless trouble to call on people who might be interested and ask their advice. This was so much Frank's own way later as to suggest that he learned it from Parkin.

Frank accepted his new position at a time when the future of the Rhodes Scholarships looked bright, partly as a result of the war, which had quickened interest in England, partly because the recently established Doctorate of Philosophy, so essential to academic status in America, would appeal to men who must consider professional as well as personal advantage. A marked increase in the number of candidates seemed virtually certain. And the proposal that committees of selection should be made up of former Rhodes Scholars seemed likely to be approved and to result in eliminating unsuitable candidates and increasing the proportion who would be outstanding.

With much to look forward to, the new Secretary at the moment had little to do, since competitions had been suspended for the duration of the war. He had discussed plans with Parkin, who sent him a memorandum, "Outline of Work for Aydelotte," listing ten responsibilities, simpler and subtler combined:

> Distributing the papers for the Examination in October, after finding out what States have candidates.
> Forming lists of all qualified candidates during the years when no elections are held [one in every three].
> Arranging for local secretaries in each state to be centres of information.
> Plan for American Circulars and publication of Memoranda for first selection after the war.
> Arranging Committees of Selection for places where it is decided to apply the new plans.
> Considering methods of election, including further examination outside Responsions.
> Formation of local organizations of ex-Rhodes Scholars to look after the interests of the scholarships.
> Lists of Canadians in the hope of getting co-operative work.
> Forwarding co-operation between American and British Universities in regard to graduate work and degrees.

Promoting a determination in the United States that the country shall
be well and worthily represented at Oxford.

Parkin did not think of two incidental activities which eventually fell
to the Secretary's lot. One, to run what was almost an employment
office for former Rhodes Scholars, proved to be particularly effective
because unofficial and personal. When Frank recommended a man, he
was doing a favor to the employer. And when the Rhodes men reached
the age and experience to be considered for college presidencies, Frank
acquired a reputation as Kingmaker.

Host to the British Universities Mission

A second future side line—arranging itineraries for visiting Englishmen—he tried out before the war ended by helping entertain the British
Universities Mission. They came in the autumn of 1918, invited to this
country by the Council of National Defense for a two months' tour
with a view to finding "the best means of procuring closer co-operation
between British and American educational institutions." Frank served on
the committee which planned their visit and went with them on their
travels. It was an enlightening experience to know this group and to see
American institutions through their sharply observant eyes. There were
seven in the mission, chosen to represent a variety of institutions, academic ranks, and subjects of special interest. The chairman, A. E. Shipley,
was Vice-Chancellor of Cambridge and a zoologist; from Oxford, the
senior tutor at Queen's, the Rev. E. M. Walker; John Joly, professor of
geology and mineralogy, Trinity College, Dublin; Miss Caroline Spurgeon, professor of English literature, Bedford College, University of
London; and from the provincial universities, Sir Henry Miers, Vice-
Chancellor of Manchester and professor of crystallography; Miss Rose
Sidgwick, lecturer on modern history, Birmingham; Sir Henry Jones,
professor of moral philosophy, Glasgow. In the weeks between October
18 and December 7 they visited colleges and universities in twenty-five
cities, including Montreal and Toronto, going west as far as Minneapolis
and Des Moines, south to New Orleans, returning to New York by way
of Tuskegee, Chapel Hill, and Charlottesville. They celebrated the Armistice with their Allies and, sad to say, endured the influenza epidemic
which took the life of one member, Rose Sidgwick.

During the long hours on the train Frank welcomed the chance to
talk with E. M. Walker of Oxford about the requirement that candidates

for Rhodes Scholarships must take Responsions, the qualifying examination in mathematics, Latin, and Greek. Frank "put to him very strongly the point that (this requirement) . . . had the effect practically speaking of confining the Rhodes Scholarships to classical students."[1]

Before the trip ended, Frank, in his role of editor, had collected reports from four of the mission and seventeen of their hosts to use in the January *Oxonian*, devoted to "Results of the British Universities Mission." His editorial sums up points of substantial agreement as to what had been gained and what should be done next. The gains: "good feeling between American and British institutions"; understanding by the British of "educational facilities in the United States"; new interest in sending American students to England, and also for some subjects to France and Italy, this on Shipley's recommendation; a new sense of the advantage to Americans of exchanging the German influence toward "narrow specialization" for English "breadth and humanity," commonly achieved without sacrificing thoroughness. The next steps most often stressed were to raise stipends for students who would cross the ocean in both directions and to simplify English regulations—not in any way to lower standards, but to make matriculation less cumbersome. Frank was happy about the whole enterprise; he thought it bound to add to the importance of the Rhodes Scholarships and to strengthen Anglo-American friendship.[2]

In an outburst of eagerness to extend the circle, he wrote his Canadian friend and Rhodes Scholar classmate Frank Parker Day:

> I have just been traveling with the Mission from the British Universities which visited the States in the fall, and my head is full of plans working to closer academic relations between the United States and the British Empire. I do not know how you feel about it, but it seems to me that this is the moment to do everything possible to bind the English speaking nations together.[3]

Asking Advice

To another old friend, Leonard Cronkhite, he wrote describing his new position and asking advice on proposals that were still in the air:

> I want to receive constantly the benefit of your advice. . . . My feeling is not that the Rhodes Trust has put me personally in charge of competitions, but that they are using me as a means of collecting the best efforts and thought of all the ex-Rhodes Scholars. I am very anxious to know what

you will think of the methods I am proposing for capitalizing our joint intelligence and good will toward the scheme.

    1. to add one Rhodes Scholar at least to every Committee of Selection in the United States in order that the Oxford point of view may enter into every selection.

    2. to substitute in a number of states where the local committees have not worked well and where there are Rhodes Scholars whose position and judgment makes them suitable, Committees entirely composed of Rhodes Scholars in the place of the present Committees composed of college presidents.

    3. to substitute in a few districts like New England, New York and New Jersey, and Indiana and Illinois, Regional Committees which shall make the selections for two or three states, traveling about from one state to the other.[4]

In this letter Frank pursues the policy he may have learned from Parkin, but made unalterably his own. The first step—asking for advice—disarmed opposition, aroused interest, and might well elicit something new. A firm belief in this last point saved him from the taint of hypocrisy: he did not pretend to be interested in other people's opinions as a way of winning them with flattery. He honestly hoped for an inspired suggestion to adopt with full credit to the donor. But he did have a second motive: by arousing interest in a project before it was fully formed, he hoped to involve the person who gave advice, make him feel responsible, and win his support. It was part of his policy also to offer his adviser a list of possibilities as a focus for discussion. If the list included a proposal likely to be controversial, he would place it last, leading off with a point that could hardly be questioned. So, here, he begins with the idea of adding a single Rhodes Scholar to a selection committee, going on to a second possibility also easy to accept: to compose these committees in some states entirely of Rhodes Scholars. This could not alarm anyone except perhaps a displaced college President. But the third point, to substitute regional for state committees, even when limited to a few districts, might prove to be dynamite, a threat to cherished "states rights." That Frank already had an even more serious threat in mind seems likely: to change the area of selection from state to region. Soon he began to ask advice directly on this point and continued to discuss it for a decade until it finally gained the support of the majority of Rhodes Scholars and was put into effect by Act of Parliament. The mention of a regional committee to Leonard Cronkhite served as an early feeler from a man whose patience in a good cause could be formidable.

New Plan of Selection

Early in 1919 the new Secretary's enforced leisure was broken by the Rhodes Trustees' announcement of resumed elections the following October—not only resumed, but in twice the usual number, adding the group for whom there had been no competition in 1918 to the one now due. They reported also the welcome news that they would no longer require the "qualifying examination" in mathematics, Latin, and Greek. In the April *Oxonian* the editor explained that while the Trustees' action had no bearing on University requirements, there was a strong movement among the dons also to waive this examination for graduates of foreign universities who were admitted to Oxford with advanced standing as candidates for research degrees. A triumphant "Postscript" to the July issue, probably written when the *Oxonian* had already gone to press, reports a statute on this point passed by Convocation on June 17, proposed by E. M. Walker, who explained that "a graduate of an approved American university is now qualified for Senior status and he is excused Greek." Frank could rejoice that his talks with Dr. Walker had helped remove an obstacle to the keenest competition.

The "new plan," as Frank referred to it in this Postscript, was substantially what the three Secretaries recommended; to form committees of selection of "ex-Rhodes Scholars acting under the chairmanship of some man of position in the state"; where the number of Rhodes Scholars was too small in a state, it would be served by "peripatetic committees from neighboring states." Frank reported that Wylie had come over at the end of May to help put the new plan in operation and that one or both of them had "visited most of the Eastern, Middle Western and Southern States," preparing for the competitions. Everywhere they had heard "the warmest approval of the new plan."

While the two were traveling together, Wylie became convinced that even Frank's vitality could not stand the strain of teaching at Tech in addition to the details inevitable in setting up the plan, and he recommended that the Trustees should "claim the whole of Aydelotte's time for the coming year" and pay his full salary: "he is singularly well qualified, as well by his personal qualities as by the position he has made for himself in the academic world of America, to make [his] contribution a valuable one" not only to the election of future Rhodes Scholars but to the unity of the "Rhodes Scholar body" through bringing them together to do important work.[5] The Trustees wisely followed Wylie's recommendation, and President Maclaurin handsomely granted Frank leave of absence for 1919–1920.

The new plan had the great advantage of simplicity for the candidate. As Frank described procedure, "He simply fills out an application blank giving certain information about himself . . . and the names of men to whom he wishes to refer. His record is then investigated by the committee, the more promising candidates are summoned for a personal interview, and the selection is made." No more collecting a scrapbook of thirty-three testimonials such as Frank himself had prepared for the Indiana committee.

Visit to Oxford

In the spring after the plan was first tried out, Frank went to England to report progress to the Trustees, appearing in Oxford in his new role of American Secretary. Rhodes Scholars in residence who caught a glimpse of him, perhaps on his bicycle pedaling down the High, liked what they saw: a vigorous man, looking younger than his age of forty, and with an air of enjoying himself. Finding that one of the Scholars, Brand Blanshard of Michigan and Merton, was about to take a B.Sc., but had no gown to wear, Frank remembered that his own handsome black silk gown served for the B.Sc. as well as the B.Litt. and lent it to the new graduate, the first of many kindnesses to the Blanshards.

Frank made good use of his time in Oxford for Rhodes Trust business and his own research. He wrote his friend Warner Fite (new professor of philosophy at Princeton) what he had accomplished on both counts. Concerned as he was to send first-rate men to Oxford, he had been troubled by the tendency of some committees to overestimate the all-round man. Too many who were all-round mediocre had succeeded in winning appointments. Distinction in at least one line he thought absolutely essential. Now the Rhodes Trust had passed an interpretation which should clear the air: "We are saying that while the first-class all-round man is what we want, yet in the absence of such an ideal combination, Committees should choose a man who has some claim either to intellectual or personal distinction over an all-round man of a lower grade of excellence."[6] This was a position from which Frank never wavered. A student or a teacher, a program or an institution, must at some point achieve excellence—as he put it later—"to redeem democracy from mediocrity."

Frank was happy to give Warner Fite the further news that he had made progress in his research on Robert Greene and was "at least in sight of the finish." The Oxford University Press had agreed to publish this book and another as soon as it was completed. Both were fated to be crowded out by other interests. At the moment Frank had "also taken a firm resolve to live a somewhat easier life in the future."

The resolve would commend itself to anyone who had tried to keep track of his recent activities. While it was true in the war years that many men attempted more than was comfortable, particularly men who had been refused for military service, Frank had seemed positively to glory in overwork. He was teaching full time at M.I.T. and editing the *American Oxonian* in the fall of 1917 when he began his weekly trips to New York to give the course for the telephone company, traveled with Parkin, and put *The Oxford Stamp* through the press. In the second semester, still with his extra teaching, he began to plan the War Issues Course which he took on full time in June. By October he was off with the British Universities Mission, having helped make their arrangements in the intervals of correspondence for the course. The English department at M.I.T. showed a marvelous tolerance for absence in the national emergency.

If Frank could do so much and do it well, it was because he had a gift, rare even among good managers, for putting his mind completely on one thing at a time. He gave himself with gusto to the absorbing present, excluding alien worries until their time came in turn.

Personal Life

Meanwhile he had personal problems, some uncomfortable, others pleasantly exciting, all requiring time to consider. Marie had a serious operation in April, 1918. Frank decided he should stay with her in the operating room and surprisingly was allowed to do so. Riborg Mann wrote his congratulations on her recovery and also a word of friendly scolding, "You foolish boy, to attend operations!"[7] The operation brought heavy expenses and a renewed loan from the Sullivan Bank. He was never completely free from debt until after he went to Swarthmore. However, Frank's extra salary of $6,000 a year from the Rhodes Trust brought relief from financial pressure, and early in 1919 he and Marie ventured to buy a house. "We passed papers last week," he wrote a friend, "and are now the trembling owners of the property," 14 Kirkland Place.[8]

The house had a delightful simplicity and excellent location in the heart of old Cambridge, east of Harvard Square, standing at the end of a street with no through traffic to make hazards for William. Another asset for William: his back yard nearly joined that of his great friend Peter Sprague, son of W. M. W. Sprague, professor of finance in the Harvard School of Business. To buy a house meant that the Aydelottes had a feeling of permanence in Frank's two positions. They did not expect to move for a long time.

Always a casually hospitable family, now with their own house they began a program of constant entertaining, as pleasant as it seemed effortless. When we Blanshards arrived in Cambridge for Brand's year of graduate work at Harvard, we were welcomed at a dinner at 14 Kirkland Place. There were only two other guests, Leonard Cronkhite and his wife. Frank and Marie liked best a table of six and hoped never to go above eight, the maximum for general conversation. Not content merely to do their duty by a returned Rhodes Scholar, they invited us again in the spring after their position at Swarthmore had been announced. We went for lunch and met William, a slender, serious boy of eleven (his impishness outgrown). Marie's pretty young cousin, Gretchen Warren's daughter Marjorie, a student at Radcliffe, was staying with the Aydelottes while her mother went abroad. Through the years there was likely to be an extra member of the household, one of Frank's or Marie's nieces or nephews, or a favorite friend of William's. His parents did all they could to save him from the loneliness of an only child. Once in Swarthmore, when my husband was at work abroad, I spent several months in one of their hospitable guest rooms.

They were no sooner settled in Kirkland Place than Frank began to have offers, some too attractive to be dismissed without careful thought. He was at a good age to take an important position, and his name had become well known, partly through his essays and articles, partly through his nationwide correspondence for the War Issues Course, partly through his new position with the Rhodes Trust. The University of Iowa wanted him as professor of English. Nicholas Murray Butler invited him to Columbia to organize a course growing out of War Issues which would be given throughout the country "under the general administrative oversight of Extension Teaching."[9] Frank turned down both, but not until after he had visited Iowa and carried on considerable correspondence. At Columbia he disliked the idea of being an "extension professor," which hardly conformed to his vision of what he wanted most to do. He wrote to John Coss of Columbia:

> I believe my greatest usefulness is in the line which I have already marked out for myself, making the teaching of English literature a means of spreading the ideals of the Anglo-Saxon Race. I am interested in that project both from the point of view of teaching and of research, and I do not believe . . . I can afford to step aside.

At this time Frank began to be considered as a possible college President and was asked by the Fisk Agency if he would care to be recommended. He replied politely that while he had a high regard for agencies, he would not want one to nominate him for a presidency, "believing that no individual should push his own claims for a position of such importance and such responsibility." This was during his leave of absence from M.I.T. on Rhodes Trust business. The next fall he was approached directly by colleges needing Presidents: a "nibble from Lehigh" and an offer from Idaho, both of which he declined.[10]

Then came an invitation he found more tempting to the presidency of Reed College in Oregon. Frank and Marie went out to Portland and liked both college and city. A relatively new institution, Reed had admitted its first class only nine years earlier, attracting attention at once by its serious purpose and the quality of its famous first President, William Trufant Foster. The statement of aim in its first catalogue would surely scare away any but the most ambitious students: "Intercollegiate athletics, fraternities, sororities, and most of the diversions that men are pleased to call college life as distinguished from college work have no place at Reed College. . . . Only those who want to work, and to work hard, and to gain the greatest possible benefits from their studies are welcomed." Frank balanced the pros and cons in a letter to Warner Fite. Reed was blessedly free from "the two evils" of "Alumni and intercollegiate athletics" and had the great positive advantages of an excellent Board of Regents—"a group of the finest men I have ever seen in such a position . . . all men of character and cultivation"—and of an unusually good environment. "Portland is more like Boston than any city on the Pacific Coast and, in fact, is more like the traditional idea of Boston than Boston is itself." He was tempted by the chance to build up a faculty. Feeling that in his war job he had proved to be a good judge of men, he was confident that he could soon "get together a faculty which would be hard to equal," adding, "I think I should have the sense to leave them to do their jobs in freedom." But here, as in any presidency, he would have to sacrifice teaching and research. And at Reed there was also financial pressure. He would need to spend many years raising money before he could devote himself to the college program. When he finally refused the offer, he wrote about it to an old friend of his Indiana days, Joseph Swain, then at Swarthmore, ending with warm praise of Reed and its future: "I feel that it is a place with high intellectual ideals and that it is likely some day to become an important institution."[11]

Frank's reluctance to assume heavy financial burdens may have been sharpened by the recent sad turn of events at M.I.T. President Maclaurin, after ten years of arduous and successful money-raising, having at last reached the point where he could concentrate on educational problems, died suddenly of pneumonia at forty-nine, his resistance undermined by incessant work. At Reed also Frank had before him the warning of President Foster's resignation at what should have been his prime, his health impaired by overexertion and unequal to the fund-raising campaigns that lay ahead.

When Frank reported his decision against Reed to his venerable Cambridge friend George Herbert Palmer, emeritus professor of philosophy, Palmer wrote him in terms which showed both a New England skepticism about the West and relief that he was not to lose the Aydelottes: "The more I have considered it, the more I have feared you would be injured by the western entanglement. The west is a place of hopes, only occasionally of fulfillments. You are too important where you are to let yourself loose in Space." The letter ends with a word about the "little Poetry Club" that met on Sunday evenings at Professor Palmer's house, which both Marie and Frank enjoyed. At the next session they would read *Much Ado about Nothing*.[12]

Statistical Study of Rhodes Scholars

Having refused the Reed offer, Frank became engrossed in his two jobs of teaching at M.I.T. and managing the work for the Rhodes Trust. In the latter he had organized an important project, the first statistical study of the records of American former Rhodes Scholars from the pioneers of 1904 through the Class of 1916: a total of 351 appointees, of whom 331 were living. The study was in the hands of a former Rhodes

Scholar, then professor of mathematics at Brown University, R. W. Burgess. To his request for information there were 303 replies. He asked for data about the men's records before going to Oxford and after their return as well as during their stay—data which would be useful in measuring the present success of the Rhodes plan and in providing a standard for appraising future improvement.

Frank knew that these statistics could serve to check a widespread impression for which some of the Rhodes men, including himself, were partly responsible. Because they so often urged the need of improving methods of selection and appointing only the best men, the American public had jumped to the conclusion that those already sent had been failures. Rumors were also spreading that the best American students were not competing and that "an Oxford career interferes with a man's success in the United States."

Burgess' figures showed that all these impressions were unfounded. The men selected had included a large proportion of high-ranking students in their American colleges: three-fourths had done "the grade of work indicated by election to Phi Beta Kappa." Their academic prowess at Oxford, measured by final honors examinations, showed a higher percentage of First and Second Classes than did the total group of candidates for honors. As to their careers after returning home, the statistics indicated a success hardly to be expected in that period from men so young—from twenty-five to forty. In the profession claiming the largest number, education, with a total of 114, 95 were in colleges and universities, 70 per cent of them with professorial rank, 36 already full professors.

Frank seized on these figures, quoting them at meetings of educators before they appeared in the *Oxonian* of January, 1921.[13] In that number he published an editorial pointing to the report's effective refutation of common criticisms, but taking occasion at the same time to say that the Rhodes Scholars' record was not as good as they intended to make it. "The best of the men who have gone over in the past are the best that the country produces; the poorest of them have been far below our American average, and the success of the scheme is simply a matter of eliminating the weaker men." Here there was the difficulty that each state in the Union had equal representation, even though the states were strikingly uneven in interest in the Scholarships and in the number and ability of candidates. To eliminate the weaker men would mean that some committees must have courage to refuse to appoint if no candidate appeared who was "qualified to make a creditable Rhodes Scholar." Frank was moving steadily toward the plan of appointing not by states but by regions.

With all his interest in the techniques of selection, he never lost sight of Rhode's hope of furthering peace. He wrote eloquently on this point to one of his Sullivan High School classmates:

> In my opinion these Scholarships offer the most wonderful intellectual opportunity which is at present within the reach of American boys, and they have an international significance which is even greater than their importance to a man's individual career.
>
> In these days when it looks almost as if the destruction of civilization which was not accomplished by the war is being completed by a peace which is worse than war, I put my faith more and more not in political alliances but in the slow growth of understanding between nations which will be the result of these international educational relations. More understanding and more goodwill between the English-speaking countries seems to be something which we are on our way to achieving and seems to me to be about the one thing which the world needs more than anything else at present.[14]

British Fellowship Plan

When Frank mentioned "these international educational relations," he had in mind not only the Rhodes Scholarships but the possibility of a reciprocal plan for bringing British students to the United States. He had been playing with this idea for a long time and had worked out details which he formulated in a letter to Max Farrand, Director of the Commonwealth Fund.[15] At the moment nothing came of it. The next February he was trying to interest two educators in the scheme, James Rowland Angell of Yale and S. P. Capen of the University of Buffalo, hoping that with their support he might prevail on someone to become an American Cecil Rhodes. In June he wrote again to Angell: "The British Fellowship plan is sidetracked for the present but I am not letting up in my efforts." These efforts eventually bore fruit in social science fellowships given by the Laura Spelman Rockefeller Memorial and in the more extensive Commonwealth Fellowships established by Edward S. Harkness. The story will be told in a later chapter.

Presidency of Swarthmore

At last Frank had the offer of a college presidency which succeeded in wooing him away from Cambridge. This came from Swarthmore, where he was asked to follow Joseph Swain. Although at first he thought there was no chance of his accepting, he agreed to visit the college as a courtesy to his old friend, taking Marie with him. Unexpectedly they found themselves deeply impressed by the Quaker Board of Managers and felt that "here was something different from the ordinary college, more solidly founded on . . . character." Also as a practical man, Frank was glad to see that it had "a very sound basis financially"; a new President would be free to devote himself at once to the program.[16] He wrote about Swarthmore to Warner Fite: "It needs improvement on the academic side, but they have the money necessary to make that, and I gather from what I saw of the members of the Faculty that a good deal could be done in a very short time. The rivalry of Haverford and Bryn Mawr also Quaker Colleges would make the whole task of academic improvement infinitely easier." He liked the possibility of continuing his work for the Rhodes Trust: "They are very keen to have me go ahead with the Rhodes Scholarships."[17]

Warner Fite, a graduate of Haverford, looked down on Swarthmore, both academically and socially, and wrote by return mail to warn Frank of pitfalls. In curriculum "Swarthmore has only rather recently come into the rank of real colleges." To locate the Rhodes Trust there struck him as "a bit amusing." As to the relation with Haverford, in his own time the only connection had been football. On the social side the two institutions appealed to entirely different groups, with Haverford's clientele "undoubtedly superior in culture and social position," as was true also of Bryn Mawr. Warner Fite went on to explain the contrast between "the Main Line" of the Pennsylvania Railroad, with its aristocratic suburbs, including Haverford and Bryn Mawr, and Swarthmore's middle-class Media Line. "In brief, to be president of Haverford would give you a position of importance in Philadelphia. To be president of Swarthmore would not. But this is perhaps unimportant." Fite's attitude may have influenced the Aydelottes later to value connections with Philadelphia and to determine that social life, like everything else at Swarthmore, should not be mediocre.

Fite's advice might have been supported at that time by more objective critics. Frank probably heard the same comments from others who wished him well. But they left him unperturbed, perhaps even piqued his interest. He wrote to Fite that in the past twenty-five years conditions had changed. Swarthmore had become much stronger academically, and there was no reason why the improvement "should not continue at the same rate or go forward even more rapidly." There was adequate means; the Board was interested and willing to give him a free hand. And, of course, the fact that something needed to be done appealed to him. From what he had seen of the faculties of the three Quaker colleges and knew of their resources, he believed "that Swarthmore can be made fully as strong as either Haverford or Bryn Mawr." That this had, indeed, come to pass when Frank left Swarthmore nineteen years later would probably have been admitted even on the Main Line.

Frank delayed his final decision until he could compare the "Swarthmore job" carefully with other offers coming his way, most of which he would have been "very glad to have received at any time up to the present." One he found particularly tempting was "the headship of the two Departments of English Literature and Composition at the University of Minnesota." This would have been in some ways "a bigger job than Swarthmore since the number of instructors combined must be something like twice that of the Swarthmore Faculty entire." To help him make up his mind he visited the college again, this time without seeing any of the Board, so that he could discuss his ideas with some of the faculty.[18] He called on leading members one by one, saying that he had been offered the presidency, but before accepting, wanted to get their reactions to his "educational ideas."

> The proposal which I had in mind was to make a distinction between the Pass and the Honors degree. I thought of instigating something that would be called Honors work for the two final years of the undergraduate course, which would be both freer and more difficult than the ordinary course. For Honors work there were to be no term grades or examinations. Instead the whole Honors program was to be tested by final examinations at the end of the Senior year, . . . to be conducted by external examiners. This was of course, simply an application of Honors work at Oxford to an American college. It was the answers I received from members of the Faculty . . . which determined me to accept the Swarthmore invitation.

Son of Martha

What Marie thought of the move from Cambridge is not known. She may have found it less attractive than Frank because it meant leaving relatives she liked. Especially she would miss her cousin, Gretchen Warren, who had been a comfort while Frank was away during the war. Marie, like many women, turned for strength to religion, in her case to the Indian mysticism of Vedanta. She had hoped that Frank might share her interest, as she wrote him once when he was out of town. He answered affectionately but honestly in the tone of a son of Martha to a daughter of Mary:

> I have not gone with you to Vedanta not because I was not interested but simply because of the pressure of a million things. It is grotesque how unimportant these things are in comparison but there they are and all together constitute my bit toward making the kingdom of God come on earth. Every time I go away I think I will go to Vedanta with you as soon as I get back and talk with you more about religion—and then I get back into the whirl—the mixture, as Lucretia Mott calls it.[19]

Marie hoped there would be less "whirl" at Swarthmore, but wherever Frank went, he attracted work with a magnetic pull. And Vedanta became unimportant to Marie as she found greater support in Christian Science.

Withdrawal from the Oxonian

Before going to Swarthmore, Frank resigned the editorship of the *American Oxonian.* He announced in the April number that his successor would be Professor C. F. Tucker Brooke of Yale and summarized what he had tried to do in the past seven and a half years: in addition to providing Rhodes Scholars and other Oxonians with news of Oxford and each other, and printing matter of interest to prospective candidates, "to express the intellectual results of the Rhodes Scholarships in education, scholarship, and public affairs."[20] Pointing to the magazine's need of endowment, he took the lead in promising to contribute royalties from books on Oxford: *The Oxford Stamp* and the forthcoming *Oxford of Today,* which he edited with L. A. Crosby.[21] One bit of unfinished business had to do with closer cooperation with Canadian Rhodes Scholars. Years before, when the first number of the *American Oxonian* appeared, Frank's great friend, the Canadian T. M. Papineau, wrote proposing that the new journal become a *North American Oxonian,* for both Canada and the United States. Before anything could be done the war broke out; Papineau enlisted and was killed two years later. Frank hoped the time was now "ripe for going on with it." (The idea did not gain support.)

In the month when Frank retired as editor he started a new venture with "the first Southern reunion of Rhodes Scholars." Fifteen of them gathered to meet him at Nashville, representing committees of selection from the states of Missouri, Tennessee, Kentucky, Alabama, and Mississippi. This experiment with a local reunion succeeded so well that Frank proposed holding half a dozen more the next year. "Problems concerning the Scholarships differ from one part of the country to another, and can perhaps be better thrashed out in small groups of from ten to twenty-five."[22]

Through his success in teaching English and his novel success with engineers, Frank had been given positions of leadership in professional organizations; he was President of the New England Association of Teachers of English and on the Council of the Society for the Promotion of Engineering Education. In this latter field he was to continue his work, thanks to a flourishing department of engineering at Swarthmore.

Welcome from Swarthmore Students

When he had finally agreed to accept the presidency, the students' newspaper, the *Phoenix* (March 8, 1921), carried an important headline: "Professor Frank Aydelotte Elected Unanimously by the Board of Managers as Swarthmore's New President"; below it was an impressive account of the new President's war record and educational ideals, with a photograph of a youthful, serious face, large ears, and an almost hairless head. The camera caught a look that was direct and somewhat fierce. No Adonis, certainly, but once seen, not forgotten. The *Phoenix* welcomed the new President in a cordial editorial, presumably and appropriately written by the editor in chief, Alan Valentine.[23] Its writer was to be the first Rhodes Scholar from Swarthmore and later its Dean of Men, the first Master of Pierson College at Yale, and President of the University of Rochester.

FOREWORD TO CHAPTERS NINE
THROUGH FOURTEEN

To Frank Aydelotte, his most important work was as President of Swarthmore College. Two months before he died, he wrote to his second successor in office, Courtney Smith; "Swarthmore in a certain sense has been my life. As I look back on past years it seems to me that everything I did before 1920 was preparation for the administration of Swarthmore and that everything I have done since 1940 has been the application of the lessons I learned at Swarthmore to all sorts and kinds of educational situations."

This period occupied almost half of his professional life—twice the time he spent in any other position. So it seems appropriate to devote over one-third of his biography to Swarthmore, or six of the seventeen chapters. Two of these discuss the character of the college and the man; one speaks of his work with foundations during these years; the others recount three parts of the Swarthmore story.

When the new President came to Swarthmore he brought with him the office of the American Secretary to the Rhodes Trustees. Four years later he added a third responsibility—for planning and organizing the John Simon Guggenheim Memorial Foundation Fellowships, staying on as chairman of the Educational Advisory Board. The last two were not volunteer activities, but positions earning substantial salaries, undertaken with the cordial consent of the Swarthmore Board of Managers.

Frank Aydelotte kept these lines of work distinct by separating them physically, each in its own office with a secretary and files, the Rhodes Trust Office across from the President's, the Guggenheim in New York. I propose to adapt his plan by the physical separation into chapters.

CHAPTER NINE

FORTUNATE PLACE AND TIME

The Swarthmore Scene

WHEN Frank Aydelotte became the seventh President of Swarthmore in 1921, the college had 510 students, about equally divided between men and women, a faculty of 47, and a Board of Managers of 32. All would be important to him. He wanted to keep the enrollment small, believing that American education had suffered from a mistaken regard for numbers. It was his idea that the growing throng of students in the United States should be cared for, not by building larger and larger institutions, but by a greater number of small ones which might combine for some purposes in federations similar to the University of Oxford. The only increases he hoped to see at Swarthmore were in the number of teachers, the size of their salaries, and the volumes in the library.

Frank liked the college site in a commuting suburb, with the right balance between country quiet and Philadelphia's theatres, music, and art. The campus was a park of great trees and green lawns sweeping from the railroad up a hill to Parrish Hall, past a knot of buildings in the rear, across the athletic fields, and on to wooded slopes dipping down to a little river—altogether more than two hundred acres. Parrish Hall, originally the only building, still set a Quakerly tone, outside and in, with its gray stone walls, and front doors opening on a row of three portraits: Lucretia Mott in bonnet and shawl, Isaac Hopper wearing knee breeches, and a lady in an indeterminate style of white dress with long, starched full skirt. She was Susan Cunningham, teacher of mathematics for many college generations, known for her learning and characteristic command to a floundering student: "Use thee gumption."

On the ground floor of Parrish Hall's middle section was the college dining room, and above it, Collection Hall, large enough to seat the whole body of students and faculty. In the wings the women's dormitories occupied the three upper floors, with offices and classrooms below. The men's dormitory, Wharton Hall, at the edge of the woods, would soon have a new neighbor in a lodge for the Phi Kappa Psi fraternity, the first of a proposed group of five. As the use of these lodges was to be purely social, they would not affect men's living in Wharton and taking their meals in the college dining room. The six women's "fraternities"—a term used at Swarthmore for women's groups as well as men's—had as yet no plans to build.[1]

A fraternity man himself, member of Sigma Nu, Frank was well disposed toward these groups, though aware that their activities might come to overshadow all-college functions.

In athletics he had already banned subsidies for football players. The emphasis at Swarthmore he knew to be the usual one of developing teams for intercollegiate competition, but he hoped to change it in the direction of his "Spectators and Sports":[2] encouraging everyone to play something for fun and reducing spectators in numbers and influence. Other Swarthmore activities followed customary lines: departmental clubs, glee clubs, and Little Theatre. One of the oldest activities, started soon after the fire that almost destroyed Parrish Hall in 1881, was the newspaper called the *Phoenix*, "as coming from a college which had just risen from its ashes."[3]

His chief interest, of course, was in the curriculum which he had described to Warner Fite as not outstanding but good, a sound basis for what he wanted to do. The liberal arts program made the usual distinction between the first two years, devoted mainly to meeting requirements, and the last two, which permitted greater freedom of choice and some concentration on a major subject. Prescribed subjects included two foreign languages, English literature and composition, mathematics or astronomy, a laboratory science, and one of the "social sciences." Progress toward a degree was measured in the customary way by what Frank called "academic book-keeping" of hours and quality points. He proposed to substitute a less mechanical system for honors students.

As a concession to vocational interests, practical courses were offered in two departments, education and engineering. Frank recognized that the training of teachers had long been a responsibility of Friends, but was reluctant to see a student divert from liberal courses the eighteen hours of education required for a teachers' certificate. As to engineering, the Swarthmore program, like the one he had known at M.I.T., supported technical work with courses in liberal arts, on the ground that these would prepare students for the human side of engineering when they would need "to meet men of education and culture on equal terms."[4] Engineering students received the degree of Bachelor of Arts until the Bachelor of Science was introduced for the Class of 1927.

Frank took coeducation for granted, aware of its hazards and advantages. He thought the presence of both sexes made students more perceptive and discriminating than those in separate colleges, but more difficult to handle. "You can fool women alone about some things," he said, "and men alone about other things, but put men and women in college together, and you can't fool them at all!" The completeness of coeducation at Swarthmore impressed him favorably. Men and women students had meals together three times a day. Meeting each other so often and particularly at breakfast, still sleepy and sometimes cross, they were likely to lose illusions, to be less prone to overemphasize social life than in a college where separation heightened glamour. He welcomed the rule that students could not be formally engaged until after one of them was graduated. This and other strict social regulations helped him tolerate the Swarthmore nickname of "Little Quaker Matchbox."

At the same time he saw a subtle danger to his campaign for more rigorous and independent work in an attitude of Swarthmore men. Like men in other coeducational colleges, they had grown skeptical of the academic system, partly because women did so well in it. Women succeeded, in the men's opinion, through being conscientious and thorough; they got high grades and were elected to Phi Beta Kappa, often in the proportion of three women to one man. Study was for the girls, said the men. As for themselves, they would do just enough to stay in college so that they could give their best efforts to the football team or the *Phoenix*. Frank would have to break through this prejudice before his program could get the men's attention, not to speak of rousing their interest and enthusiasm. No wonder he would tend to measure academic progress at Swarthmore partly in terms of an increased proportion of men in honors work and Phi Beta Kappa.

The location of the President's office, at almost the exact center of the ground floor of Parrish Hall, seemed right for a man who did not want to miss anything. Close to the dining room, on the main hall where everyone passed more than once a day, the office was easily reached by anyone who wanted to see the President. For him it was a strategic point where he could keep his finger on the college pulse.

The President's house was somewhat more retired. It stood on the edge of the campus, a dignified gray stone structure with a mansard roof. The chief physical charm was its outlook, with most of the windows facing south on an expanse of lawn separated from the campus by a hedge which often burst into white blossoms in time for the Commencement luncheon under the trees. Beyond the hedge a path through the Meeting House woods joined a broad walk leading to Parrish Hall and the President's office. Every morning when Frank left home, he hurtled across the campus as if impatient to be in the thick of things.

The circumstances of his appointment at Swarthmore were fortunate both for him and for the college. On his side, he recognized the advantages of the Friendly connection and of following the strong administration of Joseph Swain. From the standpoint of the college, the new President's ideas, experience, and special skills gave him a long head start over most newcomers to office.

Swarthmore was a Quaker college, but hardly a college of Quakers. Of the students, less than a fourth were children of Friends, and the proportion on the faculty was even smaller. But the Board of Managers held to the rule of electing only Friends and served as liaison between the Society and the college. They kept the college aware of its Friendly background in various ways, not least effectively by simply being themselves.

To see the Managers when they assembled at Swarthmore was to feel an almost formidable impact of good sense, integrity, and independence. Frank liked these qualities as he liked the Quaker virtue of keeping an open mind and considering any idea on its merits. This, together with the Friends' belief in educating every individual according to his talents, Frank hoped would predispose the Board to listen to his new plans for the ablest students. He liked the Quaker way of conducting business, reaching decisions not by counting votes, but by the "sense of the meeting"—a conclusion on which there seemed to be substantial agreement. The Clerk would state this conclusion as he saw it, to which individuals would respond by saying "I approve" or by raising an objection. Objections were aired in further discussion until the Clerk formulated what everyone would accept. The method appealed to Frank's preference for carrying points by consent. Indeed, he was a natural Quaker, sharing the qualities he admired.

The college had another Quaker asset in the Friends' Historical Library, begun in 1870 with a gift of $1,000 from Anson Lapham. The collection had grown to include an impressive number of books, Meeting records, and other manuscripts, forming a useful research center in Quaker history. Frank saw the library as a source of intellectual leadership among Friends, just as he saw in the tradition that the college should provide teachers for Friends' schools a chance to serve Friends' education. He wanted to make the most of what he found at Swarthmore as well as to develop ideas of his own.

He also appreciated the influence of the Meeting House which stood on the campus and was the focus of college religious life, even though it belonged not to the college but to the village Monthly Meeting. New-comers were likely to attend First Day Meeting at least once out of curiosity. Frank went regularly, sat with the elders on the facing benches, and often spoke. Other members of the administration and faculty and a number of students commonly attended, whatever their denomination. Every year some of them, profiting from the silence and the novel ministry, joined Meeting as "convinced Friends." In spite of Frank's sympathy with Friends, he himself did not join until after he had given up his office, offering two more or less whimsical explanations. He would not deprive the Friends of the supreme example of their broad-mindedness: a non-Quaker President of a Quaker College. More seriously, knowing that the time might come when the Managers would be opposed to something he thought important, he said that such a situation would be less painful if he were not a Friend.

Frank was lucky in following Joseph Swain. Swain had accepted the office in 1902 after nine years as the successful head of Indiana University. Because he was a Friend, he listened to a call which could hardly be said to carry professional advancement: "The only college under the care of the religious society to which I belong, has made an appeal to me, which I cannot gain my own consent to refuse."[5] In President Swain's nineteen years at Swarthmore he succeeded in three undertakings of advantage to his successor: straightening out difficulties between the Managers and the President, gaining a more adequate endowment, and advancing the intellectual life of the college, largely by good appointments to the faculty.

According to the traditional relation between the Managers and the President—essentially that of a corporation and its secretary—the Managers made all important decisions and had complete control of finances. This should not have caused trouble among such reasonable people as the Quakers, except for the fact that the college from the beginning had two aims, not sharply distinguished nor necessarily incompatible, one of which seemed of first importance to the Board, the other to the President. The aim of serving the Hicksite Friends by giving their children a suitable education, originally called "guarded," had been the concern of the Founders and continued to stand first with the Managers. The second aim, to build a college equal to the best institutions of learning in the country, appealed more strongly to a professional educator. This difference in emphasis was acknowledged by the early President Edward Magill in his *Sixty-five Years in the Life of a Teacher*,[6] which introduced Frank Aydelotte to Swarthmore history. Edward Magill is discussing the man proposed for his successor, Charles De Garmo:

> Although not a Friend in name, he was one in principle, and I felt assured that his being of a Friends' family would help him with our Board. That he was of such a family I considered to be of importance on their account; but that he was a scholar and a born educator . . . was of far greater importance if he was to attempt to make our college take an honored place among the colleges of our State and country.[7]

Charles De Garmo more than lived up to Magill's expectations in his program for the college, but could not interest the Managers in financing it, and after seven years of frustration he resigned to become professor of "pedagogics" at Cornell. The next President seemed to be precisely what the Managers wanted, a man well known for his devotion to Friends' concerns, William Birdsall, then principal of a Friends' school in Philadelphia. But handicapped as he was by inexperience in higher education, he could not deal adequately with college academic problems. When he resigned, his four years in office had helped the Managers understand as never before that academic excellence was no frill, but essential to Swarthmore's future.[8] At this point they turned to a man who might advance both aims, Joseph Swain, loyal alike to the Friends and to the best in education.

Swain saw that no President could succeed in the existing relation to the Board and that the endowment of $400,000 could not meet rising costs. Making his acceptance contingent on the promise that both difficulties would be met, he stipulated that the Managers should guarantee to increase the endowment to a million dollars within two or three years. (Owing largely to his efforts, it amounted to three and a half millions at the end of his successor's first year.) On the side of administration Swain asked for "certain guaranteed Presidential powers: the power of appointing all teachers, subject to Board approval, the power to veto salary changes made by the Managers, and the right to dismiss members of the Faculty." The change is described by Homer Babbidge, later President of the University of Conneticut at Storrs, in his unpublished "Swarthmore College in the Nineteenth Century": "What Swain sought and what the Managers agreed to, was a shift in the role of the Board from that of combined judicial and executive agency to that of repository of the institution's conscience, and an elevation of the President from administrative assistant to executive head of the College."

In accepting the loss of power the Managers showed their confidence in Joseph Swain and their willingness to do what seemed best for the college. But old habits die hard. Even as late as Frank's administration there was an occasional stirring of the buried preference for a program tailored to Friends' children rather than one which gave Swarthmore "an honored place among the colleges of our State and country."

On the intellectual side Swain's achievements had been notable. He persuaded William Sproul, Swarthmore alumnus, member of the Board, and Governor of Pennsylvania, to give and endow an observatory, with a large telescope and other equipment far in advance of undergraduate needs. With these attractions, Swain lured away from Indiana his friend John A. Miller, distinguished teacher of mathematics and astronomy, whose expeditions to photograph total eclipses of the sun added to college prestige. Swain succeeded also in building the much-needed library by raising money to match a Carnegie grant. And of first importance was the quality of the faculty he appointed, including a high proportion of excellent teachers, ready to consider with open mind the new President's proposals.

Well-Timed Idea

When Frank Aydelotte urged the claims of unusually able students, at Swarthmore and elsewhere, he spoke to a receptive audience. Their interest represented a fortunate change in attitude in little more than a decade. As recently as 1909, when President Arthur Twining Hadley of Yale proposed a similar plan, he won no support from his alumni and little from his faculty. Both groups questioned special opportunities for a minority of gifted students, still believing that in a democracy what was good for the majority (the average) should be everybody's fare.

President Hadley, looking for ways of stimulating the intellectual interests of undergraduates, had said: "I frankly own that I should be glad to see the English system of separating honor men from pass men introduced at Yale."[9] To which the Alumni Advisory Council replied: "While opportunities for the minority who are keen for study should consistently be improved, the main purpose of Yale—as to undergraduates, at least—is to fit the majority for useful work in the world. No scheme out of line with this thought would, we are satisfied, be approved by the alumni."[10]

Among the Yale faculty the issue had been complicated by departmental differences. Discussion of a proposed honors program dragged through compromise after compromise, all in the interests of "the ordinary student," until what finally went through offered the honors student little or nothing. To quote the historian of Yale, George Wilson Pierson, the faculty "refused to deprive the ordinary student, no matter how dull or frivolous or uninterested he might be, of the slightest opportunity. Instead they had restricted the Honors man, kept him from really specializing."[11] The same miscalled "equalitarianism," which in fact favored the average student, still dominated American education.

Much had happened by 1921 to change this point of view. The end of the war had brought spectacular increases in enrollment of colleges and universities, with no corresponding additions to faculty and equipment, a condition which was rapidly producing the evils of "mass education." At the same time, new developments in psychological testing and in the philosophy of education had drawn attention to the needs of individuals and to the importance in a democracy of preparing the ablest for leadership. A word on each point.

Between 1910 and 1920 the number of students in colleges and universities throughout the United States had risen by 60 percent, four times the increase in population and about double the increase in faculty members.[12] With virtually twice the number of students per teacher, a decrease in personal contact was inevitable. A Yale senior who entered college in 1919 described conditions which he deplored: "Every class of which I have been one of the fifty or more members has been purely a lecture course, and instead of being a person . . . I am now merely a suit of clothes pinned together by four or five seat numbers."[13]

Psychological tests, brought into prominence by the Army's wartime use, had disclosed such range and variety of *ability to learn* as to make the concept of the "average student" virtually meaningless. Now it was to "individuals" that educators must turn their attention. Similarly in philosophy the influential John Dewey stressed the education of "individuals" as the responsibility of a democracy, with special emphasis on those with unusual gifts. His *Democracy and Education* (1916) spoke to the condition of many thoughtful readers.[14]

Three of Dewey's points are relevant here. First, that when a democracy fulfills its duty of providing individuals with equal educational opportunities, "equal" means not identical but equivalent. *Advantages* are equal when every student has what he requires to bring his individual capacities to full growth. Dewey's second point: that democracy, as a kind of social order without hereditary rulers or a self-perpetuating bureaucracy, can benefit from the leadership of the ablest citizens, wherever born, provided they can be singled out in youth and given adequate education. (Dewey seems to take for granted that the voters in their wisdom will cast their ballots for these well-trained, ablest citizens.) To Dewey's followers the conclusion is clear: that such a program as honors work, designed expressly for the ablest students, should be acclaimed for its supreme social importance—a *sine qua non* of the best government in a democracy. When these two points are understood, early reproaches against the honors program as "undemocratic" seem not merely stupid but antisocial.

To be convinced so far is to see the force of a third point: that the method in education must be experimental. Educators must test ways of discovering the range of students' abilities, of identifying those with special gifts, of providing a variety of opportunities that can be accepted as equivalent. There is no doubt that these principles of John Dewey's and knowledge of their application in experiments with children helped prepare educators and a growing public to listen to Frank Aydelotte's proposals for an experiment with the abler college students.

It must be said at once that Frank Aydelotte was not a "Deweyite." He could agree with these points of Dewey's, but not without qualifications. He had reservations about psychological tests, sharing the skepticism of Alexis Carrel, who had remarked that "psychological tests are an excellent means of selecting large numbers of people for unimportant jobs." And though ready to experiment endlessly with methods of teaching which should stimulate students to find their own best speed and depth, to avoid dullness and preserve spontaneity, he was opposed to experiments with the subject matter and organization of the curriculum in which some progressive educators threw overboard the values of a liberal arts course of study, substituting individualized programs often called "functional" or "life-enhancing." Such programs, made famous later by experiments at Sarah Lawrence and Bennington, were already foreshadowed in some slight degree at Reed College and, beginning in

1921, at Antioch. Frank Aydelotte never doubted that education should be "liberal," that some subjects were more valuable than others, that some writers had the accent of greatness, and that some works were masterpieces—points he would always keep in mind when planning a curriculum or a single course.

In the prevailing climate of opinion Frank Aydelotte's inaugural address seemed both novel and important. An apt introduction to his address was provided by the spokesman for the University of Oxford, Roger B. Merriman, Balliol '97–'99, professor of history at Harvard.[15] After paying tribute to the new President as one of Oxford's "most indispensable and effective servants," through whose efforts the Rhodes Scholarships had been firmly established with high standards and "the value of an Oxford career has come to be appreciated in the United States," Professor Merriman went on to define the English heritage in education in terms of two ideas: a college is responsible for a student's "moral as well as his social growth"; a college education should aim "not primarily to impart information, but rather to give the student intellectual power" so that he learns "how to teach himself." These ideas, in eclipse during the years when Americans imitated the German universities in manufacturing "highly trained specialists" rather than "thinking men and women," are coming to light again and can take effect most easily in a college small enough for close contacts between faculty and students.

Frank Aydelotte prefaced his proposals to adapt Oxford aims for the benefit of "students of exceptional ability" by expressing warm appreciation of Swarthmore's debt to Joseph Swain and to its heritage of liberal traditions from the Society of Friends.[16] He went on to note the serious need in America for leaders who would make clear that material advances were not important in themselves, but rather as means to producing "human beings of finer quality." Hitherto the students of largest capacity had not found commensurate opportunities in college. To make good this lack would be his chief concern.

Then, with the zeal of a crusader, he made a statement which would be quoted in the college catalogue as an introduction to honors work from 1922 through 1939:

> We are educating more students up to a fair average than any country in the world, but we are wastefully allowing the capacity of the average to prevent us from bringing the best up to the standards they could reach. Our most important task at the present is to check this waste. The

method of doing it seems clear: to give to those students who are really
interested in the intellectual life harder and more independent work than
could profitably be given to those whose devotion to matters of the
intellect is less keen, to demand of the former, in the course of their four
years work, a standard of attainment for the A.B. degree distinctly higher
than we require of them at present.

This speech stood out among inaugural addresses for its definite
program, focused on intellectual quality, in contrast to the usual vague
idealism or emphasis on material needs. Witness the New York *Evening
Post's* comparison of his address with four others delivered at about the
same time.[17] The new President of Cornell had "turned aside from the
question of immediate academic needs to the urgent duty of educated
men and women everywhere in the present world crisis." At William
and Mary the audience had heard "a sermon on the national needs of
education and the necessity of higher standards for the teaching profession." The President of the University of the State of New York, also
State Commissioner of Education, "pictures the immensity of the problem
of providing schools for all the children of all the people, and points out
that, no matter what the cost, the American people will not turn back in
its program of education." The most striking contrast lay between the
two Pennsylvania speakers, the Presidents of State College and Swarthmore,

> the former calling upon the State of Pennsylvania to make his institution
> a vast State university, the latter urging that the most pressing problem is
> improvement of the quality of college education, to the end that we may
> not merely provide abundance of educational opportunity, as we now
> do, but that we shall substitute qualitative for quantitative standards in
> American colleges and provide the best possible intellectual training for a
> superior type of American youth.

The reporter concludes hopefully that with the "real problems before
American colleges" there are also "real opportunities" such "as have
never been known before," particularly the one brought to the fore by
President Aydelotte, of viewing "in their proper perspective the problems
involved in numbers and quality."

In that reporter's mind there is no lingering trace of the prejudice in
favor of "the average" which only twelve years earlier had blocked
President Hadley's efforts at Yale.

CHAPTER TEN

PORTRAIT OF A MAN OF ACTION

FRANK AYDELOTTE impressed his Swarthmore colleagues as an engine of inexhaustible energy, delighting in strenuous exercise of mind and muscle. He was like the war horse in the *Book of Job* who "rejoiceth in his strength ... he saith among the trumpets, Ha, ha." "Work, golf and work" described his "hobbies."[1]

It was true that he hardly distinguished work from play, showing the same zest for both. Taking for granted that his colleagues were like-minded, he involved them in prodigious undertakings with an air of inviting them to share in a lark. They usually found themselves responding in the same spirit. Henry Moe of the Guggenheim Foundation who worked with him intimately, remarked: "When Frank Aydelotte was interested in something, he steeped himself in it, and made it fascinating." Courtney Smith said of his energy that it was "the kind needed for administration," with a "divine quality" of courage and optimism which "makes anything his vision produces seem feasible."[2]

A portrait of Frank Aydelotte in action would show him in discussion with a group small enough so that everyone could be heard, large enough for variety. He could infuse a committee with the liveliness of a seminar, tapping each member for his special contribution and spurring them all to go on thinking. One result: a remarkably unified college. As John Nason, then his assistant and later his successor, put it: "Swarthmore College has a board, an administration, and a faculty, but for practical purposes it is one unit, and the college embodies the deepest convictions and the matured judgments of all its constituent members."[3]

A few brief accounts of his ways of working with different elements in the college community may help to fill in the colors of his portrait.

Working with the Faculty

Frank Aydelotte made a good start with the faculty before he agreed to become President by asking their opinion of his ideas on honors work. Their response helped convince him that he should accept—the first of many joint decisions.

They welcomed the honors program both for themselves and for their abler students. It was inspiriting to think of what they might do with no more than five or six students in a group. They had faith in the new President's plans because he came with a reputation for success in his own teaching; indeed, when honors work was in its experimental stage, they often asked him to conduct a seminar himself so that they could observe how he did it.

Another fortunate result of his teaching experience: he knew that the more intensive the teaching, the heavier the toll on a teacher's resources of strength and knowledge and the greater the need for replenishment. Accordingly he set a goal for doubling in both time and money the usual allowance for leaves of absence, stating that they were intended to keep members of the faculty "intellectually alive." Whether their study would produce books was for them to decide. (No threat of "publish or perish.") Privately he had every confidence that teachers with alert minds would write books, and better ones if free from what was already known in some quarters as "the academic rat-race."

The faculty never became too large to permit members to see the President easily and establish a friendly basis for working together. This basis was the stronger because at Swarthmore, as in many colleges, the President was also virtually Dean of the Faculty, presiding at their meetings and serving as chairman of their Instruction Committee. He kept the number of meetings low, bringing the whole faculty together only when they had to take action on important business. He preferred more personal and informal ways of reaching decisions. "It was characteristic of Frank Aydelotte," said Patrick Malin, "that when he wanted your judgment, he would come and knock at your door." He liked to ask advice, partly to benefit from a variety of opinions, partly to give those who would be involved in a plan a share in making it.

Throughout his administration the President and faculty continued to work well together because they liked and trusted each other. Frank's colleagues particularly liked his *joie de vivre* and courage. This last, as one of them wrote, was the temperamental courage of the man who genuinely enjoys the fray and lacks the organ that would tell him when he is beaten. In Frank Aydelotte there is more than a touch of his own Elizabethan seamen, who felt that life was at its best when they could swing about their decks with the enemy closing in and all guns going. . . . This sort of courage is contagious. In fact it spread through all the staff in the form of heightened morale.

The President's confidence in his faculty

was nothing short of epic. It was hardly a debatable point with him that he had the best college faculty in the United States; he exulted over them individually and collectively, and kept breaking out into little "whoops of blessing" over them, reading their books with pride, sending them notes of appreciation, calling them in continually to give him advice.

What more natural than that "the making and executing of plans was a communal business. . . . His most fruitful ideas are so largely shaped in discussion that, as he would be the first to say, they are group products rather than private ones." This helped explain the lack of faculty opposition to the President's proposals of something like a revolution in educational methods. The revolution was accepted "with hardly a dissenting voice," because

the new program never seemed, and never was, an imposition from above. It was elaborated in endless conversations with his faculty, in which he unburdened his mind to every section of it, sometimes getting firmly sat upon, but generally bouncing up again with some ebullient compromise that somehow saved his main point and everybody else's face.[4]

His communal planning was largely his own invention. He wanted the faculty to follow something like the procedure of a Friends' business meeting, where everyone with a concern expresses it freely until they reach some kind of unity. But his meetings should be small: sometimes a group of those particularly interested in a point, sometimes only one person at a time. Convinced that he often heard the frankest expression when he talked to men singly, uninhibited by the presence of colleagues who might disagree, he arranged interviews, listening to opinions he could weigh rather than count, even disregard altogether if he thought them unsound. It was a kind of imaginary Friends' business meeting where the President as Clerk saw and heard participants who never saw or heard the whole group, but when he reached a sense of the meeting, they found it acceptable. Sometimes their consensus of opinion needed to be taken to a faculty meeting for formal action; more often a meeting seemed superfluous.

The President liked this flexibility, the chance to "proceed as way opens," in the Quaker phrase. After a series of interviews he could drop a point if it had struck no spark or had brought out too many strong differences to be reconciled at the moment. He could do this the more easily because he had probably put any view of his own in the form of a question and because he had talked to only one man at a time. With no pressure from him and no marshaling of opposing forces, he could reopen an issue when circumstances seemed more favorable.

Occasionally he raised a point at faculty lunches held for members of departments assembled by Divisions. These were weekly affairs, the Divisions of the Humanities and Social Sciences meeting in one room, the Divisions of Mathematical—Natural Sciences and Engineering in another, with a passage between, and doors left open. They could exchange ideas. He attended when he could, usually joining the Humanities and Social Sciences, more as a benevolent bystander than a participant. Because he seldom spoke, he was heard with greater attention when he did introduce a topic; often his presence seemed hardly noticed. For so dynamic a man, he could play himself down surprisingly when he saw fit. Whenever he consulted the faculty he took care to concentrate on points of policy that should interest them. He would not bore them with procedures. "The administration exists," he would say, "to save the faculty's time." He would not make the mistake of some Utopian communities which required everyone to discuss and vote on everything, including the week's menus, with the result that there was not enough time left to produce the food.

In the most important area of his cooperation with the faculty—the choice of new members—his practice was to set up a special committee for each appointment. This committee included representatives of the department with a vacancy, also of others in closely related subjects: teachers whose point of view would be at once sympathetic and detached. When the philosophy department was looking for a new member, it profited by advice from psychologists and political scientists. Committee and President worked together until they could agree unanimously on the candidate to invite. Then he was asked to come to Swarthmore for an interview and, if he was a married man, to bring his wife. Together they should decide whether they would fit in as a family.

Occasionally the Swarthmore selectors were so hard to please that they went through a forest of possibilities and picked up a crooked stick in the end. But this happened rarely.

To keep the faculty in a healthy state of growth and contentment, Frank made various provisions, the first a Faculty Traveling Expense Fund, helping teachers attend meetings of learned societies. He mentioned this in the *Annual Report* of his first year in office as one of "a large number of influences upon the improvement of the academic standards of the College."[5] Soon he set a faculty committee to work on a system of tenure, adopted at a meeting on February 25, 1924. This provided indefinite tenure for full professors and terms of five years for associate and three years for assistant professors. An instructor's appointment was to be renewed year by year to a maximum of five reappointments. A statement to this effect was drawn up and accepted by the faculty as in accord with good practices at that time.

The largest item in his budget, and the one which grew most rapidly, was instruction salaries. During his administration, while the number of the faculty was doubled, the amount for salaries was tripled. He was interested also in housing the faculty well. The college built a group of houses after a practical and charming plan drawn by one of the first new professors, the Aydelottes' old friend Alfred Brooks. Faculty families could put up houses of their own on college property. And thanks to Mrs. Aydelotte's help, social relations with the faculty, indeed, with the whole community, were friendly.

President's Wife

One of the portraits in Parrish Hall shows Frank Aydelotte in the scarlet gown of his Oxford honorary degree, seated by his wife, true to fact in representing them together. The caption, "Frank and Marie Aydelotte, President of Swarthmore College," said more than the one who made it may have realized. But it was true that Mrs. Aydelotte did her full share of work for the college, especially in the delicate areas of personal relations and official entertaining.

Fortunately she looked the part of a gracious First Lady. With a high-bred manner and pleasant voice, she carried herself well and dressed becomingly in conservative taste. Social life in a Quaker setting appealed to her for its simplicity, though she was not sorry when the President of the Board recommended that she add a touch of elegance.

Because the college community was small, Mr. and Mrs. Aydelotte could call on newcomers early in the year, inviting them to dinner so soon that they felt royally welcomed. Mrs. Aydelotte herself made a point of taking a present to a new baby, or a book to amuse a child who had been ill. Both the Aydelottes liked to help young people in emergencies. Robert Spiller remembers that he and his family stayed in the Aydelotte house while their own was being painted—this in the summer when the President's family were out of town. And Patrick Malin recalls a similar occasion when his children were small. Frank Aydelotte offered the use of his study, saying, "It must be noisy for you at home."

Both the Aydelottes wanted their house to be the center of college hospitality. Frank liked to brighten a committee meeting by holding it in his study, serving tea. They entertained many student groups to discuss college problems or to celebrate a special event. There was a dinner for the football squad at the end of the season: huge roasts of beef and mountains of potatoes. The women's honor society of Mortar Board initiated new members in the spring, with appropriately dainty refreshments. An element of pleasant homeliness was added by the Aydelottes' official greeter, their large shaggy Briard (French sheep dog) Denny, his black disheveled hair falling over small bright eyes. Bounding awkwardly in affectionate welcome, Denny was an incongruous figure in that stately house and gave it an unexpectedly informal charm.

When the President had a conference with out-of-town visitors late in the morning, he often took them home for lunch on half an hour's notice, obviously proud of his wife's easy coping with the situation. She coped also with a continuous stream of house guests—distinguished lecturers, Oxford dons coming for advice on their American tours, relatives invited for a little rest, and friends of Bill's. The Comptroller used to say, "The Aydelottes run a hotel," adding, "Don't think their entertaining allowance covers all that!"

Mrs. Aydelotte had faced the fact that she must have a staff large enough for entertaining, combined with all sorts of emergencies. On the day of a formal dinner for a British statesman, there might be an unexpected guest or two for lunch, a visitor to be met at the Philadelphia station, or an injured student to be taken to the hospital. A staff of four— cook, two maids, and chauffeur—proved to be only just adequate. Even then food could not be elaborate, scrambled eggs sufficing for anybody's lunch. Mrs. Aydelotte had another aim in providing simple meals: to encourage young faculty wives without help to take their turn at entertaining.

She disciplined herself to avoid doing anything that might cause even a hint of difficulty for her husband. She even told me once that it was dangerous for a woman in her position to say anything witty or quotable; such remarks might make her seem uncomfortably clever and frighten people! On social occasions when she appeared with Mr. Aydelotte, she talked very little, convinced that he was the one everyone wanted to hear. When he was away and she represented the family, she took care not to act as though she spoke for him. Indeed, even at meetings of committees to which she belonged in her own right, she rarely volunteered an opinion; someone might take it to be the President's.

While this determined self-control made her seem more aloof than she was, and less interesting, it had its compensations. "The less she spoke, the more she heard," and with a chance to observe other people's reactions. She learned a great deal about the college and about human traits and motives, becoming a wise counselor to anyone who asked her advice. It was generally believed that her husband never appointed anyone without consulting her and postponed any important decision until he had her opinion. He acknowledged his debt by saying, "I married an angel."

The art of personal relationships practiced by both the Aydelottes required time and attention which would have been impossible in a large institution. If someone mentioned this to Frank he would reply, "Another advantage of a small college. Individuals count."

Working with the Administration

When Frank Aydelotte said, "The administration exists to save the faculty's time," he stated a fact and expressed a point of view. It is a fact that administrative officers are the hewers of wood and drawers of water, the Marthas of the college world. In the symbol of the essential college, Mark Hopkins sits on one end of a log and a student on the other; there is no Dean. None is needed until something goes wrong with the log. Frank's point of view would seem shocking in institutions where officers, not teachers, are thought to constitute the higher echelon. At Swarthmore every administrator hoped to teach a course often enough to preserve his faculty status. Aydelotte himself came with this intention, but was able to carry it out only rarely at first and later not at all. One reason for his defection, as for that of other would-be teachers in an administration, was lack of time to keep up with his subject.

The President coddled the faculty, careful to see that they were not overworked or underpaid, but regarded the administration as an extension of himself, expecting them to be ready to work almost as long and hard. He pointed out proudly that when the budget item for faculty salaries had tripled, he had kept the increase for administration down to less than two-thirds. His procedures differed in dealing with the two groups, notably in making appointments and in his ways of working with them. While an appointment to the faculty was the result of prolonged discussion between the President and a committee, a new member of the administration was chosen by the President without necessarily asking anyone's advice. He worked with the faculty by consulting them; with the administration, by delegating responsibility. These differences were accepted without question, if, indeed, they were noticed. Administration and faculty alike enjoyed working with the President and felt lucky to be connected with Swarthmore at a time when he made it such a lively and famous place.

One member of the community who saw him from the points of view of both faculty and administration is Edith Philips, long the chairman of the department of romance languages and for a year the Acting Dean of Women. Though one who much preferred teaching to administration, she recalls that he was "exciting to work with," that he "made administrative problems interesting," and that he combined qualities rarely found together: he was "always available, always seemed to have time, no sense of pressure," and that nevertheless he was a "quick decider." Most important, he was "never defeated."

The administrative staff was small; usually two Deans, the Comptroller (a new officer), a Vice-President without function except in the President's absence, a Superintendent of Buildings and Grounds, a House Director, a dietitian, a librarian, and a few secretaries and assistants. The President liked this simplicity. He thought most institutions were top-heavy and was amused to hear of some with so many Deans as to require a Dean of Deans to keep them in order.

When there was an administrative vacancy to fill, the President seemed to rely on hunches. His colleagues, observing through the years the persons he appointed, came to recognize some of the qualities he wanted in his staff. The physical vitality required to enjoy hard work was essential; also the practical imagination to see needs and make plans to meet them. He wanted people who were versatile and flexible, interested in the variety of work likely to fall to every member of a small administration, ready to fit into sudden changes of program or schedule.

There should be no clock watchers, no devotees of red tape or rules without exceptions. At last, when he was resigning, he stated explicitly the qualities he valued particularly in the staff he was bequeathing to his successor:

> They have been chosen on the principle of seeking for each position an expert in that particular work. . . . They have in addition the ability to work together as a team, and they are furthermore each of them devoted to the great intellectual aims of the College. This seems to me very important. The administration of a college should be different from that of an engineering firm, or a trust company, or a hotel, because the aims of a college are different; only that person who can see how any engineering or financial or housekeeping problem is related to the problem of education will be able to conduct the affairs of his or her department in such a way as to contribute most to this central educational purpose.[6]

For the responsibility he gave them, he sometimes appointed persons who were surprisingly young. This has since raised the question whether he looked for yes men. And it is true that he preferred colleagues who would say Yes to the aim of honors work; why threaten his program by bringing in opponents? But if he favored youth, it was not because he wanted rubber stamps, but rather because he believed that administrators commonly succeeded through a kind of knack or flair more than through experience or training. This could be recognized early.

No sooner was he President-elect than he had to fill the positions of Dean and Dean of Women and this time chose a man and a woman not much younger than himself: Raymond Walters, Registrar of Lehigh and one of its alumni, and Ethel Brewster, already Acting Dean of Women, a Swarthmore graduate, and a dedicated teacher of Latin. Raymond Walters was an editor of *School and Society*, well acquainted with the field of education and also with the press. Warm-hearted and enthusiastic, he was a "horse for work," the President's words of praise. Ethel Brewster, equally energetic, had been familiar with Swarthmore mores since she was a freshman in 1905. She could give useful pointers to the two newcomers. Unlike them, she was cautious and a worrier. "Someone probably ought to worry," said Frank Aydelotte. "Better Ethel Brewster than I." He liked to tease her by suggesting something preposterous and watching her react in the alarmed belief that she must save him and the college from disaster.

The Deans divided responsibilities for students, Dean Walters for the men and Dean Brewster for the women: admissions, course advising, room assignments, problems of health and welfare. Each had a few all-college functions: Dean Walters took charge of records, publicity, and editing publications; Dean Brewster managed the Calendar, arrangements for meetings, and social regulations. It was also her privilege to accompany the President to meetings of the Board of Managers, according to the Quaker custom of representing a mixed group, like the Swarthmore faculty, with a man and a woman.

In his work on the budget, the President found that college finances needed to be centralized in one office and appointed as Comptroller an old friend from Indiana University, Nicholas O. Pittenger, as confident of his devotion to academic needs as of his skill in balancing the budget. "Pitt" had built up a flourishing book store at Indiana, where he had also managed the university dining room and dormitories with a like success. A country boy, he had grown into a tall, lank man with a Lincolnian air and a gift for pithy sayings and homespun wisdom. Having worked hard for years to put himself through Indiana University while he helped support brothers and sisters, he greatly prized his education, especially for what a humanist would call "enlargement of mind." He liked to quote a Hoosier farmer's boy who said, "I went to college to get something to think about while I follow the mules." Frank was devoted to Pitt as a friend and admired his canny management and his talent for getting along with students, especially for helping those with overdue bills earn money to pay them; above all, for making his first concern in a budget the "educational value to the students." He prided himself on never cutting a budget "solely for the sake of cutting it," implying that such economies might be expected of a Comptroller!

The President had a sharp eye for promising young men assistants, who justified his confidence by their work at Swarthmore and in later positions elsewhere. Among them was Detlev Bronk, first Associate Dean of Men, who left soon to become Director of the Johnson Foundation of the University of Pennsylvania Medical School, later President of Johns Hopkins University, and Rockefeller University. After him Alan Valentine, briefly in the Rhodes Trust Office and Dean of Men before going, as we have noted, to Yale as the first Master of Pierson College, then to Rochester as President of the University. John W. Nason, assistant in both the Rhodes and the President's offices, followed Frank as President (1940–1953), resigning to become Head of the Foreign Policy Association. Ten years later he returned to academic life as President of his Alma Mater, Carleton College.

Two young men who assisted Frank Aydelotte in the Rhodes Trust Office in Princeton, Courtney Smith and Gilmore Stott, eventually moved to Swarthmore. Gilmore Stott went first as a teacher of philosophy. Courtney Smith followed John Nason as President, taking the Rhodes Trust Office with him, and Stott served as his right-hand man in both offices while continuing to teach philosophy. A third assistant in the Princeton Rhodes office, James Hester, became President of New York University. Another of Frank Aydelotte's jewels was Henry Moe, whose first job after he returned from Oxford was to organize the Guggenheim Fellowships, eventually becoming President of the Foundation and recipient of many honors. With the exception of Detlev Bronk, all these men were old Rhodes Scholars, a group to which the American Secretary deserved to have the inside track.

He was equally good at finding secretaries who were technically perfect, tireless workers, at their best in emergencies, and devoted to their jobs. Two outstanding ones: Emma Abbett, whom he appointed in Washington for the War Issues Course, took to M.I.T. and then to Swarthmore, was with him for a total of twenty-two years; Elsa Palmer Jenkins, wife of Howard Jenkins, professor of engineering, and mother of four children, was secretary in the Rhodes Trust Office for Frank Aydelotte's last sixteen years. "He made us feel that what we were doing was so important," she remarked, in words that help explain his hold on his staff.

Young men who had not worked with Frank Aydelotte but simply seen him in action felt rewarded by what they had learned. Maurice Cramer, a schoolmate of William Aydelotte's and a frequent house guest, said he could recognize in administrators scattered over the country traits that they had at least partially absorbed from Frank Aydelotte—his "optimism and resourcefulness" and his generous warmth toward those he worked with. When Maurice himself became the chairman of the humanities staff of thirty or forty teachers at the University of Chicago, he remembers often asking himself how Aydelotte would have dealt with a situation. He was sure that Bill, too, had learned from his father the importance of a painstaking search in making appointments; he did it so well during a year as visiting professor and acting chairman of the history department at the University of Iowa that he was invited to stay and drop both temporary titles. Tom Jones, President of Earlham and of Fiske, told Maurice he had asked Frank Aydelotte how to be a college President, had discussed finances with him, and had learned much of value; indeed, Jones seemed to Maurice to have Frank's manner of conducting discussions. All agreed that Frank was one President who kept the faculty point of view. He wanted to make Swarthmore the kind of place where he would have liked to teach.

Initiating New Members

He seemed casual in his way of training a novice, preferring to let him see what to do rather than to tell him. Often the President would ask the newcomer's help, and they would jointly plan a program, thinking out the details together. Or the President would seek advice on a letter he had written. He was not easily pleased with his own efforts of this kind and would have a letter typed again and again until it was right. "Form letters," he deplored as not precisely appropriate for anyone. And after helping to revise the President's letter, his associates were less inclined to send out loose ones of their own.

A young colleague, encouraged to take a question to the President, found him ready to give it his full attention. In my own office, the perennial and most delicate problems had to do with women's admissions. We might have to reject candidates who were at the head of their class in high school, but still below our highest group. I would show him a complaining letter from parents or principals, inclined myself at first to argue the case, to point out where the student had not measured up to the best. The President saved me from such a mistake: "You can never persuade these people that their girls could have fallen down in anything. All you can say is that of course they're wonderful, but the ones we took are more wonderful still." Sometimes, when I felt uncomfortably like St. Peter at the heavenly gate, the President would restore my perspective by a facetious remark. Once, just before we sent out notices of our action on applications, he asked me to comment on the top group of rejections, which would surely bring some protests directly to him. I spoke sorrowfully about losing these girls, describing their talents so warmly that he finally stopped me. "Look here," he said, "why shouldn't we just exchange these lists, and accept the second lot?"

Delegating Responsibility

A college President faces a difficulty when he delegates responsibility; he wants to show confidence in his assistants by not checking up on what he has turned over to them and yet must keep in touch with their progress. Aydelotte solved the problem through the simple friendliness of a small community where he might come across staff members several times a day. He "took an interest." When one of my seasonal occupations was editing the college catalogue, at about the time I should have it well in hand he would stop me in the hall and ask, "How's the catalogue going?" He asked it eagerly, with the air of expecting good news. Or he would remark to his staff in general, "Be sure to let me know what you're doing so I can back you up." Since that was what he did, his assistants felt repaid for keeping him informed.

Having delegated responsibility, a President may be guilty of two kinds of lapse: he may override an assistant's decisions; he may forget whom he has asked to do something and assign it to someone else. The first occurred only once in my experience with Frank Aydelotte. I was in charge of Collection programs and had asked a woman member of the faculty to talk about some work she was doing in Philadelphia. Apparently the President felt she lacked force and would be dull. Having to choose between overruling an assistant for once and inflicting probable boredom on the whole college, he decided quickly to suggest a substitute—then changed the subject. I did not enjoy breaking the news to my speaker, but fortunately she seemed relieved. When he lapsed in assigning a particular job to one person only, it was generally on minor matters and in the haste of leaving for a business trip. Sometimes he would tell more than one of his four women helpers in Parrish Hall to do so and so. (The four were his two secretaries, the House Director, and the Dean of Women.) The first time I saw one of the others doing what he had asked me to do, I was aghast at having lost the President's confidence. After I learned what had happened, I always compared notes on last-minute instructions. If two or more of us had been assigned the same task, we could draw lots!

Qualities as a Colleague

Everyone enjoyed working with the President because somehow he made our enterprises exhilarating. This was a natural gift which he guarded by a determination to have no truck with dullness. Dullness he saw as a creeping infection, and he took drastic precautions against it, as in the case above. He would not call any meeting unless he could make it lively, sometimes by the sheer speed of putting it through. He would analyze issues briskly, hold discussion to the point, keep everyone alert.

We enjoyed our work, again, because he expected a great deal of us and was ready with appreciation. We found ourselves rising to occasions in a way to surprise and delight us. The President handled the affairs of office much as he played golf, always hoping to top his past score, and his pleasure in the game was contagious.

At the same time it must be admitted that he was inclined to expect more of us than was comfortable. Left to himself, he would have preferred not to have an official closing hour for any office. The Deans usually did stay on to organize their plans for the next day. But on Saturday, when our offices were supposedly shut at noon, the Deans' secretaries liked to leave punctually enough to catch the only convenient train to Philadelphia. Often about half past twelve, the President would come into our outer office, look around, and say in a puzzled way, "Where *is* everybody?"

Because the Deans, following the President's example expected to answer the call of duty whenever it might sound, the college telephone operator would not hesitate to give me the call in the middle of Saturday or Sunday afternoon, or even on Labor Day, saying that parents with a daughter had dropped into Parrish Hall, hoping to talk to someone about admissions. Swarthmore under Aydelotte was not likely to disappoint them. It must be confessed that we took some pride in being like dependable old fire-engine horses, ready to leap into harness at the sound of a gong.

Sometimes the call of duty came from the President himself, long after office hours, requiring instant breaking of a social engagement. This might seem hard to a young man with a charming wife, dressed to go out to a gala dinner. Of one such young man Mrs. Aydelotte said to me in a tone of satisfaction, "He has begun not to mind breaking engagements when Frank needs him." From seasoned members of the staff there was no protest.

In any work with the President, we could count on pleasant personal relations. No one could be more courteous to his co-workers. Gilmore Stott observes that he never gave orders.

> I cannot remember that . . . Frank Aydelotte ever told me to do anything in any form approaching the imperative mood; he would simply describe a state of affairs—several times if necessary!—and in a happy penumbra of "I'd be very grateful if so and so" and "warmest thanks for such and such," those of us who have been his associates have found ourselves catching his vision and pursuing his plan.

If we had not caught his vision, what then? Courtney Smith had the answer: "He would have kept coming back." He kept the way open for coming back by avoiding what less diplomatic people liked to do; he did not "take a firm stand," did not "bring things to a head." Since he exerted none of the pressure which arouses resistance, we were the more ready to accept his line, particularly after reflecting how right he had generally been.

It was characteristic of him to ignore anything that had gone wrong if it could not be corrected. "He didn't notice what shouldn't be noticed," said Gilmore Stott. One instance of this tact on the part of both the Aydelottes. They had planned an unusually festive reception to follow a lecture by the Master of Balliol College, A. D. Lindsay, inviting appropriate dignitaries from Philadelphia. But when they brought the speaker home, they saw only faculty members responsible for arrangements. No one else came. No one had sent regrets. The host and hostess carried it off so well that those present thought no more than that they were privileged to be included in a small party. Two weeks later Mrs. Aydelotte found all the invitations addressed and stamped. They had been ready for mailing well ahead of time and stowed away by a secretary who had forgotten to come back for them. Relieved to know what had happened, they decided not to say anything about it. "You've been working her too hard," said Mrs. Aydelotte. "After this, I'll check on mailings."

On rare occasions the President spoke sharply to a young colleague who had made a blunder which should not be repeated. Once when I called a meeting of instructors in a new kind of course to ask what they thought of it, he scolded me for not seeing them one at a time. "There wasn't enough business to be interesting," he said. He made the rebuke so impersonally as to leave no scar. Habitually he kept what someone described as "a pleasant distance," aloof from the kind of involvement which takes offense or, at the other end of the spectrum, demands personal devotion. While he did expect a great deal of his colleagues, what he asked was not loyalty to himself, but the loyalty of a team to the college. "He was conscious of himself as an instrument," said Courtney Smith. And Albert Einstein said of him to Mrs. Aydelotte: "It is rare to find someone who is devoted and independent and without vanity."

The Art of Saving Time

To use his time economically was a necessity for a man who wanted to do so much. Frank Aydelotte made it also an art. His son remembers one of his methods: to avoid anything routine. "He liked to limit his efforts to creative work, to solving a problem. . . . I recall his saying that it was his practice to do a thing only once, for the first time, and that when it had to be done again he would leave it for someone else to do." When routine was the business of a meeting, he stayed away. This happened even when he was chairman. He let someone else conduct meetings of the Instruction Committee called to consider student petitions connected with honors work. This practice of his struck me only recently in rereading committee minutes when I noted where his name did not appear among those present. Then I remembered his excusing himself fairly often: "Can you manage without me today?" he would say. "So and so is coming down." Apparently he preferred not to declare a principle for his absences which might irritate those of us for whom there was no such escape.

His power to concentrate and to see when to make quick decisions helped him use his time to advantage. He could be so completely absorbed in the moment as to forget even the triumphs of the day before. Less than twenty-four hours after a Board meeting where all his proposals had been approved, I congratulated him on "the fine meeting." "Meeting?" he repeated politely. "The Managers' " I said, "where everything went so well." "Oh yes," he said, breaking into a grin, "that was yesterday." When questions were brought to him, he recognized instantly which could be answered at once—commonly those having to do with practical arrangements. If someone asked his approval of a program for a group of visitors, he would read it, call Emma Abbett to bring her "shorthand book," and dictate necessary memoranda in his caller's presence. The program was launched, and he could forget it.

Fortunately he recognized equally well a decision he could not make quickly—one involving complicated adjustments, especially of personalities. He would feel his way, ask advice, reach a tentative decision, change his mind, until he finally saw his course. At that point he took time to tell anyone who had a share in an abandoned project that he had given it up. This prevented the disappointments likely to bring against a President the charge that "he always agrees with the last man he talks to."

Now and then he saved time somewhat disreputably by breaking engagements to speak away from Swarthmore. He would accept more invitations than anyone should undertake, partly because he hated to refuse what seemed at the moment a reasonable request, partly from an insatiable interest in a host of educational and international topics. Occasionally, he had to cancel because he had caught a cold from overwork. But I am thinking rather of occasions when he dispatched a telegram saying simply that he regretted his inability to keep an appointment. His son thinks "this gave him a feeling of liberation and of time gained: it was a way in which he could shake himself free of existing commitments." Was this in the spirit of the half-whimsical essay he had written long before when he was teaching at Indiana, "On Not Doing One's Duty"? Or was he showing devotion under dubious circumstances to a value which he placed in his highest category: spontaneity, indispensable to any kind of creative thought?

Another of his interests might seem incompatible with saving time: to be easily accessible. In the close quarters of a small college he thought it would be absurd to have to make an appointment with the President weeks in advance. If teachers or students had to wait so long, they would be likely not to come at all. So he introduced the practice of sandwiching in an appointment on the very day it was requested. The usual result was that a caller came eagerly and gratefully, resolved to be brief. This, in fact, did save the President's time in the long run and made the system work. Often after five minutes or less, his caller went away, amazed at what had been settled.

When outsiders dropped in unexpectedly, they also saw the President for a moment before being handed over to someone else. They could not resent this, having arrived unannounced, and usually found the substitute appropriate. If a father had come to talk about his daughter's admission and insisted on seeing the President, he would soon find himself ushered into my office by the President himself, who would say with a twinkle, "Here's the person who really knows about these things."

Relations with Students

Anything important to the students interested the President: athletics, fraternities, and other "activities," better food in the college dining room and better orchestras for college dances. He seized opportunities to hear their opinions, expecting them to be sound. He enjoyed their gaiety and high spirits. But above all he prized evidence of intellectual ability and took pains to show his feeling.

James Perkins, '34, later President of Cornell University, remembers when he first noticed this Aydelotte trait at the beginning of his freshman year. He and a classmate, Ben Moore, were crossing the campus one evening when Frank Aydelotte suddenly appeared. "He squinted at us in that owlish manner that was his trademark and said, 'I hear you boys did very well in the placement examinations; congratulations!' " The boys were pleased and startled. How did he know their names and ratings? How extraordinary for him to take the trouble to speak about them! Then they realized that "to Aydelotte it was a first-priority matter" to know who had done well in the examinations and "to seek them out" and congratulate them. "Immediately and forever it was clear that this college gave top priority to the intellectual development of its students. The President could not have said anything that would have been equally convincing."[7]

James Perkins was right that the President wanted to know which freshmen had started well. He always asked the Deans to make a list of holders of good scholarships and high test ratings and took pains to remember them. Sometimes he studied photographs of an incoming class in the Dean's files. The relation between President and students *should* be personal, he thought, and often *could* be in a small college.

He and his wife took a first step toward a personal relation with freshmen by inviting them to their house early in the year. As seniors the class came again for a farewell luncheon. Meanwhile some of them would have seen the President with student committees whom he consulted, but all had a chance to understand what he thought important by hearing him speak at "Collection."

Collection, the student assembly with required attendance, was held daily in his first years, later once a week. Many of the faculty attended, sitting on the platform with the President, who usually presided and often spoke.

On one occasion he discussed the purpose of Collection, to serve as "a kind of unifying point for the College," a place for contributions "to the great subject of what education means in this college, what the college stands for, what are our ideals for the undergraduate program and for life outside." Such a program he took to be "essentially religious," his test of religion being not dogma, but deeds.

Everything I say to you from this platform I stand behind as a part of my religion. I am a good deal more interested in the religion which is acted through the week than in that which is preached on Sundays, and it is my hope that Collection may have some influence on the religion which we as faculty and student body act out in our daily lives.[8]

He implies here what becomes clear in his talks at Collection and also in his Baccalaureate addresses, that religion meant for him not theology, but the serious concern for morality—ideals of personality and conceptions of the ends of life. He spoke on "Intensity," "Intellectual Curiosity," "Serious Athletics," with references at Baccalaureate to service with a humanitarian slant. It was significant of his regard for sports, rightly played, that he called attention more than once to the moral training gained from athletics: "lessons of . . . scrupulous fairness, of generosity to opponents and of self control in crucial situations"—in a word, the "civilized virtue" of sportsmanship.

At the first Collection of his first year, an occasion when he could expect an attentive audience, he discussed the virtue of intensity, citing as an example the football player's concentration of energy in order to play at the top of his form. If he finds himself falling short, he does not resort to excuses, but settles down to harder effort. This experience suggests the pattern for achieving intellectual excellence as well. "If we can all of us, Freshman and Senior, student and faculty alike, live and work with the same intensity of effort which makes athletic sports so valuable a part of our moral training, my first wish for the College will be fulfilled."[9]

His second Collection wish was for intellectual curiosity, the trait which impelled a person to keep on asking questions and go on learning. In two Baccalaureate addresses he told the seniors what perspective he hoped they had gained on their education. First, a sense of *noblesse oblige:* through the advantages of their college training they had incurred a debt of service to society. "You may serve society by your cleverness, by your knowledge, by your technical skill; but you will serve best, be your walk in life high or low, by your humanity—by that understanding of the motives of others and that willingness to cooperate with them which alone makes society possible."[10] For another senior class his wish was that they had gained an ideal which would hold their lifelong loyalty: "The most precious thing in life is to spend your efforts, to give unity to your personality and to your career, in the service of some ideal which will last beyond you."[11]

While he planned his talks carefully, he usually did not write them out, preferring to speak to the students directly. A secretary was generally on hand to take down what he said. He rarely said anything humorous, but his seriousness was not solemn; rather, lightened by his tone of exulting in a challenge. Students spoke of being impressed by his "moral authority," his acceptance of "moral absolutes in the universe," and they found his talks "singularly appealing," an "inspiriting experience."

At times students attended Friends' Meeting in the hope that the President would be present and speak. He rarely spoke first, preferring to develop someone else's idea, often waiting until the end of a meeting to bring the train of thought as a whole into unity. Older members of Meeting wished he were "more religious," more inclined to speak about Christian doctrines or the Scriptures. But students generally responded to his emphasis on self-discipline and service.

On one of the few occasions when he taught a course, he made an impression which a student described vividly thirty years later, moved to do so after his death by the lack among many tributes of any reference to his teaching. The student was Marion Hall, '29; the course on some of his favorite nineteenth-century writers. He was usually late, she remembered.

> In he came, coattails flying. Came? Blew. Strode. Exploded. . . . He took long fast steps from the door to the low platform. . . . There was always a pause . . . while he shuffled papers and caught his breath, and everybody got very very quiet. Then he started. He grasped the upper edges of the lectern, a hand on each side, and leaned forward across it, and started talking. . . . It was good stuff, solid stuff, but there was no art in it. . . . It was straight exposition, and it was up to you to follow if you could. . . . I can't remember a thing about his lectures on Huxley or Ruskin, and very little on Arnold. But Carlyle! . . . Perhaps it was just that it is easier to strike sparks with Carlyle, than with, say, Ruskin. But I remember the sparks. . . . There was . . . a sort of electricity; he communicated excitement. You took it in with more than your mind: you could feel it on the back of your neck, like poetry.

Marion concluded with a comparison of a teacher and an educator which Frank Aydelotte would have accepted, perhaps with a pang at not having chosen the better part: "I am very glad I took the course, because a good teacher is personal to you, and an educator is not. And he was a good teacher."[12]

In day-to-day contacts, President and students remained on good terms, even when they did not see precisely eye to eye. His frankness in stating where he stood pleased the students. When he said that he was "socially conservative" and expected the college to be so, in the interests of the greatest "intellectual freedom," they might not agree, but respected his forthrightness. The *Phoenix* reported what he did and said, always fairly and sometimes with enthusiasm. When he announced that the Men's Student Government was "on trial"[13] because they hesitated to enforce their own ruling against sophomores who indulged in "physical intimidation" of freshmen, the reporter simply asked whether the President implied a threat, intimating that he might have left the men in greater freedom to make their own decision. After a suitable resolution censuring the sophomores had been passed by the Men's Student Government, the story went around that someone asked the President whether they were no longer "on trial." To which he replied, "They're always on trial when they take any action," adding with a grin, "just like the President."

He surprised and amused the college by inventing ingenious penalties for misdemeanors outside the jurisdiction of Student Government. When some freshmen showed less than fitting respect for works of art by smearing mustaches on Benjamin West's paintings of gods and godlings, he first made sure that the daubs could be easily removed, then set the culprits to writing papers based on a little research in art history, promising to read them himself.

Sometimes he regarded a student prank as a game he too could play. Finding a Ford coupé in the front hall of Parrish, he startled onlookers by seizing the wheel, asking them to push the car so that he could drive it down the front steps. He descended in a series of controlled bumps and climbed out at the bottom, saying gleefully, "I've always wanted to do that. It worked, just as I thought, to brake hard on every step."

While such stories gave students a sudden glimpse of a friendly, amusing human being, he was still to most of them a "remote and legendary figure," according to an account by an alumnus, Laurence Lafore, '38, of his own undergraduate impressions.

> With the few students whom business or chance brought into contact with him, he was incredibly friendly and informal; he met them . . . on terms which suggested that the student and his ideas and work were of great importance to him and to the College. I remember hearing about the experience of one student from England, who had fallen ill just before the Christmas holidays and had spent them in the President's house. The

rest of us were astounded by the reports of Mr. Aydelotte's interest, and by the fact that he had spent hours discussing life and the world with the sick freshman. It was as if we had heard that Jupiter had sat down for a serious talk on theology with a Roman slave.

But for most of us he was remote. Despite that remoteness the students were intensely aware of him. He had placed his stamp not only upon the College but upon our view and knowledge of it. Not all the undergraduates of my day approved of what he stood for. There were complaints on the one hand about what were thought of as excessively high standards and the "intellectualism" bred of honors work; and on the other hand, complaints about the President's conservatism, even conventionality in social affairs. But all of us shared, I think, in the enthusiasm for what we knew to be an "adventure in education." And all of us, even the critics, felt that this was Aydelotte's college, that he had made it what it was and that, in a sense, he was making the students what they were. His personality and philosophy were pervasive as well as Jove-like.

The criticisms of his policies which were heard among undergraduates were always upon the level of abstract and impersonal, even philosophical, discussion, which I think would have been a satisfaction to him. We argued about his Collection speeches the way we might have argued in an honors seminar, the way he himself might have argued. There was never, I believe, any question in the mind of any undergraduate about his personal power or integrity, or, I am tempted to say, majesty. He was immune from the carping and complaints and the disrespect of superiors which is the pride and birthright of college students.[14]

It is the custom at Swarthmore for each class to publish a yearbook, the *Halcyon*, in the spring of their junior year, with a dedication to a favorite member of the community—to Frank Aydelotte at the end of his first year and his last. While both dedications show sincere feeling for the President, there is a striking difference between the almost childish baldness of the first and the more mature perceptiveness of the second—a difference that would seem to represent a change in the quality of student life which took place in his administration.

In 1922 the Class of 1923 expressed "its unlimited appreciation of his interest in the Student Body and the welfare of the College." In 1940 the inscription ran: "Appreciative of our good fortune in coming to Swarthmore at a time when his graciousness and sincere enthusiasm have influenced every phase of our college life, we, the Class of 1941, dedicate our *Halcyon* to Frank Aydelotte and his Swarthmore."

Relation to the Board of Managers

At Swarthmore, as at most educational institutions, the President's relationship to the Board of Managers was complex and delicate. The Board had final authority on two important points: the President's tenure of office and the control of college finances. The Board had appointed him and at any time could ask for his resignation. Because they had charge of investments and could give or withhold approval of his budget, they had power of life and death over his educational policies. At the same time, recognizing that they were not experts in academic matters, they looked to him for leadership. He must educate them to an understanding of his plans for the college and so earn their official support.

When Frank Aydelotte took office, all the Board of eighteen men and fourteen women were Quakers, and most of them had been students at Swarthmore. They were bound by conscience and loyalty to take their duties seriously. A lay group, including only one professional educator, the retiring President, Joseph Swain, the majority of the men were in business, connected with substantial firms in building, banking, retail trade, hotel keeping, publishing, and horticulture. Some of the women had once taught, but now as public-spirited wives of prosperous husbands gave their time generously to Quaker good works. The Managers brought the common sense of intelligent, well-disposed men and women to bear on college problems.

As the President was ex officio a member of every Board committee, he saw small groups of Managers often. Once a month either the full Board or half its members who constituted the Executive Committee held a meeting at Swarthmore, attended by the President and the Dean of Women. The President was the focus of interest at every session, constantly consulted on committee reports, finally taking the floor to give an account of the state of the college. He would draw a lively picture of able teachers, clever students, and distinguished visitors from Europe, mingling in a stimulating atmosphere where discussion thrived. The Managers enjoyed his reports and listened with keen attention and respect to his discussions of education. They also liked him as a man, and several became his close personal friends.

On the rare occasions when there was a serious difference between the Board and the President, it rose from the traditional conflict of aims which had not been wholly resolved by Joseph Swain. Some members might object to an emphasis they thought overintellectual, representing ambition for worldly recognition rather than service to the Society of Friends. Fortunately there was a group, including the President of the Corporation, Wilson M. Powell, who usually carried conviction that both ends were being pursued successfully.

Wilson Powell gave Frank Aydelotte strong support during the ten years when they worked closely together and became one of his greatest friends. A graduate of Harvard and a distinguished New York lawyer, Powell combined Quaker integrity and forthrightness with unusual knowledge of academic progress in other institutions and the will to meet the highest standards at Swarthmore. Also, as a man of the world, it has already been said that he wanted the college to be mindful of the quality of its social life, easily convincing the Aydelottes to add to the amenities. William Aydelotte retains some boyish memories on this point. When the two families spent several summers near each other, linen napkins replaced paper when Wilson came to lunch; and years later, on the sad occasion of Wilson Powell's death, Frank returned from the memorial service to report that "it was just as Wilson would have wanted—all the ushers in morning coats."

At this service, Frank paid affectionate and eloquent tribute to Powell as a friend and a trustee:

> I count as one of the great privileges of my life the years of my association with Wilson Powell, in an educational enterprise which lay so near the hearts of both of us that friendship and official relations were intermingled and neither of us knew where the one began and the other left off.... I sometimes think that the conception of the duties of a trustee as Wilson Powell exemplified them represent America's finest contribution to the ideal of unselfish public service.[15]

Other members of the Board also were the Aydelottes' warm friends, seeking them out as companions for a vacation or a game. Dr. Edward Martin, brilliant Philadelphia surgeon, their neighbor in Media and affectionate guardian of their health, invited them to stay with him and his wife in Florida for many a delightful winter month. Later Henry Turner, able construction engineer, was also a Florida host for the Aydelottes. Charles F. Jenkins, editor of the *Farm Journal*, who followed Wilson Powell as President of the Corporation, went with his wife to Spain to travel with the Aydelottes and often entertained them at Buck Hill. Claude Smith, fellow Hoosier and golf enthusiast, relished Frank's zest and skill in matches of the Quaker "Ozone Club."

Relations with Alumni

Swarthmore alumni had their first opportunity to hear the President-elect when he visited the college on Alumni Day, June 11, 1921. He spoke at their banquet, leaving a happy impression of warmth and sincerity. Paying tribute to his predecessors, he praised Joseph Swain, his good friend since his student years at Indiana, and quoted Edward Magill's autobiography as the basis of appreciative comments on Swarthmore tradition. Edward Magill had raised Swarthmore standards, while limiting his sights to what could be effectively done. In both lines the new President hoped to follow. "Whether we have many students or few, whether we teach many subjects or few is not so important as that we should truly educate those we admit."[16] After the banquet he departed, feeling that the retiring President's last Commencement should be his alone.

Every year Frank Aydelotte visited alumni groups, giving news of the college and sketching plans for the future. He urged them to come to Swarthmore and say what they thought of it. "Alumni serve their college as much by taking an active interest as by giving money." This was a new line from a college President, and the alumni liked it.

He was on more slippery ground when he discussed new policies in athletics. Having accepted the presidency on condition that financial subsidies to athletes should be banned, he had gone on to emphasize sports for everyone, instead of giving first place to developing teams to win games with other colleges. No question but that these moves, taken together, would end forever what some alumni regarded as the "great days" when Swarthmore had a record of victories in football over Columbia, Cornell, Pennsylvania, and the Navy, all in a single year. These alumni were not mollified by the President's hope of attracting athletes who were primarily good students through a system of scholarships similar to the Rhodes plan, based on the requirement of a distinguished academic record combined with force of character, leadership, and the physical vigor to do well in sports.

Before the end of his first February, Frank Aydelotte found a "friend of the college" to give funds for an experiment with scholarships of this kind, five a year, each with an annual stipend of $500 for four years—unusually large for those days. They were called "Open Scholarships" because anyone could compete. On the campus a rumor flew that the generous "friend" was an alumnus who had formerly been keen to support good athletes, but was now beguiled by the idea of discovering bright boys who might also shine on a team. Alumni skeptics would reserve approval until teams including Open Scholars showed the right proportion of victories.

Of course, alumni in general could not fail to be proud of Swarthmore's growing recognition, but some of them would have been glad if it had depended less on intellectual achievements. Their attitude was natural in those years when students with strong academic interests were in the minority in most colleges and not much admired. It was only after the alumni body had absorbed generations of graduates who had come through the honors program themselves or had witnessed its stimulating effect on the whole college that alumni opinion could be expected to view the new emphasis on ideas with enthusiasm. Then alumni doubt gave way to pride.

Alumni and Managers, faculty and students, constituted what Frank Aydelotte once called the "Four Horse Team."[17] Thanks to his skill and good will in working with them severally, the team usually pulled together.

CHAPTER ELEVEN

THE START AT SWARTHMORE

1921–1925

The Adventure with Honors Courses

AFTER the inauguration the last delegate had scarcely departed when Frank Aydelotte was waited upon by members of the faculty who were completely in sympathy with his idea of an honors program, asking, "When do we begin?" At once he appointed a committee to lay plans for the following September, but two irrepressibly lively teachers, R. C. Brooks in political science and Jesse Holmes in philosophy, decided to make a trial run.

Hearing that honors students might be taught in small groups like graduate seminars, they decided to test this method the very next semester in two small senior courses. Each course met once a week, leaving the students otherwise in "unprecedented freedom" to read at their own rate. As both teachers were adept at leading discussion, their experiment proved to be the best possible advertisement for honors courses. When plans for the next year were announced, the *Phoenix* could say that the honors method was already in use and heartily approved: "The higher value of the new plan as estimated by students who are now studying under both the old and new systems, promises well of any arrangement that may be made to extend this program."[1]

Frank chuckled over his faculty's jumping the gun, pleased with their initiative. He had wanted the experiment to begin in a small way, involving at every stage only teachers and students who felt ready and eager for it. This was particularly important for the instructors of the first years when they undertook the new kind of teaching in addition to a full schedule and with no extra salary. He hoped they would volunteer and regard the work as a privilege.

The program was launched in 1922–1923 in two Divisions: English
Literature, comprising English, history, and philosophy; the Social Sciences, political science, economics, history, and philosophy.[2] In the first
year there were four teachers, including the two who had made the trial
run, all of them unusual personalities.

Robert Clarkson Brooks, promoter in chief of honors work and its
first historian, professor of political science and authority on Swiss government, was a stocky man with the rolling gait of a sea captain; he had
copious firsthand information about the Democratic party, even to the
unsavory goings-on of some of its bosses. Jesse Holmes, professor of
philosophy with a doctorate in chemistry, Quaker from Nebraska who
said "thee" to students, was called "Ducky," not always behind his back.
Jesse, with his twinkling eyes, wind-blown gray hair, and sturdy look of
a mountain climber, several times Socialist candidate for Governor of
Pennsylvania, was a lively and unsentimental speaker in Friends' Meetings
and a popular Chautauqua lecturer. William Isaac Hull, Quaker professor
of history with emphasis on international relations and the Society of
Friends, followed pacifist principles with a quiet inflexibility, combined
with a surprising reputation for rivaling Jehu when he drove a car.
Harold Clarke Goddard, perceptive and subtle professor of English,
devoted to good music, Russian novels, and Thoreau, had a gift for the
right word in a literary judgment and in the appraisal of a student,
personal or intellectual. Of many members of the faculty who responded
to the President's hope for honors work, these four were in a position to
go ahead at once.

At the beginning a few principles were accepted. Honors work
should be restricted to the two upper classes and should replace the usual
program of five courses meeting fifteen hours a week. Instead of "taking
courses," an honors student would "study subjects," reading extensively
from bibliographies provided by his teachers and writing frequent essays
based on his reading. With this greater freedom he would be required to
meet severer standards. In place of course examinations at the end of
each semester, the measure of his achievement would be a special set of
comprehensive examinations, written and oral, at the end of his two
years' work.

One question left open briefly had to do with method of teaching:
individual tutorials versus small seminars. The impromptu experiments
by Professors Brooks and Holmes helped to bring in a verdict for
seminars as affording stimulating discussion, made all the livelier if two

teachers were on hand to exchange opinions and show students how to argue a case. Professor Brooks urged this practice, which remained in vogue until instructors felt they needed all their time for their own seminars. Another question, on the degree of specialization desirable for undergraduates, was answered in favor of variety with unity: a student's honors program should combine related subjects, probably three or four, which would support each other in an integrated whole. The model here was Modern Greats at Oxford (known as P.P.E.)—political science, philosophy, and economics. Again with Oxford as the model, it was agreed that honors examiners should be, not the students' own teachers, but members of the faculty in other institutions—"external examiners."

In the first year eleven students were accepted: eight juniors beginning the regular two years' work; three seniors who had talked their teachers into letting them have the one year possible. These three studied political science, philosophy, and economics and took their examinations in these subjects. The proposed use of external examiners, an unfamiliar practice in American education, seemed dubious to some of the faculty. They could not feel sure that strangers would do the students justice. Frank Aydelotte himself was convinced that they would not only be fair to students but prove useful to the faculty as objective critics of a novel enterprise. If they were enthusiastic about it, they could be useful again in forwarding its reputation. But he wanted the faculty to be equally convinced and so was ready to compromise. In this first year, 1923, one examiner was a member of the Swarthmore faculty, R. C. Brooks, and there were only two from outside.

Those two seem to have been chosen as much for their prestige and friendliness as for their objectivity. One was Harry A. Overstreet, professor of philosophy at the College of the City of New York, a student at Balliol in 1899—a warm, sympathetic person and a teacher and writer with enthusiastic followers. The other, J. Russell Smith, professor of economic geography at Columbia, member of the Society of Friends and one of its most distinguished educators, belonged to the Swarthmore Meeting and lived on the edge of the campus. The examiners sent questions and received students' papers by mail, then joined Professor Brooks at Swarthmore for oral examinations. They agreed that no one of the three candidates deserved First Honors; two should receive Second Honors and one Third Honors. (These ratings were soon replaced by the more attractive Highest Honors, High Honors, and Honors.) Their decisions seemed fair to the Swarthmore faculty and their presence so stimulating that by common consent all honors examiners thereafter were "external." They lived up to expectation.

Incidentally, external examiners improved the relation between honors students and their instructors. The students soon saw that these strangers were passing judgment on teachers as well as taught and came quickly to regard their fellow sufferers as allies in preparing for the common day of reckoning.

In the second and third experimental years the growth was satisfactory: from the original number of eleven students to eighteen, then to thirty; from two Divisions to four (adding French, and Mathematics, Astronomy, and Physics) and in the third year a fifth, Classics. Meanwhile the program became famous somewhat prematurely. After only one year, it was placed in a fierce light of publicity when the National Research Council asked Frank Aydelotte to edit a survey of honors courses throughout the country. The Council sent questionnaires to member institutions of the Association of American Colleges and Universities, the returns to be analyzed by the editor. His report, published in January, 1924, carried a preface by Vernon Kellogg: "President Aydelotte's name gives the report a special prestige because of his well-known large personal knowledge of both English and American honors systems and his devoted efforts to introduce into American college and university practice more particular attention to the individual student."[3]

The report included brief accounts of forty-five honors programs. Eight of these besides Swarthmore replaced the regular curriculum with one redesigned as a whole. The other thirty-six based honors on additions to the usual courses, such as a thesis or other piece of work on an advanced level. The editor described these without comment, though convinced that no such makeshifts could provide what was needed by the abler students. A year later, when the Council asked him to prepare a second edition,[4] he found that the more adventurous class had doubled, and the other expanded from thirty-six to seventy-five. Clearly the concern to do something for the abler students was gaining strength, and in Frank's opinion, much of the credit was due to the National Research Council. In addition to their surveys of honors courses, they were publishing papers on other methods of "breaking the academic lock-step" and had sponsored a conference on the whole subject for colleges and universities in the Middle West, calling more attention to Swarthmore by inviting Frank Aydelotte to be one of the chief speakers.[5]

With this expansion of a system adapted to individual needs, it was natural to ask how far it should go. Would such instruction be profitable not only for a select group but for all students? Frank discussed this question in his *Report* of December, 1924 and offered an immediate answer based on expediency.[6] While experience at Swarthmore had shown that an unexpectedly large number of students, thirty in that year, had been attracted by honors work and had done it well, its high cost made restriction unavoidable. This being the case, he wasted no time on further discussion of what was at the moment only a theoretical question.

But even if there had been no financial obstacle to making honors work universal, I venture to suggest that he would have opposed it on other grounds. To him, honors work meant not simply an individual plan for independent study but one recognized as too difficult to be attempted by everyone. To undertake it was a distinction and an honor. To put it through successfully meant graduation *with honors*. He approved of intellectual competition and thought it more interesting among competitors who, like seeded players in a tennis tournament, were acknowledged to belong to a superior group.

Frank Aydelotte's *Annual Reports* of these four years call attention to other intellectual events: academic standards raised by limiting enrollment and by the operation of the new Open Scholarships for men; the recognition by Sigma Xi of Swarthmore's scientific work; two expeditions from the Sproul Observatory to photograph eclipses of the sun; and graduate work in astronomy and mathematics.

Improving Academic Standards

One way to improve academic standards is to admit better students. Frank saw that this was happening at Swarthmore, thanks to a highly selective admissions policy, made possible by an increase of applicants and a strictly limited enrollment. The flood of applicants resulted partly from postwar prosperity, which had sent the number of candidates soaring in many colleges all over the country. There was also a sudden special interest in Swarthmore, which sprang, no doubt, from the reputation of the honors experiment and other activities of the new President, including the experimental establishment of Open Scholarships for men.[7]

These scholarships stood out among those available to high-school seniors for their generous size and the freedom from limitations commonly imposed by donors. The stipend, $500 a year for four years, offered more than twice the annual yield of the average at Swarthmore and would cover most of the total charge of $600 for tuition, room, and board. Where donors of other scholarships were likely to stipulate that recipients should be men or women, graduates of a particular school, residents of a geographical district, members of a religious denomination, these scholarships were open to any boy on the basis of qualifications modeled on the Rhodes Scholarships: academic standing, leadership, and physical vigor.

The response in number of candidates had been astonishingly quick: in the first year, 209 competitors from 23 states. Also, since some boys who had not won scholarships could afford to come without help, they did so. In the first two years, in addition to ten Open Scholars, forty-three of the other applicants enrolled, forming a fine nucleus of unusually able men. By 1924 Frank could say that three years of competitive admission had already improved the quality of work, if judged only by the striking decrease in students who had to be dropped. He praised the admissions committees for their extensive use of the still uncommon personal interview which he had recommended on the basis of his experience in choosing Rhodes Scholars.[8] Given students whose paper records are all outstanding, a face-to-face encounter vastly helps a committee decide which have the character, energy, and what Frank called the "juice" for a program requiring independence, hard work, and spark. This implies what was the fact: that Swarthmore committees on admissions and scholarships were on the lookout for future honors students.

With such opportunities for selection, if the quality of students had *not* improved—and with it, the quality of work—both the admissions officers and the teaching staff would have felt gravely at fault.

Swarthmore Chapter of Sigma Xi

A chapter of Sigma Xi was formally installed at Swarthmore on April 27, 1923, the only chapter of the Society in a small college. The President welcomed this as a tribute to the science departments who had done research of high quality. "The acceptance of this chapter should be felt by the College as a pledge that we will do all that our resources allow to further research in Science and . . . that we shall not wish to confine our encouragement of research to Science alone but to extend it to all departments of the College."[9]

Eclipse Expeditions

The most notable research at that time was by John Miller, based on photographing total eclipses of the sun at Yerbanis in Mexico (September, 1923) and at the less exotic locale of New Haven, Connecticut (January, 1925). Frank's own part was to help raise money, since it was agreed that the expeditions should not be financed by college funds. The one to Mexico cost ten thousand dollars and six weeks' work for eleven men. Fortunately Wilson Powell was interested, contributed generously himself, and got the support of the Rubel Foundation.

Since the date when the eclipse could be observed from Yerbanis fell before college opened, a few lucky undergraduates joined the expedition. One of them wrote a full and dramatic account for the first issue of the *Phoenix*, giving the whole college a share in the hazards and excitement.[10]

Yerbanis had been chosen for the expedition's camp as a point where the duration of the total eclipse would be relatively long—three minutes— and the September weather likely to be good. Otherwise the place had no advantages: "no trees, no running water, no ice, no milk, no accommodations, poor drinking water." During the six weeks of setting up telescopes and cameras, members lived in tents they had brought with them and imported all their food and supplies.

Contrary to predictions of good weather, the expedition was almost rained out. The skies were overcast until within the hour of totality, when they cleared providentially for almost the entire three minutes, giving time to take the photographs which would be studied for information about the sun's corona of gases: its shape, chemical composition, motion, and rotation. Successful use was made also of two large Einstein cameras, each weighing over two tons, to test Einstein's theory of "the deflection of light waves that pass through distorted space." Of all the expeditions to observe this eclipse, including those from the Yerkes, Lick, and Mt. Wilson Observatories, Swarthmore had the best weather and the most satisfactory results.

Again in New Haven on January 24, 1925, Miller had his usual luck. "In spite of the unfavorable time of year and the fact that the eclipse took place at nine o'clock in the morning, weather conditions were perfect and the expedition was extraordinarily successful."[11] Students used to say that Miller was bound to be lucky since he was the sort of man that was certain to have heaven on his side.

Frank, delighted to learn something new, studied plates and reports and plied Miller with questions. Then he expounded the subject, according to the astronomers, with rather surprising accuracy.

Graduate Work in Astronomy and Mathematics

Between Miller's two expeditions the President announced that the department of mathematics and astronomy would "provide postgraduate teaching for a limited number of students."[12] This was his one stand in favor of graduate students at Swarthmore, qualified only to the extent that the number should be "limited." He expressed confidence that the work could be well done with the Sproul Observatory's "splendid equipment" and that it would help meet the demand for such training, which "exceeds the supply." He knew also what he did not mention here, that this department in the past had trained occasional graduate students successfully and could not well be denied the privilege.

Though ready to consider special cases, he was in general opposed to graduate work at Swarthmore on the ground that a small college faculty could succeed in an important enterprise only if they gave it full attention, and at that time they were already engrossed in honors work. If they tried to develop a Graduate School as well, they would risk disaster in both. For members of the faculty who needed stimulus and help in research beyond that of advanced undergraduates, why not bring in postdoctoral fellows? Later he took steps to do this in zoology and psychology.

Student Activities

The President soon showed his interest in applying what he had learned at Oxford to student activities as well as to the curriculum. In his second year at Swarthmore he gave special attention to debating and athletics.

Debating had not been one of his favorite lines at Oxford, though he had joined the Union, describing it in a letter to his mother as modeled on the House of Commons and often a proving ground for future Members of Parliament. Almost by accident he undertook to test the merits of English debating with an American audience. Hearing that the first Union debaters to come to the United States would shortly arrive, he arranged an early engagement for them at Swarthmore, described the English method to his students, and found them eager to try it. The differences, as he explained them to the Board of Managers, favored the

Union, since speakers were expected to support only causes they believed in, and audiences, having a chance to take part, were more likely to be interested.

> On the English theory, a debate is an occasion not primarily for exhibiting the argumentative skill of the speakers, but rather for influencing and ascertaining the opinions of the auditors. The decision is made not by a picked group of judges on the merits of the speaking, but by vote of the entire audience on the merits of the question. Voluntary speakers from the floor are given an opportunity to take part after the speakers on the paper have finished. It is a tradition of the English method that a man should speak according to his convictions.[13]

The common Oxford practice was not to pit one team against another, but to divide each so that two members of one joined forces with one member of the other. Accordingly, at Swarthmore two Oxford men and one Swarthmore woman supported the affirmative; two Swarthmore men and one Oxonian, the negative. The question: "Resolved, that the United States should immediately enter the League of Nations." After spirited discussion by the speakers and from the floor, the audience voted, 414 to 327, in favor of the motion. The English style made such a good impression that it was adopted at once for other debates and used for years to come.

Serious Athletics

There was nothing accidental in Frank's choice of another importation: the Oxford attitude toward sports. He had already made a point of this in the essay "Spectators and Sports" (*The Oxford Stamp*), where he took exception to the corrupting effect in America of crowds of spectators who have never been players and who are less interested in the sport or in sportmanship than in victory for their team. At Oxford, in contrast, virtually everyone played or had played some game: spectators almost ceased to exist, and such few as did appear knew how to see the game from the players' point of view. It was not surprising, then, that in a Collection speech on "Serious Athletics,"[14] he said that his ambition for Swarthmore would be realized if every student played a game and a large number played well enough to represent the college on a team.

This statement from a college President was novel enough to get a headline in the Philadelphia *Evening Bulletin*, "Athletics for all, Swarthmore Plan." The reporter described Aydelotte as an advocate "of athletics for their own sake, and not for the mere glory of a college team triumphing over its rivals. . . . The greatest value of sports is their moral value." The New York *Evening Journal* took notice also: "More athletes and fewer spectators, is the slogan of Dr. Frank Aydelotte, President of Swarthmore College, in his desire to raise the standard of college athletics. This system is used at Oxford University."[15]

The President hoped that Swarthmore's athletes would prove to be good students and was delighted when he could announce to the alumni in 1923 that the scholastic average of the football squad for the past two seasons was higher than that of the highest men's fraternity.[16] He was happy to congratulate the Graduate Manager of Athletics on the percentage of men engaged in sports in that year, 1922–1923: 84 per cent of the total of 256. In 1924–1925, 76 per cent were trying out for teams and about one-fourth getting their letters in at least one sport.[17] The teams won a satisfactory proportion of victories, doing particularly well in lacrosse. The President could not greet with unqualified rejoicing a reduction of gate receipts at football games which increased the need of subsidy. But he realized he must accept the loss with the gains and began to urge endowment for athletics and freedom from any financial dependence on spectators.

Fraternities

Within a month after the inauguration, the Phi Kappa Psi fraternity opened its lodge, the first of five which the college had agreed to let the men's fraternities build on the campus. (The women's request to follow suit came later.) The lodges were not dormitories, but simple social centers; all would be planned by the same architects, constructed of the same local stone, and arranged in a group to be connected by colonnades and called The Cloisters. Each would conform to a price limit of $25,000. With these original specifications Frank had nothing to do. When he announced the completion of the first lodge he made no comment beyond saying that it was "comfortable and attractive," adding "to the beauty of the campus."[18]

But already he was concerned about fraternity social life, which was by-passing college regulations and overshadowing college functions. The first controversial issue to test the new President's relation to the students in his first year had to do with dances given for the fraternities off the campus. If he had been confused or irritable, he might have lost what would have been hard to regain. In fact, he showed a tact, imagination, and strength which won student respect. Since to the students the episode had importance out of all proportion to its intrinsic seriousness, it may be told in some detail.

Frank found that these dances given off campus involved breaking rules in spirit though not in letter, and this with the aid of alumni and alumnae—sensitive and influential elements in the Swarthmore community. According to college regulations, dances should be held on campus and only on Saturday night in order not to interrupt the week's work. But there was no rule forbidding students to be away from their dormitories overnight during the week, provided the women registered their hostesses' names and addresses. So the practice had grown up of someone's giving a dance for a fraternity away from Swarthmore, on any night, arranging to have women guests entertained in the neighborhood. Another objection important to the President: the number of these dances, in addition to those scheduled legally on the Calendar, had increased to a point where successful all-college dances had almost ceased to exist. The result: a loss of inclusive social life possible in a small institution and essential to the best college spirit.

In a situation where it seemed out of the question not to offend someone, the new President proceeded serenely, assuming that everyone wanted what was best for the college and that all concerned groups should have a voice. Then with some fanfare of publicity in the *Phoenix*, he appointed a Committee of Thirty, including twenty students—ten men and ten women—seven representatives of faculty and administration, and three alumni, one woman and two men. The preponderance of student members, two-thirds of the thirty—more than enough to carry a vote—disarmed suspicion that anything was being "put over" at student expense.

The President waited to call the first meeting until after the football season when students were ready for a new interest.[19] He invited the committee to the President's house—a pleasant social touch—and no doubt served refreshments. There he explained his concern for the spirit of a rule and for promoting a social program for the whole college. He mentioned also a possible new feature: a college prom to which alumni could be invited: Then he asked the group to consider not only eliminating the invited off-campus dances but also, *as an experiment,* limiting scheduled fraternity dances to one a year instead of two, so releasing

more Saturday nights for all-college affairs. At one point he dropped
the remark that the Calendar would be improved if instead of giving
one fraternity exclusive right to a Saturday night, two or three fraternity
dances could be held on the same night. When his whole speech came
out in the *Phoenix* his last suggestion caused an uproar of objections
which he considered carefully and found to have some weight. Since
the disputed point had seemed to him his least important one, he withdrew it in a statement in the next *Phoenix,* an act which seemed to the
students to show fairness and courage.[20] Thereafter he left the committee
to hold discussions uninhibited by his presence, and on the day when
they took their final vote, he was out of town for a speaking engagement. Dean Walters telegraphed him the result of the vote: no more
not quite legal off-campus dances, consent of all but one fraternity to
the experiment of scheduling only one dance a year, unanimous approval of a college prom. The President sent back an open telegram of
congratulations to the Committee of Thirty. When the prom was held
in April, the *Phoenix* gave it a glowing headline: "Greatest Social Event
of Season is Acclaimed Triumph by Students."[21]

In 1923, when two more fraternity lodges were built—by Delta
Upsilon and Phi Sigma Kappa—Frank was ready with a considered
opinion of the place of fraternities at Swarthmore. The location of the
lodges in a group on the campus he saw as a symbol of fraternity loyalty
to the college: "In its unity, the group is almost unique and should be a
constant reminder to the men of the college of that fact which, in the
rush of fraternity rivalry, sometimes tends to be forgotten, that above all
fraternities is the college which makes them possible and to which the
undergraduates' first loyalty is due."[22]

Admitting the social value of a fraternity to its members, he believed
that the college should guarantee similar opportunities for all students,
and consequently he welcomed a new organization, the Wharton Club,
to which all nonfraternity men automatically belonged. The Wharton
Club would have its own lodge "as an organic part of the group," thus
"giving to the men of Swarthmore a social life open to every undergraduate . . . on terms as democratic as it was possible to make them."
His conclusion left no doubt of his position: "No other plan would have
been consistent with the traditions of this college," referring to the early
Quaker traditions which antedated secret societies.

Frank's hope for the Wharton Club was never realized. The club
never built a lodge, not because of opposition from the fraternities nor

from lack of funds, which could surely have been raised, but because of the indifference of the nonfraternity men themselves. Most of them saw little attraction in a club held together by a bond that was chiefly negative: nonmembership in a fraternity. Also some of them were lone wolves by nature and preference, emphatically not clubbable men. This was one of the rare times when an ingenious idea of the President's failed to strike fire.

Support of the Quaker Connection

Frank's pride in Swarthmore's Quaker background made him want to be no less active in the Society of Friends than if he had been a member. In the summer after his first year at Swarthmore, he took part in the biennial Friends' General Conference, held this year in Richmond, Indiana. In discussing the topic "Quakerism and Democracy," he showed how alike they are in an ideal of group responsibility to be shared by every individual: responsibility for religious ministry in a Quaker Meeting, for government through intelligent voting in a democracy. In both ideals "the key to ... full realization ... lies in education" which should give each person a chance to develop his special abilities.[23]

Two years later, when the Friends General Conference met in Ocean City, Frank was on hand to discuss efforts to raise academic standards at Swarthmore and found that the Friends' Conference Committee on Education had a similar concern for the improvement of Friends' schools. All agreed that the first step should be a survey of the schools, and the man to undertake it, the professor of education at Swarthmore, W. Carson Ryan. Frank welcomed this cooperation as a service to Friends and of a kind to promote academic values. Here was a step toward reconciliation of the traditional conflict between the President's concern that the college should meet the best possible academic standards and the Managers' concern that it should serve the Society.[24]

Another step was in sight when he wrote his *Report* for 1924–1925, with the leading section on "Quakerism and Higher Education."[25] Referring with satisfaction to the increase in the number of Friends in college and the higher proportion of Friends than of non-Friends in honors courses, he went on to mention the less happy fact of a higher proportion of Friends among those dropped for failure. This had given rise to discussion by the Managers of "the real purpose of the college" and to their decision "to draw up a considered statement of policy" addressed to all members of the Society and all graduates of the college. The President's summary of their letter shows that it gave him unqualified support.

> The object of this letter is to make clear that the Board approves un-reservedly the improvement in the level of academic work which has already been made at the college, and stands solidly behind the faculty in the effort . . . to raise this level. The Board asks that "parents and pro-spective students share its enthusiasm for a college that is a college and not a social club," and calls attention very gravely to the responsibility of parents for the success or failure of their children in school and college. It emphasizes the fact that the task of early education is not one that can be left to the schools alone, but is one in which the parents must cooperate, more particularly in developing in their children intellectual ambition and habits of faithful work.

The President sees this responsibility as one which Quaker parents can meet particularly well because of their traditional seriousness and independence of worldly standards. He urges them to oppose the skepti-cism of "intellectual accomplishment"—a skepticism which "democracy must fight in order to produce a civilization of high intellectual and spiritual value." If Quaker parents teach their children from kindergarten through college to respect intellectual accomplishment and the habits necessary to achieve it, they will begin to make a distinctively Friendly contribution to high education.

Less than two years after Frank wrote so appreciatively of the Man-agers' support, they showed what seemed a change in heart. That story will be told in a later chapter.[26]

A Favorable Press

Newspaper comments on Frank's athletic policy have already shown that he got a good press. Fortunately for himself and the college, he appealed to reporters. When the Philadelphia *Evening Bulletin* was col-lecting answers to the question "What books would you choose to have if marooned on an island?" Frank was a natural person to approach, and he rewarded the interviewer with an unusual idea. Turning his back on both "great books" for consolation and practical guides to survival, he would plan to use his solitude for specialized study. "Let all the books deal with or be related to one subject . . . When they have been thor-oughly studied the castaway will be something of a master. If he ever gets out of his fix he will have something to show the world." He himself, as an Elizabethan scholar, "would take Shakespeare and the works of nine Elizabethans that dovetail with his work." Smatterings he would not allow himself: "Promiscuous reading, although it gives a variety of information well worth having, is really the school-boy way of reading. It lacks the character of culture. It does not matter so much what a man has not read. It is what he has read that counts."[27]

The *Bulletin* got another good story of a snowball fight outside the men's dormitory which showed the President in a hospitable light. Snowballs had broken all the windows in two students' rooms, making "their sleeping quarters a cold damp place. Dr. Frank Aydelotte . . . heard of their predicament and invited them to be his guests in his home. The two men slumbered on feather beds while their envious attackers continued to use cots.[28] Again a *Bulletin* reporter amused himself by describing the elaborate proceedings Swarthmore's President went through to fulfill his promise to the senior class to bring them ivy from Oxford to plant on Class Day. He had gone to England in April on business for a foundation and dug up a healthy sprig of ivy at Brasenose, only to learn on board the *Aquitania* that it could not enter the United States without a permit from the Department of Agriculture. Forthwith he radioed the senior president to arrange this through Frank's secretary, whose sister happened to be secretary to Senator Hiram Johnson. The permit duly meeting the boat, the ivy had to go to Washington "to be inspected for foreign vermin." The reporter concludes: "If the plant survives these tests (for plant lice) and does not die of the (red) tape worm before it reaches Swarthmore, the class of 1924 will plant it in the shadow of Parrish Hall on Commencement Day."[29] (The ivy did, in fact, survive, but was planted in the quadrangle of the new Worth dormitory for women.)

Personal Life

These four years of hard work and excitement for Frank proved equally strenuous for Marie. She was troubled about William, who did not make the transition from Cambridge easily. He missed his friends, especially Peter Sprague. After the Hockings' school, Swarthmore public school was bound to seem dull. The first half-year proved so difficult that his parents tried the drastic experiment of sending him back to Cambridge to stay with the Spragues for another term at Shady Hill. This also did not work. Returning to Swarthmore, he studied at home with an unusual tutor, Walter Matos, clergyman and learned bachelor, who had specialized in astronomy so successfully as to be elected a Fellow of the Royal Astronomical Society. He was "Volunteer Observer in the Sproul Observatory" as well as rector of the little Swarthmore Episcopal Church when he took on William's education. Two years of tutoring accomplished so much that William was able to enter the senior class at the William Penn Charter School and be graduated at fifteen.

Too young for college, William took a postgraduate year at Penn Charter, where he met another boy with his own enthusiasm for study and ideas, Maurice Cramer. They began what proved to be a long friendship. Though they went to different colleges, Maurice to Princeton and Bill, as he was now called, to Harvard, Maurice spent so many vacations with the Aydelottes that he seemed like a second son.

Marie had another personal responsibility: for the aunt who had helped to bring her up after her mother died, Mrs. Lewis B. Monroe (mother of Mrs. George Barnard). "Lambie," as she was called affectionately, lived on the quiet third floor of the President's house and gave Marie the support of adult companionship during Frank's long absences when he was speaking to college groups and carrying on Rhodes Scholarship business.

He missed Marie sadly and tried to make up for lack of talk by writing full accounts of people he saw and questions on his mind. Sometimes he felt uneasy. Was he neglecting her? Did he except too much? On a strenuous two-week trip from Chicago which took him to Iowa City, Lincoln, Kansas City, St. Louis, Sullivan, and Cleveland, he wrote a contrite loving letter from Sullivan, where he had stopped to see his parents:

> These last few weeks I realize that I must have been a terrible person to live with—both for you and Auntie. I am going to let down now and be more human. I can't ever say to you Darling how much I love you— how you are the whole centre of my life—I can't put it into words and when I get off and think about it I am afraid I fail too often to say it in my manner as well. I am going to take life more easily and want you to. Nothing would pay me for letting you get too tired at this job. I want you in some way to help me more in what I am doing and divide up more on shopping as we used to in the old days.[30]

Frank and Marie were popular in Philadelphia and entered into city life so far as they could find time. They subscribed for seats in a box at

The Orchestra. Frank particularly enjoyed his membership in two Philadelphia organizations, the Franklin Inn Club of local literary men and the American Philosophical Society, founded by Benjamin Franklin, with nationwide and foreign membership. Wanting to give active support to Cecil Rhodes's favorite cause of international peace, he helped organize the Pennsylvania Chapter of the League of Nations Non-Partisan Association.

Marie also was drawn into Philadelphia public life when she took part in a new venture, the Women's City Club, of which she became the first president in 1924. This was one of twenty-eight such clubs in "cities throughout the world," founded to bring together able women who represented a variety of pursuits—"society, professions and business."[31] Each club maintained a house where members could invite distinguished women visitors to discuss topics of importance, the hope being to build enlightened public opinion which might carry weight in community and world affairs.

Though Marie filled her difficult position in Swarthmore remarkably well, thanks to almost superhuman efforts to do what was best for Frank and never to say anything that might give offense, she must have enjoyed escaping to the relatively free atmosphere of the Women's Club where she was expected to speak out. Frank was glad she had the responsibility and gave her the benefit of his own experience. Once, when she faced a crucial session on building a clubhouse, he wrote her careful advice:

> As I think over your plans I believe all three are O.K.: it just depends on price and that depends on enthusiasm. I should advise the cheapest but let the Club take the responsibility for spending more if they want to. Make your explanation very clear in your head: tabulate it on paper: make them all understand it with wearisome iteration. Make the cost clear and the resources of the Club, then throw it open for discussion. You might select advocates of each plan to hold forth about it. Try to keep them from fighting and to agree in advance to stand by the will of the majority or leave it to the Board. Keep your detachment and sense of humor in the discussion, don't take any violent side yourself. Say "I should like the most expensive if we had the money but favor the cheapest since we haven't."[32]

Thanks to his coaching and her own good sense, Marie's administration went well.

If Frank and Marie remembered Warner Fite's condescending remarks

VI: Frank and Marie Aydelotte with their son William, ca. 1927. Photo:
William Shewell Ellis.

VII: Two Swarthmore commencements. Above, Frank Aydelotte with Lady Wylie, 1933. Below, with Albert Einstein, 1938.

about the negligible position of Swarthmore's President in Philadelphia, they must have been amused and not displeased to see him proved wrong.

Golf and Florida Vacations

To ease the strain of these early years, Frank was persuaded to do two things for fun: play golf and take a winter vacation in Florida. Joseph Swain was the first to urge the charms of golf. Frank described his efforts to an old Indiana friend:

> Dr. Swain is now doing his level best to overcome what appears to be my most serious defect as an administrator, namely my poor game of golf. He and I are going out this afternoon for another, but I fear vain attempt to enable me to crack 100. I wish you were here to go with us.[33]

Frank had reason to find golf difficult because of his stiff right elbow, but he managed to overcome the handicap in football and rowing; why not again? His early lessons produced no apparent improvement, but with a vacation in Florida, his game took a forward leap.

He tells the story of his first trip to Florida (1924) with due thanks to Dr. Edward Martin. Frank had been working hard setting up plans for the Guggenheim Fellowships when he went to see Martin about a member of the faculty who was ill and seemed not to be getting proper attention.

> Dr. Martin heard the case, gave me what I thought was a most satisfactory opinion and I got up to thank him and leave. He motioned me to sit down again and said "Young man, I want to talk to you about yourself. You are riding for a fall and I want you to come away with Mrs. Martin and me to Palm Beach for a month." I said, "Dr. Martin, I can't leave Swarthmore for a month. I don't know what would happen to the college." He said, "You might have to leave for good if you don't look out." This was at the end of November, just before the annual meeting of our Board in December. Dr. Martin talked to the Board about this, got them all excited, and the result was that it was unanimously voted that Marie and I should go to Palm Beach for a month.[34]

They went the next week and again every year so long as the Martins lived. After they died, another friend on the Board, Henry Turner, invited Frank and Marie to his house at Lake Wales, and later still they stayed at the Highland Park Club nearby.

In Florida Frank was preoccupied with golf. Dr. Martin found a professional who taught him well, and from a mediocre player he became a very good one. He enjoyed learning, throwing himself into golf with boyish abandon, dressing in golf clothes on the train so that he wouldn't waste a minute in getting to the course, and playing again just before he took the train to go north, boarding it in plus fours.[35] He devoured all the best books on the subject; indeed, his son reports that his books on golf alone occupied five feet of shelf space. He could make the game fascinating even to listeners who never expected to wield a driver. Eventually (1935) he was elected to a famous Quaker golf club, the Ozone Club, as the first non-Quaker. A fellow member, Claude Smith, one of the Swarthmore Managers, recalled that Frank played seventy-five Ozone games and was always "a great competitor with many scores in the low 80's."[36]

Red-Letter Days

Three dates in one month of Frank Aydelotte's calendar for 1925 deserved to be printed in bright red: February 17, 23, and 28, the first two celebrating events in his extra-Swarthmore activities, the third a high point in the honors experiment.

On February 17, 1925, *The London Times* carried an item about the new Commonwealth Fellowships, established to bring British students to the United States. The plan was based on suggestions made by Aydelotte to Max Farrand of the Commonwealth Fund, handsomely acknowledged by Mr. Farrand. New York newspapers of February 23 announced the Guggenheim Fellowships, with Frank Aydelotte as chairman of the Foundation's Educational Advisory Board. His part in both enterprises will be told in the next chapter.

Of first importance to the experiment with honors work was the five-year subsidy from the General Education Board made public on February 28. The subsidy would bring the college $20,000 for 1925–1926, $40,000 for 1926–1927, and $60,000 a year for the next three years, a total of $240,000. The grant depended on an agreement that at the end of the five years the Board of Managers would provide additional endowment "to continue the work on the same scale of expenditure."[37] Events leading up to this gift involve an old acquaintance who was becoming a warm friend and an encounter between honors students and a representative of the General Education Board.

The old acquaintance was Abraham Flexner, who had helped Frank in Louisville with advice on how to learn enough Greek to pass an examination for a Rhodes Scholarship. Since then they had rarely met. Recently Flexner had asked Frank to be chairman of a committee under the General Education Board to study the teaching of English. Flexner tells the story in *I Remember*: "When Aydelotte told me what he was doing at Swarthmore, I advised him not to abandon his experiment. 'Have you enough money to carry on the experiment properly?' I inquired. He replied in the negative. 'Why don't you ask us for it?' I suggested. The result was a five-year grant."[38]

As Frank Aydelotte remembered it, before the grant was confirmed, a representative of the Board came to Swarthmore, arriving at the end of term when everything was over except a meeting of honors students and instructors to discuss difficulties. Frank would have preferred a regular seminar and took the visitor to the meeting with some misgivings. He describes the incident in *Breaking the Academic Lockstep*:

> My worst fears were immediately realized. As soon as the meeting was opened one student after another began to hold forth on the defects of honors work. The requirements were vague. There were no definite assignments of so many pages to read, so many exercises to do, so many dates to learn. Instead they had to wrestle for themselves with a topic and a bibliography: they never knew how much would be expected of them they did not know when they were through, they missed the definiteness of course work where specific tasks were assigned day by day, so that a man could know when he had finished his work and when he was free to play.
>
> My heart sank and I thought I perceived that our visitor was embarrassed. But before I or any member of the faculty had time to reply to these objections, other undergraduates took up the discussion. They pointed out somewhat more sharply than would have been courteous on the part of a professor, that the whole theory of honors work was to place upon the student the responsibility for his own education, they intimated that possibly those who felt the need for such daily spoon-feeding were not themselves suited to the demands of independent study, they pointed out that undergraduates could hardly expect to develop initiative and independence unless they were given precisely the freedom which honors work offered. A lively discussion followed, which continued for two or three hours entirely between the students with hardly a word from any member of the faculty. When we left, our visitor pronounced the meeting the most impressive academic exercise he had ever attended and in due time the much needed financial assistance was forthcoming.[39]

The money was important, of course, but no more than the recognition. When the President announced the gift at a Swarthmore Alumni Club dinner, he paid a warm tribute to the faculty and students who had earned it:

> It is, in my opinion, to the scholarship and enthusiasm of the faculty and to the success which our honors students have made in work of this new, severe, and independent type, that we owe the generous grant from the General Education Board. . . . Success in this undertaking, if we are able to achieve it, will mean infinitely more than increased appropriations or endowment—it will mean a contribution of significance to American higher education.[40]

The *Phoenix* which reported this speech carried also an editorial solidly behind the experiment in honors work: "The Rockefeller Foundation has issued the challenge, the world watches, and if success is to be won, if Swarthmore is to be worthy of this trust reposed in her, every effort must be expended from every source available to justify faith in this work."

A month later, in fairness to an opposing point of view, the *Phoenix* published a student's letter which struck a sour note in the general rejoicing. The writer deplored the probable effect of the subsidy on the college admissions policy,

> eliminating most of the red blooded men and women . . . substituting that vile species designated as "Greasy Grinds" for the robust, virile type that has made Swarthmore glorious in the past. . . . Let other colleges, founded with specialized intellectual aims project them in this enlarged Honors plan, but there is no excuse for sacrificing Swarthmore's established pre-eminence in the field of producing well rounded men and women, for the sake of attempting an alien and undesirable success in cultivating mental geniuses.[41]

Appearing at the beginning of spring vacation, the letter seems to have been forgotten in the month before the next *Phoenix*. There was no answer; no one seconded the criticism. But the critic's point of view in less extreme form would reappear from time to time among Friends and alumni who preferred the old Swarthmore to the new.

This year another foundation, the Carnegie Corporation, expressed confidence in Frank Aydelotte's plans for Swarthmore with a gift of $50,000 toward endowing the library. The moving spirit was undoubtedly his friend Frederick P. Keppel, President of the Corporation. In 1918, when Keppel was third Assistant Secretary of War, he had come to know Frank through the War Issues Course. Recently he had visited Swarthmore as Commencement speaker.

Members of the Society of Friends also chose this time to be generous: Joanna Wharton Lippincott, with a gift of $25,000 for research in astronomy; William J. Cooper, whose legacy of $100,000 was intended to provide "lectures and musical entertainments . . . to enrich the intellectual and artistic life of the college";[42] Mr. and Mrs. Daniel S. White of the Class of 1875, who celebrated their fiftieth anniversary by founding three Open Scholarships for Women (modeled, like the ones for men, on the Rhodes Scholarships).

Altogether Frank Aydelotte had reason to take pleasure in the state of the college at what was for him a special Commencement, the graduation of students who had been freshmen in his first year. They asked him to give their Baccalaureate Sermon, including part of the talk he had made at their and his first Collection.

In these first years at Swarthmore no event was more important to him in both his professional and personal life than his discovery of Abraham Flexner as a like-minded, stimulating co-worker in education and an extremely congenial friend. When the Flexners came to stay with the Aydelottes, the talk at dinner made the future of American education seem the most exciting prospect in the world—so much to be done, and all so fascinating. Both men had a background of enthusiastic, dedicated teaching. Both had a passion for "excellence," with fires partly kindled from the same source, Matthew Arnold, and his "doctrine of the saving power of the 'remnant.'" Both agreed wholeheartedly with Jules Cambon, as quoted by Flexner: "We have to defend the country against mediocrity, mediocrity of soul, mediocrity of ideas, mediocrity of action. We must also fight it in ourselves."[43]

With all their agreement on ends, the two were likely to bring them about in very different ways. Abraham Flexner was inclined to rely on ridicule or sarcasm to needle individuals and institutions into overcoming weaknesses. Frank Aydelotte, preferring the more irenic line that nothing is so good it couldn't be better, persuaded people to work for improvements in the spirit of a golfer trying to lower his strokes. His devotion to games made him value good teamwork, while Abraham Flexner was something of a lone wolf. These differences were not without advantages. The two men supplemented each other well and delighted in each other's company for twenty years.

CHAPTER TWELVE

ON HIS METTLE

1925–1931

WHEN Frank Aydelotte was congratulated on the subsidy from the General Education Board he said cheerily, "Money is easy enough to get. The hard thing is to spend it right." Now that he had funds for expanding honors work by adding teachers and increasing the endowment of the library, would he be able to use them so that his program would more than fulfill its promise?

In these critical years, while chiefly concerned with the fate of his experiment, he took steps to extend some of its principles and advantages to the curriculum in general. When the time came to raise money for endowment to replace the subsidy, he carried the chief responsibility. Since planning new ventures and surmounting obstacles were meat and drink to him, these were among the happiest years of his life.

Choosing New Teachers

The President determined to make appointments slowly, guarding against even one mistake, which in a small college might prove disastrous. As always, he set up a faculty committee to help him with each choice.

Fortunately Frank Aydelotte and the faculty agreed on the kind of teacher they wanted. They would avoid the "small college type," far more interested in his students than his subject and consequently not likely to grow. They would avoid also the "graduate school type," so wrapped up in research as to consider students something of an intrusion. Swarthmore needed men and women who were enthusiastic about their subject, who found students stimulating and research a means to better teaching as well as a possible contribution to knowledge. Of course, these are the teachers most institutions would hope to find. Frank Ayde-lotte never doubted that he could discover them in good supply and, with the help of the faculty, persuade them to come to Swarthmore. He knew that some of them would be temperamental, but why not? "When you want teachers who can't be dull, you're bound to get a few prima donnas."

President and faculty agreed again that new teachers must have the vitality indispensable to honors seminars and almost equally important in courses. A candidate's gift for the two kinds of teaching had to be considered, since every teacher was expected to do both, partly to prevent a cleavage in the faculty, partly to guarantee to students in courses their share of the best instruction.

When President and committee found a candidate who seemed to meet their requirements, they asked him to come to Swarthmore for interviews, with his wife if he were a married man. The visitors commonly stayed at the President's house so that Mrs. Aydelotte could welcome them and form an opinion to pass on to her husband. Candidate after candidate might be invited until one seemed right for an offer. If he did not accept, it was all to do again.

A candidate sometimes accepted, to his own surprise. He may have come for an interview largely as a matter of courtesy and found himself persuaded. This happened to one of the two men appointed in the spring of 1925, Brand Blanshard, whose change of opinion I could witness as his wife.

Brand was teaching at the University of Michigan, his alma mater, and was happy to be there. When he was urged by a fellow Rhodes Scholar, Frank Aydelotte, to visit Swarthmore, how could he refuse? We took the train from Ann Arbor, interested in seeing a place we had heard praised, but that was all. After a series of talks with men who exulted in new opportunities for more effective teaching, Brand took a fresh look at Swarthmore, with its limited enrollment and expanding faculty.

Michigan, like most other universities in 1925, had grown enormously, first with the influx of returning soldiers and then of sons and daughters of families newly prosperous since the war. Large lecture courses had become larger. The stress on mass education depressed an old Rhodes Scholar. To Brand at thirty-two, ambitious to teach well, honors work offered great attractions. The community also appealed to him, with a peaceful setting for work and the stimulus of sympathetic, lively colleagues. Swarthmore lived up to his expectations so well that he stayed there happily twenty years, leaving then partly because he felt that the strenuous kind of teaching was a young man's work.

The other man appointed in the spring of 1925, Frederick J. Manning of Yale, eventually became professor of history and for many years chairman of the department. The two were chosen early enough to be asked to serve as honors examiners while they could still qualify as "external." The President liked the practice of giving new appointees a chance to take a close but still objective look at the system before they became part of it.

During these six years twenty-nine full-time members were added to the faculty who became some of Swarthmore's most influential teachers. Only seven were Rhodes Scholars—evidence of restraint on the President's part! Seventeen of the twenty-nine stayed on until they retired.[1]

Honors Teachers in Action

As the wife of an honors teacher, I found I was expected to support the system of holding seminars in faculty living rooms. My role was to serve a substantial tea. This was in the spirit of the Aydelottes' way of inviting committees to meet in their house, with refreshments to give a festive touch.

But the purpose of tea for honors seminars, I soon discovered, was more than social. Seminars were so long and discussion so strenuous that both instructors and students needed replenishment. Arriving at half past one and often still going at half past five, they leaned heavily on midafternoon sandwiches and cake. Faculty wives provided bountifully, meeting the cost from the family budget. Eventually, when I had work which kept me away from home in the afternoon, I put first among our maid's duties to serve tea to honors students. One maid responded by producing culinary marvels with an eagerness I could not understand until she explained she was competing with the maid of a neighbor. The girls had heard that at the end of the year students would take a vote on the best seminar food. This rumor apparently started in a facetious student publication, a *Seminar Guide*, which did say that the quality of food should not be overlooked in the choice of a seminar. Though the maids found they were to be rewarded only by lavish praise from week to week, they seemed to lose nothing of their zeal.

College pride in an educational experiment struck some foreign visitors as unique. When a group of them from Columbia had completed a tour of Swarthmore, one of them said: "We have visited many colleges in your country. At all of them except Swarthmore they said: Oh, you must see our new library, or our laboratory, or our new gymnasium. At Swarthmore you said: 'Come in and we will tell you about an experiment in education that we are making.' "[2]

The President relished such observations and sometimes quoted them "in the family." He also greatly enjoyed an account of honors teachers in action by a visitor who was a good friend of his and of the college, the novelist Dorothy Canfield Fisher. Bred in three universities, Kansas, Ohio State, and Columbia, where her father had been respectively a professor, the President, and the librarian, she had always known teachers and now saw those at Swarthmore partly through the eyes of her daughter, a junior honors student. She gives her impressions in a peculiarly warm and enthusiastic article, "Melting the Faculty Ice," which begins: "Everybody expects great artists to be absorbed by their art—singers to keep coming back to music, painters to canvases—but who ever heard college professors in any hour of social leisure talk about teaching? Teaching, remember; not research work or writing books! Well, I have! I have been traveling in a new country."[3]

Meeting them at dinner, she expected to hear them talk about trips to Europe, but with only a word or two on that subject, "they were all off on a warm debate on how best to keep the balance, in a group studying the fine arts, between exposition by the teacher and discussion by the students." Then following a brief exchange on a recent novel,

> a turn of phrase had plunged everybody into what seemed a serial continuation of one of those perpetual controversies which never get settled. It was a new one to me—not about the relative merits of clay or grass tennis courts, nor fly fishing versus worm bait, but whether it is better to have papers read aloud in conference or passed around beforehand as a basis for discussion. Feeling ran high; those present exchanged black looks and bitter words, like people disagreeing over informative bids at bridge.
>
> Neither party could talk down the other, and by common consent the topic was switched to student personalities—what would be called gossip in less intellectual circles. . . . All the interest—it was a live interest, full of heat and conviction—was centered on the students' potential brain power. They glowed with the prayerful anxiety of athletic coaches and trainers exchanging impressions of bodily possibilities. You've heard them:

"Strong as a bull, stands up under punishment, but is clumsy on his pins. You're crazy to think of making a tackle out of him. He belongs on the crew."

Transposed into intellectual qualities I was hearing just such appraisals: "Quick witted, yes; but no staying powers. He'll never get beyond thinking in flashes." Or: "No, she's not slow. She doesn't go jumping all over the place from one idea to another. But she never wastes time scrambling out from half-baked nonsense either. I consider her one of the best minds in the class."[4]

I had the impression that they did not intentionally go on working in play time, but that they could not help it, any more than an artist can help that incessant preoccupation with his art which makes him less of a generally agreeable conversationalist and more of an artist. The point was that they took their profession more than seriously: rather with something of the primitive vitality of athletes and the savage intensity of artists—fighting tooth and nail, as artists always do, with the difficulties of their medium. . . . They had the varying moods of athletes and artist. . . . Sometimes they were exalted by a sense of unconquerable power. Sometimes they fell into a tragic distrust of themselves, their calling, their raw material, their methods; into that sour certainty of failure which poisons the life of artists and athletes who are off their game. In short they were teachers who cared immensely about teaching well.[5]

When she visited three seminars, she found each teacher ensconced in his living room with four or five students, using his own distinctive method to develop the subject and stimulate discussion. One professor let the meeting turn into a "glorified bull session." Another in constitutional history gave what amounted "almost to an informal lecture," a "brilliant exposition . . . of the attitude of our Supreme Court in applying English common law." Here Mrs. Fisher recognized a student attitude quite unlike one she remembered from her own student days when it was the thing to "get a line" on a professor either to "give him what he wants" or "get him going on something" so that he wouldn't ask awkward questions. Instead a girl came out with a flat challenge: "But, professor, you always say the Justices are thinking of precedents and property rights when they make their decisions. How can you know what they think?" The professor "reached into the bookshelves behind him, and, by direct quotation from Supreme Court decisions, established his point." The girl was silenced, but Mrs. Fisher could feel her thinking, "All the same, that *is* the way he always interprets those decisions." The professor seemed to feel it, too, to "get what she had meant rather than what she had said."

To Mrs. Fisher's surprise, he added, "But you are right. I have a strong personal bias in this matter. I won't admit that I do more than exaggerate. But I want you to be sure to look up and read the authorities who have the opposite bias."[6]

This friendly honesty between teacher and student Mrs. Fisher took to be partly the result of small numbers. With four or five students the relation can be direct and simple, a minimum of pretense on either side. This makes it easier for the teacher to understand and meet each student's needs.

Mrs. Fisher thought she saw this done in a seminar in ethics, conducted on a different theory from the "glorified bull session" of the previous day.

> After half an hour of listening to the intimate intellectual give-and-take between the mature, experienced mind of the professor and the questing young spirits I had an almost mystical vision of those conventionally dressed young people, not as faces and hands and collars and silk stockings but as living fires. I saw them flickering and smoking, flaring up in brilliant flashes of intuition, their boldest, richest flames blown about helplessly by their inexperience while with care and patience the older man went about the business of trimming and shaping them into clarity and steadiness. Yes, of course he must have been a very fine teacher, who would have done good work, no doubt, as many a teacher has, with a gong in the hall to tell him when to stop, lecturing . . . to huge classes of students practically unknown to him. But the best he could have done for those hordes, compared to the certainty of his help to these responsive young minds, would have been like a sign painter's work compared to Whistler's.[7]

From the students' point of view, Mrs. Fisher gathered that the close relation to their teachers depended partly on the use of external examiners. As a student would put it: your own teacher "is not the one who is going to determine your marks by an examination he himself draws up, but the one whose heart is set on having you pass the test as well as you possibly can," for his own credit as well as yours. Mrs. Fisher saw that the advantage of this relationship would not be limited to the students. Teachers also would do better work when freed from the frustrations of mass production which has turned too many of them into "hacks and routineers."[8]

For Frank Aydelotte such impressions as hers and those of other visitors confirmed his belief that his role at Swarthmore was largely "to release the creative energies of other minds." He saw clearly how much teachers gave to their work and how great was their need for replenishment. As he explained to the Managers:

> For the teacher Honors work is at once more stimulating, more interesting, and more exacting than ordinary instruction. It requires better brains and sounder scholarship. It offers a constant challenge, and it denies to the teacher both the ease and the danger of the familiar grooves of constantly repeated courses.
>
> To be a success with Honors students, the teacher must be himself a student, constantly broadening and deepening his own scholarship. This means that if we are to expect a continuation of the admirable work now being done by the members of our staff, the college must provide for them more frequent opportunities for leave of absence, more time and more money for research than has been possible in the past. It seems clear that the minimum should be one years' leave in seven on full salary, or a half year on full salary one year in three. This is almost double the provision which we are able to make at present.[9]

Two Crises in the Honors Program

In the spring of 1926 there was a crisis in the final honors examinations. Twelve candidates with a major in English literature (the largest group so far in any subject) looked forward to having the first Oxford don as an external examiner, Helen Darbishire of Somerville College, then visiting professor at Wellesley. She had accepted the invitation to examine partly because she and Frank Aydelotte had worked at Oxford with the same tutor, Ernest de Selincourt.

The students had not found Miss Darbishire's written examinations disconcerting and thought her friendly and skillful in their orals. Consequently no one was prepared for her Draconian verdict that only five of the twelve deserved honors of any level. For six of the other seven she recommended pass degrees, and for one, a failure. This last was no surprise. The man who failed had given far more time to acting in plays than to reading in the library. But the other unfortunates had worked hard and, from their instructors' point of view, satisfactorily.

Before the sad results were announced, the instructors had a chance to ask Miss Darbishire some questions, but came away still puzzled. Since her province was the more important half of a student's program—work in the major subject—her decision could not be contested unless the college proposed to repudiate the system of external examiners, a possibility no one wished to consider. The list of honors was posted with omissions which shocked the community.

Of those immediately involved, the instructors took it harder than the students, asking themselves agonized questions. Had they in the first place admitted students to honors work too generously, including some who were not sufficiently able and mature? In seminars, had they allowed the discussion too often to drift into pleasant bypaths instead of keeping to the main track? In criticizing students' papers, did they value personal reactions more than objective appraisals, stated precisely? Or was it simply a mistake to invite a foreign examiner whose experience and expectations might be remote from those of her American colleagues?

This last question helped to save face. If an American examiner had found less than half the candidates worthy of honors, the effect might have been disastrous to the whole experiment, discouraging younger students from attempting it, raising doubts about its merits outside Swarthmore. The subsidy itself might have been jeopardized, having been granted for such time as the plan continued to succeed. But an examiner from Oxford in English literature was a judge whom few American departments would meet with complete confidence. The blow was softened for the students who got only pass degrees by the concern of their teachers, whose need of comfort seemed greater than their own. And the President's attitude helped enormously. He refused to be downcast, discussing the whole incident as useful experience. An honors teacher in English, Robert E. Spiller, writing some years later on "Ten Years of Outside Examiners," without mentioning Miss Darbishire, noted points which she had undoubtedly helped confirm:

> The most apparent effect of outside examiners upon the teaching process is an increased emphasis upon central and essential knowledge, and a careful examination of the success of various methods of imparting that knowledge. Personal opinions may still be discussed by teacher and student, but they lose their absolute values and must be related to the accepted body of knowledge and judgment in the field.[10]

A second threat to honors work, less public than the first but potentially more dangerous, took shape at the Managers' annual meeting in December, 1927, in a proposal to subject the program to careful and critical study. The proposers, a small but powerful group, convinced that the old athletic Swarthmore prepared men well to succeed in a highly competitive world, had never liked the intellectual emphasis under Aydelotte, but tolerated it so long as the proportion of students involved seemed unimportant. Indeed, only two years earlier they had concurred in a letter from the Managers to Friends and alumni supporting high standards. But now, with almost 23 per cent of the seniors reading for honors and greater growth made possible by the subsidy, these critics took alarm, all the more as the time approached when the Managers would be obliged to replace the subsidy with an addition to the college endowment. It was a request on this point from the President which brought their opposition into the open. He asked the Board's approval of his applying to the General Education Board for help in raising the two millions which would be needed in two years.

The resulting discussion made another group uneasy, those with the Managers' traditionally dominant concern for children of Friends. Were these children now in danger of being sacrificed to an intellectual and perhaps a too worldly ambition? A vote might have shown a majority in favor of the present program, but to take such a vote would go counter to Friendly practice. The Managers could not ignore serious questions about policy. Accepting the sense of the meeting, they appointed a committee to reconsider the whole experiment.

The Board minutes report the President's reaction in words with an Aydelotte ring. He "heartily concurred" in the need for such a study, feeling "very strongly that it was necessary for the Board to take a definite stand at this time, and that it would be quite impossible for the College to go ahead with so ambitious a program unless the Board was solidly behind it."[11] Then a jaunty move: while the committee investigated, he and his wife would go to Egypt and Spain. Having recently decided against a leave of absence on the ground that he had too much to do at Swarthmore, he now saw the wisdom of being off the scene so that he could not possibly be said to exert pressure on the committee. When Charles Jenkins was appointed chairman, Frank wrote him urging that the committee include "those members of the Board who are not clear as to the wisdom of Honors work," adding: "While it is a matter of regret to me to learn that some members do not believe in what we are doing, since that is the case, I am extremely glad that the Board has decided to conduct this investigation." Frank left no doubt of what was at stake for Swarthmore:

> I hope the decision can be made as promptly as is consistent with careful study of the problem, since the consequences of a repudiation of Honors work would be far-reaching. A negative decision would inevitably cause

us to sacrifice the position of leadership which the college now admittedly holds throughout the country, and which scores of colleges are straining at the leash to take from us. It would probably result in stopping at once the subsidy granted us by the General Education Board year by year, and it would make it very difficult for the college to tap sources outside the Swarthmore group in the provision of endowment for the future. It would destroy the wonderful morale of our faculty and probably result in the loss of many of our best men who have been attracted here largely by the extraordinary interest and importance of the work which we are doing. It would undoubtedly lower the quality of the students who now seek admission to the college.[12]

He wrote from Florida where he and Marie rested and played golf before boarding the *Aquitania* late in January.

The investigating committee did, indeed, include members of the opposition, but also three of the remarkable older women on the Board who gave Frank strong support: Lucy Biddle Lewis, Emma C. Bancroft, and Caroline Hallowell Worth. Lucy Biddle Lewis, chairman of the Managers' Instruction Committee, was the one best informed about the academic progress of the college, which she approved at every step. Of the three she was the most intellectual, a dedicated pacifist on rational, humanitarian grounds, who could argue well for her position. Emma Bancroft, chairman of the Household Committee which gave advice on dormitory and dining-room management, was a woman of shrewd practical judgment and a sense of proportion about the minutiae of housekeeping, always duly subordinating them to academic ends. Caroline Worth, also on the Household Committee and later its chairman, combined practicality with worldly wisdom, and a reasonable degree of "plainness" with elegance and style. Banded together, their intelligence and courage made them impressive advocates. Mrs. Worth spoke for all three in a steamer letter to the Aydelottes:

Mrs. Bancroft and Mrs. Lucy Biddle Lewis lunched with me when we threshed out this major subject [honors work] and several minor ones: we decided we wanted our college to keep the position she held in the academic world, obtained thro' the guidance of her President. We marvelled that any one could desire an old-fashioned institution built upon athletic prowess—it was simply incomprehensible to us.[13]

Like Frank's other supporters, they felt a special responsibility when he was too far away to speak for himself. Astute strategist that he was, he undoubtedly foresaw this when he departed from the field of conflict.

Meanwhile the Vice-President, Professor John Miller, kept in touch with Board activities and on February 18 sent a triumphant cable to the Aydelottes in Cairo: "Honors Committee work practically complete Enthusiastically advocate Honors courses Unqualifiedly support your policy Everything fine here." Charles Jenkins made his official report to the Managers on March 6, recommending that honors work be continued:

> We have found among the students, the faculty, the administrative officers, those skilled in educational work, and among our own clientele in the Society of Friends and among the alumni, a deep conviction that in introducing this system of study Swarthmore College has taken a great step forward. The experiment has brought freshness and vigor to intellectual college life and has in the few years it has been in force profoundly impressed those in whose hands rests the responsibility for the educational development of the country.
>
> We recommend to the Board that there be no hesitancy in going forward with the development of the plan and that the college should continue to afford exceptional students the opportunity of making full use of their abilities.[14]

Years later, when I asked the President what he would have done if the report had been unfavorable, he answered quickly, "I should have resigned," adding, "Of course I didn't make any such threat."

Miller's cable had given Frank a free mind for his next private venture, a trip to Spain. He would follow his usual practice in a foreign country of studying the language. "You have to know something of the language," he would say, "to get any insight into the people." Deciding that a good way to train his ear was to go to the same play several times, he attended seven performances of *Quiero No Quiero* until he knew it almost by heart. It was a dull play, he said, but all the better, since there was nothing to distract him from the sounds and meanings of words. Meanwhile Charles Jenkins and his wife joined the Aydelottes in Spain to celebrate the happy outcome at Swarthmore.

The conflict sparked at the Managers' December meeting by the President's proposal to ask the General Education Board for help in endowing honors work ended appropriately when he announced in June that the request had been made and had brought in a pledge of $675,000 toward the desired two million. This was eleven months before the campaign was officially launched.

Through an ironical coincidence, at that same December Managers' meeting the President announced an event related to the honors program which would add to college prestige, the publication of Professor R. C. Brooks's book, *Reading for Honors at Swarthmore*, with a commendatory introduction by that formidable critic of American education, Abraham Flexner.

Flexner began with some characteristic strictures on American colleges and universities for playing down to "the average or less than average," for their "predilection toward mediocrity," their inevitable failure to produce the excellence required for good government and a "proper contribution to civilization." By contrast, his approval of the Swarthmore experiment was all the more telling.

> The honors work at Swarthmore is frankly an endeavor to spot and to develop excellence. It recognizes the inequalities of natural endowment; it proposes exceptional care and opportunity for the unusual—the unusual in respect to ability, industry or both. It assumes that exceptional ability will in America, as elsewhere, respond to exceptional opportunity; and it implies the hope that, somehow, sometime, we shall be intelligent enough to find in politics, art, science and literature an outlet for the unusual, as we have already abundantly found appropriate outlets for the unusual in business and industry. . . .
>
> Towards the Swarthmore campus many eyes are now turning in the hope of seeing an essential task fearlessly, thoroughly, and in the best sense, democratically performed.[15]

Honors Work Full Grown

Although Frank Aydelotte wanted his experiment to proceed slowly, he might have been taken aback if he had foreseen the length of time before all departments would become involved. The first catalogue account of the beginnings in English literature and the social sciences (December, 1922) stated that by the next academic year "Honors work will be started in all or nearly all of the other subjects taught in the College."[16] In fact, it was five years before all but one department were included, the last coming in three years later in 1930.

If the President was disappointed in the delay, he understood it and did nothing to hurry anyone. Some departments wanted to wait until they had students who would be sure to do well. Other departments, notably in the sciences, already provided their small number of majors with ample individual attention and opportunities to go at their own speed and questioned what they would gain by a change of system. Since they finally did change, they must have recognized advantages, perhaps no more than the satisfaction of sharing in an important experiment, including the ordeal by external examiners. The President was repaid for his patience by cordial faculty support.

Faculty unity was the stronger because from the beginning all honors instructors taught courses also, and by the time the system was well established, a teacher divided his time about equally between the two. Then a teaching program commonly consisted of two courses and two seminars.

In admitting students to honors work, members of the faculty did not announce that certain sophomores were eligible, but waited for those interested to apply and to submit a plan of work. This had two advantages: that a student was accepted partly on the basis of effective planning; that he could not belittle the system by saying that, of course, he had been accepted, but decided against it. Everyone must have a sense of privilege.

After eight years of trial and success, honors work had reached a stage that seemed definitive, though flexible. It was described by the Instruction Committee in a statement published in the catalogue of 1931 and reprinted virtually unchanged throughout President Aydelotte's administration. The statement used the term "Division" in a new way. Whereas it had denoted a group of departments cooperating in an honors program—there being ten such groups—it now referred to four logically distinct areas of the curriculum: "Divisions" of the Humanities, the Social Sciences, Mathematics and the Natural Sciences, and Engineering. Two departments, history and philosophy, belonged in two Divisions, the Humanities and the Social Sciences. This year for the first time the catalogue statement included the list of honors examiners (for 1930), a total of twenty.

The introduction to "Honors Work" was the familiar passage from Frank Aydelotte's inaugural address on the need of greater opportunities for the abler students. Then a brief description:

> Honors work is offered in four divisions and is under the supervision of committees of the departments which compose those divisions. Small groups of students meet their instructors for weekly conferences; in scientific subjects they may spend much additional time in the laboratory. The work is so planned that a student takes not more than two subjects in any one semester. He devotes half the time of his two years of honors work to the subject of his major interest and divides the other half

between two related subjects within his division, unless special exceptions are permitted under the rules of his division or are approved by the Instruction Committee of the Faculty.

Honors students are excused from ordinary examinations and class requirements and their work is not graded from semester to semester. Instead, they are expected to spend their time in mastering a definitely outlined field of knowledge, and at the end of their senior year to take written and oral examinations given by examiners from other institutions. . . .

External examiners may recommend degrees with Honors, High Honors, Highest Honors, or without Honors. In this last case a student's instructors decide whether he should be granted a degree in course.[17]

Two sections, "Procedure for Admission to Honors Work" and "Departmental Statements," outline the mechanics of the program. A candidate must file a formal application in the spring of his sophomore year with the chairman of his major department, giving his proposed choice of minors. "His acceptance by the division depends in part upon the quality of his previous work, . . . but mainly upon his seeming capacity for assuming the responsibility of honors work."[18] Each departmental statement lists the prerequisite courses for major and minors to be taken in the first two years and the topics of final examinations for which honors seminars prepare. So a candidate includes in his application his choice of eight final examinations, which in effect outlines his complete honors program of four seminars in his major and four divided between his minors. As his work progresses, he may, with reason, modify his plan.

Between 1925 and 1931 the number of honors students had more than doubled: 52 to 115. At the same time the percentage of the combined junior and senior classes in the program had gone from 19 per cent of 269 to 44 per cent of 261. One growth that pleased Frank Aydelotte was in the proportion of men to women both in numbers and in standing. Making the comparison among senior honors students, 41 per cent were men in 1925, 61 per cent in 1931. Of those receiving awards of High or Highest Honors, the men advanced from 40 per cent to 64 per cent, and in elections to Phi Beta Kappa, from 35 per cent to 65 percent.[19] The President rejoiced, not from antifeminist prejudices, but because he had felt from the beginning that honors work would not take firm hold at Swarthmore and elsewhere until it appealed to men as difficult and valuable enough to be worth taking in all seriousness.

An occasional skeptic from the Swarthmore faculty as well as from some other institution questioned whether too many students were given the privilege of honors work. Were there, in fact, from 38 per cent to 40 per cent of the juniors and seniors who "deserved" to be taught by a method so costly of instructors' time? One answer: that students without the highest grades but with a real ambition to do the work should be allowed to try. If they did not measure up, they would go back to regular courses. This policy appealed to the President, convinced as he was that some students who had dawdled in courses might exert themselves in a seminar of really keen students. A "late bloomer" who sees a classmate produce an excellent paper may be moved to a bit of burgeoning himself.

A second answer became clear as experience showed that honors students in substantial numbers made a powerful impact on the whole college. Here was a conspicuous group of respected juniors and seniors committed to an intellectual way of life which they obviously found exciting. They walked briskly to the library looking important. They surged into the college dining room from a seminar, still arguing. They made what they were doing too exhilarating to miss—a pleasure which even an ambitious freshman might begin to enjoy in his own courses and expect to find all through college, whether in or outside honors work.

No one could fail to be impressed by community interest on the fateful day in late May when distinguished professors from other institutions assembled to give public oral examinations. The college rocked with excitement as observers crowded into examination rooms to hear friends and favorites put through their paces, came out to repeat brilliant or funny exchanges, and gathered when the honors list was posted to greet the results with whistles and groans.

At this time the President had been known to console someone—a disappointed instructor or student—with the remark that "Honors examinations and the day of judgement are not one event, but two," adding cryptically, "No one was ever harmed by missing Highest Honors except someone who didn't deserve it."

Honors Work and the Educational Program

While honors work quickened the students' intellectual interests, it also gave an impetus to better teaching and improvements in the academic program.

The Managers' Committee had begun their study with a question about teaching raised by several members of the Board: had the experiment worked to the disadvantage of students in course? Those who asked apparently feared that teachers engrossed in something new might neglect their more routine work. But in fact the committee found nothing of the kind, reporting rather "that through the development of the Honors courses with a greatly enlarged and strengthened faculty, the quality of the teaching throughout the college has been much benefited."[20] The faculty would have thought this likely to happen because the same teachers taught both honors and course students, and what they learned from conducting honors seminars, they would expect to apply in all their work, so far as possible. For example, instructors began to meet course students in small groups from time to time for more intimate discussion; there were more long-term assignments based on full bibliographies; there was more emphasis on the writing of essays based on critical reading.

Some principles of honors work were applied to other aspects of the curriculum when the President appointed the new and important Instruction Committee to undertake "a fundamental reconsideration of the entire educational program of the college." The committee included eight members besides the chairman: six from the faculty and the two Deans, the Dean of Women to be secretary. My book of minutes has helped me describe what we accomplished. Our committee usually gathered at four o'clock in the President's study, where we began with tea poured by Mrs. Aydelotte, and as welcome to us at the end of a busy day as to any honors seminar. Indeed, our meetings seemed like lively seminars with the President guiding discussion.

When we came together first in November, 1926, Frank Aydelotte suggested that our first topic should be "Required Work" and noted the direction in which changes might be made: the substitution of standards of achievement for fixed number of hours and credits. This would mean that the mathematics requirement, now stated as passing a certain course, could be met by a qualifying examination; that freshman English would be waived for students who did well in an examination—they could go into advanced work at once; that the foreign language requirement should be restated as "proficiency in one language or a reading knowledge of two," again to be measured by tests which would serve also for placement in advanced courses. Here was a transfer of values from honors work. Requirements would be understood in terms of meeting standards. Freshmen with special training or ability should not be "held back by the pace of the average," but should go at once into the advanced work for which they proved to be ready. The President welcomed this flexibility at a time when rigidity still often counted as an academic virtue; he welcomed also the chance to remove some causes of boredom. Hereafter no Swarthmore student need be bored by repeating what he already knew.

The committee liked these proposals, recommending them to the faculty, who put them into effect for the class entering in 1927. The plan carried the provision that in any course, whether required or not, a department should stand ready to give a placement test to a student who hoped to qualify for advanced work. That first year a smiling, round-faced young man asked to be examined on first-year chemistry, saying he wanted to make it his major. The department, astounded that anyone thought he could by-pass their own introduction, drew up a particularly stiff set of questions which the boy answered without a mistake. Where-upon no one could have been more pleased than the chemists, except perhaps the President.

In the first year the committee put through a new requirement for students in course at their own request: a comprehensive examination in their major subject at the end of the senior year. It had become clear that honors examinations gave a student the opportunity to survey and correlate two years' work in his major and minor subjects. Now a comprehensive examination for seniors in course would give them a similar chance.[21]

Intellectual Plums

From the time when the William J. Cooper Foundation began to support a program of lectures and concerts to "enrich the intellectual and artistic life of the college" and the village of Swarthmore, Frank Aydelotte had wanted to add a lectureship which would bring a distinguished person into residence for a month, to take part in seminars and classes and meet faculty and students informally. In a small, compact community like Swarthmore, such a visitor might make a significant impression.

This was precisely what happened when the Cooper Foundation Lectureship was launched in January, 1929, by A. D. Lindsay, Master of Balliol College, Oxford. Lindsay gave a series of lectures on *Essentials of Democracy*, to be published as the first volume of Cooper Foundation Lectures, appropriately including a discussion of the democracy characteristic of the Society of Friends.[22] He proved to be an ideal Lecturer in Residence—an approachable, generous, and lively member of every group he joined. The lecturers who followed him each in his own way furthered the President's aim: "to give the students . . . stimulus . . . from contact with . . . the world's great minds."

Frank Aydelotte took pride also in an unusual enterprise started in Swarthmore in 1929–1930, a study of unemployment financed by an anonymous friend of the college. The Board of Managers appointed Professor Paul H. Douglas of the University of Chicago (later Senator from Illinois) to take charge of the study. He established his headquarters in the college library with a Chicago colleague, Aaron Director, to help him. They produced a book, published in June, 1931, *The Problem of Unemployment*, which attracted wide attention by its timely subject and thoughtful conclusions. It received favorable reviews in many periodicals, the *New York Times Book Review* praising it as "the best of a thick harvest of books on unemployment."[23]

These two respected economists, at work on a subject of world importance, made their impact on the community, revealing a scientific approach to the depression and the possibilities of research as a career. Students took a proprietary interest in the book, many of them reading it carefully as they did the long and able review in the *Phoenix*. To the President, these effects on the undergraduates ranked high among the values of the venture.

Student Activities

The President observed that some kinds of student activities contributed notably to the quality of college life. One he reported to the Managers was the undergraduates' action when Professor Hull's opposition to the Big Navy Bill subjected him to attack by an official of the Daughters of the American Revolution, who demanded that he be removed from the Swarthmore faculty and deported from the United States. Though student opinion was divided on the merits of the bill, "the undergraduates were a unit in upholding the principle of free speech and the right of any citizen to express himself . . . on any questions . . . before Congress. . . . At a special meeting of the entire student body" a resolution was passed, deploring the stand of the D.A.R. official and expressing admiration for Dr. Hull: "We are firmly convinced that Dr. Hull has reached his decision through intimate research and intensive study in the field of International Relations. He has, in our opinion, all the essential qualities for a college professor and thinking American citizen."[24]

Other events on a similarly adult level: the publication by two students of a pamphlet on the textile mills of North Carolina, *Southern Labor in Revolt*;[25] a two-day conference at the college on the coal industry, with the Liberal Club as prime mover; a performance by one hundred students of four scenes from Rimsky-Korsakov's *Sadko*, directed by Professor Alfred Swan.

Athletics

With Frank Aydelotte's belief in athletics for everyone, he was glad that the percentage of men participants had reached four-fifths in 1927–1928. Then for the third year Swarthmore won a respectable number of games, half or more. He worked toward giving up football with larger institutions, such as the University of Pennsylvania and Princeton—contests with no value for Swarthmore except from gate receipts. He looked forward to football schedules exclusively with colleges of Swarthmore's size and the financing of athletics by a special endowment. All to be accomplished in good time.

Bricks and Mortar

While Frank Aydelotte heartily agreed with Abraham Flexner's slogan for the Institute for Advanced Study in its early years, "Brains, not buildings," when he had the funds for a building that was needed, he entered into every detail. First enlisting the help of Alfred Brooks, a trained architect as well as an art historian, the President asked everyone who would use the building to read the blueprints critically. As a result, there were few mistakes.

In these years the social life of the men's and women's fraternities was made more attractive by the completion of their lodges: five buildings for the men and six small row houses for the women, the latter forming a unit with the new center of women's and college activities, Bond Hall, all in a pleasant Cotswold style of a warm gray local stone. There were several new faculty houses, each based on a comfortable and thrifty plan tested by Alfred and Ruth Brooks in a house built for themselves. Much as the President appreciated adding to the charm and comfort of student and faculty life, the new buildings he valued most in these years were two which contributed to educational aims. First was the Clement M. Biddle Memorial, a wing of the library to house the Friends historical collections. This remained an important and growing center for research in Quaker history until 1967. In that year, which saw the completion of the great McCabe Library, the Quaker collections were transferred into a still more spacious setting provided by the Cornell family, but still continuous with the main library of the college. Then there was the Clothier Memorial, with an auditorium more than large enough to seat the whole college. This imposing building, constructed in a style the President called "Quaker Gothic"—an austere Early English—with its handsome tower the most conspicuous campus landmark, provided graciously for public events: weekly Collection, plays, and concerts. From the first sketches to the formal opening, the President gave his eager attention to every phase. He was particularly glad that the buildings put up in his administration carried the names of Quaker families he had known and admired: Worth, Biddle, Clothier, and soon to be added, Edward M. Martin.[26]

Wanted: Money

Among the President's pressing responsibilities of these busy years, none was so starkly essential as an endowment to replace the General Education Board's subsidy for honors work and to ensure Swarthmore's future development. The pledge of $675,000 from the superbly beneficent General Education Board in the spring of 1928 augured well for the two-million-dollar endowment campaign scheduled for the next year, to be compressed into the month before Commencement. In the interval the President took steps toward getting additional pledges, pointing out with some amusement that he was renouncing one of the conditions on which he accepted office: he should not be asked to raise money. Wilson Powell reassured him, saying that strictly speaking, he had been consistent: "it had not been necessary to ask him." Like other Presidents who took office on the same condition, Frank abandoned it when he saw that he could not carry out his plans without more money and that he was the one best prepared to present the need to potential donors, notably to the foundations.

Fortunately he had connections with several foundations through officers who had become his friends as they knew and admired his work:

in addition to Abraham Flexner of the Rockefeller Foundation's General Education Board, Frederick Keppel of the Carnegie Corporation and Edwin Embree of the Julius Rosenwald Fund. These, with Edward Harkness, who may have been glad to make some return for Frank's help with plans for the Commonwealth Fellowships, and an "anonymous donor" interested in a fitting tribute for his friend, Dr. Edward Martin, helped alumni and Managers round out the proposed two millions. Then the President pointed out that this would do little more than replace the subsidy, without providing means for further growth and proposed going ahead while the steam was up for two millions more. Alumni and Managers agreed to this second drive, and the foundations increased their pledges, with the result that the President announced in his *Report* of December, 1929, the completion of one campaign and the successful beginning of another, with only $175,000 still to raise. In spite of the crash in the stock market, an Emergency Committee of Alumni managed to complete the fourth million by the deadline of June 30, 1930. The President reported that the combined campaigns brought in a final total of $4,084,487.93, tabulated as follows:

General Education Board	$1,350,000.00
Alumni and Board of Managers	1,027,903.13
Anonymous—for the Edward Martin Department of Biology	700,000.00
Edward S. Harkness	500,000.00
Julius Rosenwald Fund	335,000.00
Carnegie Corporation	150,000.00
Outside Sources	21,584.80
	$4,084,487.93

Among many hard-working alumni, Frank Aydelotte paid special tribute to Morris L. Clothier, '90, chairman of the Emergency Committee, and Alan C. Valentine, '21, executive secretary of both campaigns. Alan, with the help of an alumna, Elsa Palmer Jenkins, '22 (later the President's secretary), combined efficiency with remarkable economy, keeping the total cost of the two campaigns down to $18,943.50, less than one-half of 1 per cent of $4,000,000. Frank announced proudly that this cost had been included in the college budget, "leaving every dollar contributed to go to the endowment fund."[27]

Of all the generous donors, the outstanding benefactor was clearly the General Education Board, which with its earlier subsidy of $240,000 gave Swarthmore more than one and a half millions.[28] How much the campaign owed to the President was handsomely acknowledged by the Managers: "the work had been done mainly by and credit should be given to President Aydelotte." (To anticipate the happy ending: thanks to the relative financial stability of donors to Swarthmore, notwithstanding the depression, pledges amounting to $4,000,000 were paid by June 30, 1936, "to meet the conditional pledges of the General Education Board which expired on that date."[29])

Frank's new-found facility in raising money brought him both praise and friendly teasing. "Who but Aydelotte would go out for two millions and come back with four?" "When would he become a professional fund raiser?" This last question, implying that he could promote practically anything, made him uncomfortable: "I couldn't ask for money except for something I believed in." He must have winced at the caption of a *Phoenix* editorial, "A Super Salesman," even though the editorial itself was wholly laudatory, ending: "Swarthmore is indeed fortunate in having as a president not merely a distinguished leader along educational lines, but a man possessed with uncanny powers of super-salesmanship."[30] It was true enough that when he believed in something with all his heart, such as the future of Swarthmore, he approached a man or a foundation with a confident air of offering an investment with the best possible returns. His methods were described by the Comptroller, N. O. Pittenger:

> His success lies in the fact that when he talks to a man who has a million dollars to give away, he is sincerely convinced that the work to be done with the money, the ends it will serve, the educational value in prospect, has a value far greater than that of the money it may cost. The money itself is nothing. Like the highest and most successful type of salesman, he knows he has something to exchange which is well worth the price to be paid for it. No man with a high regard for money will find it easy to persuade others to part with it.[31]

Important as the four millions would be to Swarthmore's future, the President considered the campaign's intellectual results almost equally valuable. For the alumni, an increase in understanding the college emphasis on quality; for American educators generally, heightened recognition of "the trend of the times . . . in the direction of higher standards of work. . . . Our new endowment funds have come to us because of the part which the college has taken in initiating the movement toward higher standards in the undergraduate course."[32]

The campaign had also brought the college a kind of publicity— praise by educators—that was especially convincing when they happened to be parents of Swarthmore students. The recent increase of parents who were "expert judges of educational values" delighted Frank, among them two friends whose endorsements of honors work have already been quoted, Abraham Flexner and Dorothy Canfield Fisher.

Vacations

The Aydelottes, like most families in academic circles, expected to use part of the long vacation for work. The President's responsibilities for the college were continuous and once or twice kept him at his desk in Swarthmore through most of the summer months. His obligations to travel for the Rhodes Trust and the Guggenheim Foundation could be met most easily when college was not in session. In the summers of 1925 and 1929 he went to Oxford on Rhodes Scholarship business, also in 1929 to Mexico to make arrangements for Guggenheim Fellowships, and in 1930 to South America. More about these trips in another chapter.

Four particularly happy vacations in the United States were spent by some or all of the Aydelottes in one of Wilson Powell's country houses in Old Chatham, New York, with Bill's friend, Maurice Cramer, a favorite visitor. Maurice's diary and memory offer pleasant glimpses of the life there. He reports a "constant stream of guests." "Mr. A." entertained them, wrote many business letters, played golf, even built a putting green, holding "after dinner putting matches ... keen to win even if over utterly inept boys like Bill and myself." He went in for "washing and greasing his old Franklin, and teaching Bill and me to do it. I can still see his bald head sticking out from under the rear end of the car while he lay on his back on the gravel drive greasing a spring." Maurice interpreted this kind of work as "the lingering on of country frugality, of professorial frugality that really has never left him."[33] But the gusto with which he greased a spring would remind anyone who knew the old Middle West that an Indiana small-town boy delighted in his own ingenuity, triumphant at not having to pay for work which he could quite well do for himself.

Maurice remarked on "Mr. A's keen pleasure in the sunsets at Old Chatham. After supper ... he would bundle us all into the car and dash up to some near high hill from which the Hudson Valley and the mountains were visible and the sunset sky. This meant something special to him, and therefore to us all." Sunsets had begun to mean something to Frank when he was a boy in Sullivan and used to drive his mother behind the old horse, Kibus, into a wild section of Brown County where they would sit on a hilltop to see the sun set and the moon rise.

Mr. A. could be stoical. "On the drive up one summer, Mr. A had their cat on a leash; it made a silly dash for freedom; Mr. A. dashed after, tripped on a mossy log (it was in a deep woods where we were lunching), and he sprained his ankle—he rolled on the ground for a moment in pain, but never said a single word, although he was laid up from his beloved golf for quite a while."[34]

Maurice's diary pictures Mrs. Aydelotte in a happy mood; "Mr. and Mrs. Aydelotte arrived yesterday. . . . This day was perfect. Mrs. Aydelotte was glorious. She is so radiant with humor, joy, fun, love, happiness that one is carried away as by a torrent. . . . We had an uproarious evening, laughter, noisy naturalness." The entry is dated "Wednesday July 25," probably of 1928, the summer between the boys' freshman and sophomore years.

During short vacations also Maurice often visited Bill at Swarthmore and remembers family customs that impressed him: "the loving way both parents, no matter how busy things were, did the packing up for Bill whenever he was going away to College. I remember sitting in the back rooms at Swarthmore while the entire Aydelotte family consulted over what neckties, shirts, etc., should be included; it was very jolly and affectionate."[35]

Once Mrs. Aydelotte included Maurice with Bill in an especially kind plan. It was 1929 after the summer when Maurice had not been able to join them on a trip to England because of his father's illness. Mrs. Aydelotte proposed that Maurice spend the Thanksgiving vacation in Cambridge with Bill, offering the trip as a present for both boys. She wrote him:

> Do you object to a gift which has to be shared? We are very eager to give you and Bill something which is quite as much for Bill as you. . . . We want to send you a return ticket to Cambridge so that you can spend a few days there with Bill. Bill says there is no Thanksgiving present he would like better than this. I wanted to see your mother first and get her consent for I did not want her to feel I was taking you away when you might be with her. But she agrees with me that the trip would do you good and the visit be of equal benefit to you and Bill.

Once, to "bolster" Maurice when he had "pulled a boner," Mrs. Aydelotte told him of an occasion when her husband lapsed into absent-mindedness.

At the conclusion of some important Swarthmore financial drive there was a dinner to announce the results. Mr. Aydelotte was so preoccupied that he forgot to announce it. Afterwards Mrs. A. said to him, 'Frank, why didn't you make the announcement?' He was driving; he pulled the car over to the side of the road in despair, and said, 'I'll resign.' Mrs. Aydelotte told me this . . . as an illustration of how a man who appeared so poised and so much on top of things could be tired and in need of support.

He could count on her for support of every sort, particularly for that of an able and sympathetic critic who understood what he was doing and how he might do it better. According to Maurice, "Mr. Aydelotte used to try out speeches and plans on his household. Many times Mrs. A., Bill and I were expected to give advice. I recall how astute, shrewd, practical, concrete, down to earth Mrs. A.'s suggestions were. She knew how to help him reach audiences and people."[36]

In 1931, after Bill was graduated from Harvard and Maurice from Princeton, they were in Old Chatham for part of the summer, the last they would spend there together. Bill went to Cambridge, England, in September to begin work for his Ph.D. in history; Maurice to the Princeton Graduate School, for English literature.

End of a Decade

The end of these six years in 1931 coincided with the close of Frank Aydelotte's first decade, surely a moment for stocktaking and congratulations. His *Annual Report*, which he converted into a survey of the decade, showed that ten years' experience had put meat on the bones of his theories and sharpened his skill in incisive writing. But he still gave first place to points he had emphasized when he took office: the character of the liberal arts college; a student's variety of opportunities; increases in faculty salaries and freedom for research.

At this point, when he discussed the liberal arts college, he rarely echoed Newman, but described what he had observed—limitations and possibilities alike. One oddity of this distinctively American institution was to combine work done in other countries by both secondary schools and universities: it "receives its students before their secondary education is really completed; its ideal is to graduate them four years later as liberally trained men and women, ready either for the duties of active life or for specialized professional study or research. . . . Inevitably it molds the careers of its students as does no other institution."[37] This molding he took to be, above all, intellectual: the college of liberal arts was a "good place only for students with definite intellectual interests. . . . In the place of the utilitarian urge, it must have in its students that rare thing, intellectual curiosity." Ten years had made Frank Aydelotte more of a thoroughgoing intellectual. He admitted the value of "college life," but chiefly as "relaxation from work and not an end in itself." If a student is led to exaggerate its importance, he "is cheated of his birthright. He fails to mature"; he also fails to justify the expenditure of the sums necessary for faculty salaries, equipment, and attractive surroundings. "To provide such facilities for students who are merely in search of a playground or an athletic club is a waste which no nation however wealthy could or should afford." The President believed that Swarthmore students now accepted this scale of values. "Unquestionably they tend to look upon studies, athletic sports and extra curricular activities with a truer sense of proportion than was the case ten years ago." Another gratifying result: to increase the number who go on to graduate or professional schools.

Turning to trends in student social life, the President praised the efforts of faculty and administration "to bring the life of the undergraduates as far as possible up to the standard of friendliness and simplicity of the early days of the college."[38] Freshmen were no longer hazed, but "oriented" by respected seniors; the rule against maintaining automobiles was "carefully enforced." One regret he admitted: that both the men's and women's fraternities had grown to the point where the membership included 70 per cent of the men and over 77 per cent of the women—an uncomfortable situation for the minority outside.

Over against this he put a decided change for the better, from "a great social pressure toward regimentation and uniformity" to "a new freedom of spirit and greater individuality." He welcomed this, sure that it would not go too far: "With most American colleges the excess is in the direction of regimentation, and we can confidently expect a richer social and intellectual life at Swarthmore from our present tendency in the opposite direction." No question but that he liked the students as he found them: "Certainly there never was a time when the undergraduates as a group were so frank and so interesting."

When he mentioned the additions to educational endowment, he took great satisfaction in the concurrent increases in faculty salaries. He could not resist amplifying the point: "the cost of instruction has risen in ten years from $102,000 to $248,000—a larger increase, both actually and in proportion, than all the other items combined." As to leaves of absence, he could point to a good number granted at shorter intervals than seven years and with full rather than half salary. He would institute a plan for "the orderly rotation of such periods of leave" as soon as the endowment pledges were paid. On the importance of faculty research he wrote: "In the long run the success of our plan of education will depend upon our developing our Faculty as a society of scholars—men and women who are citizens of the intellectual world and not merely tourists who have visited it in search of a Ph.D. degree."[39]

A signal academic triumph in prospect was the Edward Martin Department of Biology, to be housed and staffed with provisions for both teaching and research; "I hope that it may constitute a model which we shall be able to imitate in the case of other scientific and literary departments of the College." And this should be still another point where Swarthmore might lead the way:

> If we make it our policy to restrict the number of students and the number of subjects which we teach, and if we can provide in each subject not merely for teaching but also for research, we should be able to offer at Swarthmore a unique opportunity both to our students and to the members of our faculty. . . . It is in this direction that I should like to see Swarthmore develop; to build here such an institution would be to ensure the lasting success of our contribution to American higher education.[40]

Congratulations were in order at a luncheon in Frank Aydelotte's honor given by the Swarthmore Alumni Association on June 6, 1931. Detlev Bronk, President of the Association, was toastmaster; the chief speaker, Marian Edwards Park, President of Bryn Mawr, Frank Aydelotte's neighbor in office for nine of his ten years.

Miss Park praised the President of Swarthmore for standing out against the popular veneration for numbers—the trend toward making small colleges larger—but at the same time avoiding the danger of too great homogeneity. He had achieved "variety within a small compass" through honors work. He had solved the problem of the faculty by making their position as close as possible to that of teachers in a large graduate school, with "the prerequisites of apparatus, of library, of equipment, of leisure." Even more remarkable from the worldly point of view, he had convinced two groups that he was right, "the most difficult groups . . . that anyone could find, the alumni and the foundations." As for the first: "I believe that the alumni of all colleges have chosen as their patron saint, Thomas. One can never convince all of them all of the time, and some of them will doubt to the end. But I understand that the Swarthmore of President Aydelotte's dreams will be gazed upon by the minimum of doubting alumni." With "more bitterness" she admitted his success with the foundations, intimating that in addition to his publicly acclaimed "virtues of courage and intelligence and vision" he must have certain added "mundane" virtues of "tact and persistence and wit" which have "gained him . . . the victory." Confessing that she, like other Presidents, was "admiring and critical and jealous," Miss Park conceded that he took success in his stride: "He does not call together his friends and neighbors to hear a new encomium or to rejoice over a new million; he simply sets to work to earn another encomium and to ask for another million."[41]

The subject of those tributes, when his turn came, passed on the praise to the faculty and the students, who, he said, had earned it; his own role had been to "take the obstacles out of their paths." He thanked the Board and the alumni for their generosity and "spiritual support" and above all for the Quaker "willingness to let the individual follow the dictates of his own conscience" at a time when freedom was becoming "so difficult and so rare." He told an experience in point:

> I made a speech in Philadelphia in which, as usual, I said what I thought, and later someone said to me: 'Do you realize that there are not half a dozen colleges in the country where the president can make a speech like that and keep his job?' I had not thought of it before, but it is one of the blessings of a college like this, and one which I hope you will guard jealously for all of your faculty and all your presidents.

Unfortunately there is no clue to what he said.

Recognition

In these six years Frank Aydelotte and his work at Swarthmore were recognized by honorary Doctor's Degrees from the University of Pittsburgh, Oberlin, and Yale. His friend James Rowland Angell, President of Yale, conferred the degree of Doctor of Laws upon him in 1928, with an unusually apt citation: "In recognition of your distinguished service in the successful promotion of the old ideal of liberal education by fresh and inspiring methods, and particularly of your rare combination of insight and vision with practical ingenuity and sound judgment."[42]

The bulletin on *Higher Education* issued by the United States Bureau of Education in 1927 noted the attempt of Swarthmore to develop honors courses as the "best and most promising" in the country. The report goes on to say, "No single movement in higher education has given more interest or promises more far-reaching results than this."[43]

During the Columbia Summer Session of 1931, Frank Aydelotte was invited to give one of a series of lectures on educational experiments in five institutions: Columbia, Harvard, Chicago, Wabash, and Swarthmore; and the lectures were published as a book, *Five College Plans.* Early in September he enjoyed the honor of election to the Senate of Phi Beta Kappa for a six-year term. All straws in a fair and favoring wind.

In 1933 he conceived a scheme in which two of his offices joined hands. The American Rhodes Scholars had never yet had a reunion, and he worked out a plan by which they could meet in Swarthmore at commencement time, hear some of their senior members, and spend a further day or two together. Willard Sperry (Michigan and Queen's, '04), Dean of the Harvard Divinity School, gave the baccalaureate address, and Tucker Brooke (West Virginia and Oriel, '04), Professor of English at Yale, gave the Phi Beta Kappa address. Sir Francis Wylie was to give the commencement address, but at the last moment was prevented by a virus infection, and Lady Wylie read his manuscript for him. The 114 Rhodes Scholars in attendance held a symposium on public affairs at which a recent Eastman Professor, Wesley C. Mitchell, and Wilson's Secretary of War, Newton D. Baker, were speakers. The economy was at low ebb in those days, and the irrepressible Paul Kieffer (Maryland and Oriel, '04) described a man who wanted to shoot Aimee McPherson, Huey Long, and Rudy Vallee for God, for country, and for Yale. There was a banquet at which food, humor, sentiment, and memories abounded. The reunion was a gay affair, and the campus played up the occasion by wearing its floweriest dress.

CHAPTER THIRTEEN

ADVENTURES WITH FOUNDATIONS

Rhodes Trust, Commonwealth Fund, John Simon Guggenheim Memorial

American Secretary to the Rhodes Trustees

THESE years of pressure in the President's office were also full of activity in the Rhodes office. Since the routine work of this office was handled by the experienced Emma Abbett, Frank Aydelotte was free to concentrate on the elections of Scholars, writing announcements to be posted in colleges and universities, sending notices to newspapers, framing committees of selection, arranging their interviews with candidates, and preparing press releases of new appointments.

In forming committees—now consisting, to his high satisfaction, of old Rhodes Scholars except for the chairmen—Frank took pains to find men in each state who were in touch with younger people and, if possible, sufficiently well known so that their decisions would carry weight. Here he could rely on office records and personal impressions which he kept fresh by traveling over the country, taking Rhodes Scholarship trips "for recreation," so he said. On these trips he had a chance to mention casually his idea of changing the basis for elections from states to regions, which was soon to become a conspicuous and controverted issue.

Frank saw another function of his office: to provide general information about Oxford. When postwar changes put existing handbooks out of date, he and L. A. Crosby (Maine and Trinity, '13) produced a new one, *Oxford of Today*, Frank contributing a chapter on the operation of the Scholarships in the United States. The book drew favorable reviews, one of them noting that "although . . . intended primarily as a manual

for prospective Rhodes Scholars, it is of more than ordinary interest for
the average reader who enjoys good history, is interested in education,
and desires, withal, to read of both in excellent English."[1]

When *Scribner's Magazine* presented Frank with a title, "What the
Rhodes Scholar Gets from Oxford," he produced an article with more
subtle appraisals than those of *The Oxford Stamp*. In that earlier book he
had brought together essays written before 1916, formulating his creed as
a teacher. Now, in 1923, with seven years' added maturity, including
two in a President's office, he was ready to suggest what a man gained
from Oxford on a deeper level, intellectually and otherwise. The article
was described by the *Oxonian* as "one of the meatiest and most judicial,
as well as one of the most alluring, estimates of Oxford opportunity that
we have ever read."[2] The Rhodes Scholar's intellectual gains, put briefly,
are: a B.A. degree combining the widest liberty of choice with the
greatest opportunity of mastery; a new capacity for independent work;
and an opportunity to know himself intellectually—"he may come back
to America with his intellectual creed unchanged, but he can hardly
come back without having thought through for himself the whole
foundation of his educational beliefs, a process of the highest value
whatever may be the result."

Frank emphasized again some gains noted in *The Oxford Stamp*: the
conception of sport for sport's sake and acquaintance with the delight
and value of good talk. But he went on to stress other accessions. The
Scholar comes back with a changed attitude toward his own country; he
is a better American, but less of a jingo (the jingo, like every other
blusterer, being "at heart not sure of his own cause"). He has a fresh
international outlook and a new conception of the kinship of the English-
speaking nations. Finally, he has a keener appreciation of the richness of
life. This last takes him time to recognize:

> Only in after years, on one of those visits which Americans show such a
> tendency to make back to the home of their English foster-mother, will
> he be able to see in true perspective the significance of these eager
> undergraduate days—days of intense effort, of struggle with great tasks,
> of listening to half-heeded words of great teachers, of light-hearted, high-
> spirited converse. . . . Then some night as he walks back to his lodgings
> after dinner at High Table—that stateliest of all the rites of academic
> hospitality—the moonlight on sleeping walls and towers will thrill him
> with the sense of the tangled, interwoven beauty of this life that once was
> his.

Frank's work as American Secretary was recognized in 1923 by an honor from England, election to the distinguished London club The Athenaeum. He had been proposed in 1918 by George Parkin (soon to be knighted), who wrote that the seconder would be Sir William Osler: "He was delighted to put down his name as seconder, so I hope ten or twelve years hence that you will find yourself a member of the famous old club. The chance of my being there to welcome you is very dim."[3] Although Frank had, in fact, been elected sooner, neither of his sponsors was living; Sir William Osler had died in 1919 and Sir George Parkin in 1922. The invitation came in a letter which Frank treasured because its writer was the Shakespearean scholar Sir Sidney Lee,[4] who had been one of the official readers of his thesis, *Elizabethan Rogues and Vagabonds.*

British Fellowships Plan

While still at the Massachusetts Institute of Technology, Frank began to play with the idea of finding an American Cecil Rhodes who would finance a plan to bring British students to the United States. Having let the idea drop temporarily in his first two years at Swarthmore, he picked it up again and prepared a memorandum for Beardsley Ruml, Director of the Laura Spelman Rockefeller Memorial Foundation, in the hope of interesting the Trustees.[5] Though this gave a wealth of details, Frank was not yet ready to stop "asking advice." He was going to England in the summer of 1923 and proposed to consult leading educators and others who could give valuable support when a plan was put into effect. His list of forty-one is impressive, including sixteen heads of colleges and nine professors, a total of thirteen from Oxford, five from Cambridge, four from the University of London, the editors of the *Times* and the *Spectator*, and Secretaries of several offices in Education. Five of the forty-one had been members of the British University Mission to the United States with whom Frank Aydelotte traveled in the autumn of 1918. Now, in 1923, his schedule of interviews was compressed into three and a half weeks, beginning in Oxford on July 23, ending August 16–17 in Dublin.[6]

Rewarded by cordial interest in his plan, Frank saw that the time had come to get more definite information about the probable expenses of British students in American universities, and he came home to launch a sheaf of inquiries to graduate schools. He asked Dean Woodbridge of Columbia, for example, "How much money ought a man have to live in reasonable comfort, pay his fees and expenses, buy books and clothes, pay medical doctors' and dentists' bills, etc., during the normal university year at Columbia? And how much do you think we ought to allow him to travel a certain amount through the country in the summer vacation?"[7] The answers estimating needs for the academic year ranged from eight and nine hundred dollars at state universities to two thousand at Princeton and Harvard. As to what should be added for summer travel, most people made no suggestion. When the plan was put into effect, it was sensibly flexible in financial arrangements.

Happily Frank's ideas appealed to the Spelman Trustees; they decided to offer fellowships, but only in the social sciences, on the ground that other fields were already covered by other Rockefeller funds. Frank reported these new opportunities to the London office of the American University Union, asking for help in bringing them to the attention of British educators.[8] This would be indispensable, owing to the usual Rockefeller practice of avoiding publicity. He described the method of appointment, which did not include "applications from individuals." Instead, "a representative of the scholarships will be selected in England, and he will undertake to obtain from Professors in the subjects concerned nominations of advanced students who would benefit by postgraduate study of these subjects in the United States and who would be men or women of such outstanding attainments as to deserve appointments." Then an echo of one of Cecil Rhodes's ambitions for his Scholars: "So far as possible it is the wish of the Spelman Trustees that the appointments be restricted to people who are likely after their return to be able to pass on the results of their training to others, either by teaching or by public work of some kind in their respective fields." Frank added that he would go over soon to select and recommend the man to launch the scheme "modestly and quietly" in time to let the first group begin study in the United States the following September (1924).

He sailed on March 1 and soon cabled Beardsley Ruml that he had chosen J. R. M. Butler, fellow of Trinity College, Cambridge (later Regius Professor of Modern History). Butler had agreed to "a salary of 500 plus travelling, printing and stenographic expenses." When Ruml wrote that he had confirmed the appointment, he added, "I believe the preliminary work is now over and that we may say that a fellowship plan in the social sciences has actually been begun."[9] He enclosed a check to Frank for his expenses, $1,031.67. According to Frank's secretary, Emma Abbett, his work of planning and arranging was never publicly acknowledged, somewhat to his surprise. Nevertheless, when "they" asked his advice again, he gave it without hesitation. "He cared very little who got the credit for something so long as it was well done and worth doing."

Since the Spelman Foundation operated by spending its principal and would close its books in 1928, the life of these fellowships would not be long. Consequently Frank was gratified when his plans were used again by the Commonwealth Fund as the basis of a more lasting and extensive system.

Commonwealth Fellowships

Earlier, when Frank first began to dream of British fellowships, he discussed them with the Director of the Commonwealth Fund, Max Farrand, who encouraged him to put something in writing to show to Edward S. Harkness. Frank did so, but though Mr. Harkness expressed an interest, he was not ready to do anything then.[10] Fortunately Frank was not the only American who saw the importance of bringing British students to this country. His concern was shared by a military attaché in London after the war, Colonel Oscar N. Solbert, who felt that despite all the talk about Anglo-American friendship, scarcely anything was done to help British young people know the United States at first hand. Hearing the Prince of Wales say at a banquet of the American University Union that he wished there could be a few British students at every American university to "learn about your country and your people,"[11] Colonel Solbert took occasion to ask the Prince if he might care to help interest a possible donor of fellowships—again, Edward S. Harkness. The Prince happened to be on the point of going to the United States; he played golf with Mr. Harkness; and the upshot of their talk was that the Commonwealth Fund took on the fellowships and the Prince himself agreed to sponsor the plan as Honorary Chairman of the British Board of Selection.

At that time Max Farrand, remembering his talk with Frank, told him what was in the air, adding that he would be glad to show Frank's plan to Mr. Harkness, though if it were used, the understanding would have to be that Frank's name might not be mentioned. Frank gave his plan gladly. It was adopted with only slight changes and with handsome acknowledgment of his help. Mr. Harkness wrote him a cordial personal note of thanks, which reads in part:

> I want you to know how deeply I appreciate the great help which you gave Mr. Farrand in connection with the new Plan for British Fellowships recently started by the Commonwealth Fund.

Mr. Farrand has told me on several occasions of your great kindness and willingness to help him in every possible way and of the very complete plan for such a project which you had worked out and so willingly let him have.[12]

In one of the first published accounts of the Commonwealth Fellow-ships (July, 1925), Max Farrand himself wrote: "I should like here publicly to give credit to President Aydelotte of Swarthmore for his assistance in developing the details of this plan. President Aydelotte had already been working as many of you know, upon this very subject for a number of years. He turned over his plan for our use, and it was simply adapted to meet the requirements of our directors."[13] In a private letter to Frank, Farrand said that when he had been in London making arrangements, he began his remarks everywhere by mentioning that this was Frank's plan, "and the result was that the path was clear for me in every case,"[14] sure proof that Frank's prolonged consultations in England had borne fruit. The fact that this was for someone else's picking did not trouble him. Indeed, he took satisfaction in using his experience with the Rhodes Scholarships to improve these new awards: the stipends were more generous and included transportation from a student's home in Britain to his destination in the United States, as well as provision for summer travel.

Guggenheim Fellowships

Frank Aydelotte's active connection with the Guggenheim Foundation during the first twenty-five years of the Fellowships was one of the happiest chapters in his life. To appreciate his excitement at pioneering in such an important field, we have to remember the scarcity at that time of scholarships and fellowships for study abroad and the fact that many of those offered were for only $400 or $500, not nearly enough to cover a year's expenses. A student could not afford to accept one unless he could supplement it with his savings or a loan. In 1924 Frank estimated the number of "effective" scholarships—those of $1,000 or more—as only 154 a year.

In his position as Educational Adviser to the Guggenheim Foundation, he took a leading part in determining its aim in line with his lifelong concern to give unusually talented individuals the freedom to do their best work—in this case, scholars and artists of maturity and promise. He was equally effective in problems of organization and administration, having the practical imagination both to chart a course and to foresee the details. When plans to extend the Fellowships required his presence in Mexico and South America, he enjoyed meeting able Latin Americans, but even more the sense of playing a part in good international relations.

What he accomplished, as he would have been the first to say, owed much to the quality of those who worked with him and became his warm personal friends: two old Rhodes Scholars, Carroll A. Wilson (Massachusetts and Worcester, '08), already established as legal counsel for the Guggenheim brothers; Henry Allen Moe (Scholar-at-Large, Brasenose, '19), fresh from Oxford when he agreed to help Frank set up the Foundation; Senator Simon Guggenheim himself, one of the ablest and most lovable public benefactors of his generation. Frank was devoted to him; indeed, temperamentally the two men had much in common. Part of a tribute to the Senator might have been paid verbatim to Frank: "He was sanguine, constructive, liberal; he was kind, generous and appreciative." His was "a truly American spirit of fair play, hard work, venturesome decision, and warm and confident faith in the future."[15] The Senator came to like and respect Frank so much as to offer to take him into his business, promising to make him a rich man in five years. Frank was touched by the compliment, but declined, saying that making money did not interest him half so much as spending it on education.

The first inkling that Senator and Mrs. Guggenheim were considering a possible memorial for their son, John Simon, reached Frank a day or two before he sailed to England (March 1, 1924) on behalf of the Spelman Trustees. Carroll Wilson wrote to ask his advice for the Senator, who was "interested in forming a foundation or trust for the general purpose of transmarine education."[16] Wilson said he had told the Senator that Frank was the man to consult because of his experience with the Rhodes Scholarships, and he went on to give a few preliminary facts.

The income available could amount eventually to $500,000 a year, beginning probably with $300,000, about 20 per cent to be devoted to bringing young men from South America to study in the United States, the balance for scholarships which young men and women from this country would use in Europe. Wilson said:

> I gather from my talk with him that so far as the 80 per cent is concerned, he is interested first in extending the benefits of his gift to persons of musical and artistic ability, or along other lines more remote from pure scholarship, and second, that he wishes these benefits to be applied wherever in Europe proves to be best suited to the particular beneficiary, rather than to have them confined to a single country or specific institution.

Here was a scheme on an even grander scale than the Rhodes, involving at the start $26,000 more a year, open to women as well as men, extended to include music and art, to take the recipient wherever he should prefer to go. Frank replied that he would be delighted to help, but would have to postpone meeting the Senator until his return from England in April.

During Frank's absence, Carroll Wilson prepared the Senator for profitable discussions by drawing up a masterly memorandum on problems of organization and aim.[17] Pointing out that some existing scholarships had gone begging, Wilson explained this as indicating, not lack of interest in study abroad, but failure in publicity. There must be a "high degree of publicity in the press and in educational circles"; young people must feel that an appointment is "generally recognized as an honor singling out the successful person." This had been achieved for the Rhodes Scholarships under Frank Aydelotte's direction. As to the all-important topic of "The Field for the Foundation," Wilson urged that it must be *distinctive*, not competing with the Rhodes, for example, but wider. Wilson listed areas not yet covered by any foundation, including music and art and the general foreign education of women. With so many important decisions to make and put into effect, the Senator could see the need of an extremely able "organizing secretary" who would set up the Foundation and then either stay on as permanent secretary or give over to a less experienced man.

After several talks with Frank, the Senator concluded that there was "only one man for this big work," Frank himself.[18] Carroll Wilson went as "confidential messenger" to offer the job, but Frank felt he could not leave Swarthmore with his work there only well begun. Wilson sounded him out again about a position which he could combine with the presidency of Swarthmore. "Both the Senator and Mrs. Guggenheim would of course have preferred all your time—but both felt, as I did, that they had rather acquire your responsibleness for the work on part time, than another man's on full."[19] At this point Wilson sent another memorandum to the Senator suggesting next steps: "Engage Aydelotte as responsible head of enterprise" and let him find an assistant to work closely with him and take charge of the New York office. The assistant should be a man who gives "promise of developing into the active working head of the enterprise after the extremely difficult questions of policy, which arise only at the start and in the first years, have been determined upon."[20] Wilson ended with a tentative timetable: a public announcement about

January 1, 1925, and the first Fellows on their way to Europe the following fall. At the end of June the Senator formally invited Frank to serve as "Educational Adviser to put the plan into successful operation," at a salary of $10,000 a year.[21] Frank pointed out that the work would involve some trial and error and would be likely to take at least three years. Both he and Wilson wanted to guard against the Senator's expecting final arrangements too quickly. With the approval of the Swarthmore Board of Managers, Frank accepted.

On the choice of an assistant there was no immediate decision. Frank and Wilson exchanged views through the summer, going so far as to try out a man from the west coast, but neither he nor anyone else seemed right. Then in August there returned from Oxford a Rhodes Scholar, Henry Allen Moe, whom they knew and admired, both of them having served on the committee which recommended his appointment as Scholar-at-Large. In reporting the recommendation to Dr. Parkin, Frank had stressed Moe's academic record, adding a footnote on his war service to explain temporary disabilities: Moe was then "in a naval hospital in Brooklyn recovering from injuries received for undertaking an extremely dangerous bit of duty in connection with the repair of his ship—a duty so dangerous that he was unwilling to order any of his men to undertake it, but instead took the risk himself."

Moe had done well at Oxford. He had taken a B.A. in Jurisprudence with First Class Honours, followed by a B.C.L. and an appointment as Hulme Lecturer in Law, to teach for a year. Now at the age of thirty he was returning to the United States presumably to practice law. Would he have the imagination to see the possibilities in the proposed new foundation? Frank asked him to come to Swarthmore to talk things over, and he reported to Wilson favorably. "Moe is with me and it looks as if he would do for the Guggenheim job and he is definitely interested. He is going to make a trial trip for me interviewing six or eight college Presidents in the Middle West."[22]

In this trial trip Henry Moe was introduced to Frank's way of laying the foundations for an important project by asking expert advice after first drawing up a memorandum to use as a basis for discussion. Why he wanted to consult college Presidents Frank explained in a report to the Senator, giving two reasons: "first, the obvious one that some of them would be able to contribute suggestions of value, and secondly, the psychological one, that when your plans are put into operation, they, having been in on the ground floor, will be the more interested and will

therefore be the more certain to give their valuable support."[23] The
second explanation was to Frank the more important; he had plenty of
ideas of his own.

As to the kind of memorandum he preferred, it should not be in final
form, but "sufficiently fluid so that every individual can feel that his
contribution can at least be considered." Frank might even include a
point he thought dubious. Because someone had suggested it, he would
not dismiss it out of hand, though he would not be sorry to see it
modified or given up altogether. He worked like an artist, feeling his
way. Henry Moe, with his legal background, might have expected a
memorandum to be rather like a formal brief in which a definite line
was laid down. Actually this one was no more than a page and a half of
suggestions sent recently by Frank to Carroll Wilson,[24] to be introduced
by Moe in an interview when he could make the opportunity.

Frank had noted four suggestions, two or more of which might be
combined, or one used alone.

1.   A system of supplementary grants to holders of traveling fellowships from various colleges, in order to raise the total to an amount
adequate for the expenses of a year abroad: $1,5000 to $2,000 a year.

2.   A limited number of continuation fellowships to holders of grants
under (1) who have made progress but need more time to complete
their work.

3.   A limited number of advanced research fellowships for which
applicants must already have taken a research degree and entered upon
their teaching or scholarly career—applicants who could be expected to
make important contributions to scientific, literary, or historical knowledge if it were possible for them to drop remunerative employment for a
year or two.

4.   A publication fund of $5,000 to $10,000 to bring out books and
monographs written by holders of research fellowships (3), the Trustees
having the right to publish but also the right to refuse.

(All four points, in modified form, will appear in the "Outline of
Purposes" of the Foundation.)

Between August 22 and September 26 Henry Moe interviewed the
Presidents of twelve colleges and universities: Ohio State, Butler, Wabash,
Carleton, Minnesota, Hamline, Northwestern, Chicago, Indiana, Oberlin,
Western Reserve, and Buffalo. He sent Frank two reports that made
interesting reading. He described one encounter on a hot afternoon with
a man with a gift for confident self-contradiction, who said first that it

was dangerous to send young Americans to European universities because they are "veritable hotbeds of radical thought," and the next minute, that "in international education lies one of the hopes of peace for the future." To which Moe charitably added, "It was, as I say, a very hot afternoon!"

At Minnesota he had seen the Dean of the Graduate School, Guy Stanton Ford, as well as President Coffman. Dean Ford was one of two men whose comments stand out in Moe's reports; the other was President Vinson of Western Reserve.[25]

When Dean Ford heard the first suggestion, to supplement existing inadequate traveling fellowships, he dismissed it. "The donor will not rise to pulling some other persons' irons out of the fire. That's the short answer to your first suggestion."[26] He was also against the second: to give some continuation grants to men who had held such fellowships and had made some progress, but needed more time. Here he was opposed on the ground that there would be no one to say which men deserved and needed these grants: "The system of European Universities being as it is, the professors would know next to nothing of the scholars' work." Then he asked, so Moe reported, "'Have you any other suggestions?' I outlined suggestion 3. He said, 'That is fine, but I should go farther along those lines. I should make the bulk of the fund available for advanced research fellowships. . . . There is a real gap in existing schemes right at this point; the fund could not be used to better advantage.'"

Dean Ford spoke of what such help would mean to instructors who were granted sabbatical leave on half pay but could not afford to take it. At Minnesota, he said, only "one third of one percent take their leave. They cannot make it." The situation would be wholly changed if these instructors could get a research fellowship to add to their half salary. But he was fully aware of the difficulty in interesting a donor in the instructors' age group: "donors generally want to help youth." He was confident, however, that "they would be doing more with their money if they helped older, more mature men. . . . These men make better 'American ambassadors,' they bring more to Europe. . . . And when they come back, what such men have acquired abroad is of direct social utility." He tentatively approved suggestion (4), a fund for publishing fellows' books or monographs, with the safeguard noted, that the Trustees would have the right either to publish or not, as they saw fit.

If Dean Ford, in recognizing advanced research fellowships as something new, had asked where the idea came from, the obvious answer to anyone who knew the Aydelotte history was from Frank's own experience. As an associate professor at Indiana, thirty-two years old, with a wife and child to support, holder of a research degree for which he had produced a thesis he was eager to make into a book, he had the almost unprecedented good fortune of getting a year's sabbatical leave together with a grant from the Rhodes Trustees. The two stipends permitted him to take his family to Oxford where he rewrote *Elizabethan Rogues and Vagabonds*, which was published by the Clarendon Press in a subsidized series, Oxford Historical and Literary Studies. The similarity between this opportunity of his and the one outlined in his suggestions for Guggenheim Fellowships is too close for coincidence. He wanted to extend to other ambitious and impecunious teachers such advantages as he had enjoyed.

Henry Moe found President Vinson of Western Reserve absorbed in an idea of his own for improving Mexican education. When Moe asked him what he would do if he had several millions to use for education, he answered:

> I would . . . build in Mexico a college which would be to that part of the world what Robert College is to the Near East. Mexico is the leading one of the Spanish speaking countries and is recognized by them as such; Mexico is the place for such a college. . . . They are just waking up to the advantages of education in Mexico. . . . At the present, 90 percent of the population is illiterate: a college, such as Robert College, would be a big factor in changing that.[27]

When Moe sent in his final report, he added conclusions of his own. First, that "to insure the success of a scheme . . . there must be behind it a big, statesmanlike idea, an idea . . . that strikes the imagination, is easy to grasp and to hold."[28] It was because the Rhodes Scholarships were based on "the friendship of the English-speaking peoples" that they had succeeded conspicuously, whereas other schemes, for want of such an idea, had accomplished less. Second, "The selection's the thing. The big idea behind the whole foundation is necessary to get good men, but when you have found them the thing is accomplished."

Moe was convinced that "the biggest idea" he had heard is President Vinson's, but it did not go far enough. "Senator X should make himself the Rhodes of the Western hemisphere—the big idea being Pan-American friendship." Because of differences in language and literacy, the method would have to be different from the Rhodes machinery. Logically the first step would be to carry out Vinson's idea of "a college such as Robert College of Constantinople," gathering scholars there from Mexico and Central and South America; give them the equivalent of a B.A. degree there, and then "send the best of them to the United States for graduate work." Then Moe added a large-minded second point of his own, to "send Americans to the universities of the Spanish speaking countries."

If President Vinson's proposal should not be feasible, Moe would agree with Dean Ford "that the field to take was that of young professors and instructors" and other scholars at the same stage of promising productivity. On this point more than any other he had found the Presidents agreed. He reported also fairly general if tepid approval of publishing products of the Fellows' research, always with the proviso that the Trustees could refuse to publish a particular work. All maintained that "selection was the thing," some thinking this would be easy, others difficult.

Before Henry Moe completed his trip, he had told Frank he would accept the position of secretary if he were offered it. He noted that he had received support of an important kind: his fiancée also was in favor. In response to a letter from him, she had cabled: "Idea Appeals. Seems Opportunity for Great Good."[29] She was right.

Senator Guggenheim wrote to Moe on October 20, 1924, proposing to put him in charge of the New York office of the Foundation, "but in developing and working out policies and carrying out details" he would be under the direction of the Educational Adviser, Frank Aydelotte. Moe's salary would be $5,000 a year. This was equal to the salary of many full professors at that time. Frank, always liking to do the best he could for a young assistant, wrote to Carroll Wilson to ask if Moe could be paid from October 1 instead of the date mentioned, the fifteenth: "Moe has already done six weeks of pretty hard work on the scheme for expenses, and it might be a graceful thing to do, if the Senator felt like it. . . . But there is absolutely no obligation, of course, and indeed the boy is fortunate . . . to start in such a good position, so that if you feel it is more tactful not to mention this matter to the Senator, don't do so. I will leave it to you."[30] This was the beginning of Henry Moe's remarkable career with the Guggenheim Foundation, which lasted for almost forty years.

Before Frank recommended a plan to Senator Guggenheim, he collected supporting facts and figures so that the evidence in favor of his proposals would be as decisive as possible. He showed where there were gaps in existing schemes and quoted educators who had helped to formulate his suggestions for filling the gaps, presenting these findings in thirty-six typed pages with the heading, "Endowments for Foreign Study: A Report on Systems of Scholarships now in Operation and on the Field which Might Usefully be Occupied by a New Foundation."

While the Senator considered this report, Frank went to New England for further interviews, with Henry Moe's help, partly to interest educators who eventually agreed to serve on the Foundation's Educational Advisory Board. When the Senator had made his decisions, Frank prepared a draft of the Memorandum which would announce the Fellowships, taking it with him for advice on wording from President Butler and Dean Woodbridge at Columbia, President Lowell and Professor Charles Haskins at Harvard. The resulting "Outline of Purposes" was rightly described as the result "of the best educational thought in the country."[31] The Memorandum itself is a noble document, offering a respite from the struggle to earn a living to young men and women equipped to use this freedom in distinguished constructive work.

The purpose of the Foundation sounds a call to public-spirited ambition:

> To improve the quality of education and the practice of the arts and professions in the United States, to foster research, and to provide for the cause of better international understanding, the John Simon Guggenheim Memorial Foundation Fellowships for Advanced Study Abroad offer to young men and women opportunities under the freest possible conditions to carry on advanced study and research in any field of knowledge or opportunities for the development of unusual talent in any of the fine arts, including music.

The Memorandum consists of two parts, one of regulations, the other giving Simon Guggenheim's view of the memorial to his son.

As to regulations, the keynote is flexibility. There are no restrictions of sex, race, color, creed, marital status, subject, or place of study; no strict age limits, though a candidate should be advanced enough to show undoubted promise—probably between twenty-five and thirty-five. The stipend may vary according to need, from a norm of $2,500, and may be held in addition to a sabbatical leave's salary or a fellowship from a college. Awards will be for one year, subject to renewal when this seems advisable. The two firm requirements are that candidates must have begun the constructive work which they need help to complete and "that they shall produce contributions to knowledge in their special subjects and . . . make the results of their studies publicly available. Where necessary and deemed wise the Foundation will give financial assistance towards publication." The first awards would be made for 1926–1927, in the expectation of maintaining forty to fifty Fellows a year. As if to demonstrate flexibility from the start, fifteen awards were granted a year ahead of the stated time to Fellows who went abroad in September, 1925.

These regulations echo the four points of the memorandum which Aydelotte gave to Moe before his trial run of interviews: (1) the stipend could supplement a fellowship granted by a college and (2) could be renewed; (3) holders should be experienced enough for advanced research; (4) on occasion, the Foundation might supply funds for publishing Fellows' productions. It is conceivable that the three able men, Frank Aydelotte, Carroll Wilson, and Henry Moe, without asking advice, could have drawn from these points substantially the plan announced, but what a difference in effectiveness! Thanks to laborious consultation and discussion, there was a host of interpreters and advocates who had a share in a remarkable new enterprise.

Simon Guggenheim's statement begins with a reference to his son, who died in 1922: "If he had lived, he would have continued his education in one of our great American Universities, and then upon his graduation there, would have embarked upon a course of graduate study abroad, just such as we are now endeavoring to make possible for others under this Foundation." Mr. Guggenheim goes on to mention his interest in the Rhodes Scholarships and his desire to supplement them with opportunities for older students, for women as well as men, in the hope of contributing to an even broader international understanding and to research "on the broadest possible base." He takes satisfaction that "the income of the Foundation will be spent on men and not on materials," trusting "that the result will be to increase, at least to some degree, the vitality and effectiveness of American education."

According to Carroll Wilson's first letter to Frank about a possible Guggenheim Foundation, the Senator's idea had been to divide the income between two aims: 20 per cent to bring Latin Americans to study in the United States, 80 per cent to take North Americans to Europe. While only the second was ready to go into effect, the Fellowships for Latin Americans were not forgotten. By 1930 they would be set up in Mexico, Chile, and Argentina and promised as forthcoming for Cuba and Puerto Rico.

The first announcement of the Guggenheim Fellowships for North Americans came out in the New York newspapers on February 23, 1925, almost exactly a year after Frank heard of the Senator's concern from Carroll Wilson. On February 17, 1925, *The London Times* gave the first news of the Commonwealth Fellowships to bring British students to the United States. An article in the *American Oxonian*, commenting on both schemes, mentions that both are indebted to the Rhodes Scholarships on two counts: "the donors' satisfaction with the management and consequences of the Rhodes Scholarships; . . . the personal labors and counsel of the American representative of the Rhodes Trust, Frank Aydelotte."[32]

CHAPTER FOURTEEN

SWARTHMORE: 1931–1940

Riding the Waves

WITH the completion of Frank Aydelotte's first decade, some of his colleagues wondered how they could keep him at Swarthmore. He had reached his main objectives: to establish honors work firmly but flexibly and make it well known; to add to the faculty and their salaries; to raise the necessary endowment. He had been heard to say that no man should stay anywhere more than seven years—time enough to put through one job before tackling another elsewhere. Now, after all of ten years at Swarthmore, would he be impatient to make another fresh start? Not infrequently the rumor of an offer rippled the composure of the Deans' offices. Though we agreed that none of the beckoning institutions seemed dangerously tempting, at least not to our prejudiced eyes, it was only when each rumor died that we could feel quite safe.

Frank Aydelotte may have decided that he would be deserting Swarthmore if he left before the deadline for paying endowment pledges, June 30, 1936. During the depression no one could be certain that money would come in until it was actually deposited in a sound bank. The President's secretary, Emma Abbett, who had known him well since World War I, gave another explanation for his not moving on. "All those offers come from large universities. Frank Aydelotte knows he's at his best when he can see and talk to everybody he works with. And a man who likes to have a finger in every pie as he does, ought to have the sense to avoid a large place with too many pies." The simplest explanation was at least part of the truth. He liked Swarthmore too well to leave except for a chance to do something unusual.

His last nine years coincided with a period of disasters in world affairs: the depths of the depression, the rise of Hitler, wars in China, Spain, and Ethiopia, the outbreak of the conflict in Europe which would grow into World War II. With his interest in international affairs almost as strong as in education, he read widely and critically, eager to help keep the students in touch with events in the outside world. When he spoke at Collection or wrote for college readers, he gave full measure of attention to politics and economics, national and international.

The Depression

The disaster that carried the first great threat to any college was, of course, the depression. Frank Aydelotte acknowledged the danger at the beginning of his *Annual Report* for 1931–1932: "The first question, and in many cases the most important question to be dealt with by every college President . . . this year, is the effect of business conditions upon institutions and student bodies." He was happy to be able to say that Swarthmore finances had not been disastrously affected, thanks to con- servative investments and recent additions to capital in two endowment campaigns. Investments yielded "nearly 5%." Admitting that the income from students showed a loss of $30,000, he explained this as the result of a shrinkage in the number of resident students from the Philadelphia area who saved money by living at home. This loss could be met, not by cutting costs in dining hall and dormitories (because the overhead re- mained constant), but by general tightening of the belt.[1] He could still rejoice that he did not have to reduce either the size of the faculty or their salaries.

The most profound effects of the depression on the students he took to be moral and intellectual growth: a gain in maturity and a keener interest in problems of government and politics. He said little here about students' personal financial problems because they were in the resourceful hands of the Comptroller, Nicholas O. Pittenger.

When Swarthmore parents, less fortunate than the faculty, had suffered serious losses and could not manage to keep their children in college without a scholarship or loan, "Pitt" liked to make business arrangements directly with the students. He was ready to confer at any time with those who wanted to take loans and be personally responsible for repaying them. Even through the darkest years he managed to maintain the policy of "not dismissing a student from college for purely financial reasons" and, miraculously, to improve the percentage of loans collected.[2]

As the need for scholarships became critical, especially to keep up the number of well-qualified freshmen, the faculty voted to contribute a percent of their salaries to a scholarship fund for 1933–1934, the percent increasing with the size of salary. Similar contributions from the administration, yielding a total of $30,000, raised the scholarship budget to $80,000, five times the allotted income from endowments. One result was that the college was spared the loss of some excellent applicants for admission. There was no decline in quality of work.

The President's thanks to the faculty came from the heart:

—I have felt for many years that the one thing in Swarthmore from which I have got the most solid satisfaction has been the whole-hearted devotion of the faculty to the educational task which we have set ourselves, and I feel the deepest appreciation for this striking proof of that devotion.[3]

President and faculty alike welcomed the letter of appreciation from the Managers, expressing their strong sense of solidarity:

This action of the faculty was felt by the Board to be a remarkable demonstration of loyalty to the ideals of quality for which the college stands. The maintenance of an able student body is absolutely fundamental to the type of work which Swarthmore College is trying to do. . . . Furthermore, this action is welcomed by the Board as evidence of the feeling of the faculty that they are not merely employees of the college but rather members of an organization, the corporate welfare of which is inseparable from their welfare as individuals.[4]

The next year the Board voted not to let the faculty make the sacrifices necessary to repeat their gift, but to maintain the sum of $80,000 for scholarships by tapping other resources. Their action was the more courageous as they were refusing also to allow students to accept further subsidies from the Federal Relief Administration and felt obliged to make up that amount as well. Frank Aydelotte wholly sympathized with this policy of self-reliance:

We see on every hand efforts to get as much as possible from the Government and to give as little as possible in return. This tendency, which threatens the very foundations of democracy, can only be checked if those institutions and individuals who are by any possibility able to care for themselves undertake to do so and refuse longer to allow themselves to be a charge upon the public revenue.[5]

A feeling of gratitude at being spared the worst of the depression heightened college morale. Students lucky enough to stay at Swarthmore were more determined to use their opportunities to the full. Members of the faculty tried to better their best. It was true that many of them, like the President himself, had responsibilities for relatives; he was helping to support three families in addition to his own.[6] But he carried an atmosphere of confidence, good sense, and cheer wherever he went—speaking at Collection, holding conferences in his office, standing with his wife at the head of the receiving line at college dances.

In both the great changes of the time, the depression in the United States and the rise of Fascism and Nazism in Europe, he found confirmation for his view that society must have a leadership that is at once expert and disinterested. Comparing the economic disaster with the plagues that swept over medieval Europe, he pointed out that the remedy for both lay in scientific knowledge. Medical scientists had discovered how to prevent plagues by laying bare their causes; economic scientists could do the same thing for depressions. "Never in our history was there such need for intelligent and idealistic leadership as in America today." At the first Collection of 1934–1935, the President praised "the Brain Trust method of dealing with governmental affairs," urging that it become permanent. Economic and social problems had reached a level of complication beyond the competence of the average voter. Frank was neither a socialist nor an advocate of *laissez faire;* he felt much sympathy for what he conceived as the middle course taken by the New Deal. Individual initiative was for him the indispensable source of every kind of achievement. On the other hand, the depression had made it clear that if the marginal people were to be taken care of—the aged, the sick, the jobless—social legislation, framed by experts and on an unprecedented scale, was necessary. Frank was happy that Swarthmore could contribute an economist, Clair Wilcox, to the General Code Authority of the N.R.A.

The summer vacation of 1932, Frank paid a visit to Germany and at Freiburg heard a speech by Hitler. It is clear from his comments, made to a student reporter on his return, that he had no idea of the demoniacal and almost hypnotic power that Hitler was to exercise a few years later over the German people. The speech he thought shallow and the man of no great consequence; "the better class of Germans do not follow the swastika standard, and . . . the young people are attracted only by the novelty and colorful display."[7] He was soon to be disillusioned.

Changes in Administration

In the spring of 1932 two members of the administration resigned: the Dean of the College, Raymond Walters, to become President of the University of Cincinnati; the Dean of Men, Alan Valentine, to go to Yale as Master of one of the new colleges, Pierson. Raymond Walters, who had come to Swarthmore as one of the new President's first appointments, had supported him with energy and enthusiasm. Alan Valentine, the first Swarthmore graduate to hold a Rhodes Scholarship, had returned as assistant in the Rhodes Trust Office and executive secretary of the endowment campaign, later becoming Dean of Men and assistant professor of English. Both men would be hard to replace.

When their plans were announced, the President was in Mexico at the beginning of a six months' leave of absence which would take him soon to Germany. In transit he stopped at Swarthmore to confirm two temporary appointments: Ethel H. Brewster, professor of Latin and former Dean of Women, as Acting Dean of the College; Everett L. Hunt, professor of English, as Acting Dean of Men. Both were willing to hold office for only one year, but that would give the President the opportunity to explore possibilities. Already there was a young instructor in philosophy who would eventually be an asset to the administration, a Rhodes Scholar from Minnesota who had just taken his Oxford degree. This was John Nason, soon to assist Frank Aydelotte in both the Rhodes and the President's office and in 1940 to be his successor as President of Swarthmore. But in 1932 John Nason was known simply as a vigorous, able young teacher who wielded a powerful tennis racket.

When Frank Aydelotte came back from Germany he found several members of the Board of Managers eager to recommend that the new Dean should be Harold E. B. Speight, professor of biography at Dartmouth, "convinced" member of the Society of Friends and well-liked speaker at Meeting, formerly a Unitarian minister at Kings Chapel, Boston. His sponsors were enthusiastic about what he might contribute to the religious life of the college.

Born in Yorkshire, Harold Speight was a graduate of the University of Aberdeen, where he had also taught philosophy before going into the ministry in 1912. After he joined the Friends in 1927, he returned to teaching as professor of philosophy, later of biography, at Dartmouth. Frank Aydelotte, seeing that his interests centered on personality, suggested that he come as Dean of Men rather than Dean of the College, proposing at the same time that the latter office be given up, its essential functions divided between the Deans of Men and Women. The President liked to keep the administration flexible and to reduce its numbers when he could.

Harold Speight did, indeed, speak well in Friends' Meeting and conducted Collection ably when the President was out of town. He and his wife quickly became congenial members of the college community. But his time at Swarthmore was destined to be brief. On the death of his great friend William Isaac Hull, he was offered the professorship of Quaker history. But he preferred to accept a position with the Association of College and University Presidents and became the Executive Secretary of their Commission on Teacher Education at about the time Frank Aydelotte moved to Princeton. Meanwhile Everett Hunt had been persuaded to return to the Dean's Office, this time with a change in the titles of both Deans by dropping out "of Men" and "of Women." The Deans liked the change for its implication of academic as well as other responsibilities for the whole college.

Status of Honors Work

The organization of the honors program in 1931–1932, though satisfactory enough to remain little changed for many years, brought forth a characteristic warning from the President. Honors work must not be standardized. It must continue to be a "living and growing thing, with just as little of the dull and mechanical about it as possible." In order to keep it alive, students "must branch out for themselves from the common core of reading." They must not lose "spontaneity and the spirit of adventure."

In these years the number of honors students increased, but with a corresponding rise in college enrollment, the proportion of juniors and seniors in the program changed very little.

1930–1931　Upperclassmen, 261　Honors students, 115　44.06 per cent

1939–1940　Upperclassmen, 331　Honors students, 146　44.40 per cent

The number of external examiners rose in about the same proportion, from 26 to 36, and the number of institutions they represented, from 14 to 22. Each department chose its examiners with reference to the subjects of seminars: the greater the variety of seminars, the more examiners needed. Some were invited from institutions which had expressed an interest in learning about the system. They saw it put to a severe test, but one which commonly showed the students in a good light—lively, well read, and independent. By this time students made a practice of reading their examiners' publications to get an idea of the point of view from which they would be questioned. This was not an idle attempt to "curry favor" with astute examiners by agreeing with them, but an effort to gather ammunition for self-defense.

Honors Work and the Educational Program

Already the faculty had extended the principles of honors work, changing the basis for meeting college requirements from specified courses to tests of achievement and introducing a final comprehensive examination in their major subjects for seniors in courses.[8] Now they discussed carrying the process further by reducing the normal number of a student's courses from five to four.

This step was not so clearly a gain as those already taken. There were arguments for and against the Four Course Plan. Its supporters urged that since honors students had profited by intensive work in two seminars instead of five courses, students in courses might reap similar benefits from greater concentration. Opponents conceded that such a reduction might be good for juniors and seniors, but not for freshmen and sophomores, who needed more scope for testing their interests before choosing a major subject. A compromise of requiring five courses in the first two years and four in the last two, while seemingly reasonable, was hardly practicable, since the effective use of placement tests had resulted in a mixture of under- and upperclassmen in the majority of courses. No solution immediately forthcoming, the plan which had been approved in principle in 1929 stayed in committee for several years, with no recommendation from the Instruction Committee to the faculty until 1933.

A reason for this delay, suspected by only one or two of the committee, was that the President himself was doubtful whether the change would be for the best. He agreed that in general, concentration on fewer subjects had its merits. But he saw also that freshmen and sophomores might profit by keeping the existing system, all the more if they were hoping to go into honors work and be limited to three subjects in two years. Realizing that faculty support for the plan was strong, he did not express his doubts, wanting the faculty to feel no pressure from him.

Finally, when a vote was taken and showed a majority in favor of the plan, he asked the faculty if they would be willing to postpone putting it into effect for a year, and they agreed. He hoped they might see reason to change their minds. But in fact at the year's end they reaffirmed their support and put the plan into operation in 1934–1935.[9] Now, long afterward, the incident serves as evidence against arguments of later cynics that Frank Aydelotte could let the faculty make decisions because he had always first beguiled them into accepting his point of view.

The influence of the honors system was responsible for a new requirement, of one minor subject, for students in courses. This came about after critics objected to honors work as overspecialized and the Instruction Committee undertook to find out whether students in courses actually took advantage of their freedom to study more than three subjects. What was the committee's surprise to discover that students in courses often studied nothing but their major in the senior year and perhaps no more than one course outside it as juniors! Here, indeed, was excessive specialization and need for a requirement providing some breadth.

Frank Aydelotte welcomed a chance to take stock of the honors program when he was asked by the Association of American Universities to give a paper on "Honors Work and Graduate Study" at their annual conference in 1935.[10] With fourteen years of experience behind him and four hundred honors graduates to consult, he looked forward to gathering opinions on questions he had often asked himself.

Was honors work valuable chiefly, if not exclusively, as preparation for graduate school? As such preparation, did the program prove deficient at some points, strong at others? These questions, sent out in a letter to honors graduates, brought in a flood of replies, many of them written in a spirit of grateful appreciation. Frank Aydelotte read all of them eagerly, calling in his colleagues to share something unusually well written or acute.

He found general agreement among honors students that the prime value of honors work was not as preparation for graduate study, but as a means to a liberal education.

> The honors plan "seems to our graduates a good liberal education because of the great interest it arouses, because they discover for themselves the pleasures of study, and become excited about learning . . . because they depend not upon the prodding of a teacher, but upon their own courage and self-reliance. This "more adult and more imaginative experience," as one student called it, sharpens and matures their minds as

mere classroom drill would not. . . . The student learns to plan for himself, to budget his time, to work toward a distant goal.

The former students went on to appraise the system as a preparation for graduate study. Did it provide any exceptional grasp of their particular fields, as measured in extent or depth, or any exceptional training in methods of work?

As to the extent of a student's grasp of his field, there were differences of opinion, corresponding to the organization of work in different subjects. Honors graduates in most lines reported that they had anticipated at Swarthmore part or all of the material covered in the first year of graduate courses and could begin research at once. In other subjects, notably English, they recognized gaps: no Anglo-Saxon at Swarthmore, fewer period courses of the survey type than in some other colleges. Instead, Swarthmore provided thorough study of major authors, aimed toward the understanding and appreciation of literature. This was the emphasis of the department, and one with which the President and many students felt full sympathy, even though they had to make good what they had left out when they went to graduate school.

> The Honors work in English was definitely not a pre-graduate course, and as such was much more valuable than the extensive survey courses in literature and linguistics would be. Inasmuch as the emphasis was upon the interpretative rather than the scholarly approach to literature, I should say that my experience in honors work was supplementary to graduate work rather than a direct preparation for it.[11]

Students liked the emphasis in honors work on grasping a subject in depth, "thoroughness in the mastery of a limited field." Regarding the criticism, often made, that such work was a narrowing process and overspecialized. The President quoted an honors student:

> Delving into a limited division instead of scattering one's energy over many unrelated fields is far from being a narrowing process. For the further one delves into one field, the more its relations with other fields are realized. This knowledge that the boundary lines between the various branches are unimportant is supplemented by many informal discussions with students majoring in various divisions. The discussions begun in seminars have a way of carrying over into the dormitory and being pursued long after the seminar. In this way one becomes interested in fields other than one's own, and the eagerness to learn more about them is still felt after graduation.[12]

As to training in methods, Frank Aydelotte reports that "the value of honors work to our graduates seems absolutely clear and nothing could increase the strength of their endorsement of it." They agree on the importance of preparation in three lines: "apprenticeship in scholarly work," including use of sources and organizing material; "the habit of critical analysis of conclusions as over against mere learning of facts"; "learning to work independently, to rely upon one's own efforts."[13]

Frank Aydelotte refers only indirectly to the impressions made by Swarthmore honors graduates when he mentions the generosity of the graduate schools in giving them fellowships. He barely touches on the criticism of some graduate work by honors students who have hoped to find opportunities as stimulating as those they had known at Swarthmore, and been disappointed. He shows tacit sympathy when he calls attention to "important changes ... now being made in some universities": "greater flexibility," "replacing course requirements by comprehensive examinations, and laying more emphasis on the thesis for the Doctor's degree."[14]

The report expresses the writer's pleasure in what he describes, and all the more effectively because of his restraint: "The case for honors work is too strong for me to be willing to risk overstating it."

Crisis in the Women's Fraternities

In 1931 Frank Aydelotte faced a fraternity problem far more difficult than the one he had met ten years earlier when he first came to Swarthmore. Then he had been concerned by finding college social life overshadowed by the fraternities, and he persuaded them to cut out some of their dances to give more scope for an all-college program. Now the fraternities had grown to a size and importance which raised questions about their very existence in so small a college. Members as well as nonmembers asked these questions, their answer frequently a strong No, particularly in relation to fraternities for women. The situation was complicated by the attitude of some alumnae who refused to believe that the undergraduate reformers could be acting on their own initiative and suspected the President himself of dark designs to get rid of all fraternities, beginning with the women's.

This had never, in fact, been his position. He made clear from the beginning of a discussion which lasted two years that he favored reform, not abolition, and that the questions by students should be left to them

VIII: Frances Blanshard (with her husband) during her tenure as a Swarthmore dean. Photo: Roger Russell.

IX: The British and American Secretaries to the Rhodes Trustees: Lord Lothian and Frank Aydelotte at an academic gathering.

to settle with the help of "their advisers in their alumnae body and in their national organization."[15] He urged the students to look for a solution which would benefit the college as well as the fraternities and might eventually shed light on similar problems in other colleges. When he told the women students that he expected them to be "bold, large-minded, imaginative, and wise," they knew he thought they were undertaking something important. They accepted the justice of his verdict that "for fraternities as for other organizations, the price of survival is usefulness."

To reconstruct the serious situation which threatened the President's relations with alumnae and eventually with alumni more than thirty years ago, the chief source is the *Phoenix*, supplemented by the writer's recollections. What was the position of the fraternities, and how had it changed in the past ten years? Why were the women's organizations subjected to special attack? How explain the concern of the alumnae?

At Swarthmore in 1931, as in any college which housed and fed its students, the function of both men's and women's fraternities was, in a broad sense, social. This meant supporting not only dances and other festivities but also standards of conduct. Upper-class members encouraged freshmen to take part in activities and to keep up with their work in the interest of fraternity prestige, both local and national. The national aspect was emphasized. The wearer of a pin would find a welcome from other wearers all over the country.

Choice of members usually followed a short period of "rushing" freshmen, often no more than a week at the beginning of the year. There was a system of "bidding" which required fraternities to list freshmen in order of members' preferences, and freshmen to list fraternities. An impartial committee matched the two. A freshman whose name did not appear on any fraternity list was not asked to join one. There was a ritual of initiation which gave the chosen a feeling of dedication and responsibility and, above all, the reassurance of being wanted by an important group.

Criticism of fraternities began on a high plane and remained there. No one seemed to doubt that they were well managed, helpful to their members, cooperative with each other and with college authorities. In fact, the Dean of Women relied on the seniors in a fraternity for sound advice to their freshmen on personal matters. And the seniors themselves profited from this kind of responsibility.

What student critics attacked was the operation of the fraternity system in a small college, erecting barriers between groups which could otherwise have formed a unified community. They said also that there was a special inconsistency at Swarthmore between college ideals of individual freedom and the fraternity emphasis on conformity and exclusiveness. Moreover, the claim often made for the system, that it created exceptionally congenial groups, could not be guaranteed because members were chosen on brief and superficial acquaintance. But what troubled the women most was the effect on the freshmen who were excluded. At best, they missed the benefits of belonging to a group. At worst, they suffered a shock and disappointment which might warp their attitude toward themselves and the college at the very beginning of their four years. To the Dean's office, those left out seemed likely to be sensitive, odd little girls who, with encouragement, might develop unusually fine qualities of mind and personality.

The situation was not new, of course, and the same points could be urged against the men's fraternities. How account for the outburst of dissatisfaction in 1931, with its focus primarily on the women's organizations?

The simplest answers were in terms of expansion and the building of lodges. The proportion of students in college who were fraternity members had been steadily growing; 70 per cent of the men and 77 per cent of the women were now members, the larger figure for women resulting partly from the organization of a new fraternity, granted a charter in 1930.[16] The resulting shrinkage in the nonfraternity groups, numbering in 1931 only 30 per cent of the men and 23 per cent of the women, intensified their feeling of social ostracism. The importance of fraternity membership had been further emphasized by the building of lodges on the campus: five for men, put up one at a time between 1921 and 1926; six for women, all built in 1927 (before the seventh fraternity was founded). Though the men's were larger and more elegant, they had come on the scene so gradually as to make less of an impact than the women's, which had sprung up simultaneously. The lodges were visible symbols of opportunities not open to everyone.

A more subtle explanation for the difference between men's and women's attitudes toward fraternities was offered in a *Phoenix* editorial on "The Fraternity Question": that women took far more seriously the social advantages which fraternities represented. "Basically the problem is one for both men and women to solve. However, it must be admitted that the social side of college life does play a more important part in a woman's undergraduate life than in that of a man."[17] Women knew that the social life of which nonfraternity women would be deprived included not only the friendliness of a group but also invitations to coeducational affairs given by cautious men who looked for the fraternity stamp of approval. (Witness a triumphant exclamation overheard after the women had voted decisively for abolition: "Now the men will have to decide for themselves which women are attractive!")

If nonfraternity women had been the only ones to sense the situation, their pride might have kept them from speaking out. But there were fraternity members among the leaders of the movement whose presence gave it the dignity of disinterestedness. They could not be accused of "sour grapes." A sizable group of members and nonmembers accepted a thoughtful position: "that the advantages of fraternity life to a fraternity woman are less than the disadvantages of the fraternity system to a non-fraternity woman."[18] This conviction had grown on senior officers as they helped administer the distribution of bids and were sought out by freshmen who had not received any and were sure there must have been a mistake. To see girls bewildered and hurt by this blow in their first week of college seemed intolerable to the seniors—too high a price for their own membership. When I asked one of them why she was suddenly appalled by a situation which had been so long accepted, she said she had never been close to it before, adding: "Perhaps the depression has something to do with it. When there's so much misery that can't be avoided, why add to it if there's a way out?"

Proposed solutions were listed in the *Phoenix* editorial, with the weakness of each.

> Among the remedies suggested is the idea of junior bidding, which would tend to minimize the fraternity influence during the first two years of college life. Another idea has been to decrease the numerical strength of each fraternity, thus creating more non-fraternity women, which would tend to offset the feeling of social ostracism. Still another idea is for the fraternities to increase their membership to include all the women. The first two suggestions are temporary adjustments but they still overlook the real problem of college unity and undergraduate good-will. The third is obviously out of accord with the fraternity system itself.[19]

This third remedy was precisely the one Frank Aydelotte favored: "the best solution . . . would be to expand the fraternities so as to take in all the women. . . . Then the advantages of fraternity life would be enjoyed by all."[20] While he knew as well as the editorial writer that the right to choose and exclude had been central in the fraternity system, he was convinced that a revolution on this point would be necessary to bring fraternities into harmony with contemporary ideas of education in a democracy. He hoped that Swarthmore women would attempt a change that seemed impossible and show it was not, both for their own sakes and for the benefit of fraternities in general. "My contact with national officers of a great many fraternities leads me to think that they do not consider the fraternity system perfect and that they are eager for any suggestion or any experiment which may lead to its improvement. The opportunity to make that experiment is now in your hands."[21] Then, as usual, he recommended what he thought the best plan, but when he saw that it did not appeal to either the fraternity undergraduates or the alumnae, he did not press it.

Early in the discussion of the future of women's fraternities, the organization which represented them all, Panhellenic, took the surprising but enlightened step of turning over the decision to the Women's Student Government Association, on the ground that whatever was done would affect all the women, nonfraternity as well as fraternity. One of the W.S.G.A. officers, troubled by not being able to imagine a college without women's fraternities, asked the Dean of Women what it was like at Smith, her college. She thought it would be helpful to Swarthmore women to know what went on at some other coeducational colleges and got the President's approval for sending two representatives of W.S.G.A. to Oberlin and Antioch to observe and report. They came back ready to reassure their friends that the two Ohio colleges had all the social life anyone could want. The alumna who was prime mover of the question remembers now that she enjoyed the expedition, but most of all how completely she took for granted that the Swarthmore administration thought students' views worth considering and "to be heard." She was right, thanks to the President's confidence that students could be public-spirited and sensible. The practical question, What would happen to the lodges in the event of abolition, was answered by the Board of Managers according to Frank Aydelotte's recommendation: the college would buy them from the alumnae who had raised the money to build them. This helped focus attention where it belonged, on the merits of the fraternity system.

Between January, 1932, and December, 1933, W.S.G.A. conducted a series of polls. The first, on proposed reforms, showed no decisive majority. The second, on three plans for changes in the rushing system, favored sophomore bidding by 127 to 103.[22] If this were put into effect for 1932–1933, it would mean no elections of either freshmen or sophomores, since members of the latter class had already been chosen under the old system. It was decided to ratify this virtual "moratorium" on elections and to add a provision curtailing other activities of women's fraternities for the year, in the interest of an experiment with a "social reconstruction program," to be planned and carried out by a committee of women. This would provide a variety of dances, formal and informal, and other social events, open to all Swarthmore women, who invited men to these dances, according to the custom of the women's fraternities.[23]

The program was popular from the start and became more attractive when provided with a meeting place in old Collection Hall, in the central section of the main building above the college dining room. Collection Hall had lost its original function to the new Clothier Memorial, but kept its name. Now cleared of balcony, stage, and rows of fixed seats, with a fine new fireplace at one end and groups of comfortable furniture around the walls, it made a handsome setting for teas, dancing, and ping-pong and a new social event which particularly pleased the President, called "Coffee in Collection." Once a week after dinner coffee was served in Collection Hall to students and their faculty dinner guests, regularly including the President and Mrs. Aydelotte, who often brought distinguished visitors to meet students informally. There was music adequate for dancing, but not too loud for talk.

To carry out the idea that social life should develop, wherever possible, in connection with shared interests, there was a burgeoning of "interest groups" in music, painting, writing, and so on which brought together men and women students, members of the faculty and their wives. These groups managed to pass the crucial test of being almost as lively as an honors seminar.

The women found that they liked college life uncomplicated by fraternities, and while the moratorium was still in force, they took a vote which favored abolition, 160 to 108. This seemed premature to members of the Board of Managers, who ruled that it was a "straw vote," to be followed by another the next year. Whereupon the *Phoenix* spoke out sharply: "The administration has so far shown a commendable attitude by forbearing to interfere. It would be a fine piece of hypocrisy to throttle the movement now."

At last, on December 12, 1933, the official vote plumped for abolition by 168 to 109, a larger majority than the Managers had stipulated. When the *Phoenix* reported this outcome, there was not a word of comment in an editorial or letter.[24] Editors, like most of the community, favored the women's action, but after two years' discussion, what was left to say?

Alumnae Reactions

Many fraternity alumnae reacted to abolition with dismay. A few resented what seemed the inconsistency in college policy which had encouraged their groups to build lodges and then, after only four years, allowed the undergraduates to give up fraternities and the lodges with them. Even alumnae forget that in a college generation anything may change. The regret of the Swarthmore alumnae was at losing their connection with undergraduates, a relation they had enjoyed in itself and as a means of keeping in touch with the college. But they may have felt their greatest pang as they realized that these organizations, so important through their own four years of college and beyond, now meant little except to freshmen and possibly sophomores. It was still true that freshmen suffered when they were not asked to join. But when senior fraternity women saw this suffering as out of all proportion to their own advantages, it must be clear to thoughtful alumnae, not that the suffering had increased, but that the advantages had come to seem negligible—childish things to be put away as students developed into adults. Who was responsible for this change? Largely, no doubt, the President, with his emphasis on intellectual interests. While alumnae were mistaken when they charged the President with deliberately "putting out" fraternities, they were right in holding him and his faculty responsible for a new atmosphere of excitement about ideas in which fraternities had little to offer.[25]

When the college bought the women's lodges, the alumnae of the oldest and most Quakerly fraternity, Kappa Alpha Theta, used part of the money to establish a scholarship fund for a Swarthmore woman student. Frank Aydelotte was pleased when he mentioned this, though not wholly satisfied. He said, "I had hoped that all the fraternities would use this money to do something for the college." To most persons aware of alumnae ill feeling, such an outcome would have seemed most unlikely. But he himself did not harbor grudges and could hardly believe that disappointment in one element of college life would seriously weaken loyalty to the institution as a whole.

The lodges became useful at once. Four were Class Lodges, one assigned every year to freshman women, who kept it until they were graduated, their class numerals permanently on the door. The other two, Activities Lodges, filled a great need for attractive, informal meeting places of groups of men and women carrying on manifold activities which involved discussion. After a year or two it was hard to remember how the college had got along without them.

Reactions of Fraternity Men

Undergraduate and alumni members of men's fraternities did not see eye to eye during the attacks on women's fraternities. Some alumni persisted in believing that the President was weighting the scales for abolition, no matter how strongly this was denied by the undergraduates. On Alumni Day, June 3, 1933, one float in the parade had a "large-eared caricature of Prexy, wielding an axe on the neck of a female dummy labeled 'Fraternities.' " A man who was a junior at the time reports this years later, adding, "We were shocked. The lampoon wasn't true; it wasn't cricket to do that to Prexy."[26] Prexy's supporters must have been cheered by finding a good drawing of him on the cover of the current issue of *Time* (June 5, 1933) with the caption, "He would reprieve democracy from mediocrity." Inside, an account of his career emphasized his connection with the Rhodes Scholars, then holding their first American reunion at Swarthmore.

Some undergraduate men had been seriously troubled by the women's criticism of the system. Hear one account in *Swarthmore Remembered:* "Why all the fuss about those happy table-party-giving women's fraternities? I asked a girl in the library stacks. She said, 'Have you ever in all your life been on the outside with your nose against the window pane?' I couldn't answer. I was cut, and the process of internal bleeding had begun."[27]

Arguments against the fraternities carried the members of one group to the point of deciding to withdraw their chapter from the national organization within the month after the women's vote for abolition. But owing to "various considerations," doubtless including pressure from alumni, their decision was not carried out until thirty years later.

The president of another fraternity, although devoted to "the brothers," finally made up his mind to "belong to nothing whose bylaws shut men out." Resigning as one of a small group, he wrote to break the news to Frank Aydelotte: "We know that you are in a hot spot. We hope this step we are taking will not embarrass you in any way." He repeated verbatim the President's reply, lost long ago: "If the day ever comes when I am embarrassed by anything a student does as a matter of conscience, I shall not be fit to be president of Swarthmore."[28]

Alumni Criticism Grows

While the women's abolition of their fraternities stiffened alumni resistance to similar action by the men, it also brought into the open their irritation at other changes in the college. Especially they resented the policy in athletics. They had been startled by the rumor, when Frank Aydelotte became President, that he had accepted on condition there should be no more subsidies for athletes. This could only mean a death-blow to football as it had been played at Swarthmore, with victories over far larger institutions. When the President went on to change the emphasis from preoccupation with football to developing a variety of sports involving a large number of students, he took another step away from the old athletic ascendancy, even though he proposed at the same time to establish schedules with competitors comparable to Swarthmore in size and academic standing, with whom the college could compete on even terms. The old days ended in a disastrous football game between Swarthmore and the University of Pennsylvania in October, 1932, lost by the Little Quakers by a score of 0 to 54.

In that same year, 1932–1933, the President was able to carry out his plan by which the college assumed direct responsibility for the athletic program, financing it completely and giving faculty standing to all the instructing staff in physical education, including the coaches. With the basketball season the new schedule went into effect, Swarthmore winning ten games and losing five. Similar successes in lacrosse and track pleased the President, but outraged those alumni who believed that victories in football alone, as a contact sport, were sufficient proof of masculinity.

A courageous new president of the Swarthmore Alumni Association, William W. Tomlinson, '17, decided to express publicly the disaffection among his constituents, first at a dinner of the Philadelphia Swarthmore Club in February, 1935, the next month at a meeting of the Board of Managers. In Philadelphia his hearers included Frank Aydelotte and the President of Princeton, Harold W. Dodds. While Tomlinson spoke with courtesy and dignity, he left no doubt that the alumni feared what they considered serious threats to important Swarthmore values.

In his speech, "Men Wanted," he pointed out that over the years a large majority (about 72 per cent) of Swarthmore alumni had gone into business and industry and found themselves well prepared for positions of leadership. In this highly competitive line, the qualities needed for success—courage and determination—had developed particularly by college athletics. Now that improving conditions in business and industry were again raising signs, "Men Wanted," alumni feared that Swarthmore no longer prepared men who would be wanted: "men of mentality, courage, determination, understanding and vision." The college ought to lay more emphasis on producing winning football teams. He recalled Swarthmore's recent victory, 7 to 6, over Amherst's "more powerful team," a triumph of "superior courage and determination—the will to win." The college needed more teams with "this unconquerable spirit," which would cause the same spirit to "permeate" the whole student body.

Alumni feared, again, that the college admissions policy was not taking into account "the broader qualities of manhood," that "the purely academic functions . . . are crowding out those vital activities that have to do with the development of ruggedness, courage, determination and better human understanding."[29]

As President of the Alumni Association, William Tomlinson was "all too conscious of these fears . . . dangerous and unfortunate . . . because they seem to be driving a wedge between Swarthmore and a large part of her alumni body."

If Frank Aydelotte could have replied, he would have agreed warmly that athletics developed qualities necessary for successful and sportsmanlike competition in any line. He had said as much himself in his first Collection speech as President of Swarthmore. But he would have questioned how far courage and determination could "permeate" the student body from simply watching a victorious team, preferring himself to rely on widespread participation of students representing the college on a variety of teams and reaping the benefits directly.

When the Board of Managers met the next month, William Tomlinson submitted the same lines of criticism in a clear and temperate memorandum, adding constructive suggestions. Noting again alumni fears of a decrease in the number of "well-rounded men with essentially masculine interests and qualifications," and urging the need for training winning teams in order to strengthen in the whole student body "the will to win," Tomlinson mentioned two points at which college and alumni could be brought closer together. The alumni with their variety of experience could help meet a need which had been mentioned by the President: for more vocational guidance. Also the existing lack of communication between college and alumni should be studied and rectified.[30]

Copies of this memorandum were sent to members of the Board of Managers with a statement from the President of the Board, Charles F. Jenkins, in his usual vein of hearty good sense and humor. Ready to pay careful attention to alumni criticism, he refused to take this particular criticism quite seriously and never wavered in his enthusiastic support of Frank Aydelotte and what he had accomplished. Recalling that alumni everywhere are likely to be "stand patters," he observed that some at Swarthmore longed for the old days when "with a hand-picked, country-wide recruited football team, we downed the mighty Pennsylvania and played other big colleges on equal terms." Now alumni say that "half the boys in the present Freshman Class wear spectacles," meaning that they are "dippy studes," not the desirably "husky, brawny type." Alumni complain also because students are not "het up" over fraternities at Swarthmore, though fraternities are lagging everywhere.

Then Charles Jenkins' picture of the college as he sees it:

> Swarthmore has today a forward-looking, distinguished, yes a nationally known, President, whose every waking thought is for the success of the college, who, while lacking the traditions, yet cherishes the fundamentals of Quaker faith and practice to a degree surpassed by no member of this Board. [He went on to remind the Board of relevant facts:] That Swarthmore under his guidance, even in these days of depression, has more students than ever before in its history. That from one end of the United States to the other, the college is known and respected among educators. That the college today has a larger percentage of members of Friends and children of alumni among its undergraduates than ever before in its history. That it has a capable, cultured, hand-picked faculty, the envy of institutions less fortunate than Swarthmore. That our finances are unequalled by any educational institution—barring none, and our physical property never was in such good order. . . .
>
> And I ask the Board, in all honesty to themselves, to tell me how many of these great accomplishments of the last 15 years are due to us, and how many are due to our President, his administrative staff and the faculty. Never has the stock of Swarthmore been held in such high esteem by those best qualified to judge. The dollar and cents as well as the cultural value of every Swarthmore College degree has been definitely raised in the last fifteen years.

Following William Tomlinson's suggestion that the Board should take steps to bring the alumni into a better relation with the college, Charles Jenkins proposed a joint committee "to canvass the situation." Perhaps such a committee would recommend the appointment of "a . . . permanent, paid Secretary" who, among other duties, would "assist in filling up the coming freshman class with brawny students, none under six feet, all over 200 pounds with brain cavities in proportion and high ideals to go with all and not a spectacle among them!"[31]

Frank Aydelotte took special pleasure in Charles Jenkins' facts about the increase of students from families of Friends and alumni. "Alumni may criticize the college," he said, "but the more attention it gets from educators and parents of applicants, the more they want their own children to have its advantages."

Even with the strong support of Charles Jenkins and other members of the Board, and the enthusiastic loyalty of the faculty, Frank Aydelotte had moments of discouragement which he took pains to hide. But signs of it must have crept into his correspondence with Abraham Flexner at the Institute for Advaned Study. Recently someone who was going through Institute papers asked me what happened at Swarthmore in 1935 which made Frank Aydelotte seem willing to leave.

He was particularly cast down to find alumni complaining of lack of communication with the college. They had to learn from outsiders, so they said, what was going on. Obviously they were ready to criticize without even troubling to look at his *Annual Reports*—full of information about each year's achievements and plans and written with care and skill to make them good reading. But by the time he wrote his *Report* in December, 1935, he had regained his usual nonchalance and rejoiced in what had been accomplished along the lines proposed by William Tom-. linson.[32]

He gave first place to the Board's appointment of a Joint Committee including representatives of the faculty as well as the Board and alumni. The faculty members, Everett Hunt, Clair Wilcox, and Patrick Malin, had been admirably chosen to meet the alumni on a basis of mutual respect and liking. The Joint Committee's early recommendation of a new publication "in the interests of Swarthmore College and her alumni" had already produced the first issue of the *Garnet Letter* in September. This included a comprehensive account of the college in three articles: one by the Joint Committee's faculty members on the academic program and admissions policy, planned to discover and develop "well-balanced personalities"; the second on "Athletics at Swarthmore," by the Graduate Manager, Samuel C. Palmer, '95 (also professor of botany); and "Student Life and Activities," by a young alumna Assistant to the Dean of Women, Nora Booth, '32. This last discussion introduced alumni to the popular new program of five Creative Interest Groups, each meeting about once a week, without credit, but with provision for systematic work under a faculty director: the Little Theatre Club, the Sketch Club, the Chorus and Orchestra, the Manuscript Group, and Arts and Crafts. Frank Aydelotte was proud of this community venture in the use of leisure.

Alumni Pride in the College

In the next year at Swarthmore there were three events that gave exceptional pleasure to both the President and the alumni. The Field House was completed and put to use. Pledges adding four million dollars to the endowment fund were paid in full by the deadline of June 30, 1936. The engineering department received an important official stamp of approval.

The Field House was "unique among college or university buildings" at that time, a roofed-in playing field—325 feet long and 125 feet wide—at one end a floor for basketball and tennis, the greater part an expanse of clay surface large enough for football, baseball, and lacrosse, the whole framed by a running track. Nets separating various areas made it possible to carry on several activities at once. The advantages for exercise in winter were obvious, as well as for practice in bad weather in all seasons. Alumni took special pride in the Field House because it had been conceived and designed by one of their number whom they liked and admired, Robert E. Lamb, an able engineer and chairman of the Property Committee of the Board of Managers. He had the imaginative help of the architects then responsible for most of the new college buildings, Walter Karcher and Livingston Smith. Among them they had produced, at the astonishingly low cost of ten cents a cubic foot, a handsome as well as useful building, with long simple lines of low walls and domed roof which made it a restful element in the landscape. Frank Aydelotte delighted in this new provision for athletics throughout the year, and all the more because here again Swarthmore proved the value of something new.[33]

The endowment campaign came to a dramatic finish on June 30,

1939, with the collection of "the last dollar needed to meet the conditional pledges of the General Education Board on the date when they expired." This brought in four millions, raising the total endowment to "something over seven and one-half million dollars." Frank Aydelotte paid tribute to an achievement which was

> especially remarkable because of the fact that the last of the pledges . . . were secured in June 1930, eight months after the stock market broke, and all collections had to be made during the worst business depression of modern times. . . . It is eloquent testimony to the loyalty, self-sacrifice, and financial stability of the alumni and friends of the college who made these pledges that they were able and willing to pay them under such adverse conditions.

And he acknowledged the obligation laid upon Board and faculty "to make the wisest possible use of the additional resources thus placed at their disposal."[34]

Engineering at Swarthmore seemed particularly important to many alumni because of its value not only in the profession, but as preparation for business. Some of them had been glad that Frank Aydelotte came to Swarthmore knowing engineering education through his teaching at M.I.T. But before he was appointed, the engineering program had begun to grow stronger and continued to do so along the line of honors work, according to a trend described in the same May issue of the *Garnet Letter* that discussed the new Field House. Professor Scott B. Lilly, chairman of the Division of Engineering, in an article, "Instruction in Tune with the Times," pointed out that where engineering schools had once given chiefly practical training preparing men for specific jobs in industry, they now stressed theory which could be applied in many lines. This corresponded to a change in the larger industries, which had "adopted the plan of training their own cadets."

In the ensuing uncertainty and confusion about engineering curricula, members of the Division at Swarthmore had been guided by their experience in honors work. Recognizing that honors students could best be prepared to meet unknown external examiners by emphasis on the fundamentals of engineering, their teachers saw that the same emphasis would benefit all undergraduates "who must . . . pass that same kind of test upon their entrance into industry." Seeing also the greater need of breadth in engineering education, they began to stress the fundamentals of mathematics, physics, and chemistry and work in the humanities and social sciences.[35] Professor Lilly's article prepared alumni to understand and appreciate the official stamp of approval given by a new and important rating agency, the Committee on Engineering Schools of the Engineers' Council for Professional Development. Swarthmore's engineering curricula had been approved in all three branches, mechanical, civil, and electrical.

Two years almost to the day after the Joint Committee was appointed they submitted their report to the Managers on three main topics: an alumni publication, an Alumni Executive Secretary, alumni representation on the Board of Managers. By this time the alumni publication, the *Garnet Letter* had gone through four issues (September and December, 1935; May and December, 1936). The committee recommended that an Alumni Executive Secretary be appointed who would serve also as a member of the college administration, with "a real part in the day-to-day work of the college," perhaps related to admissions and vocational counseling. In recommending that the alumni should elect representatives to the Board of Managers, notwithstanding the present preponderance of Swarthmore graduates among Board members—twenty-eight out of thirty-two—the committee acted in the interests of representative government and according to a long-established precedent, widely supported. Harvard had granted this right to alumni in 1866, Yale in 1872; the number of colleges and universities that had followed suit by 1937 was no less than 216. The recommendation now: that each year one or two members of the Board, nominated by alumni vote, should be elected for a period of four years.[36]

The next year the Alumni Association was formally reorganized with due provision for electing representatives on the Board and establishing the office of Alumni Executive Secretary. The first incumbent was a popular choice, Carl Dellmuth, '31, who served also as vocational adviser for men. A modest vocational guidance program for women was already functioning in the office of the Dean of Women. Among Carl Dellmuth's duties would be those of Alumni Recorder, performed for many years by Caroline A. Lukens, now retiring at seventy-five. Of her long and devoted service the President said: "Miss Lukens knows personally more of the graduates of Swarthmore College than any living person. She holds a unique place in the hearts of all the men and women of her time, and it is impossible that she should in any real sense have a successor.[37]

Academic Innovations
Department of Psychology

When Frank Aydelotte came to Swarthmore, he found psychology a stepchild of the curriculum. Instruction was limited to a single course, General Psychology, listed under Education and taught by a member of the department of philosophy. The situation left the new President free of commitments, and fortunately so, since he regarded the subject and its proponents with some skepticism. Freud and Jung he thought narrow and overrated. The psychologists turned out by schools of education seemed to him deficient in both scientific and liberal training. He said that if someone could recommend a psychologist who was well educated and had first-rate ability, he would gladly consider appointing him.

After much consultation and advice, such a man was found in 1933, Robert B. MacLeod, then teaching at Cornell. It was in his favor with those who admired British education that he had been born in Canada and held Bachelor's and Master's degrees from McGill. After taking his Ph.D. at Columbia, he had studied in Germany for two years, acquiring both an American and European background for research and teaching. He was young—under thirty—and would come as assistant professor and chairman of the department, then to be called Psychology and Education. Two years later a distinguished older psychologist, Professor Wolfgang Köhler, was persuaded to join him as visiting professor.

Wolfgang Köhler, former head of the Psychological Institute of the University of Berlin, and recent émigré to the United States, was a well-known leader in Gestalt psychology, "one of the most vigorous of the present-day schools," according to Professor Robert S. Woodworth of Columbia.[38] Though launched in Germany in 1912, it had become known so slowly in this country that in the 1930's it seemed "the youngest of the schools." Gestalt psychologists were experimental scientists, working in laboratories where they observed and tested the responses of animals as well as human beings. Especially they were testing the distinctive Gestalt theory of perception and learning: that perception is a dynamic process of organizing sense impressions into a pattern, a "Gestalt," as when a man gazes at the sky at night and sees stars in the forms of a dipper or a belt. This dynamic process is also central in the kind of learning that leads to discovery, that is, "insight," "seeing a combination or pattern of objects" which suggests a way of dealing with new elements among the objects.

Professor Köhler had studied this process of learning in apes during an involuntarily prolonged sojourn on the French island of Tenerife, where he had gone in 1913 to direct the anthropoid station of the Prussian Academy of Science and been interned until the end of the war. One of his famous experiments pointed clearly to the occurrence of "insight," even in animals. A chimpanzee, experienced in using a long bamboo stick to rake a banana into his cage, now sees a banana outside the cage and two sticks inside, but neither long enough to reach it. After listlessly poking about with each stick in turn, he suddenly brightens, finds he can put the two sticks together, and brings the banana within his grasp. Having once seen this, he shows he has learned it by repeating the process the next morning with no hesitation. He has learned something new through a single insight.[39]

Frank Aydelotte was disposed to think Gestalt psychologists were on the right track, convinced as he was of the value of both experiment and "insight" in solving problems. He welcomed Professor Köhler as visiting professor and hoped to persuade him to stay by providing adequate laboratories and assistants. Fortunately Swarthmore was on the point of building the Edward Martin Biological Laboratory and might make room for psychology. Again fortunately, a plan was already in prospect to make up for the lack of graduate students as research assistants by bringing in postdoctoral fellows. The year after Wolfgang Köhler became visiting professor he was joined by a former student of his in Berlin, Hans Wallach, as research associate, later to become department chairman.

By 1937–1938 the subject of psychology was well staffed and housed. Robert MacLeod had become associate professor, and Wolfgang Köhler a permanent member of the faculty. An instructor then in his third year, Edwin B. Newman, Columbia-trained, showed the promise which took him eventually to Harvard and the chairmanship of the department there. There were three postdoctoral research associates, one a Guggenheim Fellow who had found Swarthmore the best place for his particular work. The Edward Martin Biological Laboratory, in its first year, set the stage for a new era in instruction and research.

With the resources of the new building, the department of zoology also could be reorganized under a new chairman, Laurence Irving, who came from the University of Toronto after ten years in the department of physiology, where he had done special research in the chemistry of muscles. He would develop the same line at Swarthmore, soon to add a study of respiration which involved housing a porpoise in a college swimming pool. Two research associates came with him from Canada, Edgar C. Black from Toronto and L. P. Dugal from Montreal.

The Edward Martin Biological Laboratory

The opening of the building given by Fred M. Kirby in honor of Dr. Edward Martin marked the culmination of eight years of effort on the part of Frank Aydelotte. In the endowment campaign of 1929 he had first interested Mr. Kirby in making a contribution of $300,000 to support the department of biology. Soon Mr. Kirby wrote to ask what he should add to put up a building, and he received a delighted reply: "It is only because men are so much more important than buildings that I did not suggest using the sum which you originally gave us to build an adequate laboratory; such a laboratory is one of our greatest needs." Fortunately the President already had preliminary plans for a building. It would cost $200,000; a gift of $400,000 would endow the department. "With a suitable building and with endowment on such a scale as I have indicated, Dr. Martin and I are both convinced that the subject of biology could be developed here in a way that would not merely give it national but international importance."[40] After further exchanges Fred Kirby increased his total gift to $900,000—$200,000 for the building and $700,000 for endowment—in time to swell contributions to the second endowment campaign. His project, first called the Edward Martin *Institute* of Biology, was described by Detlev W. Bronk:

> By combining exceptional facilities for research with the Honors method of instruction it will make possible close personal contact between under-graduates and a faculty of eminent scientific workers. The Swarthmore student will thus have available the combined advantages of a large university and an exceptional small college. . . . Its value as an additional stimulus to the intellectual life at Swarthmore is obvious and as an active center for biological research it will bring the college increased recognition in scientific circles throughout the world.

Detlev Bronk ended with the hope, dear to the President, that this Institute would attract other donors and bring to Swarthmore "a group of institutes for sound scholarship."[41]

This use of the name "Institute" reminds us that Frank Aydelotte was already a Trustee of the Institute for Advanced Study at Princeton, to be incorporated within a month (May 20, 1930). Both ventures combined advanced research with teaching, but on different levels. The name did

not take hold at Swarthmore; a research institute as part of an undergraduate college may have seemed incongruous.

Four years later, when building conditions during the depression
made the realization of Mr. Kirby's dream still remote, Frank Aydelotte
recommended that the gift carry a minimum of restrictions in order to
be adaptable to changing conditions:

> It would, in my opinion, be the part of wisdom to make no definite
> restrictions as to what should be the relative expenditure on teaching and
> upon research, or what particular aspects of Biological Science should be
> most emphasized. An endowment which is to last in perpetuity can be
> most wisely used if the details of such expenditures are left to the
> intelligence and good-will of the authorities of the College from one
> generation to another.[42]

Writing this at the end of Robert MacLeod's first year at Swarthmore,
the President may already have thought of housing the psychology
department in the new building, though it was still unusual to include
the subject among the biological sciences. By the time the Martin Building
had reached the planning stage, Wolfgang Köhler had become an immensely effective visiting professor with undergraduates and postdoctoral
students alike. What better inducement to him to stay permanently than
an offer of quarters which he could help design.

The building was dedicated on October 2, 1937, with Dr. Martin on
the platform to pay tribute to Fred M. Kirby, who could not be present
because of illness. Dr. Martin referred to the benefits his friend had
conferred on the town of Wilkes-Barre, which "in grateful appreciation
and in honor of its first citizen, has decreed an annual Kirby Day," and
went on to suggest something of the idealism regarding education which
lay behind the generosity of so many American men of business.

> It was his wish that every student should be given ears to hear and eyes to
> see the wonder of life; that their undergraduate course should be but the
> inspiring beginning of a continued appreciation of its glory and mystery.
> Thus would each student make many, perhaps all, of his days that type of
> Kirby Day which the donor of our laboratory would most desire. . . .
>
> The spirit of research should be stimulated in all, but entire and
> exclusive devotion to it should be limited to those who have both
> aptitude and dominating urge. When this small group works in the
> laboratory or issues publications throwing added light on the workings of
> life, or makes contributions helpful against factors which curtail or

cripple it, thus would it be celebrating, as Fred M. Kirby wished, a Kirby Day.[43]

His portrait hangs in the lobby above a simple inscription: "FRED. M. KIRBY BUILT AND ENDOWED THIS LABORATORY . . . AN ENDURING TRIBUTE TO A LASTING FRIENDSHIP."

The chief speaker, James Rowland Angell, President Emeritus of Yale, praised the Martin Laboratory as "one of the greatest of recent private educational philanthropies." He took occasion to add of Swarthmore's President: "The things which President Aydelotte has done at Swarthmore have spread far beyond this campus and are written in the history of American education. Swarthmore's educational program has been watched by educators in all sections of the country, and has been widely copied."[44]

To Frank Aydelotte the occasion brought the satisfaction of hopes fulfilled, heightened by Dr. Martin's presence at the dedication he had thought he might not live to see. Six months later he died at the age of seventy-nine. The President, in his *Report* for 1938, drew a delightful sketch of a man who was at once the senior member of his Board and one of his greatest friends.

> Dr. Martin was one of the best loved men in Philadelphia. . . . He gave his whole self with the intensity of a child to every interest and responsibility: to his patients, to the Board of Education, to Swarthmore College, to a game of golf. And his whole self was something more than knowledge, be it medicine or education or human personality. He saw, with a kind of second sight, things which ordinary men do not see, and he acted on his intuitions with the certainty of a poet. This rare quality of the man was apparent at the first glance. To meet him was an experience; to know him well a great and heaven-sent privilege.
>
> Dr. Martin loved people. . . . He loved young people especially, and I am glad to think that generations of youth who never saw him will enjoy opportunities here which came into existence through his devotion to the college. His heart was always young. Men might say of him when he astonished them by playing a hole in par, "Think of it, he is seventy-nine!" They never called him old.[45]

Friends World Conference

A month before the dedication of the Martin Laboratory, Swarthmore was joint host with Haverford to a conference of Quakers from all over the world. There were about a thousand of them, including 250 from twenty-three foreign countries, who converged on the two Quaker colleges during the first week in September. Swarthmore bore the brunt of numbers: 750 delegates were housed in dormitories and in the village, 250 at Haverford. Regular sessions were held in Clothier and three public meetings in the Field House, each attended by about three thousand persons, the largest number of Quakers "ever gathered together under one roof in the entire history of the Society of Friends."

Frank Aydelotte was deeply impressed by their personalities and breadth of interest and by their concern "to link up their religious beliefs with the social and political problems of the day so as to make Quakerism in truth a 'way of life.'" According to the testimony of members of the Conference, that way of life was distinguised by

> a belief in the value of the spiritual light in every man, reverence for individual opinion, love of freedom and friendly toleration of differences, courage to face the social, economic and racial problems which divide the modern world, a deep longing for peace, an abhorrence of force, tenderness for minorities, and a fundamental adherence to the great liberal tradition which brought freedom and peace to the world in the 19th Century and is so gravely threatened in the 20th.

Frank Aydelotte was happy in his office of host: "It has been a matter of deep satisfaction to those of us at Swarthmore, who value that tradition and try to live up to it, to have had the Conference meet in this place."[46]

Personal Life

One of the effects of the depression on Frank Aydelotte's personal finances has already been mentioned: he was helping to support three families as well as his own. In June, 1933, he reported this to his brother Will, who had lost his job as an engineer a year earlier and had already received $1,450 from Frank, with the promise of more for a contemplated move to California. For several years Frank had taken for granted the responsibility for helping his parents in Sullivan. Now he began "to send something" to sister Nell, whose husband, John Rice, had just been dismissed from the faculty of Rollins College.

Frank and Marie themselves had felt the crash of 1929. Maurice Cramer recalls Mrs. Aydelotte's saying that "they had lost their savings, and would have to start again." She said it "with considerable poise and cheerfulness," as though savings were no great matter.[47] This would be her genuine feeling, partly because the Aydelottes lived by a principle that money should not be taken solemnly, partly because Frank's earned income continued to be substantial.

Beginning in 1925 he had three salaries: $6,000 from the Rhodes Trust, $10,000 and sometimes more from Senator Guggenheim, and from Swarthmore a salary which had been $10,000 in 1921, rising in 1935–1936 to $18,000, the maximum reported paid to a President in that year in a study limited to fifty-one land-grant institutions, the range of Presidents' salaries being from $7,125 to $10,200.[48] While precise comparisons are virtually impossible to make, it seems fair to say that Frank Aydelotte was better paid than most Presidents, and with his three salaries he was well-to-do.

Of course, his expenses were not low. Entertaining at the President's house cost far more than his allowance from the college. "Pitt" often mentioned this, adding, "The Aydelottes know they have to do things right." It was true that both Frank and Marie thought cheapness was poor economy and quality always important, though not to the point of ostentation. Once I heard Frank explain what might seem an extravagance, his traveling to Europe first-class. He always hoped he might meet someone whom he could interest in being generous to Swarthmore. It was the sort of hope that, in his case, had a way of being fulfilled.

In the summer of 1933 the most serious of the Aydelottes' problems was the future of John Rice. Frank was concerned for him not only as a brother-in-law but also as an old Rhodes Scholar whose record at Oxford had been excellent—a First Class in Jurisprudence—though he spoke of his time there as "three wonderful years of loafing." Afterward he had decided against law in favor of teaching classics and had been associate professor at the University of Nebraska for seven years, full professor for two years at the New Jersey College for Women, then at Rollins since 1930. The President of Rollins, Hamilton Holt, appointed him to help develop the "conference method"[49]—teaching by discussion in two-hour sessions—a method which he thought John Rice could make particularly stimulating, as indeed he did.

Long before coming to Rollins, John Rice had taken his stand as a follower of Socrates. He reveled in the Socratic method of asking questions, leading unsuspecting interlocutors to revelations of truth and folly often surprising to themselves. He had a natural turn for Socratic irony and for the role of Socratic gadfly, stinging people to think. With a genuine warmth for his students and often a barely concealed contempt for their elders, he fascinated the young and goaded many others to fury. Hamilton Holt, himself fascinated and angered by turns, came to regard him as a troublemaker who destroyed the faith of students and alienated older friends of the college. He asked John Rice to resign, and when he refused, he was dropped in spite of his having been promised tenure,[50] and in the face of a censure of the administration by an investigating committee of the American Association of University Professors. Their published report reads: "Many students said he was 'the best teacher or one of the best they had ever had.'" It was the committee's judgment that "his dismissal eliminated from the faculty a teacher who appears . . . to have done more than any other to provoke questioning, discussion, and the spirit of critical inquiry among his students, . . . and to have aimed, with exceptional success, at constructive results, both in thought and character."[51]

In the uproar of charges and investigation, some of the faculty and students had come out for the defendant and subsequently resigned or were dismissed. This was in the spring, when few positions were still open for the next year, and still fewer institutions willing to risk taking known troublemakers. It was not John Rice himself, but one of his supporters, who asked, "How about a new college?" Another said, "I know just the place, Blue Ridge, a great building in the mountains of North Carolina near Asheville, used in the summer by the Y.M.C.A., vacant in winter." John was persuaded to drive up to see it; then, naturally, he drove on to Swarthmore to talk it over on "Aydelotte's porch."

This was one of four trips to consult his brother-in-law by John and various supporters whose names appear in the Aydelottes' guest book from June to September, 1933, first in Swarthmore, twice in Old Chatham, then in Swarthmore again. The third entry, on August 2, has the heading, "Black Mountain Reunion." The new college had a name. It also had a purpose: to provide education *for* democracy through education *in* democracy. Black Mountain was to be a way of life. "The center of the curriculum . . . would be art. The democratic man . . . must be an artist."[52]

To point up obvious differences in personality between the two old Rhodes Scholars, one has only to try to imagine Frank Aydelotte's fancying himself in the role of gadfly, or John Rice's espousing Frank's conviction that "it is not enough to be right; you must also be persuasive."

At the same time, they were alike in much that both held dear: love of teaching, belief in its importance, zeal to improve education, and dislike of dullness. On the extreme point of Black Mountain philosophy, that the education of the democratic man must center on art, Frank Aydelotte would not have agreed that the curriculum must stress painting, sculpture, music, and poetry for everyone. But he had insisted on imagination as essential to fresh and constructive work in any field, and he would certainly have agreed to its value for those, in politics or elsewhere, who were working for a better social order.

Whatever their differences, John Rice sought Frank out to ask advice, counting on his sympathy and good sense. Frank had a gift for refraining from argument about premises even if he thought them dubious, saying in effect: "Given your plan, here are ways to carry it out." His verdict on Black Mountain as John reports it: "It's worth trying."

John Rice's life at Black Mountain had moments of triumph, but not a happy ending. During six years as Rector, he welcomed distinguished visitors, including John Dewey, Albert C. Barnes from his famous Foundation in Merion, and Louis Adamic. In his enthusiasm for the place and for John Rice as its leader, Adamic stayed two and a half months and wrote an article published in *Harper's Magazine:* "Education on a Mountain, The Story of Black Mountain College."[53] The article attracted students looking for something new and stimulating, as well as artist *émigrés* from Europe, who came to this country after Hitler's rise to power, among them Joseph Albers. John Rice welcomed this publicity at first. Later he deplored it as contributing to his downfall by diverting his attention from what should have been his exclusive concern: to teach well. Also it created a spirit of disunity, partly by singling him out as the leader in a community which by rights should be directed by democratically chosen representatives. At the end of six years he decided that he must leave, for his own good as well as the good of Black Mountain.[54] Some time later Frank Aydelotte heard a sad report that its finances had fallen into confusion and persuaded Nicholas O. Pittenger, retired Comptroller of Swarthmore, to go down and see what he could do. In the course of years the college distintegrated until electricity was turned off—symbol of final collapse.

So much for Frank Aydelotte's remote, benevolent relation to Black Mountain. Some day the story of the college should be written to form a chapter in the history of American Utopias.

Study and Research

Three months of a leave of absence in the second semester of 1931–1932 Frank Aydelotte spent studying Spanish in Mexico. He had visited Mexico before on business for the Guggenheim Foundation, but this was Mrs. Aydelotte's first glimpse. "Mexico outstrips all my expectations," she wrote to Maurice Cramer; "I am being lazy and enjoying it to the full." Meanwhile her husband was hard at work. "Mr. Aydelotte is studying all the time. He says nothing refreshes him like being a student again."[55] He made such progress in Spanish that he was asked to give a public lecture at the University of Mexico and chose to speak on "La Vida Literaria de Inglaterra en el Tiempo de Isabel."[56]

While in Mexico he heard of some unpublished documents in the period of his Oxford thesis on *Elizabethan Rogues and Vagabonds*. He tells the story in his sketch for a chapter in his proposed autobiography.

> One day on the golf course in Mexico, G. R. C. Conway, with whom I was playing, told me about a collection of *procesos* in the Mexican National Archives dealing with sailors who had been put on shore near where Tampico now stands by Sir John Hawkins after he lost the battle of Vera Cruz. Hawkins escaped in the *Minion*, which had a capacity of about a hundred men, with two hundred on board. It was quite evident that the food and water which they had would never suffice to take them all safely back to England and the Commander saw nothing better to do than to count off a hundred and put them on shore to take their chances, hoping to return and rescue them the year following.
>
> This was in 1568. In 1570 the Spanish Inquisition was extended to Mexico and about 1572 the members of the Mexican Inquisition heard about these English heretics who by this time seemed to have made a very fine place for themselves in Mexican life. The result was that watches and searches were instituted to apprehend the heretics and bring them into the prison of the Inquisition. There they were examined about their past lives and their ideas on religion.
>
> The Mexican Inquisition was not so cruel as the parent Inquisition in Spain. These examinations, which occupied anywhere from six months to two years, show that the Mexican Inquisitors were genuinely curious about the ideas of their English prisoners. . . . Those who were 25 or 30 years of age had lived under four different religious regimes in England: Henry VIII, Edward VI, Catholicism under Mary, and the Elizabethan settlement. They were pretty vague about the theological implications of

these changes, but very clear about what the changes meant in the conduct of the local churches.

Conway had employed young scholars to copy out and translate these *procesos*. When he told me about them I was so curious that I almost wanted to stop the game of golf right there and go and look at them. I had a certain opportunity to study the documents while we were still in Mexico, but Conway had presented a full set to the Huntington Library, and the first time I was able to arrange a leave of absence from Swarthmore [six years later] we went to Pasadena for three months of research into the adventures of the Elizabethan Seamen.[57]

Frank reveled in the chance to use these documents. He wrote to Abraham Flexner:

> I am having a wonderful time here with a piece of Elizabethan research. . . . I glanced hastily over the sixteenth century material in the Huntington Library some years ago, but I had no idea that it was as rich in that period as I now find it to be. I am also delighted to find that I am as much at home with these things as ever, and my work is a daily joy to me. I intend to keep it up from now on, getting some relief from administrative details at Swarthmore for that purpose."[58]

He produced an article which he gave as a Founders' Day address at the Huntington Library and intended to expand into a book. But the editor of the *American Historical Review*, Guy Stanton Ford, persuaded him to let the paper be published, on the ground that he was not likely to have time to finish the book in the near future. In fact, he never finished it. The paper, "Elizabethan Seamen in Mexico and Ports of the Spanish Main," appeared in the *Review* after its author had moved to the Institute for Advanced Study.[59]

Trips to England, Germany, and France

After three months in Mexico, Frank and Marie Aydelotte crossed to England early in June. They were joined by Bill, who had completed his first year at Cambridge, and by Maurice Cramer from Princeton, who had come for the trip he could not take in 1929. He and Bill agreed that the great event of their stay in Britain was a week-end house party in Scotland at Newbattle Abbey, an estate of the Marquess of Lothian whom they had first known as Philip Kerr, Secretary to the Rhodes Trustees since 1926, recently come into the title. The other guests were

Tom Jones (Lloyd George's old associate) and the heads of the four Scottish universities with their wives.[60]

Lord Lothian intended to give his historic estate to these universities for educational purposes and had invited their officials to advise him on his plan. Business was discussed after dinner when the ladies had withdrawn, leaving the gentlemen to their port, including the two young Americans, who were fascinated by the conversation and the interplay of personalities. Maurice reported in some detail Lord Lothian's opening remarks on the proposed uses of Newbattle Abbey:

> A place for adult education and for recreation of working people in connection with the University of Edinburgh; a place where scholars and teachers could have an inexpensive vacation, and come in contact with each other and with working people to the mutual enriching of all; a place where music, art, history, etc. could be taught during vacation periods to carefully selected working people who were really able and eager to learn. He was willing to turn over the mansion as it was, with its beautiful furniture and art treasures, so that it might always maintain its character as a pleasant country house. The scheme was not unlike that of Coleg Harlech in Wales, which Mr. Jones then explained.[61]

The Aydelottes and Maurice went next to Germany, where the two young men lived with the family of a professor at the University of Freiburg and studied German. Frank and Marie made the tour of German universities mentioned earlier in this chapter, in the course of which he listened to a speech by an impassioned orator named Hitler and was by no means carried away.

Their interest in German universities was partly to give Frank a better background for his work as a Trustee of the Institute for Advanced Study, incorporated in 1930 and now in the planning stage, with Abraham Flexner as Director. Flexner had been devoting this year of 1932 to finding professors for the new venture, and in June he went to Caputh near Potsdam to see Einstein, with whom he had already discussed some of his ideas when the two men met in California and Oxford. Now he found Einstein ready to accept with enthusiasm the invitation to come to the Institute as professor in its first school, mathematics. His parting words to Flexner: "Ich bin Feuer und Flamme dafür ."[62]

Again in 1934 Frank traveled with the Institute in mind when he went to Paris to look into the organization of research at the Collège de France. Earlier in that same trip he and Marie had a personal reason for going to England. Bill was completing his Ph.D. at Cambridge.

There were two more trips aboard, both to Oxford: in 1936 on Rhodes Scholarship business; notably, in 1937, when Frank was given the honorary degree of D.C.L. (Doctor of Civil Laws). According to *The London Times*,[63] the ceremony, Encaenia, was held on June 23, 1937, at noon in the Sheldonian Theatre, recently restored for use "after the ravages of the death-watch beetle." When Frank Aydelotte was presented for his degree, the public orator introduced him as "among the earliest Rhodes Scholars," adding: "His powers of administration have had full play in the presidency of Swarthmore College. Recently he has strenuously exerted himself on behalf of the Oxford appeal in America." Then a light Oxonian touch: "Oxford may give him her good wishes as an ardent golfer."

The degree entitled the holder to a soft black velvet cap and the scarlet gown that added brightness and dash to many ceremonies. Much as Frank prized his new degree, he said that he valued even more his election to an Honorary Fellowship at Brasenose College in the same year.

The personal joys and hazards of an Oxford honorary degree are described by Marie Aydelotte in a letter to Ruth Brooks, wife of Frank's old friend Alfred, written from Lord Lothian's house, Blickling Hall, at Aylsham, on July 12, 1937.

Of all our visits to England I think that this has been the most thrilling. I had not realized how much they made of an honorary D.C.L. at Oxford. Congratulations poured in upon Frank and he was royally entertained. Added to this he was much feted on his first appearance since being made a Fellow of Brasenose College. Two days after the Encaenia Queen Mary laid the corner stone of the Bodleian extension and we sat so near to her that I feel as if I know her. We went to a garden party afterwards at the Vice Chancellor's where she appeared but we did not wait to see her because we had another engagement to keep. One of the funniest things that happened was when we were visiting the Warden of All Souls and Frank was taken ill. The Archbishop of Canterbury was expected for a night on the day we were to leave and was to have occupied the lovely room where we were installed. The Warden and Mrs. Adams would not hear of Frank being disturbed and put the Archbishop (Frank insists) in the attic although Mrs. Adams said he had a very good room. Alfred will laugh at me but I must say I had a bit of a thrill in meeting the Archbishop who had crowned the new King and of talking cosily with him over some hot cocoa that night before we all went to bed!

Well the result of Frank's illness was that we gave up the golfing trip to Scotland and accepted Lord Lothian's delightful invitation to come here to recuperate. So here we are for a two weeks rest and Frank is flourishing. He does not yet feel like a game of golf but keeps his hand in by knocking out balls every afternoon on the Blickling course. He writes and reads and sleeps and you can imagine what heaven it is to be in this beautiful place all by ourselves without a care.

When the President wore his resplendent gown at the Swarthmore Commencement of 1938, he walked beside Albert Einstein, the Commencement speaker, bushy head next to head completely bald. The sight drew an exclamation from the Vice-President of the Board of Managers, Howard Cooper Johnson: "You two should get together in this matter of hair!"

End of a Full Chapter

On October 14, 1939, two days before Frank Aydelotte's fifty-ninth birthday, he shocked the Swarthmore community by announcing that he had resigned. He was going to the Institute for Advanced Study, to follow Abraham Flexner as Director. The announcement was made to the students at ten o'clock on Saturday night before it was to appear in the Philadephia papers.

The next day one of the junior editors of the *Phoenix*, Barbara Ballou, '41, wrote her parents the shattering news. She had heard it first from another editor who called her at 10:02: "Bobby? Yes. Prexy's resigned. Reasons are all very vague yet—something about his health, and working on some scientific project at Princeton with Einstein." Her letter continues,

> The whole college is very upset and wondering what we'll do without our prexy with the big ears and the lovable face ... who has made Swarthmore what it is today, made it from a usual small coed college, not into a rah-rah footballishly well-known place, but into a place with high standards and real values. ... One cares more about him than about almost anyone else who is really so remote from one's actual existence. It's almost like a nightmare from which one wants to wake up.

A week later she wrote home again, describing student reactions:

We're all used to the idea of losing Prexy now, sad though it is. ... Sunday evening about four hundred of us arrived silently on the Aydelotte lawn and sang the Alma Mater. ... Shortly afterward the porch light went on, and Dr. and Mrs. Aydelotte came out quietly and stood as we finished singing. Everyone felt chokey and still marvels at the fact that we finished. We all stood in silence for a moment, and then he thanked us and told us about his reasons for going, spoke naturally and informally as one would to one's family.[64]

The President gave a more formal message to the college in the *Phoenix* of October 17, recalling his program to provide stimulating academic work supplemented by athletics developed not to win games, but for maximum enjoyment, saying that the students were the only ones who could prove the program's success. "They have, I believe, proved it up to the hilt. In graduate schools here and abroad, in business, and in all the professions, they are demonstrating daily the value of the training they received at Swarthmore as it could be demonstrated in no other way."[65] He felt that the time had come for him to serve some of the same ends elsewhere.

> Now the opportunity comes to me to attack from another angle this central problem of the struggle against mediocrity in our higher education. Hard as it is to leave a place I love so much, I saw from the first that I must accept. The same concerns which brought me to Swarthmore now compel me to leave. My life here has been one of stirring adventure, and I have just time for one more adventure in the same cause before I am ready to retire from active work.

He went on to show how deeply he had become involved in the college: "I have been nearly twenty years at Swarthmore and have signed the diplomas of more than half the living graduates of the college. Nearly nine-tenths of the faculty are my appointments, and more than half of the members of the Board have been elected since I came in 1921." And finally, a farewell that was less poignant because he was staying through the year, dividing each week between Swarthmore and the Institute, to give the Board time to find his successor: "No one who loves Swarthmore ever really leaves it. Our graduates return so constantly that I am sometimes a little puzzled to remember whether or not they have actually taken their degrees. We shall do the same. And when we are not here in person, our affectionate loyalty and our deepest good wishes will always remain with the college as I know yours will go with us."

At the request of the seniors, the President was their Commencement speaker, and he became their fellow alumnus on the same day with an honorary L.H.D. In his speech he discussed the responsibilities of the

United States in the world crisis, the need for "faith and idealism to imagine a better future for the world . . . and the discipline and determination . . . necessary to translate that dream into reality."[66] He left the seniors conscious that they were going into a world where nothing would be easy, but where all their resources of courage and intelligence would be needed and used to the full.

When his resignation from Swarthmore was going into effect, Frank Aydelotte saw that the time had come when he could ask to join the Society of Friends. While he was in office, he thought his relations with the Managers would be on a more impersonal basis if he were not a member. Now with much pleasure he wrote to the Swarthmore Monthly Meeting that he would like to join them, and he was duly visited and recommended to the Meeting by an alumna and member of the Board of Managers, Eleanor Stabler Clark. Some years later, in 1945, he was himself elected to the Board of Managers.

To the students belongs the last word, in the dedication of the yearbook, the *Halcyon*, published by the junior class: "Appreciative of our good fortune in coming to Swarthmore at a time when his graciousness and sincere enthusiasm have influenced every phase of our college life, we, the Class of 1941, dedicate our *Halcyon* to Frank Aydelotte and his Swarthmore."

CHAPTER FIFTEEN

THE INSTITUTE FOR ADVANCED STUDY

Princeton: 1939–1947

WHEN Frank Aydelotte agreed to become Director of the Institute for Advanced Study before he could be relieved of his duties at Swarthmore, it seemed obvious that there must be a situation at Princeton which required his presence at once. This was, indeed, the case. The Institute's first Director and creator, Abraham Flexner, Frank Aydelotte's old friend and companion at arms against mediocrity in education, had become so dictatorial at seventy-three that he was faced by a movement among the faculty to force him to retire. When he did so in October, his successor was needed immediately to restore peace and good feeling. The emergency did not alarm Frank Aydelotte, who had always worked well with the faculty at Swarthmore and hoped to develop equally satisfactory relations at Princeton. Fortunately he knew the Institute well, having been an active Trustee since it was incorporated and watched it grow through nine years of existence, three of planning and six of work. Having seen Abraham Flexner bring his "dream" to life, his successor could hope to understand this brilliant novelty in American higher education: a center for the most advanced research where exceptionally able scientists and scholars "with their pupils and assistants may devote themselves to the task of pushing beyond the present limits of human knowledge and to training those who may 'carry on.'"[1] To see the significance of what Frank Aydelotte inherited, both achievements and problems, it is helpful to recall steps in the Institute's growth and aspects of its creator's personality.*

*My discussion of Frank Aydelotte's years at the Institute for Advanced Study owes a great debt to Mrs. Beatrice M. Stern, who was engaged by the Institute to carry out extensive research in its history.

Institute Prehistory

The first event in the Institute's prehistory involved both the first and second Directors. Frank Aydelotte, as American Secretary to the Rhodes Trustees, recommended that they invite Abraham Flexner to give the Rhodes Trust Memorial Lectures at Oxford in the spring of 1928, and he accepted, believing he had something to say on the subject of universities. He was relatively free at the time, on the point of retiring from the General Education Board, and welcomed the chance to clarify some of the ideas he had gained during his years of appraising plans, people, and institutions. As he accumulated facts for his lectures on American and European universities, he recognized deplorable weaknesses of many in America and began to look for means of correcting them. Eventually he came up with his dream: to create a "Paradise of Scholars," which took shape in the Institute for Advanced Study. For the chance to put his thoughts in order through these lectures he felt deeply indebted to the Rhodes Trust and to Frank Aydelotte, and he wrote affectionately to remind his successor of this debt eleven years later.

> Do you realize that without you there would have been no Institute for Advanced Study? For this Institute is a direct outgrowth of the Rhodes Lectures and you were the one human being alive who would ever have the termerity to recommend me—educational heretic that I was and am. . . . The Rhodes Lectures gave me a really marvelous opportunity and enlarged my vision as it had previously been enlarged when first I went to Germany for a prolonged stay. Hardly a day passes but that I think with gratitude of your part in the use to which I have been enabled to put what will probably be my last active years.[2]

His lectures had another connection with the Institute when he had expanded them into a book, *Universities: American, English, German,* which came to the attention of Louis Bamberger and his sister, Mrs. Felix Fuld, at an opportune moment. They had sold their great department store in Newark and were considering ways of using their fortune for the benefit of education when their advisers, Herbert Maass and Samuel Leidesdorf, impressed by reports of Flexner's knowledge and resourcefulness, called on him to ask for suggestions. This was early in 1930 when he was reading proofs of *Universities,* and he gave a set to his visitors to show their clients. Mr. Bamberger and Mrs. Fuld must have been shocked by his account of what was wrong with education. As he recalls it: "I riddled with facts, sarcasm and documents the outright and shameless humbuggery that was proving profitable at teachers' colleges; in home-study courses at Columbia, Chicago, and even my own beloved Johns Hopkins; in correspondence courses competing with work on the campus; and in the absurd topics for which the Ph.D. degree was given."[3] But devasting as he could be in attack, he was inspiring when he recommended a solution. His section on "The Idea of a Modern University" deeply impressed the two philanthropists. They asked him to come to see them several times to answer their questions and eventually decided to found the Institute for Advanced Study.

Flexner said flatly that American universities were woefully inadequate to deal with recent discoveries in the physical and biological sciences— discoveries which entailed new approaches to the social sciences and reappraisals of values in these fields and in the humanities. At such a time rigorous intellectual standards were indispensable, but unfortunately they were not to be found in the universities of the United States. The universities were failing because they were attempting too much, taking on responsibilities which did not properly belong to them. They had become a mélange of "secondary schools and colleges for boys and girls; graduate and professional schools for advanced students; 'service' stations for the general public."[4] (Among the many kinds of "service" offered, Flexner included "home study courses," practically useful work in domestic science, library science, business, and so on, which he held should be made available in detached technical schools.) Involved in so much that is irrelevant, universities could scarcely be aware of the aim with which they should be preoccupied: "intensive study of phenomena under the most favorable conditions— the phenomena of the physical world, of the social world, of the aesthetic world, and the ceaseless struggle to see things in relation—these I conceive to be the most important functions of the modern university."[5]

At the end of his second section, on "American Universities," Flexner was ready to say that since there is no such institution in this country— "no seat of learning devoted to higher teaching and research"—one should be created. He described eloquently what it might be.

It should be a free society of scholars—free, because mature persons, animated by intellectual purposes, must be left to pursue their own way. Administration should be slight and inexpensive. Scholars and scientists should participate in its government. . . . It should furnish simple surroundings—books, laboratories, and above all, tranquillity—absence of distraction either by worldly concerns or by parental responsibility for an immature student body. Provision should be made for the amenities of life in the institution and in the private life of the staff.[6]

Then a peroration forecasting what such an institution might accomplish and tribute to two sources of his inspiration: the Rockefeller Institute for Medical Research, with his brother Simon as Director; Johns Hopkins University and its creator, Daniel Coit Gilman. Both had small numbers and unprecedented standards of excellence which gave them notable influence. (Gilman was Flexner's ideal, then and always. "Those who know something of my work long after Gilman's day, at the Carnegie Foundation, the General Education Board, and the Institute for Advanced Study at Princeton, will recognize Gilman's influence in all I have done or tried to do."[7])

> What could be expected, if a modern American university were thus established? The ablest scholars and scientists would be attracted to its faculty; the most earnest students would be attracted to its laboratories and seminars. It would be small, as Gilman's Johns Hopkins was small; but its propulsive power would be momentous out of all proportion to its size. It would, like a lens, focus rays that now scatter. The Rockefeller Institute for Medical Research is limited in scope; its hospital contains less than fifty beds. But its uncompromising standards of activity and publication have given it influence in America and Europe throughout the entire field of medical education and research. A university or a school of higher learning at the level I have indicated would do as much for other disciplines and might thus in time assist the general reorganization of secondary and higher education.[8]

Flexner's vision of what might be done communicated his own enthusiasm to Mr. Bamberger and Mrs. Fuld. They warmed to the thought of a new kind of institution—on the highest peaks of learning, small in size but great in influence—and agreed to found the "Institute" on one condition: that Abraham Flexner himself would organize and direct it. When he objected that this should be the work of a younger man, Mr. Bamberger answered, "The idea is yours. You should train the younger man." Flexner postponed deciding until he could consult his wife. She answered, "You will have to do it. You have spent your life criticising other people. You can't refuse to give them a chance to criticize you."[9]

Returning to tell Mr. Bamberger that he would accept, he was asked how much money he would need to begin. His reply showed the nonchalance of a man who had spent years recommending the disposal of Rockefeller millions. He explained that he would not need much at first, but "enough to make anyone with whom I speak understand that I am in earnest." When Mr. Bamberger asked what amount would do, Flexner answered, "Five millions." "Very well," said Mr. Bamberger, "you may have it." Privately Herbert Maass mentioned a possible total of thirty millions.

Mr. Bamberger, then eighty years old, showed a wise patience in telling Flexner to take plenty of time to make his plans. "I do not care that you do anything at all during my life-time. We only want it to be right when we do it." Happily he did live to watch the Institute's progress during fourteen years.

To Abraham Flexner the opportunity seemed "little short of miraculous." Having made a career of calling attention to defects in American secondary schools, universities, and medical schools, he could now create an institution, "starting with a clean sheet, without commitments and without tradition." He was the exemplar for Pasteur's maxim which he and Frank Aydelotte both liked to quote: "Chance favors the prepared mind."

When Flexner acknowledged Daniel Coit Gilman as his model, what did this mean in terms of preparing his mind? That he observed and adopted the methods used by the President of Johns Hopkins when he established the first American graduate school offering opportunities comparable to those in Europe, and a pre-eminent medical school, both contributing notably to higher standards of American graduate and professional education. Flexner, like Gilman, would put first the problem of discovering outstanding men for the faculty and would go to the greatest lengths to find them, traveling abroad and asking advice, ignoring considerations of age, race, or creed, appointing only those who gave promise of the highest excellence. Having appointed such men, Flexner, like Gilman, would leave them free to develop research and teaching as they saw fit, without regard for the foreseen utility of what they might discover. Knowledge for its own sake was their common aim.[10]

First Steps

On May 20, 1930, the Founders signed the certificate of incorporation of an "Institute for Advanced Study—Louis Bamberger and Mrs. Felix

Fuld Foundation," with a Board of fifteen Trustees including themselves, their nephew Edgar S. Bamberger, the Director, and four men with whom they had business connections: John R. Hardin, Samuel D. Leidesdorf, Herbert H. Maass, and Percy S. Straus. There were two public figures, Alanson B. Houghton, formerly Ambassador to Germany and later to England, and Herbert H. Lehman, best known as Governor of New York. Five represented professional experience in education: Dr. Alexis Carrel, winner of a Nobel Prize in 1912 for developing an important new technique in surgery, now a member of the Rockefeller Institute for Medical Research, of which the only woman Trustee, Dr. Florence Sabin, was also a member; Dr. Lewis Weed, anatomist at the Johns Hopkins Medical School; Julius Friedenwald, who had been an undergraduate with Abraham Flexner at Johns Hopkins, now a distinguished physician in Baltimore; and Frank Aydelotte.[11] Alanson Houghton, chairman of the Board from the beginning until his death in 1941, contributed greatly to good relationships.

The purposes of the Institute were noted in preliminary statements by the Founders and the Director and at their organization meeting in the following October. The Institute for Advanced Study should be "a graduate university with a distinguished faculty and advanced students, the numbers small enough to secure the highest quality." Concentrating on two aims, pure research and the training required for it, the Institute would be unique: not like the current university which must also provide instruction for undergraduate and professional schools; not like a research institute "devoted solely to the solution of problems. It may be pictured as a wedge inserted between the two—a small university in which a limited amount of teaching and a liberal amount of research are both to be found." Its greatness would obviously depend on a preeminent faculty—in the Director's words, "not upon buildings but upon brains." A second point, almost as important: the Institute should begin experimentally in a small way, profiting by experience and not "getting too deeply involved" to change.

Before making definite plans, Abraham Flexner, following in Gilman's footsteps, traveled to centers in this country and Europe where he could profit by the experience of experts. He wanted to raise three questions: where to start—preferably with a single subject; what eminent men to try to secure for the faculty; where to place the Institute so that it could be expected to prosper. The specialists he consulted agreed that he would do well to start with mathematics. Already he himself had considered mathematics seriously. It had the advantage of being "fundamental and severe"; it dealt with intellectual concepts "for their own sake regardless of their possible usefulness" and consequently proved broadly stimulating to "scientists, philosophers, economists, poets, and musicians." The simplicity of equipment was a further advantage: "a few men, a few students, a few rooms, books, blackboards, chalk, paper and pencils."[12] So he concluded that mathematics should be the Institute's first subject and that what he called the School of Mathematics would, for the time being, constitute the Institute, always provided he could find professors distinguished enough to ensure a good start.

The first two Europeans suggested to him were Albert Einstein, without question "one of the great of all time," and Hermann Weyl, successor to Hilbert at Göttingen, eminent in classical mathematics and "one of the chief contributors to the general theory of relativity," with an unusual interest in the aesthetic: "My work always tried to unite the true with the beautiful."[13] When Einstein agreed to come, Flexner knew that the Institute's prestige was assured with mathematicians and hardly less with the general public. Somehow Einstein had caught the imagination of all kinds of people. They knew his name as the great man of science. They recognized him instantly from photographs, with his halo of gray hair, his look of high-mindedness, simplicity, and warmth. He was regarded with affection as well as veneration by Indians who initiated him into their tribe as "The Great Relative"; children who brought him candy and asked him for help with their arithmetic (which he always refused out of regard for their teachers); a Trenton taxi driver in 1965 who looked blank at first when I asked him to take me to the Institute in Princeton, then broke into a broad smile, exclaiming "Einstein!"

As to a site, the Director was told many times that the Institute should be near a university with the privilege of using its library and the advantage of stimulating surroundings. He made inquiries at Harvard first, according to Marston Morse, then a member of the Harvard department of mathematics, soon to go to the Institute as one of its distinguished professors. Professor Morse remembers that the Harvard department voted in favor of welcoming the Institute. But forces worked against this alliance, notably the Founders' strong preference for a location in New Jersey, the state where they had made their fortune. They would have liked to place the Institute in their own city of Newark, though open to conviction by the Director that academic advantages weighed heavily in favor of Princeton.

Flexner had formed a high opinion of the Princeton Graduate School when he investigated it for the General Education Board and recommended generous grants, first for the natural sciences and mathematics, later for the humanities. Before the Institute was incorporated, Princeton had a well-endowed "humanistic" laboratory under the department of art and archaeology and was training a large proportion of the country's men teachers of art history. This would promise well for the Institute's future development in humanistic studies. But for the moment the great asset was Princeton's excellent department of mathematics with its own new building, Fine Hall, housing a good library, and ready to share both with the Institute as paying guest. The School of Mathematics remained for six years in rented quarters, following a precedent set by Gilman at Johns Hopkins, and continued to make some use of them even after the Institute had a building of its own. Throughout Flexner's period of active service he rented an office for himself at 20 Nassau Street.

Complete cooperation with the university in intellectual undertakings was projected before the Institute officially opened and became effective in its first year, according to an Institute *Bulletin*:

> While the Institute and Princeton University are organically and administratively entirely distinct, the faculties and students of the two institutions cooperate in any direction that promises more favorable results than either institution could obtain alone, the students availing themselves of the courses, seminars, and opportunities for conference and direction of work in both institutions without payment of an additional fee.[14]

From the beginning one special joint enterprise was a quarterly journal, the *Annals of Mathematics*, with an editorial board consisting of representatives of both institutions.[15]

Flexner prized this relation with Princeton for many reasons, among them perhaps his own desire for academic support. Before coming to the Institute he had never been asked to teach in a college or university or to be head of one. He was not a professional educator nor a productive scholar. All this he himself admitted many times after the Institute had succeeded, when he called it "the layman's contribution to higher learning," pointing out that a professional scholar would not have had the flexibility to break through academic precedents and produce something new.[16] But at the beginning, determined as he was that the Institute should soon realize his dream and the Founders' expectations, he saw that it must not only *be* but *seem* outstanding. On both counts the connection with Princeton should prove invaluable, giving an unmistakable stamp of academic approval and providing the Director with the resources of experience and wisdom represented by Presidents Hibben and Dodds, Dean Eisenhart, and professors in whatever subjects the Institute might undertake.

In fact, the good feeling between host and guest institutions was strong enough to persist through a situation which might have caused a rupture: the Institute "raided" the Princeton department of mathematics for its first American professor of mathematics, Oswald Veblen. Before the Institute opened, Veblen lured away two more, James Waddell Alexander and John von Neumann. In each case it must be said that the raid was well conducted. Flexner took care to ask Princeton authorities for their approval.

Oswald Veblen, the nephew of Thorstein Veblen (famous for his *Theory of the Leisure Class*), began to show his interest in new ventures in education when he entered the Graduate School of the University of Chicago in 1900, only ten years after it opened, but already known for a strong department of mathematics. When Woodrow Wilson introduced the preceptorial system at Princeton, he imported Veblen as one of the first preceptors. Soon promoted to a full professorship, Veblen played an important part in developing Princeton into a "major mathematical center." A mathematician who stood high in his profession, an excellent teacher with devoted students, he seemed to Flexner a man who would bring distinction to the Institute. And so he did, but with a zest for administration which may have stood in the way of his fullest contribution to scholarship. In adding James Alexander, Veblen brought over one of his own most promising students. The youngest in the group, John von Neumann, born in 1903 in Budapest, like Weyl a student of Hilbert at Göttingen, came to Princeton as a visiting professor of mathematical physics at the age of twenty-seven and stayed on for two years before he joined the Institute faculty. Already he had published "his first great work," *Mathematical Grounding of Quantum Mechanics*, an indication that he "was to become one of those most able in our day to bridge the gap between physics and mathematics."[17] These three, added to Albert Einstein with his wind-blown look of a prophet on a mountaintop, and and Hermann Weyl with his elegance of mind, formed a faculty outstanding in personality, brilliance, and range.

The Director was determined from the first to make the Institute a model of generosity to the faculty, paying salaries which would enhance the dignity of the teaching profession, often too little respected because underpaid. And far more important, high salaries would free a man from financial worries and from the temptation to waste his energy on ways of supplementing his income. A professor should receive enough from the Institute so that he could be expected to give it his full time.

"Full time" had a special significance for Abraham Flexner from his work with the General Education Board to improve medical education. Earlier, when he had made a study of American medical schools for the Carnegie Foundation for the Advancement of Teaching, he had found students neglected by teachers who were doctors in private practice and felt that their first responsibility was for their patients. He had seen that these doctors could not be required to give up private patients and devote themselves to teaching unless they were paid much larger salaries. Later, when he joined the staff of the General Education Board, Flexner took the lead in recommending the use of Rockefeller millions to raise salaries in a number of medical schools which would agree to employ both laboratory and clinical teachers only on full time. Flexner's methods here as elsewhere tended to be brusque rather than conciliatory. According to Raymond Fosdick's story of the General Education Board, *Adventure in Giving*, "Flexner's blows on behalf of 'full time' in medical education drew blood, and his unfeigned joy in controversy left behind some wounded spirits." But the result of his work was vast improvement in the medical schools and, for himself, an almost fanatical devotion to the concept of full time.[18] While he was Director of the Institute, every *Bulletin* carried a statement that "the scale of salaries and retiring allowances is such . . . that the members of the staff may live up to the standard that has been created in the full-time departments of certain medical schools organized within recent years." To this he added in 1936 a pledge against combining part-time arrangements for some staff members and full time for others: "the Institute is pledged to its Founders to adhere strictly to the full-time basis." (During the war Flexner's stand on this point made him oppose any war service by the Institute staff and interpret his successor's permitting such service as a breach of faith, even when approved by the Founders and other Trustees.)

As to salaries, Flexner proposed that the Institute's maximum for a professor should be $15,000 a year, phenomenal in those days. It was more than three times the median reported in a study of salaries in 1930–1931, including 1,826 full professors in 51 institutions. Only twenty-four of these full professors received as much as $8,000 to $10,000; five others, $10,000 or more.[19] Flexner's proposed provision for retirement allowances would also be generous: $8,000 for a professor, $4,000 for his surviving widow.

The relations existing in most institutions between faculty and administration he thought needed improvement. The right relation, as he saw it (and as Frank Aydelotte had seen it at Swarthmore), was for the administration to relieve the faculty of routine responsibilities. At the beginning he expected to consult them regularly on matters of policy and included in the first bylaws a joint faculty-trustees Committee on Education,[20] to consider educational policies and appointments. If this bylaw had been enforced, it would have prevented later difficulties between Director and faculty, but from the start it was a dead letter, probably because Mr. Bamberger disapproved.

On one point the Director's advice on administration-faculty relations took effect: a warning against any guidance of the faculty in their work. For both teaching and research, faculty and students should be free to make their own arrangements, dispensing with regular courses, required attendance, and examinations. "Seasoned and eminent scholars . . . have usually followed their own inner light; no organizer, no administrator, no institution can do more than furnish conditions favorable to the restless prowling of an enlightened and informed human spirit."[21] This is Abraham Flexner at his most eloquent.

His three years of asking advice had brought only one important change in policy: whereas the Institute had been incorporated with power to confer the Ph.D. degree, it was now to be concerned exclusively with postdoctoral research. There were two reasons for the change: first, that there were already abundant opportunities for work leading to the Ph.D. degree but, except in medicine, few for more advanced research; second, the routine, red tape, and formal examinations involved in granting the Doctor's degree took time which the professors should have for research.

Six Years of Experiment, 1933–1939

The Institute for Advanced Study opened with everything in its favor: brilliant professors, promising postdoctoral students from a variety of well-established universities in this country and Europe. The students represented the two levels of experience Flexner had hoped for: members of faculties on leave of absence, eager to catch up with advances in their subject and to get a new impulse toward research; younger men with such recent Ph.D.'s as to have other projects they wanted to carry further. The numbers were happily small and the program flexible.

To give figures: the Institute, consisting of the School of Mathematics, came to life in the persons of the Director and a staff of seven—four professors, Alexander, Einstein, Veblen, and von Neumann, with three assistants—and twenty-three students listed as "Workers Registered," this title soon to be changed to "Members." The fifth professor, Hermann Weyl, joined them in January after completing an engagement as Cooper Foundation Lecturer at Swarthmore. Seventeen of the workers represented twelve institutions in this country: Brown, California Institute of Technology, Chicago, Columbia, Cornell, Harvard, Johns Hopkins, Ohio State, Princeton, Texas, Virginia, Yale. Six foreign students came from six universities: Cambridge, Copenhagen, Edinburgh, Jassy (Romania), Leiden, Vienna. One-third of the twenty-three were on leave from university faculties, two-thirds with doctorates they had received in the last three years. That the Institute was already trailing clouds of glory was attested by the granting of fellowships for its use by two foundations in that first year: four by the National Research Council and two by the Rockefeller Foundation. A good number of other workers had stipends from the Institute itself to cover expenses for living and travel.[22]

The program, described in the Institute *Bulletin*,[23] offered a welcome respite from the large numbers and red tape of most universities. "The workers seek the professors . . . whose interests coincide with their own," making "their own individual arrangements. No two persons during the year 1933–1934 have pursued the same course of action." Instruction is given "by individual contact with students, by seminars, by courses of lectures . . . each professor being free to follow the methods he prefers and to vary them from year to year." Four professors had seen fit to offer two seminars: one on topology by Professor Alexander and a Princeton colleague, Professor Lefschetz; the second, "differential geometry and quantum theory" by Professors Veblen and von Neumann. Modestly sandwiched between the two seminars was the statement: "Professor Einstein will continue his investigation in field theory in relation to quantum theory." A series of lectures was given by Professor von Neumann on "theory of integration, general theory of Hilbert space, and bounded operators." Beginning in January, Professor Weyl lectured on "the structure and representations of continuous groups."

The same *Bulletin* announced that "Professor Dirac" would give lectures or a seminar in 1934–1935. In the understated style of such an announcement, "Professor Dirac" is not identified as the mathematical physicist Paul A. M. Dirac, who was to be the Institute's first visiting professor—who, in 1933 at the age of thirty-one, had shared the Nobel Prize in Physics with Erwin Schrödinger. This was something anyone interested in the Institute could be expected to know.

In 1935 Professor Marston Morse of Harvard joined the School of Mathematics, and two more Schools made modest starts: Economics and Politics, and Humanistic Studies.

From the beginning Flexner had been ambitious to launch a School of Economics. He saw the subject "linked to mathematics by statistics" and indispensable to understanding the forces playing upon modern society. He liked to quote Justice Holmes: "The man of the future is the man of statistics and the master of economics." In spite of its importance, economics was getting relatively little attention: "Nowhere in the world does the subject of economics enjoy the attention it deserves—economics in the broad sense, inclusive of political theory, ethics, and other subjects that are involved therein." And for such attention as it did receive, the conditions were unfavorable. Economists were too much involved with practice, as journalists or handymen for banks. They had too little of the leisure, freedom from financial strain, and objectivity required for sound, reliable judgment. They must have the chance to be thinkers, as well as students of practice.

To provide the necessary conditions should be one of the Institute's great opportunities. As Flexner put it: "I conceived a group of economists and their associates, financially independent, unhurried, and disinterested, in closest possible contact with the phenomena of business, government, and social life and at this high level endeavoring to understand the novel phenomena taking place before our eyes." They must be able "to take the same attitude toward social phenomena that the medical scientist has now been enabled to take toward disease."[24] Flexner was proposing to ask of the men whom he would someday appoint nothing less than a new economics, with the concreteness of an empirical science, the objectivity of mathematics, and a philosophical world view.

Even while he dreamed of a clinical economics, Flexner knew that new times bring new needs, and he made provision for flexibility. He would be ready to shift the salary of a professor from one School to another, even to let a subject lapse, taking as precedent what was done in the Collège de France.

The opening of the School of Economics represented a triumph of the Director over a reluctant Founder. Mr. Bamberger as a businessman regarded economics with suspicion, considering it the work of theorists who make pronouncements without due knowledge of facts. Flexner, while admitting that some economists did show this weakness, believed that they could and would avoid it in the developments he projected at the Institute. Out of deference to the Director, Mr. Bamberger agreed to make a start, but always with the reservation that it was purely experimental and could be dropped at any time. This partly explains his not providing adequate financial support.

In its first year the School had two professors in residence, David Mitrany and Winfield Riefler, both with the combination of scholarly and practical gifts that the Director thought essential. David Mitrany, born in Bucharest in 1888, with doctor's degrees from the London School of Economics to guarantee his scholarly training, had gained insight into public events as a member of the editorial staff of the famous Liberal daily, the Manchester *Guardian*. While recently at Harvard as visiting professor of government, he had become acquainted with the Institute staff and would be welcome.

Winfield Riefler, already at thirty-eight a specialist in both domestic and foreign finance, after two years as foreign trade officer of the Department of Commerce at Buenos Aires, received his Ph.D. from the Brookings Graduate School in Washington and published *Money Rates and Money Markets in the United States*. For ten years he had worked in the Division of Research and Statistics of the Federal Reserve Board.

A third professor, Edward Earle, was on leave of absence because of ill-health. Flexner had been interested in him for some years, having unsuccessfully urged that he be included in the Institute's first Board of Trustees. Coming from an associate professorship at Columbia, where he had earned his Ph.D., he had published *Turkey, the Great Powers, and the Bagdad Railway* (1923) which won the George Louis Beer Prize for the best work of the year on European diplomacy.

The variety of interests represented by the three appointees promised well for the breadth of the new School.[25]

The School of Humanistic Studies opened with a single professor in Princeton, the art historian Erwin Panofsky, a host in himself. He established a good working arrangement with the Princeton department of art and archaeology, sharing the use of McCormick Hall. Three other recently appointed professors were engaged in research abroad: Ernst

Herzfeld in the archaeology of the Near East, E. A. Lowe in Latin paleography, Benjamin Meritt in Greek epigraphy. Soon a fifth professor was added, the only woman to hold that rank at the Institute: Miss Hetty Goldman, archaeologist excavating at Tarsus in Turkey, with a special interest in prehistoric pottery and terra-cotta figurines. Materials for future research in a new line were acquired by the purchase in 1936 (with the help of the Rockefeller Foundation) of the great Gest Oriental Library.[26]

Meanwhile the Institute was becoming a refuge for displaced European scholars, some joining the staff, others asking for help in finding openings elsewhere. To quote the Director:

> Without Hitler, many of our great scholars would still be leading happy and productive lives in their native land. And not only they: their presence in Princeton has brought thither scores of brilliant scholars, bravely and eagerly beginning life once more in the new world. We have tried to scatter them far and wide through Canada and the United States, so that they might infuse new life into struggling American institutions and yet not block the path of young Americans bent on scholarly careers. Both objects have been achieved.

And he adds philosophically:

> A quarter of a century hence, America will look back upon the happenings of this period precisely as we today look back upon the reaction following 1848—the reaction that brought to America Carl Schurz, the Brandeis family, my own parents and hundreds of other liberal idealists.[27]

Having developed more important aspects of the Institute, Flexner was prepared to say it needed a building. Already the Founders had bought a large tract of land, the Olden Farm, where they now agreed to erect Fuld Hall. At last Institute activities could be housed under one roof, with offices for Director, professors and staff, seminar rooms, library, a common room, and space for later equipment of a kitchen and dining rooms, including one for Trustees and professors. This the Director hoped might come to rival the High Table at All Souls College, Oxford,[28] in atmosphere and distinction. The opening of Fuld Hall in October, 1939, the month when Flexner retired as Director, marked the end of the Institute's first period—six years of experiment.

Taking Stock

These years of trial and error had shown Abraham Flexner that most of his original ideas were sound. He had been right to believe that American intellectual life would be quickened by an institution where distinguished scientists and scholars pursued their research and trained well-prepared younger men and women to carry it further. He had been right in his decisions that the Institute should be small and begin simply, expanding personnel and program only so far as was consistent with maintaining the highest standards. He had seen advantages accruing to the faculty from receiving high salaries; free from financial worries, they could give their work at the Institute all their energy, attention, and time. On these points he would not tolerate a suggestion of change.[29]

With all his success, Flexner reached his retirement leaving some problems unsolved, the most serious his relations with the Founders and the faculty. His disappointment in a few of the faculty he admitted in *I Remember;* any difficulties with the Founders he never mentioned, out of loyalty. In these matters his successor would have to find his way.

Relations to the Founders

Both Mr. Bamberger and Mrs. Fuld took the keenest interest in the Institute, attending Trustees' meetings faithfully and aware of every detail. Neither of them had much schooling, but perhaps for that very reason prized education all the more. Louis Bamberger had proved himself a man of remarkable practical sense in building up a great business, beginning in 1892 with a sale of stock he had bought from a bankrupt firm. The store was a family affair, his partners his twice widowed sister's husbands: Louis Frank and Felix Fuld. It owed its success to hard work, shrewdness, and vision, especially to the owners' good relations with their staff whom they called, not employees, but "co-workers." Co-workers were encouraged to form committees with considerable responsibility for administration. Each co-worker was given two days a year to visit other stores and study their methods, coming back, it was hoped, with new ideas. Anyone who made a suggestion which could be adopted was rewarded.[30] These and other benefits represented unusual procedure in those years before World War I, helping to make Bamberger's both famous and successful. Social workers praised its "righteousness"; the turnover in employment ran exceptionally low. Co-workers had too many advantages to want to leave. It was characteristic of Mr. Bamberger that when he retired from business and sold the store, he distributed a million dollars in gifts to those who had contributed notably to its success.

Mr. Bamberger, a great merchant, was also a public-spirited citizen of Newark and a loyal Jew. To the community which had supported his business he made many returns, including the building for the Newark Museum of Art. To the Hebrew University in Jerusalem he gave the endowment for the department of oriental studies, a benefaction unknown at the Institute until after his death when Frank Aydelotte visited Palestine.[31]

A description of Mr. Bamberger pictures a man who was "shy, reserved, and sparing of speech," but at the same time "expressed himself with directness and candor," whose words "lost none of their forcefulness because they were invariably spoken in a voice little louder than a whisper."[32] He had one oddity which caused his sister to watch him anxiously in meetings: he could not bear to witness clashes of opinion; they made him sick. Once when a Trustee crossed swords with Abraham Flexner, Mrs. Fuld was heard to whisper, "This man must go!" And in due course the offender was not proposed by the nominating committee for re-election.

Whatever Flexner wrote about the Founders was in terms of the highest praise. In his autobiography, he went so far as to say:

> The greatest satisfaction which I have derived from the founding and development of the Institute has been my association with the founders, Mr. Bamberger and Mrs. Fuld. Their attitude has been absolutely ideal. . . . Though their interest is keen and close and their kindness unwearying, they have never interfered with the professional development of the Institute.[33]

True, but not the whole truth. While Mr. Bamberger scrupulously kept hands off the academic programs of the three Schools, he took a firm line against the Director's proposals to involve the faculty in plans for the Institute as a whole. It was Mr. Bamberger's opposition that had nullified the early bylaw providing for a committee on education which should consist of five Trustees and three professors, with responsibility for recommending policies and appointments to the Trustees. When the Director occasionally proposed consulting the faculty on a specific point, again Mr. Bamberger said No.

These vetoes may have distressed the Director, but he thought it improper to discuss them. As a result, neither professors nor Trustees realized that in the beginning he had wanted to consult the faculty. Later he changed so completely as to forget his earlier point of view. Remarking on the dangers of any "tendency toward organization and formal consultation" of the faculty, he stated, "I was opposed to it *in toto* and from the start.[34]

The Director's consulation with the Trustees also was subject to the Founders' approval. Before a Board meeting, Flexner reported every point on which he would like the group's opinions; if Mr. Bamberger questioned an item, it was removed from the agenda. Mr. Bamberger in the role of censor might be interpreted by a stranger as one of those businessmen who give orders to employees and extend the same treatment to professors; this, as has been shown, would be a mistake. In his store there were no "underlings." His vetoes may rather have represented his determination to prevent interference with the Director's best judgment during the Institute's first critical years. Mr. Bamberger had insisted that Flexner, in spite of his age, should be Director, on the ground that the Institute was his idea and he alone could be trusted to bring it to life. He could ask advice, as he had done for three years, provided he was free from the slightest obligation to take it. There was danger of pressure from advisers in Europe, surely, but what of professors on the spot? They might urge practices imported from their conventional academic backgrounds which would retard the growth of an enterprise on uncharted ground. Flexner could resist them, of course, but what a waste of his time and energy! The Trustees, most of them with little academic experience beyond their own remote college years, were even more likely to hamper him with old-fashioned ideas. Mr. Bamberger may have been determined to put all his eggs into one basket, the clever, inventive mind of Abraham Flexner. When the Institute was well started, closer cooperation with the faculty might be feasible.

However strong this hope at the beginning, it would have faded for Mr. Bamberger as he came to know some of the faculty better. Oswald Veblen, member of the Board of Trustees, while a brilliant mathematician and inspiring teacher, acquired a reputation for being incapable of objective decisions about the welfare of the Institute as a whole. Flexner had felt obliged to tell him to act like a Trustee, not as a special representative of mathematics. And Veblen frequently urged more faculty government such as was commonly approved in universities, adding to Mr. Bamberger's conviction that professors were not flexible enough to see what was best for a new kind of institution.

Institute Finances

Another difficulty in the Director's relation to the Founders had to do with the Institute's financial future. The Founders made no commitments beyond their original promise of five million dollars, which they had paid by January, 1932, and in spite of the depression had increased by almost a third of a million. But their fortune had suffered, as figures from Moody's show. Early in September before the crash, when the Bambergers sold their store to R. H. Macy, they received a sizable block of Macy's stock, worth $225.50 a share. By November 13, the value of a share had fallen to $110. Even so, it was after this drop that they promised Abraham Flexner his five millions, no doubt expecting the market to improve. But by June, 1932, one share of this stock was worth only $17.00. Small wonder that for a time Mr. Bamberger would not consider new commitments.

As economic conditions improved, the Founders began to respond to special appeals. When land was needed, they bought a tract large enough to ensure the Institute's quiet and privacy. At last, when Flexner proposed a building, they met the cost of constructing Fuld Hall. But they did not endow it, had no clear-cut system of professors' pensions, and felt unable to offer support for expanding the faculty or adding a School.

The situation gave the Director less concern than might have been expected. In his work for the Rockerfeller Foundation he had become used to donors who could afford large gifts, to be matched by Foundation funds, but moved slowly and had to be cajoled. For example, George Eastman, when pressed by Abraham Flexner to endow a medical school at the University of Rochester, said that he would give two and a half millions toward the necessary ten, adding, "That is the best I can do now." Whereupon Abraham Flexner returned. "There's no hurry. Wait until you sell more Kodaks." After he had made two more trips to Rochester, he heard the welcome news that Mr. Eastman would increase his gift to $5,000,000, a sum large enough so that the General Education Board would match it, and Rochester would have its Eastman School of Medicine.[35] Flexner always hoped that Mr. Bamberger would do something similar.

Meanwhile the Institute appeared more prosperous than it was, thanks to gifts for special purposes from foundations as well as from the Founders. Running expenses far exceeded income on capital. The Institute was living beyond its means to an extent that would be disastrous if the gifts were not repeated. Another source of trouble was that records of promises about financial matters—pensions and the like—were incomplete, owing to the Director's reluctance to be definite about anything he expected to see changed for the better. To quote him: "I do not wish to put anything on paper which will make it difficult for me or for the Board to change, if in the course of the next months we get further light."[36] It would remain for his successor to make the financial situation clear.

Relations to the Faculty

The warmth of Flexner's first enthusiasm for all his early appointments did not remain constant as he observed that some of the faculty were producing little or nothing. He saw this to be true particularly of the ones he had brought to the Institute at an age when they had already made their reputation. In *I Remember*, he explains why he chose them, recommending that no one should repeat his mistake.

> [The Institute] had to start with a group of highly distinguished men. In choosing mathematics, a subject of which I was ignorant, I could take no chances. . . . I had to bring together a mathematical group that would at once attract the attention of their peers and in their new setting would succeed. . . I regard it as undesirable ever to repeat my perform- ance. . . . As vacancies occur henceforth whether in mathematics or other schools, they ought to be filled, not with men who have probably completed the most brilliant era of their lives, but with younger Ameri- cans, trained partly at the Institute and partly at other institutions through- out the country as well as abroad. . . . I am certain that if established men were called regularly as a matter of policy in the future, sterility would soon take place.[37]

He was disillusioned again to find that some professors could not profit by having what they had longed for: complete freedom from practical concerns. Now they yearned to help run the Institute.

> Most university professors sincerely think that they desire to devote their entire energy and attention to their several subjects; many complain, often justly—of excessive routine; but there are times when complaint is a cover for sterility, staleness, or unhappiness of one kind or an other. . . . The Institute was conceived as a paradise for scholars and such

it really is. But not all men—not all gifted men—know how to live in paradise. The earth is their proper habitation, and upon the earth, such as it is, most of them do the best of which they are capable.[38]

He comforted himself by reflecting that not many showed their failure to adjust to paradise by demanding earthly rights better left to the Director. "Most of the professors were so busy with the delights and labors of the studies they loved that few could be interested in administrative problems."

Flexner apparently never suspected that he might be oversimplifying his interpretation of productive scholars. Even those most commonly preoccupied with their work were complex human beings who could be keenly interested in practical problems, such as the choice of Institute professors or of a Director. Einstein himself admitted such interests. In Flexner's lack of experience in doing creative work, he seemed unaware that some scholars might be oppressed by a relentless expectation that they would produce and go on producing. Granted that while their ideas were bursting into bloom, scholars would revel in the freedom to attend to nothing else, what of those arid times when the reservoirs drained by a man's last production are filling up again, or so he hopes? He can only wait and see. Another fact of human nature that Flexner overlooked was that some thinkers reach their heights of creative activity as a result of prodding: a deadline to meet, a lecture to give, even the need for extra money. All such stimuli he had himself removed with much satisfaction. Of course, he had hoped that professors would vary production with seminars and conferences for members, but would not insult them with a requirement. He did not even ask for progress reports. When his scholars did not respond as he expected, he did not seem to suspect that he might have misunderstood their needs.

Abraham Flexner grew older, more disillusioned, more inclined to take matters into his own hands. Finally, in what proved to be his last year as Director (1938–1939), he appointed two professors of economics without consulting two members of the three in their School, with the result that the whole faculty seethed with resentment, the more because they thought his selections open to question. Neither man was a distinguished scholar. Indeed, neither had the formal training required for a Ph.D. and no compensating brilliance in publications or teaching. They had not taught for some years, and then chiefly classes of undergraduates.

But to Flexner, ambitious to find economists with breadth of experience in government and business, Walter Stewart and Robert Warren had much to recommend them. Both had worked for the Federal Reserve Board in the Division of Research and Statistics, Stewart as Director. Both had held responsible positions with an investment firm; they had served in turn as vice-president, and Stewart had been for nine years chairman of the board. Both were familiar with international financial problems, having served respectively as an economist in the foreign department of the Federal Reserve Bank in New York and as economic adviser to the Bank of England, later the American member of the special advisory commission of the Bank of International Settlements to investigate the ability of Germany to pay reparations under the Young Plan. Stewart was the more distinguished and was sought after by foundations: at that time he was a Trustee of the Rockefeller Foundation, the General Education Board, and the Institute for Advanced Study, all positions in which he had won the admiration and friendship of Abraham Flexner. For some years Flexner had tried to persuade him to join the Institute faculty. When he finally consented, on condition that Warren be appointed also, the Director was ready to gamble on both. Their practical experience, added to the knowledge of classical economics they must have gained in teaching, might be precisely the means of realizing his hopes for economics in a new dimension. Apparently he did not explain his appointments to the faculty. As it was, his bringing in two professors whose academic background would hardly have qualified them for the faculty of a graduate school, and at the maximum salary, aroused wonder whether his judgment was failing.

Professors' Protest

The two economists came to Princeton on January 1, 1939, when there was already a rumor that the Director would soon retire. Professors who had resented his way of making these faculty appointments now rose in wrath at the possibility of being ignored again in the choice of a Director. A faculty meeting in March passed a resolution to ask Flexner to present to the Trustees a request from the faculty to be consulted on future appointments of either a professor or a Director. Their letter, dated March 15, 1939, and signed by Albert Einstein, Hetty Goldman, and Marston Morse, read in part:

> We understand that both the responsibility and the final choice in each case rest with the Director and the Board of Trustees. Their action should

however, in our opinion, be preceded by a consultation with the faculty which should be made effective by allowing adequate time for the consideration and inquiries which are necessary in each case.

The professors earnestly desire that the above conclusions be conveyed to the Board of Trustees. We should like very much to talk these matters over with you, and to add any information which you may desire concerning the opinions expressed.[39]

Within the next ten days, the Director talked to Professors Einstein and Morse about their letter, but from their point of view with no result. Professor Einstein reports this to Frank Aydelotte as a Trustee: Flexner "neither promised to lay our letter before the Trustees, nor did he refuse this, simply and plainly. In these circumstances we have no other choice than to inform privately those Trustees with whom we happen to be in personal contact, and that is precisely the purpose of these lines."[40]

Abraham Flexner probably was in no mood to change his determination not to consult the faculty, but at the moment he knew the time had passed for their opinion to have any effect. The Founders and the Director had already agreed upon Frank Aydelotte as Flexner's successor and secured his consent to serve. Indeed, the first Director had suggested to the Founders as long ago as the summer of 1933, before the Institute opened, that his friend at Swarthmore should be his "understudy."[41] It is not clear when the understudy was informed of this role, but certainly he had begun to look forward to his new office before the faculty embarked on their campaign to be consulted.

Frank Aydelotte himself never wavered in his conviction that they should be consulted on all appointments. When he got a copy of Professor Einstein's letter to Flexner, he would have acted in character if he had asked to have the choice of Director reopened so that the faculty could be brought into the discussion. But he knew that he could not persuade the Founders and Director to consult the faculty, that he would accomplish nothing except to remove himself from the candidates for the directorship while someone else was elected by the method he had tried to change. In August he must have been glad to escape from an unalterable situation when he went to Mexico with a group attempting to arrange the resettlement of Jewish refugees.[42]

Early in August, Flexner notified the Trustees that he would retire at their meeting on October 9, his resignation to take effect on that date. Later in the month he warned his successor of pitfalls to be avoided:

Don't, for your own sake and that of the Institute underestimate the fact that you are dealing with intriguers. I freely confess that I was a baby in their hands. I took them at their word; I supposed when they said they wanted opportunities for scholarship and wanted to be free of routine they meant it. They did not mean a word of it—that is, a few or several of them. They wanted opportunities for scholarship, with high salaries, but they also wanted managerial and executive powers. They saw they could not get them through me directly; hence Veblen and a few others intrigued to get them indirectly. I should not be doing my duty by you or the Institute if I failed to give you fair warning of these facts. Veblen wants power. Maass wants importance. You will have to make them both realize from the jump that you are master—not, of course, a despotic master, but a master who insists, as I unfortunately did not, that he is to participate in every meeting, whether of the faculty or of the several groups.

Abraham Lincoln's cabinet thought they could ignore him and tried. He made them realize they could not succeed, and in short order he emerged as the real head. Your success or your failure will depend, in my judgment, in the first instance upon maintaining this position, as Simon did at the [Rockfeller] Institute [for Medical Research] from the very beginning. The position of my successor is, in one sense, stronger than mine. I hope he will never for a moment lose sight of this consideration. . . .

[signed]   With all good wishes and love to you and Marie,
                            Ever sincerely,
                            A. F.[43]

Frank Aydelotte would have read his friend's warning affectionately, without being convinced. He was prevented from taking it seriously both by temperament and experience. With too much courage and loyalty to be a schemer himself, he was slow to suspect others of devious practices. And the idea of asserting his authority as "master" seemed to him repellent and unnecessary in the light of his experience at Swarthmore, where he had carried Managers and faculty with him by Quakerly persuasion. It would have been strange if the methods that had succeeded so fully at Swarthmore had failed at Princeton. The fact is that they succeeded in both places.

Further advice from his predecessor reached Frank Aydelotte as he read the proof of Flexner's autobiography, *I Remember*, in the writer's warning against appointing professors after the end of their most productive years. The new Director could accept this more readily than Flexner's pronouncement against change: "The Institute should for the next ten years be left as it is, reserving, however, the privilege and the duty to profit by experience if unforeseen defects develop."[44] The Institute's creator seemed to believe that he had achieved what was so far perfect and would consider any change to be for the worse.

He made this more explicit in his advice to his successor, rising almost to rhapsody: "The director's main business would be to relieve the faculty of any concern about details and to preserve at any cost the soul of the Institute: for in the ten years that have now passed, the Institute has developed a soul. How fragile a thing it is! How powerful for good, if its integrity can be preserved!"

Then a warning: "If the professors are actually interested in scholarship—and that alone—and if the director is sympathetic and helpful, never losing sight of the gulf that separates the insignificant from the significant, the dream which has become, will remain, a reality—not otherwise."[45]

Frank Aydelotte, with his cheerful good sense, would read this passage as the natural and innocent rhetoric of a creator about his work, unaware that it showed an emotional attachment to the Institute likely to prevent Flexner from taking a consistently just view of any Director who followed him.

Happily, at the moment when Flexner retired, he received a due meed of praise. The New York *Times* carried an editorial, "A Critic in Ordinary," describing Flexner as

a militant educator fighting for the higher things of life and especially for the education of the "gifted." The institution of his founding bears neither his name nor that of those who furnished the funds for its building and maintenance. Out of his long criticisms, it has emerged as a constructive embodiment of his philosophy—a place in which a society of scholars may with prepared minds devote their lives to the fearless and unhampered search for truth.[46]

Flexner himself quoted in *I Remember* a letter from a neighbor at Princeton which let him know that he was honored in his own country, and for precisely what he had hoped to accomplish: "The main thing you have provided, to my mind, is the definition of pure scholarship as a visible value in American culture, or, as you once expressed it in a phrase I like to remember, the Institute has given America something excellent."[47]

Flexner set a high value on what he had wanted to achieve:

The two most important ventures in the general field of higher education during the last seventy years were the Johns Hopkins University, opened in 1876, and, I hope, the Institute for Advanced Study, opened in 1930. . . . I—a poorly educated boy—came by the merest chance into close contact with both. Gilman's ideal became my dream; over half a century later, Mr. Bamberger and Mrs. Fuld made its realization possible.[48]

Frank Aydelotte paid his formal tribute to the first Director in a resolution passed by the Institute's Trustees and faculty:

The trustees and faculty of the Institute for Advanced Study take the occasion of Dr. Flexner's retirement to record in this joint resolution their sense of permanent indebtedness to him. The character of the Institute has been determined by his great faith in the role of the creative scholar in society. It is this that led him, when he undertook to organize the Institute, to concentrate first and foremost upon the search for individuals, to insist upon complete freedom for those individuals in the pursuit of their scholarly objectives, and to endeavor to surround their lives with greater dignity. These ideals, deeply held, account for the boldness of the Institute's plan, the flexibility of its arrangements, and the severity of its standards. He built the Institute around its scholars and did not try to fit them into a pre-arranged institutional plan.

. . . Whatever prestige the Institute enjoys or may enjoy in the future, whatever service it may render to scholarship, will be based upon the foundations established by Abraham Flexner. *Exegit monumentum aere perennius.*[49]

Taking the Reins

Frank Aydelotte was happy to begin his work with his predecessor's affectionate good wishes:

Surely if ever a man was welcomed by his colleagues and his friends, you are he, and if ever a man started with the blessings and good will of all concerned, you again are he. And now give my love to you and Marie, and I hope you will have a long stretch of happy, successful, and productive work ahead of you, for I said to Dodds [the President of Princeton] that you had one great advantage over me—you are in your own right a scholar and can be one of the humanistic group. I, alas, have never been a scholar, for two years at the Johns Hopkins between 1884 and 1886 do not produce scholarship, though they do produce and did produce a reverence for it which I am now leaving in safe keeping with you.[50]

The new Director came prepared to meet the faculty's desire to take part in making appointments in the way he had found workable at Swarthmore. He would consult them, singly and in groups, until everyone was satisfied that he had been heard. As there were no openings at the Institute when he came and for the next five years, he had to postpone putting his procedure to the test. But he probably indicated to his colleagues what he would do when the time came.

Before accepting his position officially, he had asked one of the Trustees to sound out the faculty. Would they welcome him as Director? The report was favorable, one professor telling him to his face that there was nothing against him except the timing of his appointment, which had been presented to them as an accomplished fact. They should have had a chance to express themselves while the question was still open.

Lull before the War, 1939–1941

Frank Aydelotte found Abraham Flexner's dream solidly embodied in seventy-seven human beings: sixteen professors—still those who had been appointed in the first round—six in Mathematics, five in Humanistic Studies (with the addition of one visiting professor); four in Economics and Politics (a fifth on leave in England); fifteen assistants under various titles, and forty-six members—more than twice the total of thirty-five (including the Director) when the Institute opened.[51] Then there had been a single School; now there were three. Instead of depending on scattered quarters rented from Princeton, the Institute for the first time had its own Fuld Hall and, across the fields, the charming farmhouse, Olden Manor, to be converted into a dwelling for the Director. The two buildings would help him carry out one of his aims, to transform an aggregate of individuals into a community.

Olden Manor could not be occupied for another year, a postponement which eased pressure on the Aydelottes while they were shuttling between Princeton and Swarthmore. They could stay at the inn as the Flexners had done until they could give their undivided attention to making Olden Manor homelike. Meanwhile Fuld Hall presented "housekeeping" problems which Frank Aydelotte proposed to solve with the faculty's help. At once he established a precedent for cooperation by appointing a standing committee to advise him on the assignment of offices and other uses of the new building.

The faculty liked having a share in planning, liked also taking temporary responsibility for serving light lunches in the common room until the spring of 1941 when the kitchen and dining rooms were finished. At that time the faculty asked the Director to call regular meetings of the whole group at the beginning and end of each semester and to schedule three lunches between. He cordially agreed, presumably after conferring with Mr. Bamberger, who seemed ready to believe that the Institute was now strong enough not to be threatened by an organized faculty. Abraham Flexner would be dubious about these changes, but apparently did not wish to protest or make other difficulties for his successor.

Fortunately for the first Director's peace of mind, he was living in New York, rarely coming to Princeton except for meetings of the Board of Trustees. He had been a Trustee from the beginning and continued to serve until 1945.

Host to a Department of the League of Nations

In the spring of 1940 the new Director seized an opportunity resulting from the war in Europe to play host to a technical group from the League of Nations, the Economic, Financial and Transit Department. Winfield Riefler, recently in Geneva, had reported that such an invitation would be welcome. Frank Aydelotte immediately swung into action, getting help from the Rockefeller Foundation to bring the department to Princeton in the autumn: thirteen staff members and their families, under the chairmanship of Alexander Loveday of Great Britain. They represented eight foreign countries: Britain, Sweden, Eire, The Netherlands, Belgium, Czechoslovakia, Estonia, and New Zealand—a welcome addition to the international flavor of the Institute, always one of its assets.[53] The Director was happy to find offices for the staff in Fuld Hall and to see that housing was provided. With his personal devotion to the League and to the memory of Woodrow Wilson, he took special pleasure in offering this hospitality in the community where Wilson had lived when he was President of Princeton. The department celebrated the League's twenty-first birthday in Princeton, January 10, 1941. After the war, the League of Nations turned over the department to the United Nations.

The Heartening effect of the invitation on the League staff in Geneva was warmly described by President Hambro of the League Assembly:

> You can hardly imagine how much it meant at the moment—not materially, but morally and from the psychological point of view. It was more than an encouragement, it was an inspiration. It gave proof that all

the competent, unostentatious, patient, good work accomplished during twenty years—in practically every field of human activity, a work of sifting and consolidation, of collecting, classifying and presenting facts, of uniting the experts of every country in an exchange of experiences, of establishing a universal clearing-house for progressive and constructive ideas—it gave proof that this work had not been entirely wasted, but was bread thrown upon the waters.[53]

In Frank Aydelotte's second year, when he no longer had responsibilities at Swarthmore, he could do more to develop the Institute community. The Aydelottes, living now in Olden Manor, made it a center of social life, entertaining faculty and staff with their wives or husbands at least once a year, keeping open house for Institute visitors from this country and abroad, welcoming a constant procession of American friends and relatives of all ages for the night, a meal, or both. It was characteristic of the Aydelottes that the first entry in the Olden Manor guest book was on the very day they moved in, July 23, 1940: the guest, R. Schairer, London University Institute of Education. A few days later, on the same page, Ruth and Arthur Sweetser from Geneva and the League of Nations. A sampling of autographs finds two Nobel Prize winners, Niels Bohr and Linus Pauling, the portrait painter, Charles Hopkinson, and the heads of four Oxford Colleges: W. H. Beveridge of University College, Margery Fry of Somerville, Sandie [sic] Lindsay of Balliol, and R. W. Livingstone of Corpus. Cambridge was represented by the economist J. M. Keynes and by J. R. M. Butler, Master of Trinity College.

As in Swarthmore, an important member of the household was a big, gentle dog, here a Great Dane named Canute, who wagged a long, sweeping tail so destructive of objects on table tops that he usually stayed out of doors to give guests their first warm welcome.

Among the Aydelottes' favorite dinner guests was their friend Professor Albert Einstein. Mrs. Aydelotte had heard that he preferred not to talk during a meal if he could avoid seeming rude to the guests next to him, and someone suggested that he would probably like to sit among other men guests. With her impeccable social tact, Mrs. Aydelotte placed above everything the comfort of a guest, and when the guest was Professor Einstein, she seated all the men at one half of the table, the women at the other. After dinner he mingled charmingly with the ladies and entertained the whole company by playing his violin.

In the new Director's second year he began to indulge in a game he liked even better than golf: planning for the future. Remembering

Flexner's advice against repeating what he thought to be mistakes in making appointments permanent too soon, Frank played with the idea of an experimental testing of scholars and possible new subjects, writing his suggestions to Mr. Bamberger:

> If means were available to do this . . . I should [like] to bring together groups of older and younger scholars, as temporary members . . . for limited periods of time, to explore a given subject of research, with the understanding that the individuals should go back to their own institutions at the end of the period of work for which they were invited. . . . These groups might then be succeeded by others, so that over a period of years we should have the opportunity of making the best possible test of the value of research in various subjects and of the qualities of various individuals. On the basis of these tests certain subjects and individuals might be added to our permanent program if and when our financial condition made this possible.[54]

Mr. Bamberger may not have expressed any strong opinion, since the time when anyone could be added to the permanent staff was still in the distant future.

One of Frank's most interesting assignments this year, undertaken at Mr. Bamberger's request, was to report to the Trustees on the work of the three Schools. The new Director welcomed this chance to see for himself what had been accomplished and must be the basis of future programs. Flexner had not made such reports, partly, no doubt, to avoid seeming to check on the professors' use of their freedom, but a newcomer's need of information would justify his inquiry.

Determined that the Trustees should pay due attention to each School, he presented them singly at three meetings: in February, May, and October, 1941. He could speak with no trace of egotism because he was largely describing what had been done under Abraham Flexner. One result of his own efforts he did not mention: more funds for the School of Economics. In 1940 a grant from the Rockefeller Foundation of $35,000 a year for three years had been secured by matching gifts from the once reluctant Mr. Bamberger, thanks to the new Director's persuasive powers.

Of his expository powers the Trustees had impressive testimony in these three reports of 1941. He could not compare with some of his associates as an intellectual pioneer, but in catching and stating the significance of their work he was the equal of any of them. He could explain to the Trustees what Riefler was doing in finance, or Panofsky in art history, or even von Neumann in mathematical physics, in a way that made the importance of their achievement clear and its strategy intelligible. But, of course, he had done his own work in the humanities, and when he came to interpreting this School to the Board, he spoke with exceptional point and confidence:

> The function of the humanistic discipline is the critical study of that organized tradition which we call civilization and which it is the purpose of this war to preserve. We cannot, and in the long run will not, fight for what we do not understand. Our democratic way of life is not, in the last analysis, a material order; it is a spiritual point of view. It is a kind of sum total of the achievements of man's intelligence and idealism in all ages that have gone before us. It can in the end only be destroyed by being forgotten. It must be remembered and understood if men are to have the basis for still greater achievements . . . Human nature does not change; in each generation men possess the same capacities for good or evil as their forefathers. But different ages vary widely in the vividness of their understanding of the great achievements of the past. When humanistic studies flourish, life is richer and more gracious. When they decay, in the dark ages of history, man's way of life becomes brutal, poor, and mean. The natural and the social sciences teach us, among other things, the techniques of preserving our way of life in peace and war. The humanistic disciplines show us what it is we are struggling to preserve. They supply the motive for effort and sacrifice against chaos and the dark which the human race has made since the beginnings of civilization, that effort which we can never forego to make life on this planet not merely a blank animal existence but something free, gracious and spiritual, filled with ardor and meaning.[55]

On the day following this report, one of the Trustees, Alanson Houghton, wrote to congratulate the Director on its effect:

> You came into your own yesterday. . . . The spontaneous applause of the Trustees was the first instance of such enthusiastic approval that has taken place during the twelve years since the birth of the Institute. Moreover, I think Mr. Bamberger was more stirred and moved to greater interest in the possibilities of the Institute than I, at least, have ever noted before. All in all, it was a fine meeting, and one that will long be remembered.[56]

Some of the Director's own plans for the Institute showed themselves incidentally in these reports. It was clear that he planned to place more emphasis on humanistic studies. He hoped also to supplement theory in mathematics by a larger study of its applications. But he was resolved to move cautiously here; he must in no way compromise the remarkable standing already achieved. Professor von Neumann had assured him that Princeton was the equal in pure mathematical research of any of the great European centers—Cambridge, Göttingen, Moscow, Paris, Rome, and Warsaw—but the Europeans were "probably better integrated in the direction of application of mathematics to physics and other subjects." Such integration he hoped the Institute could in time achieve. Unhappily, all his plans were abruptly halted by the United States' entry into the war.

The Institute during the War

Within two months after Pearl Harbor, eight of the seventeen professors were giving part of their time to the war effort, some of them fortunately able to do it at Princeton. By May, three more were involved. When the Director reported this to the Trustees, he assured them that the war work was "extra curricular." The members of the faculty are "keeping their minds focused on what they consider to be the real job of the Institute: the advancement of knowledge regardless of its utility for war or for any other immediate purpose. These are the activities which, among others, we are fighting a war to defend, and one of the best ways to defend civilization is to advance it."[57]

The financial arrangement for professors in government service, made by the Director with the Trustees' approval, was fair to the men and generous to the government. "The Institute has made the services of members of its faculty available to the government without compensation. Where for any reason it seems advisable for one of our professors to accept payment from the government, the Institute makes up the difference between this amount and the individual's Institute salary."[58]

The work of the Institute faculty in the war effort grew out of their peacetime specialties and showed how well pure research could meet practical needs. In the School of Mathematics every professor took part, and all except Einstein and Weyl were on call away from Princeton—in Washington, Maryland, or even in England. Einstein and Weyl, serving as consultants, could go on with their own research. James Alexander flew to London to discover more accurate methods of dropping bombs from airplanes. Marston Morse, in the Office of the Army Chief of Ordnance, studied the design of bombs and the use of the proximity fuse. John von Neumann, consultant to both the Army and the Navy on shock waves and high explosives, also developed methods of constructing "high-speed computing devices." Oswald Veblen, much in demand for consultation, went from advising the Army Ordnance Department at the Aberdeen Proving Grounds to research in submarine mine warfare.

Edward Earle in the School of Economics and Politics helped organize research under the OSS, took part in drafting documents for the German surrender and the Dumbarton Oaks conference, and published *Makers of Modern Strategy*, said to be the best book in the field. Winfield Riefler drew up the first plan for the Board of Economic Warfare and was stationed in England for more than two years, "first as Assistant to Ambassador Winant, then as head of the Economic Warfare Division in London with the rank of Minister." Walter W. Stewart served as adviser to the Secretary of the Treasury, and Robert B. Warren as consultant.

Professors in the Humanistic Studies produced information for the Armed Forces, to prevent destruction of European art treasures. E. A. Lowe prepared a handbook on libraries and archives in Italy; two of the members, Rensselaer Lee and Charles de Tolnay, edited similar handbooks on art in Italy and France. Benjamin Meritt, a linguist as well as an archaeologist, supervised, the study of newspapers from thirty-six foreign language groups in the United States and also wrote a geographical handbook on Greece.

Frank Aydelotte described these ventures in his *Report* for 1945–1946, proud of the Institute's contribution, pleased to note awards to three of the faculty: a citation for Meritorious Civilian Service from the War Department to Professor Morse, the Medal for Merit from the Army Air Force to Professor Earle, the Distinguished Civilian Service Award from the Navy to Professor von Neumann.[59]

The Trustees in general shared the Director's pride and pleasure, but not Abraham Flexner. He objected, first, that the professors were violating the principle of full-time work for the Institute, the statement of which appeared in every *Bulletin*: "The Institute is pledged to its Founders to adhere strictly to the full-time basis."[60] He did not agree that exceptions were justified by war, convinced rather that distinguished scholars would serve their country better in the long run by staying at the Institute and devoting themselves to pure research. He made his position clear to one professor, Benjamin Meritt, who remembers that when he was leaving for a Washington post, Flexner told him he would much better stick to his Greek inscriptions. The creator of the Institute was angry at the thought that it had been brought to a standstill to let men examine foreign newspapers or test ballistics when they might be advancing civilization. Let less gifted men defend it! While he knew that Mr. Bamberger and at least the majority of the Board warmly supported his successor, he held Frank Aydelotte chiefly responsible.

Director in Action

When the Director listed the war work of the faculty, he gave a modest place to his own brief periods as chairman of the New Jersey Enemy Alien Hearing Board (1941–1942) and chairman of the Committee on Scientific Personnel, Office of Scientific Research and Development.[61] This last position he held only six months, in that time setting it up effectively before turning it over to a larger force—precisely the kind of spadework he reveled in.

> I have in the last six months succeeded in clearing the ground, in working out in an orderly way certain policies and procedures, and have had the satisfaction of finding that the services of my office have been eagerly welcomed by scientists engaged in government work all over the country. The result of this cordial reception has been that the work of this office has increased by leaps and bounds. It is now a full-time job, not merely for one man, but probably for a staff of two or three.[62]

His principal war work was to keep the Institute functioning for professors, members, and the group from the League of Nations. Some of his efforts went into "housekeeping"—precautions for blackouts and air raids, making do with rationed gasoline, persuading the occupants of Fuld Hall that with the reduced supply of fuel oil, they could work comfortably in offices heated to sixty-two degrees. He saw to carrying out police regulations for the Institute's "enemy aliens"—thirty-four when the war began, including twenty members and fourteen wives, almost all with their first papers toward American citizenship. The normal number of members in 1941–1942, about fifty-three, fell abruptly the next year to twenty-eight, then to twenty-four, rising in the autumn of 1944 to thirty; in 1945–1946 it returned to a peacetime figure of fifty-seven. Continuously throughout the war there was a backlog of twelve who had come into residence before Pearl Harbor, including nine scholars from abroad. Among the twelve were some experienced and exceptionally able teachers, who took charge of seminars and kept research in progress while professors came and went. It was partly thanks to them that the Director could report so favorably: "The publications of the

Faculty and Members of the Institute during the year 1943–1944 exceeded in volume and importance those for any previous year since its foundation."[63] When there was a problem of financing these publications, the Director did his best to meet it. He was obviously pleased when he could announce that he had raised money for two important works: Panofsky's *Albrecht Dürer* and de Tolnay's *Michelangelo*.

The presence of members in residence during the war incidentally gave the Director a chance to carry out something like the plan he had proposed to Mr. Bamberger for testing scholars before offering them faculty appointments. Three members in the School of Mathematics proved themselves and were given new status in 1945: two to fill vacancies left by retirements, Carl L. Siegel as professor of mathematics and Wolgang Pauli as visiting professor of theoretical physics; Kurt Gödel in the new category of "Permanent Member."

The Director's great interest in world peace made him welcome an opportunity for the Institute to play host to summer conferences on the terms of the postwar settlement.[64] Financed by a grant of $2,000 from the Rockfeller Foundation, eight conferences were held in the summer of 1943 to investigate what was needed for effective postwar planning, with the result that two studies were organized; one by a "Viner-Corbett group" to undertake "fundamental research on the problems of the peace and of world organization," the work to be done at Yale; the second study, to be made by the Universities Committee on the Post-War Settlement under Ralph Barton Perry of Harvard. Both studies would be helped by the Rockefeller Foundation, the second getting financial support also from the World Peace Foundation. An important part of the work of Ralph Barton Perry's committee would be "to mould public opinion and to stimulate public discussion."

Aydelotte pointed out that the result of the summer's discussions had no direct bearing on the Institute, but this was as it should be.

> The whole sequence of events illustrates admirably one of our functions, which is to stimulate research and to inaugurate inquiry without reference to our specific interests as an institution. Our role is not to rival other institutions of learning but to supplement and serve them, to seek not the advancement of our own prestige but the advancement of knowledge.

He saw also in the group life of the Institute a basis for hope of international cooperation:

A group ... representing a dozen nationalities (including all the Axis powers) living and working together in complete friendliness and harmony even in the midst of war, offers in miniature an illustration of how these problems can be solved by men who put first the intellectual and spiritual interests of humanity without regard to nationality, race, color or creed.

Institute Business

Even while the Institute was disrupted by the war, there were long-term problems which the Director must try to solve: continuing efforts to gain more of a share in policy-making for the faculty from Mr. Bamberger and the Trustees; establishing procedures for retirements and pensions; clarifying the budget.

One step toward greater responsibility for the faculty was to appoint a professor to the Trustees' most important committee, the Executive Committee. Heretofore, two members of the faculty had been invited to join the Board and to serve on other committees: Oswald Veblen (since 1934–1935) on Buildings and Grounds, Winfield Riefler (since 1936–1937) on Finance. Walter Stewart who had been a Trustee for five years before becoming a professor, resigned from the Board before the end of his second term because he saw a "conflict of interests" which made him oppose faculty Trustees. With this divided opinion among the faculty themselves on the propriety of their simply serving on the Board, there was certainly no pressure from them to add one of their number to the Executive Committee. Frank Aydelotte not only approved but probably recommended giving this position to Oswald Veblen. Why?

Partly, no doubt, because of the dearth of experienced Trustees. Some of the old members of the Board had resigned before completing their terms, leaving vacancies to be filled by men unfamiliar with the Institute. Veblen had been on the Board almost from the beginning. More important for Frank Aydelotte would be his belief in a generous policy toward a man who had organized the largest and most famous of the three Schools and who, as Flexner said, wanted "power." Aydelotte thought he could disarm rivals, critics, and malcontents by giving them constructive outlets for their energies, asking their advice, and treating them as reasonable beings with the best interests of their institution at heart. His method had worked at Swarthmore. Probably he did not discuss the appointment with Flexner, who had warned him against Veblen. In any event, Veblen's added power offended Flexner so deeply that he absented himself from meetings of the Trustees and the Executive Committee until urged by Mr. Bamberger to come back.

Their difference about Veblen, added to Flexner's disapproval of faculty absences for war work, heightened the tension between him and Aydelotte to a point that may have surprised them both. Through the fifteen or more years when they had worked together, always distinctly separate free agents, they had shared so many enthusiasms as hardly to be aware of the degree to which their methods were unlike. Flexner had the intensity of an attorney: now for the prosecution—ferreting out weaknesses in universities and medical schools, critically scrutinizing applications for help from the General Education Board; now for the defense—making a case for those giving promise of excellence. Aydelotte was always a team player, concentrating on his colleagues' points of strength, and a coach who knew how to turn a group into an effective team. The two men were unlike, again, in their attitudes toward power. When Flexner told Aydelotte before he took office that he must show the professors (especially Veblen, who wanted power himself) that he was "master," the advice implied that power was the necessary means to achievement and must be kept where it belonged, with the Director. A Director with power who considered sharing it with the faculty, or preferred to use persuasion, would seem to Flexner probably weak or naïve.

One of Aydelotte's problems had to do with faculty retirements and pensions, Flexner having left this area vague. In June, 1943, the Trustees approved setting the retirement age at sixty-five, with provision for extending it in special cases. Accordingly four professors would retire soon: Einstein and Veblen in 1944, Herzfeld and Lowe in 1945. The pensions Einstein and Veblen had been led to expect amounted to $8,000 a year, with $4,000 for a surviving widow. Their cases seemed clear, as also those of younger men who had taken out policies with the Teachers' Insurance and Annuity Association, the usual employer's monthly contributions being made by the Institute. The difficulty lay in an intermediate group, including Herzfeld and Lowe, who had no adequate protection from the T.I.A.A., having begun to carry insurance when they were too old to accumulate much capital. The Executive Committee recommended a minimum pension of $4,000 a year for these and other professors in a like situation, making up the difference over what each would receive from insurance.

Throughout the discussion of retirements and pensions Flexner had shown his displeasure at mean economies. A minimum pension of $4,000 was too low, he said, calling attention to the minimum of $8,000 set by the Rockefeller Institute for Medical Research. He went on to remind his successor indignantly of the sum of thirty millions originally mentioned for the Institute:

> It was on this basis that I acted, and I felt justified in continuing so to act because the Founders without request from me . . . gave the Institute additional funds and . . . bought a large site and proposed the building of Fuld Hall. Have circumstances so fundamentally altered that the Institute is so soon forced to abandon some of the characteristics that make it most notable and distinctive?[65]

After the Board accepted the Executive Committee's recommendation on pensions, the Director called in the professors one at a time and told them what they could expect. Everyone seemed "cordial and grateful" at the moment except Herzfeld and Lowe, who took the fact of a retiring age as a disagreeable surprise, having expected to remain on the active list at full salary until each had prepared his lifework for publication. Having a case, they were promised grants after sixty-five, Lowe from 1945, to go on with his *Codices Latini Antiquiores,*[66] Herzfeld from 1944, to bring out *Damascus: Studies in Architecture.*[67]

In August, Einstein and Veblen began to be dissatisfied. Einstein wanted to stay on with his full salary; Veblen wanted whatever was done for Einstein. When Einstein proposed postponing his retirement until he was seventy, Aydelotte pointed out the unwisdom of going counter to the ruling so recently passed. Then Mr. Bamberger stepped in and directed that Einstein should have what he wanted, full salary to the age of seventy, and Veblen the same. The Director said again that this would play havoc with the rule for retirement, but suggested a compromise. Einstein and Veblen should be listed as "retired" from the age of sixty-five, henceforth to receive from the Institute only the amount of $8,000, each man's pension. If Mr. Bamberger cared to supplement a pension by a special grant of $7,000 a year for five years, that should be his privilege. Mr. Bamberger agreed, and the case was settled, but much to the displeasure of Abraham Flexner.

Flexner found no fault with the amount of pension, but on no account would he postpone the retirement of Einstein and Veblen, convinced as he was that mathematicians make their greatest contribution to their subject in their forties and fifties. He expressed himself vigorously on the selfishness of the two professors, who would not give way to younger men capable of more constructive work. He seemed to hold Aydelotte alone responsible for bowing to their wishes, ignoring the intervention of Mr. Bamberger, whose word had never been gainsaid by anyone, including the first Director.

Some months earlier Aydelotte had raised other important financial questions with Mr. Bamberger and passed them on to Flexner, no doubt contributing to the latter's annoyance. Aydelotte reminded his predecessor that the budget of the Institute had not been balanced since 1938, and the deficit of 1940 would have been larger if Swarthmore had not paid his salary. There was no endowment for the salaries of Stewart and Warren, or for the maintenance of Fuld Hall, or for pensions which would cost about $30,000 a year. "The upshot of all this is that we are running at least $125,000 behind at the present moment, which is the interest on $4 million."[68]

But a balanced budget would be only the beginning. Aydelotte was bursting with plans to enlarge the program after the end of the war.

> I hope, however, that Mr. Bamberger's generosity will extend not merely to the point of covering our present commitments but will make some provisions for such interesting extensions as the development of Oriental studies, Latin American studies, and work in other fields in which I think the Institute might make a great contribution.

He ended on a note of hearty appreciation of Flexner's achievements and of hope that he himself could carry them on creditably:

> The plan which you laid down for the Institute and its method of approach to scholarship is so effective, so much needed, and promises such fruitful results that it would be nothing less than a tragedy if we were not going to be able to enter other fields. We need not enter them all at once and we can exchange one subject for another, but we need some margin to do anything.

Abraham Flexner expressed his disapproval of his successor by staying away from Trustees' meetings, as we have noted, until Mr. Bamberger asked him to attend. Then, not wishing to take issue publicly with Aydelotte, Flexner asked him to talk things over before the next regular meeting in January:

> Mr. Bamberger told me some weeks ago that he wanted me to attend the Board meetings, and I agreed to do so. I have never been in the position

of differing with you at a meeting of the Board, and I do not wish to do so, if it can possibly be avoided. I suggest that you and I try to meet toward the end of this week.[69]

Flexner's care to school himself against being nettled into speaking out proved unnecessary. This meeting was at least free from a spirit of controversy and was chiefly concerned with reports of progress, though two were along lines which Flexner must have thought objectionable. Veblen mentioned that the question of pensions had been discussed at the faculty meeting the day before, "and a resolution had been passed thanking the Director for the manner in which he had worked out his proposals to the Trustees for faculty pensions and retiring allowances." The Director was glad to say that the professors' war work had been good for the Institute's public relations: "The contribution which the Institute is making to the war effort had widened its influence and strengthened its position." If Flexner had still been Director, there would presumably have been no faculty meeting, no contribution of the Institute to the war effort. Having announced in *I Remember* that the Institute should go on for ten years as he had left it, he probably heard without enthusiasm another report by the Director of a plan for a new line of research in American civilization.

This Board meeting was the last attended by Louis Bamberger. In March he died, followed in July by Mrs. Fuld. Both Founders had taken close personal interest in the Institute until Mrs. Fuld was kept away by ill-health. Frank and Marie Aydelotte were on terms of friendship with the childless brother and sister, Frank having a filial affection for Mr. Bamberger. At the first Board meeting after his death, Frank mentioned that he had gone to Newark almost every week to have lunch with Mr. Bamberger and that Mr. Bamberger had attended all but two of the fifteen Trustees' meetings in his last five years. The Director added, "I hope that his spirit will be always with us: his modesty and sincerity, his generosity, his eagerness to be useful to humanity, and his instinct for excellence."[70]

The Founders made the Institute their residuary legatee, Mr. Bamberger's estate adding more than six millions to the endowment, Mrs. Fuld's slightly less than two millions, a total of $8,652,000, raising the sum of their gifts for endowment to $16,462,365. The Treasurer, Samuel Leidesdorf, by successful investments, increased this by four millions— not the thirty millions Abraham Flexner was led to expect, but generous and adequate provision for the future.

When Mr. Bamberger's legacy became known, the Director for the first time could be sure of an income which would not only balance the Institute's budget but leave a margin for expansion, broadened later by Mrs. Fuld's generosity and Leidesdorf's skill in finances. For the first time Frank Aydelotte could hope to be able to enlarge the faculty and support new lines of research. He, like Flexner, had dreams he would like to realize. But his hope was not fulfilled because of his unexpectedly early retirement.

Two Pressing Questions

Two questions were uppermost in the year 1944–1945: one raised by a Trustee, on the age when the Director should retire; the other, by the faculty, on the procedure for making appointments.

Shortly after the ruling that professors must retire at sixty-five, Frank Aydelotte had asked Mr. Bamberger if it should apply also to the Director. Mr. Bamberger said No, probably recalling that Flexner had been well past sixty-five when the Institute opened and carried it successfully through its important first six years. Some time after Mr. Bamberger died, the Director was surprised to have a telephone call from Herbert Maass, President of the Board and chairman of the Executive Committee, suggesting that Director and professors might well retire at the same age. As Frank Aydelotte thought this over, he was inclined to believe that Maass was not speaking for himself alone. Perhaps other Trustees and the faculty thought he should retire in the autumn of 1945. If so, he did not intend to resist. On the contrary, he replied, "I have come to feel very strongly that if members of the faculty retire at sixty-five, the Directors should do the same."[71]

Then, wanting to sound out the faculty, the Director mentioned the question of his retirement at a luncheon, where the first reaction was surprise and dismay. The idea was new to them, and they did not like it. The Director left at once in order not to hamper discussion, whereupon, according to a faculty report:

> There was further general discussion and a general expression of regret that he was considering his resignation. The essential point brought out was the strong feeling that the present Director knows how to work with scholars, and that as a result there exists a spirit of harmony and effective cooperation in the Institute which has been reflected in substantial achievements in the past five years. The general opinion was that the faculty did not want him to retire.[72]

The contrast between the faculty's regret at the thought that Frank Aydelotte might retire, and their determination five years earlier to force Abraham Flexner to go, must have struck everyone. Indeed, the language of the report, though emphasis is supplied here, could hardly fail to call attention to the difference: "the *present* Director knows how to work with scholars," implying that the *former* Director did not. Although Abraham Flexner himself had told Frank that he had the great advantage of being a scholar in his own right, the first Director, exceedingly proud and excessively sensitive, must have felt bitter toward the faculty who humiliated him by their comparison and toward the second Director as the occasion for it. It was after this episode that Flexner became openly hostile, making "representations" to the Trustees against his successor which "were investigated by the Committee on Institute Policy and found to be baseless."[73] These representations may have had to do with a quarrel which Flexner had discovered between a professor and a member in which Flexner thought the professor in the wrong, threatened him with dismissal, and reported the incident to the Director with a rebuke for not having seen the situation and dealt with it himself. Aydelotte for once did not return a soft answer, but let Flexner know he had acted beyond his authority and would not be supported. When Flexner's term as Trustee ended in 1945, he was glad not to serve again.[74]

This ends the account of the alienation of two friends which, with their differences in personality, seemed inevitable. Abraham Flexner, almost fanatically committed to the Institute in the form he had created, wanted his will to prevail over any successor. For Frank Aydelotte, incorrigibly independent, the urge to try to improve anything he touched was irresistible. But he never ceased to regret the loss of a friend who had been a delight for many years.*

As for the faculty's wish to keep Frank Aydelotte as Director, their saying that he knew "how to work with scholars" pleased him enor-

---

*When I began to work on this biography, knowing nothing about the break, I asked how I could reach Mr. Flexner. Frank Aydelotte answered, with the saddest look I had ever seen on his face, "You'll get nothing from Flexner about me." That was all. He did not live to see Flexner's final gesture against him. In rewriting *I Remember*, published in 1960 with the title *An Autobiography*, Flexner cut down almost three pages of friendly references to a single sentence. "My next choice as a Trustee of the Institute was President Frank Aydelotte of Swarthmore College, who in October 1939 succeeded me as director."[75]

mously, with the reassurance that he was realizing one of his principal aims: "cooperation with each member of the faculty on the research which he was undertaking and incidentally cooperation on the publication of his results."[76] In his first glow of pleasure, he decided that he would not retire; the faculty needed him. When one of the Trustees came to try to persuade him not to change his mind, he penciled notes of the conversation: "made it clear endorsement of the faculty meant more to me than Trustees'. Would like to retire, but would not let the faculty down."[77] The Trustees decided to compromise by deferring his retirement for two years, to take effect in October, 1947. This would give time to choose the next Director.

At the faculty meeting which adopted a resolution that the Director should stay in office beyond the age of sixty-five, Einstein raised the question about procedure for making appointments, saying: "The faculty ought always to give a majority vote, after being consulted by the Trustees, before the appointment of a Professor or Director." The minutes read, "No action."[78] Already Frank Aydelotte had expressed the general principle that faculty and Trustees should work together: "I hope that in the future development of the Institute the Board and faculty will act as a unit and that any move we make will be preceded by the fullest and freest discussion between the two groups."[79] Now, when the Faculty Committee on Policy asked specifically to have a share in appointments, he was ready to propose substantially the method which had served him well at Swarthmore. According to the committee's minutes of December 17, 1944, "Mr. Aydelotte expressed his determination, so long as he is Director, to appoint new members of the faculty only upon the recommendation of the School concerned, with competent outside advice and with full participation of the other Schools of the Institute as well as with the final approval of the faculty as a whole."

In his next report to the Trustees he went beyond this gentleman's agreement and called attention "to the importance of establishing an orderly procedure for making new appointments to the faculty," adding, "I have not raised this question before because we have never before during my directorship been in a position which would make new appointments possible."[80] Now he proposed a new Trustees' Committee on Appointments, "to which the Director can make his suggestions and which can recommend those approved to the Trustees or the Executive Committee." This new committee should recommend an appointment only when it has been approved "(1) by the department concerned, (2) by scholars outside the Institute best fitted to give advice on a particular case, (3) by the faculty."

The Director suggested that the chairman of the Committee on Appointments or, better still, all three members should attend faculty meetings called to make recommendations, a suggestion followed for the first time in May, 1945, and with somewhat curious results. The committee included the Director and two other Trustees, one of whom had been opposed to the procedure now to be tried out. He was opposed in general to involving the faculty in Institute decisions, even as advisers, partly because he had been convinced by Abraham Flexner's stand against the slightest sharing of the Director's power, partly because he refused to believe the professors capable of any decision not dictated by self-interest. No professor could consider anything but his own advantage as an individual and as a member of a School; he would find it impossible to regard the welfare of the Institute as a whole. Only the Director, according to this Trustee, could look objectively at the claims of the three Schools, could judge whether a vacancy in mathematics should be filled by appointing a professor of mathematics, or the salary used for another School, or even to introduce a new subject. The Trustee came to the Institute faculty meeting determined to prove that he was right, but instead served to demonstrate that difficulties of communication between a businessman and a group of professors could produce a farce.[81]

Ignoring a previous agreement among the three Schools, that each should fill one vacancy, he kept interrupting with remarks that were irrelevant or insulting—perhaps unintentionally. When the Director called on Professor Weyl to present the nomination of the School of Mathematics, the Trustee interrupted to inquire whether economics was not weaker than mathematics and should not therefore have preference for the appointment. When a name for the School of Economics and Politics was put forward by Professor Earle, the Trustee asked why we assumed that these people would accept? What could the Institute offer? He questioned the nomination in the Humanities on the ground that work in the candidate's line was already done by a professor who had retired, but was still active. When the Director mentioned the importance of free discussion the Trustee agreed, saying that the new procedure "held great hope that mistakes sometimes made in the past might in the future be prevented." This was taken personally by one professor who explained an irregularity in his own appointment. Finally, asked the visitor, how could he, as a Trustee, decide between the rival claims of a mathematician, an economist, and a humanist, and, in a debate with Professor Einstein, he compared himself to "a man entering a grocery store with a five dollar bill and having to decide whether to buy with it asparagus or spinach." Whereupon Professor Meritt "interrupted to beg only that if this were the dilemma the Humanities should not be classed with the spinach," releasing an outburst of suppressed hilarity.

The minutes of this meeting could be used almost verbatim as a comic skit, but the Director listened to the dialogue with courteous gravity. Fortunately in the long run he managed to bridge such gaps in communication. And before he retired, the procedure for faculty appointments was so well established that he could mention it as one of the achievements of his years in office.

Of the three professors recommended at this session, only one accepted the appointment: Wolfgang Pauli, who shortly afterward received the Nobel Prize in Physics. At a later meeting two other distinguished new professors were added, Carl L. Siegel in Mathematics and Homer A. Thompson in Humanistic Studies, contributing to research in archaeology half the year at the American School in Athens and half at the Institute.

Two Years of Grace: 1945–1947

In the first year after the war, the Institute was bursting with activity. The number of scholars at work—professors, members, and assistants— rose to ninety-two, with research in progress at "more than pre-war intensity," to quote the Director. Fortunately he had been able to mitigate what might have been a painful housing shortage by buying temporary buildings from the Federal Public Housing Authority, providing apartments for thirty-eight families. One member not troubled with a housing problem, whose presence gave the Aydelottes special pleasure, was their own son William, holder of a fellowship and lecturer in history at Princeton, at home now for two years.

High points of interest at the Institute for the Director were the Computer Project, the contribution to the building of the Firestone Library at Princeton University, and the Nobel Prize conferred on Wolfgang Pauli. Add to these Frank Aydelotte's appointment by President Truman to the Anglo-American Committee of Inquiry on Palestine and, at the end of 1946–1947, the holding of a Rhodes Scholars' Reunion. These last two will be described in the chapters that follow.

The Director encouraged faculty and Trustees to make a daring decision when they approved John von Neumann's research in the construction of an all-purpose electronic computer at a time when no other "super-brain" of such complexity had been attempted and its utility was still to be proved. To undertake it was "the greatest break so far" with the Institute's "tradition of pursuing merely theoretical studies."[82] Some of the faculty were opposed to this kind of innovation, but here as always the Director liked flexibility in recognizing a new line of probable value. "I do not believe that it is possible to schoolmaster research; an institution of this character must always be willing to gamble, to take long shots."

This particular long shot hit the bull's-eye. John von Neumann became "recognized as the world's leader in the development and construction of the high-speed computing machines . . . that have made possible the solution of problems that would otherwise require many life-times to solve."[83] Frank Aydelotte was happy to see the day in 1956 when the inventor was given the Fermi Award of $50,000 for "outstanding contributions to the design and construction of computing machines used in nuclear research," with a citation saying that Dr. von Neumann "more than anyone else foresaw the important and necessary role of super brains in the control and use of atomic energy."[84] Frank Aydelotte's own part had been to encourage von Neumann and, equally important, to secure $300,000 for construction, beginning with $100,000 from the Radio Corporation of America and $100,000 from the Navy.

When Princeton University was building the Firestone Library, a gift from the Institute seemed appropriate, and Frank Aydelotte urged that it should be generous, not only as a return for the university's hospitality to the Institute in the old library but as ensuring the right of professors and members to use the new one. He convinced the Trustees that they should give $500,000, sufficient to free the Institute from future responsibility for contributing to costs of maintenance. This was something he was glad to put through.

Wolfgang Pauli, who had come from Switzerland to the Institute as a member in 1940–1941 and throughout the war taught every year either at the Institute or on loan to Princeton, was appointed visiting professor in 1945 and later in the year won the Nobel Prize in Physics. Frank Aydelotte was delighted at the honor to Pauli and to the Institute, all the more meaningful to the community because he stayed there to receive it. On the day when the Nobel Prizes were presented in Stockholm, the twelfth of December, the Institute held a dinner in Pauli's honor and in January called a special Convocation where he was given his gold medal and diploma by the Minister of Sweden.[85] By this time Frank Aydelotte was away from Princeton, serving on the Anglo-American Committee of Inquiry on the relations between Jews and Arabs in Palestine. Professor Marston Morse, chairman of the Standing Committee in charge of administration in the Director's absence, presided at the Convocation.

In Frank Aydelotte's last Report to the Trustees, on April 18, 1947, he sketched his general idea of the government of an academic institution:

> My conception of the government of an educational institute is a bi-cameral one: the faculty constitute the lower house and the Trustees the upper. The members of the faculty are not employees in the ordinary sense; they are also a part of the governing body. No institution can be successful and harmonious which does not have suitable forms of pro-cedure by which each group can make its maximum contribution in the development of policies and in day to day administration. Eight years ago we had no such agreed method of administration. We have it now and the future development of the Institute will owe much to the creative achievement of these years.[86]

Having called attention to the necessity for cooperative formation of policies, the Director noted that the greatest advance in the last eight years had been precisely such as to make this cooperation possible: "advance in free democratic discussion of our problems and of our policies for the future."

The report ended with congratulations to the Trustees on their choice of his successor. In all appointments, temporary or permanent, "the important thing is the quality of the individual. The Trustees will continually have the question brought before them as to whether we should cultivate this subject or that. In reality the subjects which we cultivate are less important than the quality of the men whom we appoint."[87]

On the choice of Dr. J. Robert Oppenheimer as Director: "He has demonstrated his ability in science and in administration. He is by training a humanist as well. He was the first choice of the faculty as well as of the Board of Trustees and I have every confidence in predicting for him a happy and successful career as Director."

Frank Aydelotte's Contribution to the Institute

According to his report, Frank Aydelotte himself saw his chief con-tribution as organizing the Institute for cooperation between Trustees and faculty in effective administration. He would like to have been able to expand its program. On the day when he retired, his sixty-seventh birthday (October 16, 1947), a correspondent from the New York *Times,* who asked him what he thought he had accomplished, reported a brief answer: "It was a satisfaction to know that he was leaving the Institute 'with the budget balanced, the faculty considerably enlarged and the enrollment of students larger than ever before.' "[88]

Two professors at the Institute who have known it throughout its history told me how they thought his work had been important. One said: "The Institute would not be here today if Frank Aydelotte had not organized it." The second remembered "the good feeling of the faculty, their freedom to discuss"; also that Frank Aydelotte brought eminent and interesting people to the Institute, "more Nobel Prize winners here then than at any other time." All in all, he concluded: "the greatest days of the Institute were the early years of Frank Aydelotte."

THE COMMISSION ON PALESTINE

A Call from the White House

WHEN at last the war ground to a halt in 1945, Frank Aydelotte was sixty-five years old. He had come to Princeton just before the outbreak, and his high plans for the Institute had had to take second place to the overriding national claims. He looked forward eagerly to the coming of peace and the chance to give his whole mind to putting these plans into effect. But without warning the national interest stepped in again.

One day toward the end of the year he picked up his telephone to answer a call and was told that this was the White House, President Truman speaking. The President and the British Prime Minister were appointing a joint commission to advise their governments what to do about the Jewish refugees of Europe and about the future of their "homeland," Palestine. The problem was of highest urgency. Would Mr. Aydelotte serve on the commission? The President hoped very much that he would. Such a call from such a source and in such an interest could be answered, Frank felt, in only one way. He accepted at once.

The President was clearly right that the problem was urgent in the extreme. Scattered through Europe in hastily improvised camps were many thousands of Jews, the remnants of Hitler's attempted genocide. What were they to do? They did not want to go back to the towns where their friends and families had been destroyed; they wanted to be among their own people in a country of their own, and that country, of course, was Palestine. The government of Palestine was at the time in the hands of the British, who held a mandate for it from the League of Nations. President Truman had proposed to Prime Minister Attlee that the country open its doors to a hundred thousand refugees from the bulging camps of Europe.

Mr. Attlee had hesitated. He was under deep obligations to the United States and was eager to cooperate with the President. But his situation was more complicated than Mr. Truman's. In carrying out the Palestine mandate, Britain had promised to heed the interests of the Arabs as well as the Jews. The Arabs were the majority in Palestine, and they were desperately opposed to Mr. Truman's suggestion. To their ancient hostility toward the Jews there was now added the fear that they would be submerged under a Jewish majority and become second-class citizens of a land that had been theirs for twelve centuries. Palestine was tense. The Jews of the country demanded that the helpless refugees be admitted without delay. The Arabs protested that this would certainly be the spearhead of an unlimited Jewish invasion. The British were caught in the middle, where they were pressed and indeed terrorized by both parties, and Mr. Attlee felt the need of American support. American power and prestige were then at their acme; the two countries were joint victors in the war, and whatever might be done about the refugees or about Palestine would be far more likely to succeed if it had the United States behind it. Mr. Attlee therefore replied to Mr. Truman's request by proposing that a joint commission be appointed, consisting of six British and six American members, whose names would command general respect; that the commission be asked to look into these questions immediately; and that the two governments should use the commission's recommendations as the guidelines of their joint policy. President Truman assented cordially. Among the six Americans he named to the commission was Frank Aydelotte.

The call admitted of no delay. The camps for displaced persons were being maintained at great cost in money and misery, and the tension in Palestine was mounting daily. Frank would have been grateful for a year or two in which to accumulate background, for he had no more than a layman's knowledge of the Middle East and its tortured problems. Unhappily these were problems on which the specialists themselves were divided, and what the President and Prime Minister wanted was men with open minds, quick apprehension, and responsible judgment. The commissioners were instructed to begin work at the earliest possible moment, to study the situation at first hand both in Europe and Palestine, and to have their report in the hands of the British and American governments within a hundred and twenty days. By telephone, telegraph, and mail the appointees got in touch with each other and agreed to meet in Washington early in January, 1946, to plan their campaign.

Frank arrived in Washington with much curiosity as to what manner of men his colleagues would be. They would have to travel together under makeshift conditions, share rooms in hotels, boats, and trains, criticize each other's ideas over exotic meals and through long sessions by day and by night, and hammer out some sort of agreement on issues charged with emotion. The American and British contingents each had a chairman of its own. Both were judges, but apart from that they were a curiously contrasting pair. The British chairman, Sir John Singleton, judge of the King's Bench, London, was formal and precise, "a bachelor in his sixties, lean, pink-faced, and as British in appearance as a character out of Dickens. One could hardly imagine him other than in his silver wig of office."[1] His opposite number was Joseph C. Hutcheson, Jr., of the Fifth Federal Circuit Court of Texas. To the British, who were not familiar with the tongue and ways of the American Southwest, this hearty, salty Texan was a surprising apparition. While the commission was still in Washington, he took them round one day to present them to the august Justices of the Supreme Court. The company, duly awed by the magnificent pile in which the Justices sat, and escorted in silence down the lofty marble corridors, were startled by a voice booming from an open door, "Where the hell are you, Texas Joe?" It was Chief Justice Harlan Stone, in search of his old friend from the West. The commission was to be startled again in Vienna when at a military dinner the orchestra played a Texas song in honor of Judge Hutcheson. The judge "suddenly threw back his head, opened his mouth, and emitted a rafter-shaking 'Yippee-ee.'"[2] But the commissioners gradually learned that along with his breeziness there was a large charity, good sense, and humor in their Lincolnian colleague. He could face angry emirs in Cairo and angry crowds in Jerusalem with the same coolness with which he had run the Ku Klux Klan out of his home city of Houston.

Frank's other American colleagues were also notably individual. Only one of them, James G. McDonald, had had much experience with the problems of refugees, but he had had so much of it as High Commissioner of the League of Nations for German refugees that it was difficult for him throughout to take the Arab claims quite seriously. William Phillips, former American Ambassador to Italy, was "the best-looking, the best-dressed and the best-mannered member of the committee. . . . He suffered much in the hundred and twenty days of our investigation," wrote one of the members, "from the bickering of his colleagues. We would probably have behaved much worse had he not been there to

remind us how gentlemen behave."[3] Frank W. Buxton had won a
Pulitzer Prize for Journalism as editor of the Boston *Herald*. Bartley
Crum was a Republican corporation lawyer from California. But he was
far from conforming to the pattern of such a person. He was an outspoken
liberal. He had been a campaign manager for Wendell Willkie in 1940,
had bolted his party in 1944 to head the Independent Republicans for
Roosevelt, had fought the employment practices of southern railroads
regarding Negroes, had chaired a Spanish refugee rally at Madison
Square Garden, and at the moment of his appointment was preparing to
leave for Spain to defend two members of the anti-Franco underground
who were in danger of execution. Someone in the State Department
thought this too radical a record and tried to block the appointment;
when the list of commissioners was published, Crum's name did not
appear. It was only after Mr. Truman had cabled Secretary of State
Byrnes in Moscow for clearance that the President felt able to issue his
invitation.

Plainly the American contingent was a diverse group. So was the
British contingent; perhaps even more so. At the right end of its
spectrum was Major Reginald Manningham-Buller, Conservative member of Parliament, whose views of the Empire seemed to some of his
colleagues Kiplingesque. At the other end was a former Oxford don,
Richard H. S. Crossman, classical scholar, Socialist, and an editor of the
New Statesman and Nation. Like many other young men of the thirties,
he had once been far to the left, but after watching with growing
alienation the trials and the tyranny in Russia, he sadly edited a book,
The God That Failed, in which he and others of his leftist friends reported
their disillusionment. Crossman was destined to a distinguished role in
the Labor party and became, under Harold Wilson, the majority leader
of the House of Commons. There was also a Labor member of the
House of Lords, Baron Morrison of Tottenham, who, though long
associated with London, revealed his origins by an unmistakable Scots
burr. The remaining two commissioners were Wilfrid Crick, a London
banker of bankers, cautious, reserved, and exact, and Sir Frederick Leggett,
a friend of Foreign Minister Bevin, who had achieved great success as a
conciliator in labor disputes.

If Frank Aydelotte was much interested in the quirks and angles of
his new colleagues, they were also much interested in him. They were
struck, like everyone else, by his friendliness and his bubbling *joie de
vivre*. Crossman put it in the slightly sour way that was characteristic of

him when dealing with Americans: "Professor Aydelotte was the only academic of the Committee, but his abilities were more administrative than professorial. . . . He showed a remarkable resemblance to Happy of *Snow White and the Seven Dwarfs*, not only in his appearance but in his sunny temperament."[4]

These were the twelve new apostles to the Jews and Gentiles. They set out hopefully on their high and difficult mission. They assembled for the first time in Washington in the early days of January, 1946. There were formalities to attend to and a strategy to be laid out. Together they called on President Truman. He told them that an unprecedented torrent of mail had been descending on the White House on the problem of displaced persons, that he was deeply concerned about the position of these innocent people, and that he urgently hoped the commission could give him its judgment within the alloted time. The visitors were impressed by the obvious sincerity of his interest. The Britons particularly liked his modesty. "Mr. Truman," said one of them, by way of a little ice-breaking, "I have often wondered how it feels to be President." "I don't feel that I am," replied Mr. Truman, who had taken over from Roosevelt only in the preceding April; "I feel that I am trying to carry on for someone else."[5] The acting Secretary of State, Dean Acheson, gave the group a luncheon and his hearty Godspeed.

What would be the best strategy for the four-month enterprise? They must obviously tap the best sources of opinion on each of their two great problems: the refugees and Palestine. For the present, they were on American soil, and it would be best to begin there. America was the chief supporter, financial and moral, of the Zionist movement; indeed there were far more Jews in the City of New York than in the whole of Palestine. The commissioners decided to begin their hearings where they were, in Washington. They would then move on to London, from which half their authority derived and where every kind of opinion was represented. They were less clear what course to follow afterward. They could not, as a whole, with advisers and secretaries attached, lumber about to all the refugee centers of Europe; yet they must gain as full an impression as possible of the facts, the needs, and the desires of the displaced persons. In the end they decided to break up for this purpose into smaller teams. Aydelotte, Crick, and Manningham-Buller would take as their special field the refugees in the British Zone of Germany. The two chairmen, Singleton and Hutcheson, together with Buxton and Morrison, would go to Berlin. McDonald and Phillips would go to Paris and study the refugees under French control. Leggett, Crossman, and Crum would go first to the American Zone in Germany, then on into Austria and Czechoslovakia. When these hasty missions were completed, the group would reassemble in Cairo to compare notes and get a full statement of the Arab side of the case. Then they would go on to Jerusalem for an exposure to the winds of feeling and opinion in Palestine itself. Finally, it was agreed that they would fly back to Switzerland in April and try to hammer out their report in some quiet spot before the tourist season began.

The Washington Hearing

For their hearings in Washington, the State Department placed commodious chambers at their disposal on the second floor of its huge office building. The hearings were public, and for eight days a succession of witnesses, Jewish, Arab, and neutral, appeared by invitation to present their views and answer questions. It soon became plain, and it was underscored by all the later hearings, that there was no agreement on any point before them except the despair and need of the refugees. On this their first witness was an authority. He was Earl Harrison, Dean of the Pennsylvania Law School, whose report on the refugees of Europe had been the occasion of Truman's appeal to Attlee. He had gone to Europe with the idea that the German Jews should remain on German soil with the aid necessary to their readjustment. He came back convinced that this would not do. You could not send terrified people back into communities that had sought to destroy them and where, for all they knew, pogroms might recur. These people, even if they were shopkeepers or bookkeepers, would rather go and swing pickaxes on the stony soil of Palestine than be plunged again into the fear and hatred from which they had escaped.

But, granting their need and their desire, should Palestine be opened to them? The replies that the commission received from its witnesses were, as a rule, either an impatient, expostulatory, and emphatic Yes or an icy No, with comparatively few answers lying between. The most emphatic of the Yea-sayers were, of course, the Zionists, whose chief spokesman in this country, Rabbi Stephen S. Wise, appeared as an early witness. The Zionists were committed to a separate and sovereign Jewish nation. Their legal case was based on the Balfour Declaration, made by the British Foreign Secretary during World War I, when Allenby's army was about to take Jerusalem. Palestine was then part of the Turkish empire; the British were at war with the Turks; they were eager for Jewish support. The famous Declaration was a promise that when the war was over, their support would have its reward:

> His Majesty's government views with favor the establishment in Palestine of a national home for the Jewish people and will use their best endeavours to facilitate the achievement of that object, it being clearly understood that nothing shall be done which may prejudice the civil and religious rights of existing non-Jewish communities in Palestine.

The Zionists held that this was a straightforward commitment by the conqueror of Palestine that the Jews would be established there as a sovereign nation and would be able to go there at will. Rabbi Wise thought that both Balfour and Wilson read the Declaration in this sense, and he had discussed the matter with both. From his diary he quoted a statement made to him by Balfour: "This means that all Jews who may at any time in the future wish or require to dwell in Palestine shall be free to do so." It was true that in Palestine as it was, the Jews were greatly outnumbered by Arabs. But if their immigration was to be free, as seemed clearly intended, the time must have been envisaged when they would form a majority and by any democratic standard would be entitled to govern. Indeed, the very clauses inserted to safeguard Arab rights, the Zionists argued, implied an acceptance of Jewish control, for they are the kind of clauses designed to protect a weaker group from a stronger.

In America there was a vast reservoir of Jews from which the commission could draw competent witnesses, but unhappily there were very few Arabs. Perhaps the most distinguished of these was Dr. Philip Hitti, professor of Semitic literature at Princeton, a Christian by religion though an Arab by race. Dr. Hitti testified that in his opinion the Zionism espoused by Dr. Wise was illegal, impracticable, and immoral. The Palestine that was on everyone's lips was a myth; there was no such country; it was really the southern part of Syria; and its association with the Jews in the American mind was largely the mischievous product of Sunday schools, whose omnipresent maps of Palestine made it the seat of Jewish cities and Jewish heroes. But it had been Arab land for many centuries; it was a homeland of Arabs still; and for anyone to tell these Arabs that they must open their gates to a tide of alien immigration, whether they wanted it or not, was imperialistic and dictatorial.

"Dr. Hitti," Crossman asked, "your view is that anything like a Zionist solution could only be imposed by force on the Arabs?"

"Yes, sir," Dr. Hitti replied.

"And that any Arab solution could only be imposed by force on the Zionists?"

"That is correct."

"Your criticism of the British government is the attempted reconciliation of Jews and Arabs?"

"Yes, sir, absolutely. . . . "

Suppose the goal of a Jewish state were eliminated, asked Judge Hutcheson: would the Arabs then agree to Jewish immigration?

"Frankly, no," said Dr. Hitti, "Jewish immigration seems to us an attenuated form of conquest."[6]

Here was the commission's first personal confrontation with the tangled mass of antagonisms that was called the Palestine question. Dr. Wise and Dr. Hitti were both authorities and both honest men, and their flatly contradictory testimony was disquieting. But there was another witness whose testimony, at least to the British members, was still more disquieting. This was Frank Aydelotte's friend and colleague at Princeton, Albert Einstein. It may be thought strange that a mathematician and physicist should have been called in as an authority on a tangled political issue. But two things may well be remembered. One is that Einstein was himself a refugee from the regime of Hitler, which had deprived him of his German citizenship and confiscated his property. The other is the atmosphere of adulation in which, at that time, he lived. His opinion on anything whatever, from physics to art or astrology, was accepted as a sort of Delphic oracle. His name stood by a long distance first among all living scientists, and even to persons who knew nothing of his teaching his face was as familiar as that of some star of the screen. He tried to slip quietly into the audience room while another witness was testifying, but the crowd at once recognized the familiar face with its great aureole of white hair and broke into an applause so vigorous that it had to be called to order by Judge Hutcheson. When Einstein's own turn came and he began his testimony in a quiet voice, there was such a general pressing forward to hear him that again the proceedings had to be stopped while order was restored.

Einstein spoke gently and smilingly, but what he said was in the

X: Two close British friends. Above, Sir Carleton Allen. Below, Sir Francis Wylie.

XI: Rhodes Scholars' reunion, Princeton, 1947; Frank and Marie Aydelotte,
Lady Elton, and Lord Elton receiving on the lawn beside the Director's house.
Photo: R. V. C. Whitehead, Jr.

sharpest contrast to his manner. He was skeptical to the point of cynicism about British aims in Palestine and indeed about the value of anything the commission might accomplish. Britain, he maintained, was in Palestine for the same reason that it was in colonies all over the world, to exploit them in its own interest; and everywhere it used the same method, namely, to get on its side the big landowners, who were its agents in the exploitation. The British government, instead of desiring and trying to heal the breach between Jews and Arabs, was deliberately keeping hostility alive, in order to make its presence there necessary. This was more than the British commissioners could happily take, as they made clear by their countenances and their questions. Here Frank Aydelotte was with them. He asked his colleague how a government whose success depended on keeping order among its subjects could really profit by inciting disorder. Einstein replied that intense conflict was, indeed, to no one's advantage, but "a little enmity" served the purposes of the governors well.

The British group plied their distinguished witness with irritated questions. Crossman wanted to know whether, if the British had so bungled the matter, he thought the Americans would do better; did he think the United States would be prepared to take military responsibility for what happened if an unlimited refugee tide started pouring into Palestine? Einstein answered that he had no such idea in mind; the country should be placed under the control of an international organization. Crossman persisted: Who would furnish the army? Would there be soldiers from two countries, or five, or fifty, or more? Einstein was vague; such matters, he thought, "could be arranged." Bartley Crum chided him about his view that the commission was merely a "smoke screen" for the machinations of the Colonial Office. "Dr. Einstein," he said, "our British and American colleagues are doing everything in their power to find a speedy solution of the Palestine problem. I, for one, think it is wrong for you, as a citizen of the world, to say that this committee is a smoke screen. Believe me, sir, it is not."[7] Einstein asked how he could be so sure of that. Crum replied that he knew it from his own activities on the committee. Einstein smiled benignly and suggested that the Colonial Office could use a committee in ways that the committee did not surmise.

London and a Collapse

When the hearings were over in Washington, the commissioners packed their bags for London. They sailed on January 18 from New

York on the *Queen Elizabeth*. The great ship had been completed just as the war began and so far had been used only as a troopship; its cabins were battered and dingy and its portholes still covered with black paint. Frank found himself in a room with two colleagues and six double-deck beds. Before two days had passed, the ship was pitching and rolling in a wild midwinter storm, and Frank recorded that the chairs were piling up in heaps and the dishes crashing in pieces on the floor.[8] For a day the big *Queen* was the only ship still in motion on the Atlantic. With a stoical devotion to their work, the commission decided, nevertheless, to hold two sessions daily to explore each other's minds and compare tentative conclusions.

For Frank the plan did not work out, for he became a casualty. The long sessions in Washington, with hearings by day and conferences by night, had left him very weary, and a cold was coming on as he boarded the ship. When Marie was not with him to make him take care of himself, he was not a good patient, for he was habitually so sanguine that he would keep on driving himself in the belief that there was nothing much wrong and that whatever was troubling him would go away if he refused to acknowledge it. But the cold hung on and grew worse. He kept waking in the night in paroxysms of coughing. After two or three days of fighting it, he decided to surrender: "I frankly gave up today, Darling," he wrote in the journal he kept for Marie, "stayed in bed for all meals, had the doctor up to see me twice and decided to give my cold a chance." But he went on characteristically, "I have had lots of visitors and in our discussions have kept up with the work of the Committee. I also dictated some letters and have done a lot of reading." There was one minor comfort: "Everyone is afraid of my cold and is sleeping elsewhere, so I have the room to myself and can turn on the lights to read if I wake up in the night, which is a great luxury."

The ship docked at Southampton on Wednesday, the twenty-third, in the afternoon, and the party, holding diplomatic passports, were able to march through the customs. Frank got to London in time for a nine-o'clock dinner at the Hyde Park Hotel and noted in his diary at 11:00 P.M., "We have a meeting tomorrow at 10:00 A.M. and an invitation to visit the House of Commons in the afternoon." But he woke up in the morning with a temperature of 101. He telephoned to his friend C. K. Allen, Oxford Secretary of the Rhodes Trust, who insisted that he come to Rhodes House and stay till he was fit again. On Friday an official car was placed at his disposal and he was driven to Oxford and put to bed by the kindly Allens. After five days with them, he returned to London, trusting that all would be well. He resumed his part in the hearings, still hoping that in the following week he would be able to fly with the group to Germany. But at this point his doctor put his foot down. There would be no Germany for him, and no conference in Vienna, where the members were to assemble after their continental inquiries. Indeed, if he did not capitulate to the infection that was prostrating him, the nature of which was still unclear, there might be no Egypt and no Palestine. He bowed to medical advice in bitter disappointment.

On the day after his return to London, he added to his sorrow a little of the sorrow of a friend, which was far greater than his own. He had come to know Leopold Amery as one of the Rhodes Trustees, a former Secretary of State for India, and a much respected senior statesman. Amery called in the evening at his hotel. "It was nice of him to come to see me," Frank writes. "He had a good deal to say about Palestine and brought a book on the subject which I had not seen. But I soon found that he really came to tell me about John." John was Amery's elder son, and the one black sheep of a distinguished family, so different from all the others that he was probably the strange product of wayward genes. Constantly in trouble with the law (he was convicted more than seventy times for automobile offenses), financially and maritally irresponsible, he ended by going over to the Nazis in the middle of the war, broadcasting against his own country, and even trying to organize a legion of British prisoners to fight for the Germans against the Russians.[9] Fleeing from Germany when it was overrun, he was captured by partisans in Italy, turned over to the British, and brought home for trial. He was obviously guilty and made no attempt at defense, so the judge could only put on his black cap and pronounce sentence of death. John was executed shortly afterward. The suffering of his family may be imagined. Frank wrote that night:

> It was a moving story. The boy was not all bad—only a kind of rebel against society and at the end a fervent opponent of Communism. He never lost the love of his father and mother and brother. Although they disapproved, they could see why he did what he did. The boy pleaded guilty to save his family the anguish of a trial. Having pled guilty the judge had no option, since the only penalty under this old law of 1351 was death. The father, mother and brother spent the evening before his death with him in his cell. Amery says he kept them almost cheerful with his affectionate intetest in all they would do in the future. The next

morning John thanked his jailors and executioner for their consideration and kindness. I could see it did Amery good to tell me the story and I felt moved and honored by his confidence.

The hearings in London continued, with much repetition of what had been heard in Washington. "Dr. Baeck, head of the Jews in Germany, just out of prison camp," was one of the witnesses, and "since no one else seemed to feel moved to do so," Frank wrote, "I congratulated him publicly on his fair and deeply touching statement of the plight of the Jews." Patrick Malin, whom Frank had brought to the economics department at Swarthmore and who had recently been working with the European refugees, also testified helpfully. Malin was a brilliant and dedicated Quaker who went on to the headship of the American Civil Liberties Union and then to the presidency of Robert College, Constantinople. Between hearings, Frank liked to dash over to the Athenaeum, where he was a member, and where he met a surprising number of people who reminded him of visits to his house in Swarthmore. In company he was cheerful, but in fact he could barely drag himself about. His temperature kept shooting capriciously up and down the scale, and since with his lame elbow he found it hard to shake the thermometer down, he devised a highly efficacious method of spinning it by attaching it to the middle of a length of string, turning it over till the string was well twisted, and then pulling both ends.

For ten days this went on. His doctors advised him to go into a nursing home, but neither in London nor in Oxford could they find a suitable one that was not full. He decided to accept a standing invitation from Lord Elton, General Secretary of the Rhodes Trust, to come down to his estate at Adderley, some twenty miles from Oxford. He wrote of his four or five days there: "My visit with the Eltons was one of the most delightful that I have ever made anywhere." They had a fine old house, built in 1656, but with all the comforts of efficient central heating, and Frank allowed himself to relax, read detective stories, and sleep. At the end of the visit, Lord Elton drove him to Oxford again, where he spent three hours at the Radcliffe Infirmary undergoing a battery of tests. The resulting report was that he had been suffering from a very severe chest infection that had left changes in his blood, and he was casually told that he "should be ready to travel in three or four weeks. That is devastating." Happily, two weeks with the hospitable Allens at Rhodes House, punctuated with the delights of occasional dinners at his old college of Brasenose, made him more or less travel-worthy again.

On to Cairo

It was Monday, February 25, before he reached London on his way to rejoin the commission. A message was waiting for him reporting that his colleagues had finished both their visits to European camps and their session in Vienna and were expecting to forgather in Cairo at the week's end. He promptly reserved a passage from Hurn Airport, near Bourne-mouth, for Friday morning, which would, if all went well, land him in Cairo at five the following morning. Reporting at his hotel in Bournemouth about ten on Thursday night, he found that he had been put in a room with a stranger. By paying an extra guinea, he got "a wretched little room, cold as ice," to himself, and by dint of sleeping in woolen underwear, heavy pajamas, and wool socks, with his overcoat over the bedclothes, he got a fair amount of sleep. He was up early, eager to be off. The weather was dull, cold, and misty, but British pilots were inured to taking off in almost any weather; what was more important to them was the weather at their next port of call. And the reports from Marseilles were bad. The Dakota plane that had left at the same time on the day before had almost reached the city when it had to turn round and come all the way back to Bournemouth; the passengers were still huddled in the airport waiting to try again. Two or three hours after Frank's flying time, the announcement came that his plane would not leave that day, and on returning to his hotel, he noted that "there are now passengers for 3 Dakotas of 3 successive days sitting around this hotel."

Next morning he was up shortly after five, and the plane did finally take off. It was unheated; the temperature "was below freezing in the plane most of the morning and the windows were heavily coated with frost." The passengers were supplied with flying suits, but Frank notes in his journal: "This morning after we left I suffered intensely from cold feet. Finally I took off my big felt boots and chafed each foot in turn a long time, then took off my second pair of heavy socks and in 15 minutes my feet were nice and warm. Apparently the boots were not quite big enough and the extra socks impeded the circulation." He had dinner at the Air Force mess on the island of Malta, and "a kind of breakfast" at 1:30 A.M. at the airport of Tobruk, in north Africa, with eggs and beans served by German prisoners of war. The plane descended at Cairo about four that morning, but on the opposite side of the city from his hotel, which he reached at last about half past six.

All this was not what a doctor would order for someone who had been fighting a lung infection for weeks. But he attended the commission meeting that morning, and when Judge Hutcheson, who was a keen golfer, proposed a game in the afternoon, Frank persuaded himself that "18 holes in the sunshine would do me more good than sleep." Hutcheson asked him how much of a golfer he was, to which Frank replied that he kept his average in the 80's. The judge was obviously skeptical, and after taking two of the first three holes, began to joke Frank about those 80's. The jokes were premature. Long out of practice and with borrowed clubs, Frank came in with an 85, eleven strokes up on his colleague.

He had lost less than he feared by his month of illness. The hearings tended to reproduce, over and over, the familiar positions, though the witnesses in Cairo put the Arab case with especially fervent anger, directing it against both Jews and British. Feelings in the city were tense. On Frank's second day in Cairo, the commission was supposed to meet with the commanding officers of the British army in the Middle East, but there was a general strike that day in honor of students killed in protests against the British, and it was considered unsafe for the group to enter the city. They did so next day, but under an escort of police cars, and when Frank went out for a further round of golf with the judge, the pair were followed about the links by a guard of two to four policemen. When, after three or four days in Egypt, the members entrained for Palestine, they found the situation, if anything, still more tense. Their train was preceded by an engine pushing a single car in order to absorb possible bomb explosions on the track, and soldiers were stationed in every car. From the hotel in Jerusalem, Frank wrote soon after:

> We live in an atmosphere of suspicion and intrigue. You must be careful that no conversation is overheard and must lock up all papers every time you leave your room. An agent of the security police sits in the hall outside our rooms and notes in a book every time we go out or in, and we are not allowed to go out, much less to enter the old city inside the walls, without an armed guard.

At the door of the building where the members had their offices there were rolls of barbed wire and a whole squad of policemen. "All Jerusalem is excited by our coming. The papers are full of it. . . . It is hard to realize the tension and excitement, and the eagerness of each side to get a decision in their favor."

Palestine from the Inside

The commission reached Jerusalem on March 6. That afternoon Frank and a few others were driven out by the British High Commissioner to see the Church of the Nativity at Bethlehem, supposed to be built on the site of the manger familiar in Christian story. The church was a disappointment, "ugly and tawdry." It was in the joint control of three sects—Greek Orthodox, Armenian, and Roman Catholic—who maintained a continual petty squabble about their rights and their differing ceremonies. "It seems a pity," Frank commented, "that the Holy places in the Christian religion cannot have more beauty and dignity." As the group came out, Lord Morrison remarked, "As agnostics, my wife and I would like to send everyone to Bethlehem." The next day was free, and the entire commission went the rounds of the Jerusalem shrines, being careful to visit as impartially as they could the Holy Sepulchre, the Mosque of Omar, and the Wailing Wall. The old city inside the walls struck Frank as "inconceivably crowded and unsanitary," and the group were glad to get back to their clean rooms at the King David Hotel. That afternoon they were given a tremendous reception by the High Commissioner, with about two hundred guests chosen from all the warring parties, including "Generals, Excellencies, Patriarchs, Beatitudes, Eminences, Chief Rabbis, and one Reverendissimus." The hopes entertained of the commission by all parties were embarrassingly high.

The hearings in Jerusalem went on through the month of March, and the whole gamut of opinions found voice once more, sometimes clamorously. The two witnesses with whom Frank was most impressed personally were Chaim Weizmann and Judah Magnes, both of whom, (particularly Magnes) seemed to him great men. "Today," wrote Crossman in his journal, "we had Weizmann who looks like a weary and humane version of Lenin, very tired, very ill, too old and too pro-British to control his extremists. He spoke for two hours with a magnificent mixture of passion and scientific detachment. . . . He is the first witness who has frankly and openly admitted that the issue is not between right and wrong but between the greater and the lesser injustice."[10] Weizmann was the world leader of the Zionist movement. He had first made his name as a scientist. As a Jew he had not been able to enter a Russian

university, so he migrated to the west, where he took a doctorate at
Fribourg in Switzerland, was appointed lecturer in chemistry in the
University of Manchester, England, became a British subject in 1910,
and rendered valuable services to the British government in World War
I through helping to develop synthetic rubber. He had also been instru-
mental in securing from Balfour the famous "Declaration." Frank and
William Phillips went out one night to dine with him in his house at
Rehovoth. It was a splendid residence, built for him, Frank noted with
pleasure, by a Guggenheim Fellow, Eric Mendelssohn. It stood on a
hilltop, with that rarity in Palestine, a fine green lawn, and surrounded
with acres of citrus trees. Inside were polished stone floors, thick rugs,
and attractive works of art. Weizmann had first seen the place, "a bare
hill in a swamp," nearly thirty years before, as he looked out from
Allenby's camp, pitched a half-mile away.[11]

Magnes was a man of less fame and less force than Weizmann, but he
was a rare embodiment of quiet reasonableness in a land where reasonableness was too often interpreted as weakness or even treason. This
selfless objectivity lent weight to his judgment, and Frank thought his
testimony "the high water mark of our hearings." After it was over,
Frank and several colleagues went out to the university to continue the
talk in Magnes' office and see the institution of which he was the head.

There were occasional interludes of a few hours or even days in the
hearings, and Frank used these in trying to satisfy his insatiable curiosity
about the people, their way of life, and the fragments that still remained
of their fabulous past. With three of his colleagues he visited Gaza,
Beersheba, and Hebron in one long day. At Hebron "the Mayor and the
leading Moslem prelates showed us every detail of the mosque enclosing
the tombs of Abraham and Sara, Isaac and Rebecca, Leah and Jacob."
On another day he visited the large Jewish Potash Works on the Dead
Sea, which employed a thousand Jews and a thousand Arabs, working
peacefully together. He inspected and was much impressed by one of the
Jewish kibbutzim, colonies conducted on socialist principles. This one
had developed an ingenious process of desalting a stretch of marshland
near the Dead Sea and had converted it into fertile soil. The residents,
Frank notes, "have schools, libraries, wireless, etc., and seem happy,
though the life would not appeal to me because of its appalling lack of
privacy." He visited the headquarters of the Druses, the strange sect that
holds an eclectic religion, with about equal ingredients of Christianity,
Judaism, and Islam. The hosts were four brothers, all in their seventies or

eighties, and all with black robes, flowing beards, and white turbans. The conversation "consisted chiefly of compliments, at which they outdid us completely." Crossman remembers this conversation as

> rising from crag to crag of flattery for one hour and a quarter, during which I ate chocolate cake, Turkish delight, crystallized fruits, and drank tea, followed by the three cups of bitter coffee which are the mark of the highest hospitality. There was one awkward moment when someone interrupted the ceremonial duet with a breezy question—whether the sheik thought he lived so long because he didn't smoke. This was followed by an appalling pause, since a Druse is forbidden by religion to smoke, but forbidden by courtesy to suggest that guests can be wrong. The old gentleman finally replied: "Death takes us each when God wills."[12]

At Haifa, the principal port of Palestine, Frank found the city about evenly divided between Jews and Arabs, who got on fairly well together, though the greater drive of the Jews had produced very much better schools. A visit followed to Mt. Tabor, which rises straight up for 1,800 feet at the edge of the Esdraelon Plain and commands a magnificent view of it. At the top of the mountain is a Franciscan monastery, where Frank lunched with the Father Superior. For two or three days he played truant with Phillips to visit the American University at Beirut, Lebanon, passing Tyre and Sidon on the way. Then, under the guidance of Mr. Wadsworth, the American minister to Lebanon and Syria, they drove over the snow-covered mountains, 9,000 feet high, to Damascus, "the oldest city in the world." Frank was thrilled to be driven down the biblical "street that is called straight, which is not very straight and is certainly very narrow, full of people and donkeys and horse carts and dogs and children." Then back to Jerusalem along the Sea of Galilee and past the site of the Sermon on the Mount and the distribution of loaves and fishes. When commissioners were known to be coming, Frank recorded, "everywhere we had mayors and municipal councils out to meet us, were regaled with endless cups of coffee, and ate enormous meals."

One trip was taken alone on a Sunday and was a labor of love. He knew that at Ramallah, a half-hour away from Jerusalem, two American Friends, Willard Jones and his wife, were running a Quaker school, where there was a weekly Quaker meeting. Hiring a car one Sunday morning, and accompanied by the inevitable bodyguard, he drove out to Ramallah and attended the meeting, to the Jones's surprise and delight.

He had a letter from his home meeting at Princeton, which was read out by Willard Jones, and then he spoke to the audience in English, which was translated into Arabic as he went along. "My police bodyguard," he writes, "stuck with me throughout, attended the meeting and sat facing me in the audience while I sat on the facing bench. He sang church hymns lustily and I discovered afterwards that both he and the chauffeur are Arab Christians and have a high opinion of the Quakers."

Wherever he went, the problems of the commission were brewing and vegetating in his mind. Every Arab or Jew he met was a possible source of new light, or a corrective of false impressions, or a touchstone by which to test a tentative proposal. He knew that for a full grasp of the situation he would need to spend years in the Palestine community and master the languages of its people. The case was too urgent for that, but he was satisfied that in a month of talk and travel the commission could acquaint itself with all the main relevant facts. Definite impressions of the contending parties gradually crystallized in his mind. For the British who had charge of the country under the mandate he had great respect. "All these English civil servants are high class men who are invincibly fair and honest. But Palestine is too much for them—perhaps too much for anybody." As for the indigenous warring groups, "Jews and Arabs are very much alike—volatile, imaginative, sensitive, and completely unreasonable. . . . The difference is that the Jews have an idea which the Arabs do not have. They can support an indefinite number of people on any small fraction of Palestine provided they have freedom to do it. That is the argument for partition."

Flight to Lausanne

After three crowded weeks in Palestine, the commission had a huge baggage of impressions to carry on to Lausanne for sifting and reflection. The members were happy to escape from the heated hearings and exhausting travels where, Frank wrote, "we have not had enough rest and enough time to think." They were given a fine send-off. On March 26, Frank wrote at midnight after a strenuous day: "At 5:00 P.M. I went to a big farewell tea given by the Government in our honor, with all Jerusalem and nearly all Palestine there." After tea he had a final talk with Dr. Magnes, dinner with Edwin Samuel, the son of Lord Samuel, the former High Commissioner, and an evening with Brahms and Mendelssohn at an orchestral concert. Next day he packed his bags, and on the morning of the twenty-eighth he boarded a plane with his colleagues at the Lydda airport. He jotted down shortly after the take-off: "We flew directly out to sea over Jaffa and Tel Aviv, and the Mediterranean looks deep blue in the sunlight. . . . We are all cheerful at having our faces turned toward home even though the real job is yet to be done." The weary group reached Malta at nine in the evening, only to find that the Governor had arranged a huge dinner party of forty to fifty people at which they sat down at ten o'clock. "Fortunately I had a white shirt in my overnight bag." But he found Governor-General Campbell and his wife "simply delightful people" with whom he had instant common ground, for Malta had just held its Rhodes Scholarship elections, and the Governor-General had presided over the committee of selection. That night he spent in his host's residence, the Palace of Sant Anton, built by the Knights Templars in the seventeenth century. "My bedroom was about 20 by 20 and I am sure the ceiling was 20 feet high."

Next day: Lausanne. There was no compelling reason for going there in particular, but some member of the commission knew the Hotel Beau Rivage as a place of peace and quiet, and that was what they now wanted above everything. "We are all tired and tempers are rather short, mine included," Frank wrote. "I must get a Bible tomorrow, for that is the best outside reading connected with our problem. . . . The sheer fatigue of all this is beyond anything I can describe." A day or two later the choice of Lausanne was justifying itself in the rising spirits of the group. "This is one of the loveliest spots on earth. The peace and quiet of this morning, with the lake, the mountains, the Hotel gardens full of spring flowers and a distant bell striking the hour are all beyond words. It is a kind of return from the frontier to civilization again."

The peace of Lausanne, as Frank confessed, was needed for frayed nerves as well as tired brains. Considering what sharp-edged individuals many of the commission were, they bore the attrition of each other's company rather well. But the speech and prejudices of Texas are not those of Oxford or London, and the habits of thought of a British Conservative are not those of a British Laborite or an American Democrat, and tension was inevitable. After some weeks of interrogating witnesses, the members could anticipate with boredom the kind of questions each colleague would ask. The two chairmen were judges who had been in the habit of controlling their courtrooms with a firm hand and felt their authority somewhat wounded by the free and easy equality assumed by their colleagues. Further, the two found each other rather hard to bear, and the American chairman was sometimes inclined to make the decisions of his compatriots a matter of personal loyalty. To the Americans, some of the British members seemed immovably pro-Arab in their sympathies; to the British, some of the Americans seemed naïvely ready to give the Jews whatever they wanted, regardless of the cost to the Arabs. Fortunately, the divisions in the committee were not generally along national lines. Crossman and Leggett often found themselves agreeing with the majority of the American group; Phillips and Aydelotte often lined up with the British majority. From time to time, after stormy sessions, any sort of unanimity seemed impossible, and the members went to bed in deep dejection. On these occasions, Sir Frederick Leggett was invaluable. He was a labor conciliator by profession, with a fund of experience of how to bring disputants to a compromise and a fund of humorous stories of how it had been done. The only unfailing method, he held, was to lock the disputants in a room together without food or drink.[13] In the present case, he suggested that it would be astonishing if twelve men with such different preconceptions did agree, and that the best way of writing their final report was to deal with factual matters first, where there was sure to be the most agreement, and formulate later the recommendations supposed to grow out of these facts. The commission followed his wise advice.

A Refuge for the Refugees

There were two main questions at Lausanne. The first and more immediate one was what to do about the displaced Jews; the second and long-range one, what regime to support for Palestine. On the first question agreement was quickly arrived at. "We recommend that 100,000 certificates be authorized immediately for the admission into Palestine of Jews who have been the victims of Nazi and Fascist persecution."[14] The commissioners knew that this would provoke an Arab storm. But three circumstances seem to have worked together in their minds to convince them that there was no alternative.

One was the overwhelming impression of misery that the visitors had brought back from the camps of Europe. The people in these camps were dominated by one passionate thought: to get away, to leave behind forever those who had murdered their families and their friends, to be at last among their own kind in a land of their own, even if it were a pile of rocks. "For the mass of Jewish Displaced Persons who had survived the massacre of war in concentration camps," says Norman Bentwich, "the initials 'D.P.' meant 'Destination Palestine.' "[15] Crum and Sir Frederick Leggett, who visited the American Zone in Germany, went first to Zeilsheim, where a poll had just been taken in the camps of the neighborhood, asking two questions: "Do you wish to remain in Europe? If not, where do you want to go?" Of 18,311 persons polled, 18,298 wanted to leave Europe, and 17,712 wanted to go to Palestine.[16] In another poll, Crum was told, the D.P.'s were asked to report a second choice if Palestine were not open to them, and hundreds wrote "Crematorium."

Who could blame them? This frantic desire to escape was the product of their misery, of betrayal by their communities, of the long-smoldering emotional aversion for the Jews that had spread through all central and eastern Europe and was blown into a conflagration by Hitler's demented hatred. Vienna was a city where many of the ablest representatives of the arts, the sciences, and commerce were Jews. It was reported to the commission that out of 152,000 persons in Vienna in 1942 who had professed the Jewish faith, only 4,000 were alive four years later.

The first and strongest consideration, then, that moved the commission to recommend that 100,000 refugees be admitted to Palestine at once was the sheer pitifulness of their plight. The second consideration was that no other country would take them. The Arabs pointed out that they had already done more for the Jews than any other country, that there were twelve times as many Jews on their territory in 1948 as in 1918. If President Truman was so much concerned about these people, why did he not push the American door at least slightly ajar? The answer came that the United States had a long-standing quota system for immigrants, and there was no hope of immediately changing it. The British, French, and Soviet empires had immense open spaces in Australia, Africa, and Siberia, but when any suggestion was made that they might be opened to Jews, these powers all looked in the other direction.

A third reason for the commission's action was what was happening in Palestine. Legally the British White Paper of 1939 was still in force, limiting immigration to an average of 15,000 per year over a period of five years. This the Palestinian Jews simply would not accept, law or no law; they had too many friends and relatives in the camps who were passionate to join them. Immediately after a speech by Foreign Secretary Bevin in the Commons announcing that the limitation would remain until the commission submitted its report, disorder amounting almost to chaos broke out in Palestine. The Jews throughout the country went on strike for twelve hours. At Tel Aviv a Jewish mob set government buildings on fire. The secret radio of Haganah, the illegal but powerful Jewish defense force, charged on the day after the speech: "What Hitler did in wiping out millions of our brethren is now being completed by the policy of the British government."[17] The Jewish extremist underground, organized in the Irgun and the Stern Gang, demanded open war on their British rulers. When four terrorists were caught and executed, sixty thousand citizens of Tel Aviv took part in their funeral. And both in Palestine and other countries adjoining the Mediterranean, Jewish communities bought or chartered vessels, large and small, to carry to the homeland groups of tattered, wandering Jews who had filtered down to the seacoasts. These refugees were landed stealthily at night along the Palestinian water front and vanished instantly into the Jewish population.

There was no way to stop all this short of civil war between the British governors of Palestine and their half-frenzied subjects. For such a war neither the governors nor the British people had any heart. They as well as the Americans were moved by Chaim Weizmann's words, "The leaky boats in which our refugees come to Palestine are their *Mayflowers*, the *Mayflowers* of a whole generation." The British governors had no stomach for their role of standing on the shore and pushing these pathetic boats away; it was a role imposed on them by the Arab majority of their subjects. As the commission said in its report, "Absolute, unqualified refusal of the Arabs to acquiesce in the admission of a single Jew to Palestine is the outstanding feature of Arab politics today."[18] The commission thought it was time the rulers as well as the refugees had some support.

Strains in the Commission

The dozen colleagues, holed up in the Beau Rivage, sighed in relief at finding themselves in agreement on the first of their problems. When they turned to the second—what recommendation to make as to the permanent future of Palestine—difference deep and emotional broke out at once, and at times the colleagues were hardly on speaking terms with one another. They had reached the point where they were dealing with values rather than facts, and the values they assigned to many factors involved—the interests of the Arabs, the needs of the Jews, the economic security of Britain, the importance of Western civilization in the Middle

East, and many others—were bound to be affected by their national loyalties and their personal likes and aversions. After a fortnight of Lausanne, Frank was writing, for Marie's eyes alone, some reflections on his colleagues.

> It is interesting to me that the British members of the Committee are much more individual than the Americans. Crum and Buxton support our Judge in whatever he says, and McDonald more or less goes along by the expedient of being more extreme than the Judge on the Jewish and anti-British side. Phillips and I maintain our independence and are freely accused by the Judge of disloyalty. On the British side Sir John Singleton and Manningham-Buller take the position of upholding the British administration in every respect. Crossman is opposed and agrees more or less with us. Leggett takes a line more or less parallel to Phillips and me. Lord Morrison is a little more anti-Jewish and Crick still more.

None of the commissioners was a Jew, and none, of course, an Arab; they were all in a sense outsiders, and that made for objectivity. Having all been brought up in a time when rational judgments in moral matters were considered to be more attainable than they now are, they started out with the assumption that there was a best course waiting to be found, however hard its discovery might be.

Nevertheless it looked for a time at Lausanne as if nothing less than three or four separate reports could express the mind of the group. The possibility loomed that McDonald would write a minority report endorsing the Jewish Agency almost *in toto*, but he was dissuaded, probably by the prospect that if he did, some of the English members would write another minority report in precisely the opposite sense. "Members were tired and belligerent and likely to magnify trifles," Frank noted. "Crossman, Manningham-Buller, Phillips and I have emphasized the importance of unity and of letting questions alone on which we cannot agree, partly in the interest of Anglo-American unity, partly for the sake of saving lives in Palestine." These efforts paid off. The commission was able in the end to write a report that was signed by every member.

From the outset at Lausanne it was clear to the members that no solution was possible that would do justice to all the parties. As Weizmann himself had remarked, the "just" solution was merely the one that was least unjust. Bartley Crum recalled that Wendell Willkie had once said to him after visiting the Middle East, "Bart, the Arabs have a good case in Palestine. There is only one thing wrong with it. The Jews have a better case." The commission approached the issue, as Willkie did, with the desire to weigh goods and evils against each other and a healthy skepticism of any glib solution. Palestine had become for them "a country of unlimited impossibilities."

The Palestine Alternatives

Looked at in the abstract, however, the possibilities could be numbered on one hand; in principle there were just four of them. Confronted by a country of two component and rival populations, like Palestine, and given freedom of proposal, as the commissioners were, what could they do with the country? They could turn it over to the Arab majority; this was what the Arab witnesses had insisted was the only democratic solution. Or they could give it to the Jewish minority; that was the vehement demand of Ben Gurion and the Zionists. Or they could break it in two, giving to each an appropriate part; that was the proposal of the group which, before the present one, had studied the situation most thoroughly, the Peel Commission. Or, finally, they could federate the two communities under a single government, somewhat after the manner of the Swiss cantons. There were apparently leanings within the committee toward each of these views, which meant that the utmost openness of mind and readiness to compromise were imperative. The group published their conclusions, but not the deliberations leading to them, which went on behind closed doors. But their discussion was evidently a process of elimination, and it is not too difficult to infer from the printed report what the main considerations were.

The Case for the Arabs

The case for giving the land to the Arabs was simple and formidable. They were in possession, and they had been so for twelve hundred years. Everywhere else the occupation of a land for twelve centuries would be taken as conferring an absolute title to it. The Jews claimed it, indeed, as their homeland. But how much respect would an Englishman pay to the claim of a group of Saxons to Dorset on the ground that it had been unjustly taken away from them as recently as 1066? What would an American say to a committee of Indians who argued that the present inhabitants should turn over Massachusetts on the ground that they had held it only since the seventeenth century? The Arabs were established in Palestine long before the Normans landed in England, long before

America was even heard of. The country was theirs by a title that their critics would not dream of impugning anywhere else.

Again, Palestine should be under Arab control by any fair interpretation of democracy. The Arabs at the end of the war represented about two-thirds of the people, the Jews one-third. On any issue between the two people, therefore, the Arabs would outvote the Jews about two to one. The complexion of the government was, of course, such an issue, and there was not the slightest doubt about the major Arab desire. They wanted to govern themselves. To impose on them the rule of an alien minority, or to force on them an immigration policy that would turn their majority into a minority, was the opposite of democracy, and for the democratic countries appointing the commission to take that line would be sheer hypocrisy.

To this it was often replied that it would be better for the Arabs if they would let the more progressive Jewish minority take charge and show them the way. Their reply was, Who is to judge what is better for us? We have our own standards, which by those of the westernized Jews are feudal standards. We admit that it is shocking to us to see Jewish women parading our streets in shorts and Jewish organizers attempting to replace our system—the rule of ancient and respected Arab families— by the leveling socialism of the Jewish kibbutzim. They say their ways are modern and ours are feudal, but we happen to like our ways and do not want them undermined. And whether they are better or not, we surely have a right to our own preferences. For anyone else to prescribe them to us is tyranny.

Furthermore, a Jewish state would be not only an imposition on the Arabs of Palestine but a standing threat to all the Arab states of the Middle-East. "No other subject," the commission wrote in its report, "has occupied so much the attention of the Arab League or has done so much to unite its membership as has the question of Palestine."[19] The country is an enclave in Arab territory; it is bound to the north, the east, and the south by Arab countries; and to place it in non-Arab hands would drive a wedge into the heart of the Arab League. This would not be so important if the Jews of Palestine represented only themselves. But the Arabs were convinced that this was not so; that the Jewish immigration was really the beachhead of a Western invasion; that behind it was the money of the Rothschilds, the drive of the American oil companies, all the technology and aggressiveness of an alien West that had never understood the Arabs or been interested in them. Azzam Pasha, the

Secretary-General of the Arab League, told the commissioners in Cairo that he did not object to the returning of Jews as Jews to Palestine; what he and his people objected to was their returing as "Westerners in disguise." "The Jew," he went on, "has returned a Russified Jew, a Polish Jew, a German Jew, an English Jew. He has turned back with a totally different conception of things; he has turned back a Westerner and not an Easterner."[20] He was the spearhead of a fundamentally hostile civilization.

The commissioners felt the force of the Arab case, and its appeal was strengthened by the personal impression made by the educated Arab witnesses. "The Arab intelligentsia," said Crossman in Cairo, "as I was to find later in Jerusalem, is intensely attractive to the educated Englishman. They have a French elegance of mind and of expression and are a fascinating mixture of cynical melancholy, shrewd business sense and ingenuous idealism. . . . The educated Arabs are people of immense interest and charm."[21] Through the Jewish witnesses were in the majority, no one could question that the Arabs had had a sympathetic hearing.

The Case for the Jews

Unfortunately for the peace of mind of the commissioners, and of everyone else who has faced this tortured issue, the case of the Jews seemed equally strong. Palestine had been officially promised to them as their national home. The promise had been given by the British government, which held the country by right of conquest in World War I. Its control and responsibility had been recognized by the League of Nations. The promise had the support of both English parties, of both houses of the American Congress, of a sequence of American Presidents. There was, of course, that tragic ambiguity in the meaning of "national home," but as Balfour had explained to Wise, it meant at least that the Jews could go there if they wished, and that meant in turn that they would almost certainly become a majority and gain political control.

And their case was far stronger in 1946 than it was in 1917, when the promise was first made. The great intervening fact had been the rise of Hitler. If the Jews needed a land of their own in 1917, that need had become overriding and desperate in 1946. Central Europe had become uninhabitable for them by reason of persecution; other countries closed the door on them; and even if the Palestinian Arab majority did not want them, the moral claim—the claim of needy and suffering humanity—

seemed to have gained a clear ascendancy over the merely legal case. This tiny piece of the vast Arab dominions had been the Jews' ancient home; it was identified with them in the thought of mankind; it was the land of their Temple, of Moses and the tables of the law, of David and Solomon, of the whole succession of Old Testament prophets. It was the one place toward which the Jews of the Diaspora, in every generation, had turned their eyes as to a land that was primitively and spiritually theirs, as the Greeks of the world turned toward Athens and the Moslems toward Mecca. "If I forget thee, O Jerusalem, let my right hand forget her cunning."

But the case was much stronger still. If the ancient Jews had laid the foundations of the Jewish claim, the modern Jews had fortified it enormously by what they had built on these foundations. To the English or American traveler, most of Palestine seems a barren stretch of rock and desert. For centuries, few people lived there, and it was supposed incapable of supporting many more. Montesquieu said sweepingly in his *Persian Letters*: "Since the destruction of Jerusalem by Hadrian, Palestine has been uninhabited."[22] Under Turkish rule, the Arab peasants cultivated their tiny patches of sandy soil with ox and camel, hoe and sickle, knowing nothing of irrigation and crop rotation, and the country was ridden with poverty, malaria, and exploitation by absentee landlords. One would have supposed that the last people to make anything out of this inhospitable land were the Jews, who were notoriously an urban people, seldom to be found on farms. But as Aydelotte noted repeatedly in his journal, the Zionist Jews were people with "a great idea." They were out to show themselves and the world that they could make their desert blossom like the rose, and, incredibly, they did it. In their kibbutzim men and women both worked hard on the soil. The immigrants built water towers, turned pools and swamps into reservoirs, dammed the Jordan to produce electric power, planted millions of forest and citrus trees, started agricultural colleges for women as well as men, and exploited the Dead Sea for its chemicals. Oxen were replaced by Western tractors and bulldozers. Skycrapers shot up in Tel Aviv and Haifa, and modern hotels were constructed to accommodate the stream of devotees visiting the ancient shrines. These were almost entirely Jewish enterprises. "Everywhere," the commissioners noted, "is to be seen a marked disparity between the standards of living, however measured, of the Arab and Jewish communities. Jewish wages are consistently higher than Arab, those for unskilled labor being more than twice as high."[23] Though the

Arabs had many just grounds of complaint about their treatment, they were economically better off than before the Jewish influx.

To these economic achievements must be added another which undoubtedly strengthened the Jewish claim, though in a more nebulous way. The Jews stood on a higher plateau of civilization and culture than the Arab world about them. Balfour no doubt had this in mind when he made the Declaration. "The Jews," he said, "are among the most gifted races. They have great material aptitudes, great intellectual talents, but only one ideal, to return to Zion. By depriving them of that ideal, the world has diminished their virtues and stimulated their defects. If we can help them to attain that ideal, we shall restore them their dignity."[24] "Here, indeed," said the commission, "is a miracle both of physical achievement and of spiritual endeavor, which justifies the dreams of those Jews and Gentiles who first conceived the idea of the National Home."[25] Writing shortly before the appearance of the commission report, the Palestine correspondent of *The London Times* commented in a leading article: "There is little civilized here today that has not been brought about or developed by the Jews."[26] They built a university in Jerusalem where many of the leading scholars of the world have lectured. The Jerusalem symphony orchestra compares not unfavorably with those of great cities of the West. Jewish archaeologists have been reconstructing heroic passages of the nation's past from the ruins of Masada, and Jewish scholars have been interpreting the Dead Sea Scrolls. A Hebrew Encyclopaedia, on the lines of the Britannica, has been published, and "amongst the original subscribers were five hundred bus-drivers, members of a transport co-operative."[27] With the help of Western science, the old scourge of malaria has been largely eliminated; clean and efficient modern hospitals have been erected in the cities; a Sick Fund, somewhat like the American Blue Cross and employing hundreds of doctors and nurses, had 700,000 persons eligible for its services by 1950, and in that year the child mortality of Israel was reported as the lowest in the world.[28] In most Arab countries the majority of the people are illiterate; in Egypt the rate is 73 per cent, in Iraq, 85 per cent, in Morocco 86 per cent, in Iran 87 per cent.[29] On the other hand, the commission found that "practically every Jewish child has the opportunity for primary education, and those who can afford the fees have ample opportunity for technical, secondary and university education in Palestine."[30]

This cultural superiority of Jew to Arab is no accident. It is rooted in the Jewish respect for the things of the mind, which for many centuries has been ingrained in the Jewish tradition. In spite of the cold shoulder that the Jews have so often received in the Western countries, they have contributed to the cultural achievement of those countries in an amount quite out of proportion to their numbers. The great revolutions of the last century in politics, in psychology, and in physical science have been fathered by Jews: Marx, Freud, and Einstein. In philosophy this extraordinary people has produced Bergson, Husserl, Alexander, Buber, the German and American Cohens, Carnap, Reichenbach, Ayer, and Schlick. They produced Ehrlich in medicine, Michelson and Oppenheimer in physics, Haber in chemistry, Namier in history, Heifetz, Rubinstein, Menuhin, and Horowitz in music, Chagall, Pissarro, Rothenstein, and Epstein in art. "Suffering is the badge of all our tribe," said Shylock; and when one recalls how much of it has been due to ignorant racial disdain, one reads with pleasure the retort of Disraeli to a Briton who taunted him with his descent, that when his critic's ancestors were savages painting themselves blue with woad in their primitive forests, his own ancestors were writing the Proverbs and the Psalms.

Of course, the argument that all this creates a title to ownership or control is a dangerous one, forming a stock weapon in the armory of colonialism. It can be justly used only as a supplement to other considerations and even then only when the superior culture shows a spirit of *noblesse oblige*. And it has to be admitted that the Jews have shown too little of this spirit. One member of the commission, after visiting an orthodox kibbutz and talking at length with its leaders, wrote: "Hard as I tried, I did not discover any trace of serious thought on the real problem of getting on with the Arabs. They seemed to assume that the Jews had the right to the country and that the Arabs were inferior people whom the Jews, when they got their state, would tolerate and permit to exist as a minority."[31] It is this arrogance in many Jews, with the resulting sense among the Arabs of being second-class citizens, people of the ghetto, in what they regard as their own land, that has been the worm at the core of Palestine and the chief cause of the enduring hatred of Arab for Jew. The Jews, who have suffered so much from being ghettoized in other countries, have not shown, in their treatment of the Arabs, that they have adequately learned the lesson of this experience. The commission was frequently irritated further by the claim of Jewish witnesses that they should have all the rights and privileges of their British or American citizenship while also professing allegiance to their own country overseas, which might, of course, come into conflict with their other country. The Jews have exhibited genius in many forms, but, sadly enough, one of the commonest forms is the genius for getting themselves disliked.

The commission members tried not to let these irritations infect their judgment. They asked themselves whether the Jews had exhibited such gifts on the one hand, and such contributions to the country on the other, as to justify special consideration. On both counts the commission thought they had. On the consideration to be accorded to gifts of intellect and energy one could predict Frank Aydelotte's stand. He was not a democrat, if that meant democracy in the field of values , which he would have called a contradiction in terms; and he had no doubt that the education, the science, the standards of health, the music and art that the Jews had imported into the Middle East were an enormous advance over what its people had known before. He wrote:

> Curiously enough, my own views have changed. I left Washington pretty strongly anti-Zionist and very much of Lessing Rosenwald's opinion. But when you see at first hand what these Jews have done in Palestine, you cannot vote to destroy it. They are making, in my opinion, the greatest creative effort in the modern world. I am against a Jewish state but all for letting the Jews have a free chance to continue their material and cultural work. The Arabs do not understand it, are not equal to anything like it, and would destroy all that the Jews have done and are doing if they had the power. This we must not let them do.

Did the group arrogance of the Jews confine the benefits of their achievement to their own people alone? The commission thought not, though they wished the Zionists were less nationalistic. The most articulate member of the commission, Crossman, probably spoke for many besides himself when he wrote:

> The choice was between two injustices, and we had to decide which injustice was the lesser. Looking at the position of the Palestinian Arab, I had to admit that no Western colonist in any other country had done so little harm [as the Jew] or disturbed so little the life of the indigenous people. Arab patriotism and Arab self-respect had been deeply affronted and would continue to be affronted by the development of the national home; but if I believed in social progress, I had to admit that the Jews had set going revolutionary forces in the Middle East which, in the long run, would benefit the Arabs. It was by reacting to the Zionist invader that the Arab was learning to fend for himself in an industrial world.[32]

Partition or Neutral Government?

The arguments, then, for a Jewish Palestine seemed to be as persuasive as those for an Arab Palestine. But both demands obviously could not be satisfied. It had been the conclusion of the Peel Commission in its weighty report of nine years earlier that the two claims were so strong, yet so clearly incompatible, that the only rational course was to break the country in two and give to each community a small but separate and sovereign state. There were practical difficulties in drawing such a line between such communities, as was tragically shown in India a few years later, but the Peel Commission offered maps to show that the line could be drawn without mass injustice to either side.

Crossman went back to this Peel Report and attempted to persuade his colleagues that the present commission, like the earlier one, should come out for partition. He did not succeed. Why? Primarily because the proposal implied that amity and cooperation between the two peoples was impossible, and the majority of the members could not get themselves to accept this. The root of Arab animosity against the Jew was the cultural disparity between the two peoples. Partition was more likely to crystallize this disparity than to remove it. The minority in each country would still be repressed; the hatred between the two new nations would continue; each would feel insecure in the presence of the other's enmity; each, therefore, would build up armaments, spending for defense sums urgently needed for education and health; and at the end of the vista would probably lie war.

Other alternatives failing, the commission concluded that what was imperative was the sort of government control which, without canceling Jewish energy or hope, would gradually raise the Arabs to the level of their Jewish neighbors and thus cut the root of hatred. This purpose would not be served either by a Jewish or by an Arab Palestine or by either half of a divided Palestine. It must be achieved, if at all, by a neutral government sufficiently powerful to keep the peace while the injustices suffered by each side, and more particularly by the Arabs, were little by little rectified. What government should that be? The only reasonable choice was the present mandatory, whose conduct of the government should be under the trusteeship of the United Nations.

In the month at Lausanne the colleagues talked themselves into unanimity on most of the larger issues. They drafted a report that made ten recommendations. It would be tedious to recite these. The main ones were the immediate admission of 100,000 immigrants, the refusal to turn the country, or the half of it, over to either party, the continuation of the mandate, and the insistence that the mandatory power concern itself above all with removing the educational and economic gap that divided the two peoples. On the important issue of future immigration the members were unable to agree, so their recommendation was left vague. "The possibility of the country sustaining a largely increased population at a decent standard of living depends on its economic future," and it was to be left to the mandatory power to decide whether at any given moment the absorptive limit of the country had been reached.

While Frank Aydelotte thought the recommendations of the report were sound, he was not very happy about its form. "Most of it," he confided to his journal, "is pretty carelessly written and can hardly stand comparison with the well written Peel report. I tried to do my part of it better, but most of our members are very slow to realize the importance of good English. They really cannot tell the difference between good English and bad." But this was the explosion of a testy moment; some of his colleagues, Crossman, for example, wrote very well indeed. At the end, everyone was in high spirits. Frank wrote on Saturday, April 20,

> Well, the great report was signed by us all at 8:30 this morning. I was up at 6:30 and went over it from 7:00 to 8:00 for a final check. I am so pleased with it that I think our agreement little short of a miracle. . . . After the signing we six Americans gathered in the Judge's room to congratulate him and each other and to wish him a safe journey home. It may be the excitement of the moment, but some of our members think we have produced a great report. The Judge's voice broke as he made us a little farewell speech. The satisfaction that we all feel and the relief that the long grind is over are more than I can express. . . . We have been working under the dark shadow of possible civil war in Palestine, with the loss of thousands of Jewish, Arab and British lives, and that fact has done something to weaken merely personal prejudices. But it still remains a miracle that twelve such different individuals from two countries should have made an agreed report and that that report should be as good as it is.

Homeward Bound

Two original copies of the report were typed, one for the President and one for the Prime Minister. Judge Hutcheson flew off that very day to carry one of them to Mr. Truman, and Sir John Singleton to take the other to Mr. Attlee, both of them happy in being able to submit the report within the limit of a hundred and twenty days that had been set for them. Next day was Easter Sunday, but Frank put it to use by traveling to Zurich by train and discussing with Wolfgang Pauli the possibility of his returning to Princeton. Frank was due to leave Geneva by plane the next morning, but was delayed for a full day by bad weather. He spent Monday evening at "a sentimental and lugubrious French movie of the kind they love—good for my French but hard on me otherwise." Whenever he left his room, he was anxious about his copy of the precious report. "With all the journalists about, it is impossible to feel easy about this document until Truman and Attlee make it public. The sooner they do that the better. I don't feel too sure that Drew Pearson may not have had the substance of it yesterday." He locked it in his brief case and locked the brief case in his wardrobe.

He was due to leave Lausanne early in the morning of Easter Monday. After a delay of twenty-four hours, he got away on Tuesday, reaching Shannon, Ireland, in the evening. The plane was supposed to take off again in an hour, but owing to a report of bad weather over the north Atlantic, it was grounded, and Frank was taken to a hotel at Ennis, sixteen miles away. "Rooms with baths are, of course, non-existent. I felt the sheets in my room, they were cold and damp; evidently the room had not been used for some time, and I don't suppose it has been heated since 1939." Next morning there was a steady cold drizzle; the travelers waited for word till noon and were then told that they would have to spend another night in the hotel. On Thursday morning they were roused at five o'clock in order to make an eight-o'clock departure from Shannon. Something was wrong with an engine, which required two further hours of work. When the plane reached Gander in Newfoundland, it was reported that the weather was unfavorable in New York, and the weary travelers spent the night in a barrack. Frank finally reached LaGuardia Field on Friday afternoon. The strenuous adventure was over. He had reflected about it during the long waits for his plane. "I am . . . oh so glad to be on my way home. I thought a little of chucking the whole thing in London when I was all alone in bed in the Hyde Park Hotel feeling very rotten, with C. K. and the doctor urging me to do just that. I never really could have chucked it, and if I had done so I should have missed one of the great experiences of my life."

The Response in the West

Having put so much thought and labor into their report, the commissioners waited impatiently for the public reaction to it. It was released on May 1, and *The Times* of London carried that day an editorial of cautious approval: "An attempt has been made to lift the issues above the current partisan contentions of those who support and those who oppose the Zionist creed, and to treat them in a spirit of impartial justice." Next day *The Times* lumbered into a more positive position. "The more closely the report is studied, the clearer becomes the conviction that the solution envisaged should commend itself to responsible sections of public opinion in every country. Those who criticize the report may be fairly asked for their alternatives." The *Nation* of New York, not usually easy to please, carried an article of hearty praise, calling the report "an extremely able document—thorough, comprehensive, sympathetic, and fair."

But the American and British heads of state, in announcing receipt of the document, both struck jarring notes. To President Truman what stood out in it was less the proposals for a permanent solution in Palestine than the endorsement of his request for a quota of refugees, and in his shout of welcome over this, the other proposals were faintly heard. Prime Minister Attlee, who presented the substance of the report to the Commons on May 1, gave it a disappointingly qualified welcome. He and Mr. Bevin, who was at the moment in Paris, had apparently hoped for a different kind of recommendation, one that would have enabled Britain to leave Palestine altogether and would thus have helped her to get off an increasingly painful hook. No doubt they hoped, too, that if the commission did not see its way to such a policy, it would at least recommend that the United States share the military burden in Palestine. Since the commission did neither, Mr. Attlee felt cornered and baffled. If he admitted the 100,000 immigrants, the whole Arab community would be at his throat. If he did not admit them, the Jewish community, which was already seething with revolt, might become unmanageable except by a large British army of occupation. Hence in presenting the report to the Commons, his words of thanks to the commissioners were quickly followed by an ominous qualification: "It is clear from the facts presented in the report regarding the illegal armies maintained in Palestine, and their recent activities, that it would not be possible for the government of Palestine to admit so large a body of immigrants unless and until these formations have been disbanded and their arms surrendered."

The Response in the East

If the British government's response was tepid, there was little that was either tepid or temperate in the response in Palestine. When the terms of the report were known, an immediate din of protest rose from both sides. Here and there in the din, a quiet Jewish voice could be heard giving its approval; for example, those of Frank's respected friend Judah Magnes and of Norman Bentwich. But Bentwich, while giving his support, admitted sadly: "There are no half-tones in the register of vision of the Semitic peoples. All is extreme and superlative."[33] Each side tended to see in the recommendations only the denial of something to which it was utterly committed. The Jews wanted a nation, a sovereign Hebrew homeland, and it was clearly being refused to them. The Arabs wanted an end, immediate and final, to the tide that threatened to engulf them, and here was a cool announcement that the tide would continue to pour in. If these hopes were to be thwarted, nothing that the commission could add in the way of promise or qualification, no guarantees to the Jews of security and freedom, no pleas to the Arabs for refugees who must find a home here or nowhere, seemed to the heated partisans anything but contemptible evasions.

They acted accordingly. The Arab Higher Committee immediately called a general twelve-hour strike to protest the report. The Arab newspapers rejected the recommendations of the commission *in toto*. A hastily called meeting of the Pan-Arab organization in Cairo declared that "a revolt throughout the Islamic and Arab east would follow any attempt to put them into effect." Die-hard pan-Arabs called for a jihad, or holy war, to wrest back Palestine from the infidel. "In Jerusalem the Arab temper flared most angrily. A mob surged from the Mosque of Omar, shouted, 'Death to the Americans and British!' and stoned a column of Tommies. . . . Tanks rumbled up to the Damascus Gate. The 100,000 British troops in the Holy Land were alerted."[34]

The response of the Jews was even more violent. Haganah, the formidable underground army of the Jews, estimated at eighty thousand and enlisting the secret support of most of the Jewish community, began to blow up the radar stations erected by the British to detect the approach of illegal ships; they wrecked bridges linking the country with Syria and Transjordan; they kidnaped six British officers and held them as hostages for the safety of captured Irgun gunmen. Early in July, the British Governor-General, Sir Alan Cunningham, seized the headquarters of the Jewish Agency, the nearest thing to a Jewish government in

Palestine, and rounded up a thousand Jews suspected of making trouble. Thirty-one of them were convicted of carrying firearms and sentenced to fifteen years' imprisonment. Such severity seemed only to intensify the violence on the other side. Before the month was out, the King David Hotel in which Frank Aydelotte and his colleagues had stayed was blown up by Jewish terrorists with the loss of ninety-one lives.

And still the refugees poured in. The British, hating the whole business, sent the cruiser *Ajax*, famous for running down the *Graf Spee* in the war, to the Palestine coast with other ships to cut the immigrants off. Two small sailing craft, called from their condition "floating sewers" and carrying 1,286 immigrants, were intercepted and their miserable human cargo shipped to concentration camps in Cyprus. A thousand Jews, swarming toward the harbor where the incomers hoped to land, found it surrounded with barbed wire and tried, despite a British warning, to crash through. The troops opened fire on them, killing three and wounding seven. Cunningham turned the screws tighter. He threw a cordon round the entire city of Tel Aviv and had every house searched. He invaded the Great Synagogue itself, the largest in Palestine, and beneath it unearthed a cache of weapons, ammunition, counterfeiting equipment, and $800,000 worth of forged bonds. The British and the Jews were on the verge of open war.

Defeat

The commissioners read these things in the newspapers with sinking spirits. Their plan depended in the last resort on the recognition by both Jews and Arabs that their interests would be promoted by it and on their cooperation in making it work. If either of them refused to cooperate, there was no hope, and now they were both refusing.

President Truman was determined, however, that his recommendation regarding the refugees should be put into effect, and he appointed a three-man committee of his Cabinet, Byrnes (State), Patterson (War), and Snyder (Treasury), to see it through. Obviously this part of the report could not be carried out by itself, and the American Cabinet members accordingly arranged to meet with a similar group from the British Cabinet to consider what to do. They concluded jointly that to force the 100,000 refugees upon a hostile Arab majority was impracticable and that there was now nothing for it but to return to the view of the Peel Commission that the country should be broken up. They recommended a division into three domains, to be under the respective control of the Jews, the Arabs, and the British, who were to retain a sort of trusteeship for Jerusalem. Herbert Morrison explained the plan to the British Parliament, and Winston Churchill rumbled that if America declined to concur in it and to help enforce it, Britain should wash its hands of the whole distasteful business and dump it into the lap of the newly formed United Nations. When the plan was presented to the American Cabinet with Secretary Byrnes' support, it was voted down in a stormy session in which the opposition was led by Henry Wallace.

This last little fact is significant. Wallace had moved far to the left and was finding the promise of the new Russia strangely attractive. And the Russian policy in the Near East, though not much advertised, was one of steady pressure against the hopes of the Jews to become a nation and against America and Britain as their friends. Molotov and his office took little stock in compassion as a national motive. They knew the value of the Arab oil fields to the Western powers; they saw in Zionism a Western pawn pushed as far east as possible; and they were determined to stiffen the Arab resistance by all available means. While Wallace and American liberals were hailing the Russian achievement in the war and drinking toasts to Russian-American friendship, the Russians were trying to destroy the influence of their recent allies in the Middle East. This came out clearly in August, when Professor Victor Lutsky of the Palestine Desk of the Soviet Foreign Office declared (1) that Zionism was really an imperialist-capitalist campaign to set up in Palestine a bourgeois state, (2) that its ideals did not have the support of the Jewish masses, and (3) that Palestine did and should belong to the Arabs. Whereas the British and American people regarded their assistance to the unhappy Jews as a work of mercy, the strategists of Moscow regarded it as imperialist aggression.

The Rest Is History

What if the recommendations worked out so laboriously and earnestly by Aydelotte and the commission had been given a chance in Palestine? One can never say with certainty what would have happened if what did happen had not happened; and considering that Palestine was a compound of so many volatile elements, prediction about it can hardly be more than conjecture. But in the light of what took place in the twenty years that followed, one can only think that the Arabs would have been well advised to accept the plan. The Jews might have been persuaded to accept it. The Irgun and Stern Gang, who perpetrated the worst atrocities, were fanatical irregulars, not the representatives of the Jewish people; such leaders as Chaim Weizmann, who was friendly to Britain, had far more general respect. But the Arabs, who had more to gain by the terms of the report than the Jews, worked their own ruin by their intransigence. They insisted on seeing in Britain an enemy instead of their chief protector against the formidably efficient Jewish nationalism. And when it became clear to the British that they would have to go on fighting not only the Jewish minority but also the Arab majority, they at last concluded that they had had enough. They announced in 1947 that they would terminate their mandate on May 15, 1948, wipe their hands of Palestine, and bring the Tommies home.

The rest is history, falling beyond the story of the commission. Suffice it to say that even before the British withdrew, both sides were looking forward to the now inevitable war, the Jews preparing to set up their state, the surrounding Arab nations to drive the Jews into the sea. The war occupied the last half of 1948. By the end of the year the Arabs were everywhere routed and the Jews at last in firm possession of their state. The new country of Israel was admitted to the United Nations on May 11, 1949, but still with the flat refusal of all her Arab neighbors to recognize her existence. She overran the Gaza Strip and the Sinai Peninsula in 1956, but gave them back to Egypt under U.N. pressure. In 1967 the Arab nations, led by Nasser of Egypt, thought the time for vengeance had finally come. They closed the Gulf of Aqaba and massed their armies on Israel's borders. This time embattled Jews took, not six months, but six days to settle their accounts, and the war was a re-enactment of the Jewish legend of David and Goliath. Under the plan of the commission, the Arabs of Palestine would have been given a share in the modernity that Jewish skill and energy were bringing to their country. They were too proud to accept it on the terms offered. Three wars later they found their last state worse than their first.

CHAPTER SEVENTEEN

THE QUIET YEARS

SERVICE on the Anglo-American Commission was the last important work that Frank Aydelotte undertook. He was sixty-six—not truly old by current reckoning or by his own feeling; indeed, only a man who was pretty sound of wind and limb could have run the gauntlet of those months of broken nights, strange and irregular meals, and interminable anxious discussions. He came home with many plans for the Institute which he had had to lay aside because of the war and was now eager to put into effect.

In this he was handicapped by lack of time. The war had been unkind to him. Its beginning had virtually coincided with his coming to the Institute, and now that the war and the commission were over he had only a year to go. The Board had power to extend his term if it wished, but it had already delayed his retirement from sixty-five to sixty-seven, and he would not ask or hint a further extension. He told himself that he would welcome retirement. But in his heart he would have welcomed still more an appeal to stay long enough to carry through some of the plans the war had vetoed. When the Board showed no interest in this and looked round urgently for a successor, he was secretly disappointed. The hurt was not wholly rational, but neither is human nature. At sixty-seven he found himself on the shelf, which is the last place where a man of his temperament could sit in comfort. His connection with the Institute was not severed completely, for he continued as a Trustee and still kept a small office where he went daily to deal with his correspondence. He had long held the conviction that when an executive is out, he should stay out and not come back like a shade to haunt his successor; and he acted accordingly. He was succeeded in the fall of 1947 by J. Robert Oppenheimer, the distinguished physicist who had developed the atomic bomb at Los Alamos. Frank and Marie remained in their house on Battle Road, and Mr. and Mrs. Oppenheimer kindly saw to it that though the official ties were broken, the social ties remained firm.

Reunion at Princeton

Frank's closing months at the Institute were brightened by the sort of occasion he reveled in: a reunion of Rhodes Scholars. When the American Rhodes men had last met at Swarthmore in 1933, they resolved on another reunion in five years, but this was abandoned under the cloud of impending war, and it was fourteen years before they assembled again. Two hundred and twenty-two of them, many accompanied by their wives, came to Princeton in June, 1947, almost feeling themselves in Oxford as they wandered in ivied quadrangles and saw the moon come up from behind the Graduate College tower, which has seemed to many a tranplanted Magdalen. It is no small task to organize the housing, feeding, recreation, and conferences for such a meeting, and the Aydelottes, loyally aided by the weather, won general praise for their unobtrusive but meticulous arrangements. Lord Elton said to the assembled scholars: "It has been an inspiration to see for the first time at close quarters what I should have called the magnificent machine of the American Rhodes Scholarships, were it not that any metaphor drawn from the mechanical must do much less than justice to the all-persuasive kindliness and humanity of Frank Aydelotte's administration."[1]

That such praise was well grounded came out clearly in the reunion business meeting, which was held in a hall of the Institute. A question much in the minds of the Rhodes Scholars was how the new district plan, a scheme of Frank's devising, was working out. The plan had involved breaking the country into eight districts and appointing the best men from each district rather than the best man from each state, and there had been some feeling that this was an invasion of states' rights. Frank presented a report in which, for the first time, it was possible to answer the main questions statistically. It was true some of the educationally weaker states had gained very few appointments under the new plan. On the other hand, Frank was able to show that on a population basis, the plan had awarded more scholarships to small states than to large ones. On the most important question of all, whether the new system was getting better men, he produced evidence that for anyone who believed in Oxford's own tests could only be decisive. In the period from 1904 to 1930, the percentage of American Rhodes men who had gained First or Second Classes at Oxford was 61.97, a disappointing performance. In the period since the district plan had gone into effect the percentage had risen to 81.56, a most impressive leap. The Americans and Canadians, whose scores were the same, were consistently below the Australians and above the South Africans. They should no doubt have been better, but the advance they had achieved over the appointees of the older system was so marked that there has never since been a serious proposal to reinstate that system.

In 1947 the war was still in everyone's mind, and many of the Scholars had only lately returned from service. The youngest of them, Nicholas Katzenbach, gave a modest speech, describing how he had used his time in a German prison camp to study toward his Princeton degree and his later Rhodes appointment (he has since served as Attorney-General and Under Secretary of State). R. P. Brandt (Missouri and Lincoln, '18), a former president of the Gridiron Club, of Washington, reminded his colleagues of the increasing part of Rhodes men in the government; there were already a hundred and fifty of them in and about the capitol. Francis Miller (New York and Trinity, '19) told what was known of the German Rhodes Scholars who had worked in the anti-Nazi underground; at least three had been involved in the plot against Hilter and had been executed. The assembled scholars accepted as both right and characteristically British Lord Elton's announcement that "the names of all those who fell in this war will shortly be added to the memorial of the rotunda at Rhodes House, and, as before, those of the German Rhodes Scholars will be among them."[2]

The British Ambassador, Lord Inverchapel, addressed the company at their formal dinner and discussed what Rhodes would have thought of the new commonwealth that had replaced the British empire. He admitted that Rhodes was an out-and-out imperialist who was capable, at least in his youth, of wild and irresponsible ambitions. At the age of twenty-four he made

> that almost unbelievable first will, under which Britain, in almost Hitlerian style, was to colonize the world and so establish a power so overwhelming that wars would cease on the earth. Britons were to settle the whole of Africa, South America, large portions of the Middle East, Cyprus, Crete, various Pacific Islands, Malaya, and the Chinese and Japanese coastlines. They were to proceed to colonize the United States and, having revoked the Declaration of Independence, to complete the process.[3]

Rhodes's attitude toward native Africans remained to the end that of a paternal imperialist; "the native," he said flatly, "is to be treated as a child," and he would have looked with skepticism at the attempts at self-government of the new African republics. But in the matter of his will, which he revised and rerevised, the years brought to this strange man a riper judgement. The will in its final form, while still far-ranging in conception, was much more realistic in its provisions and contented itself with trying to bring about better understanding between Britain, the United States, and Germany. As regards Germany, it failed. As regards Britain and America, it was an extraordinary sucess.

The most moving speech of the reunion, however, was undoubtedly that of Lord Elton, the new Secretary of the Rhodes Trust, whom most of his American auditors were hearing for the first time. Elton's effortless eloquence was often touched with poetic feeling, and when such a speaker had Oxford as his theme—even the worried and overcrowded postwar Oxford—his words were bound to take wings. "The under-graduates," said Elton,

> as elsewhere, are older than usual, and thanks to our conscription are likely to remain so. And oddly enough, the chief complaint of their tutors is that they are too conscientious and work too hard. This is possibly a complaint which few members of my distinguished audience were accustomed to hear from their instructors in their own undergrad-uate days, but it is not unnatural that veterans should take themselves and the bleak post-war world somewhat seriously. But all these are temporary characteristics. The essential Oxford is ageless—unchangeable and un-changed. Long after we are forgotten punts will nose along the banks of Cherwell under showers of falling hawthorn blossom in May, and in the Colleges, talk as uninhibited as any in the world will range everything in heaven and earth, while clock after clock strikes midnight across the silent city.[4]

Routine of the Later Years

With the reunion over, Frank could devote the summer to winding up his affairs at the Institute, and in October he handed over his post to Oppenheimer. His work with the Rhodes Trust and the Guggenheim Foundation continued. But it soon became clear that the seemingly inexhaustible reservoir of energy that he could once draw on so confi-dently was lowering its level. A slow hardening of the arteries had set in, and he found that while fresh and clearheaded in the morning, he tired rapidly and had to keep shortening his working day. It was more difficult to focus his thought, more difficult to come to those quick intuitive decisions that he had formerly found so easy and so exhilarating.

The present writer remembers being called into conference with him in New York in 1950 or 1951 about the Eastman chair at Oxford. He looked much as ever, and the "weather of his soul," his sunny, affectionate *joie de vivre*, was unchanged, but there were unwontedly long silences in which his thought seemed to have drifted to far-off things. He would take the *Times*, that voracious consumer of mornings, to the office with him, but instead of dispatching it in minutes, as he once did, would linger over it musingly while decisions and secretaries waited. The increasing vagueness of that sharp and alert mind was noted with concern by his friends.

One humble friend, whose devotion was unaffected by any change, he lost early. This was his Great Dane, Canute. He enjoyed being welcomed by the deep-chested bay of this huge warden of Olden Manor, who would bound out to meet him when he came home and plant his great paws on Frank's shoulders in elephantine greeting. Dogs and their masters are sometimes alleged to be alike, and if Canute had not had a generous share of his master's pleasant disposition, he would have been in the eyes of the neighbors too much like the hound of the Baskervilles to be allowed at large. The devotion between master and henchman was wholehearted and reciprocal. Unhappily when Canute was four years old, he caught some sort of infection that was beyond remedy. Frank took him to a veterinary surgeon, asked that he be put painlessly to sleep, waited till the injection took effect, and went home with the sad sense that he had lost the most unquestioning of all his friends.

Frank's habits in these years remained much as before. He had been able in 1946 to give the inaugural address of his good friend Gilbert White at Haverford, but the abrupt and strenuous expeditions to give Commencement addresses and chair educational conferences were now steadily cut down. Fortunately he was not worried about money, for his astute business advisers at Swarthmore had given such prudent counsel about investments that his old age was secure. The summers he spent in his attractive little house in Waterford, Connecticut, with its lawns running down to the Sound, and he was able to spend a month or two of each winter in Florida. In these later years his southern Mecca was Lake Wales, where his friend Henry Turner placed a comfortable cottage at his disposal. A special charm for him about Lake Wales was that it was the headquarters of the Highland Park Club, a group of Quaker golfers of whom he was always a leading spirit while among them. Of a Sunday morning these substantial men of business would go to the early Quaker meeting and worship in silence and sincerity. But there was nothing grim about their Quakerism, and immediately after the meeting they would be off to the links together for eighteen holes of golf and greenery. Frank preferred a fast game. His friend Claude Smith said of him that he played the game just as he lived, gloriously and rapidly; and he recalled that when Frank once invited a fellow golfer to do a round with him in the morning, beginning at nine o'clock in the interest of an engagement at 11:45, the invitee declined, saying, "I do not choose to run." On the course at Lake Wales when Frank was seventy-three, he made a hole in one and received an ovation at dinner in the club house; he was as pleased as a small boy over a home run.

Frank was perhaps closer to the Friends after leaving Swarthmore than before. He was now a member of the Society, and he regularly attended the tiny meeting in Princeton. For some years after his arrival there, the meeting was held in a room granted by the university but Frank changed this practice by a characteristic venture in persuasion. There was an old meetinghouse on the borders of the town belonging to a group of very conservative Friends who were making no regular use of it. Frank went to see the leading members of this group and suggested to them that their meetinghouse would serve a larger purpose if it were made over to the Princeton Friends as a permanent place of worship. After discussing the matter among themselves they acceded to the proposal, though with some misgivings about the sort of views that would find utterance there. The little meeting house was duly done over, and the Princeton Friends had a home of their own. Frank was a regular attendant and spoke when he felt moved to do so, as at Swarthmore; but some of the meetings, and those not the least profitable, were held in unbroken silence.

He kept to his daily routine, though the hours were less crowded than before. He was up at 7:30, had breakfast at 8:30, and walked to his office. After lunch he liked a bit of golf, if it was only a round of putting or practice driving. The home on Battle Road remained a hospitable place, with frequent guests for dinner, for the night, or for the weekend. Frank would attend an occasional concert or listen for a while to music on the radio, but he had no marked ear or love for music, and though he had held for years a box at the Philadephia Orchestra, his support for it was rather a civic gesture than an expression of personal taste. When no guests were on hand, he liked to retire early to his room and read himself to sleep. He had a wide range of literary appetite, and though not a particularly rapid reader, he was good at getting the gist of a book by skimming it. His interest in English essayists remained keen, but surrounded as he was by scientists in his Princeton days, he felt it imperative to follow them as best he could. Scientists with a gift for semipopular exposition like Eddington and Jeans were a much appreciated help, but when it came to the uncompromising "pros" like von Neumann and Einstein, Weyl and Gödel, he was left far behind. He had done little in mathematics, and to appraise the significance of such people he had to take counsel. Still, of the art of taking counsel he was a master.

Marie

In 1952 the tenor of this quiet life was shatteringly broken. Frank was a delegate to the Friends' World Conference in Oxford, and in June he and Marie set out happily by air. Marie had never flown before. She was a little apprehensive about the flight, as most people are about a first adventure of this kind, but so far as health was concerned, there seemed to be no ground for anxiety. She was a Christian Scientist, and her faith had done a good deal to relieve illnesses from which she had suffered from childhood—illnesses that in the currency of a later day would probably be called psychosomatic. Frank was grateful for what her belief had done for her, though he could not subscribe to it himself and had insisted that she have an occasional medical check, which she submitted to by way of gratifying him. The transatlantic flight went off without incident. Lord Elton met them at the London airport and drove them to Oxford, where they were greeted with friendly warmth by the Allens and established at Rhodes House. They were delighted, as always, to be in Oxford again, and their pleasure was the greater because their son William, on a research visit to England, was staying at the time at the Athenaeum in London. Marie talked gaily with him that evening by telephone.

When Frank, on waking next morning, called to Marie, she did not answer. He went to her bedside, saw that something was gravely wrong, and called down the stairs to Dorothy Allen to come at once. Dorothy came and knew immediately what had happened. She called a doctor, but nothing could be done. Marie had died in her sleep.

Frank was in a daze. The vagueness from which he was suffering deepened; it was as if he did not quite realize the tragedy that had overtaken him or know how to cope with it. William came down from

London, and with the help of Oxford friends a simple Christian Science ceremony was arranged, attended by the family's closest friends in England, Sir Francis and Lady Wylie, Sir Carleton and Lady Allen, and Lord and Lady Elton. Frank and Marie had agreed that cremation was to be preferred to burial, and her body was accordingly cremated at Oxford. Her ashes returned with Frank to America, and they rest in family ground near the sea at Waterford.

It is easier as a rule to note and appraise the achievements of a successful man than of a successful woman. The man has held some important post, or made a fortune, or headed an institution, or rehabilitated a business, or achieved degrees or awards of record. Frank's accomplishments are there for anyone to see. Marie held (and wanted) no important post; she earned no money, never took a degree or headed an institution, and her only business was being her husband's wife. Such a person is sometimes praised by saying that "she made her husband possible." Even when this is not true in any literal sense it may signify much. A driving man of business who seems to be made of flint may be something of a child at the day's end; he can fight a good fight for so many hours a day, but not all the time; there must be some nook or haven where he can get out of it all if he is not to break. He may have a need that is quite belied by his confident exterior for someone who believes in him not on evidence, and therefore waveringly, but because he is he—some ear into which he can pour his troubles with the certainty that they will be listened to, someone who will cheer with him when he is up and be concerned about him when he is down. He may know very well that those with whom he works respect him, while knowing too that none of them would lose an hour's sleep if he were to vanish from the earth and that some of them would seize with pleasure the chance to move into his place. His sense of security needs a deeper anchorage than the mere respect of his colleagues.

Some men have been fortunate enough to have this. There is one person—and one is enough—to whom they are everything, for whom the light would go out of the sky if anything happened to them; and these men, besides an extra reason for being, have their own sort of insurance in the climate of their home. Marie was the home climate of Frank's life. Whatever he might need at the time was for her the prime concern. She was ready to make herself over, as indeed she did, if his way of life called for it. He was much away from home, often worried with large undertakings whose success was precarious, and sometimes, as

XII: Frank and Marie Aydelotte. Portrait by Charles Hopkinson; courtesy Swarthmore College.

XIII: Frank Aydelotte on shipboard, June 1953, en route to his last Rhodes Scholars' reunion. Cunard Line photo by W. A. Probst.

in his Rhodes reform and at Princeton, involved in painful personal struggles. It was an incalculable source of strength to him to know that however much of a beating he had to take when out on the high seas, there was always an enveloping affection waiting for him in his home port.

Marie was a very feminine woman, as Frank was a very masculine man. He just missed being what is called a "rough diamond," and throughout the years, in spite of the polishing attrition of Harvard, Oxford, Swarthmore, and Princeton, she could never be quite certain that through the urbane accents of the scholar and educator there would not come echoes of a more raucous voice, that of the all-Indiana football end. It was her function not only to give security to her formidable husband but also in a sense to civilize him. She seemed to know by instinct things that he had to labor to acquire. She was by nature delicate and sensitive of feeling; he had the capacity for this, too, but he was an extrovert and man of action, embarrassed in the presence of sentiment, reluctant to surrender himself to it, and likely to be silent when he did feel it. Even his son hardly knew how he felt on such matters as religion or the relation of men and women. Frank was ill at ease when such subjects came up, preferring not to talk about them. He was capable, of course, of very deep feeling. At the birth of their son, Marie had been in great pain; indeed, an operation was necessary that made further mother-hood impossible for her. Frank was in an anguish of apprehension about the two persons most precious to him, and when it was over, the sight of the mother asleep with the small object that had almost taken her life printed itself on his memory. After that he could never read dry-eyed the passage in *Antony and Cleopatra* where the Queen, with the asp at her breast, cries out:

> Peace, peace!
> Does thou not see the baby at my breast
> That sucks the nurse asleep?

Though Frank was by no means obtuse in matters of feeling, he was less alive and responsive to them than Marie, and there is no doubt that with the years her greater sensitiveness passed in a measure into his own perceptions and feelings. Whatever may be true of women, it seems to be true of men that the best of them combine masculine with feminine qualities, and Marie saw to it that such shoots of imaginative tenderness as appeared in Frank's tougher terrain had their chance to grow.

Fiftieth Rhodes Anniversary

A year later, in June, 1953, Frank returned to England for the fiftieth anniversary of the founding of the Rhodes Scholarships at Oxford. The reader may ask whether to Rhodes reunions there is to be no end, to which one answer would, be, Probably not; why should there be? More seriously, the celebration of 1953 was a unique affair. It was a double jubilee, the hundredth anniversary of the birth of Cecil Rhodes and the fiftieth anniversary of his Scholars' first appearance at Oxford. It was by far the largest assembly of Rhodes men that has ever been held. And it was the last that Frank attended.

He crossed in leisurely fashion on the *Britannic*, which carried so massive a contingent of Americans (179 appeared at the celebration) that it was almost a Rhodesian cruise ship. Frank was the only member who knew almost all the others, and he was the recognized dean of the company. At the Oxford meeting he could surrender himself, as he could not at the Princeton one, to the renewing of old friendships, without any responsiblity for the success of the proceedings. That was fortunate, for to house and feed 400 returning scholars and 274 wives, with garden parties as main items on the agenda, and in defiance of the temperamental British weather, was a risk of heroic proportions. The coronation of the young Queen had taken place a little earlier in the month and was greeted by a deluge. Happily for the Rhodes visitors, the Oxford skies were never bluer and the "emerald lawns" never greener. The Trustees had somewhere found the most enormous marquee in England and pitched it in the grounds of Rhodes House, where more than nine hundred persons sat down to the jubilee banquet. This is reported to have been the largest dinner in the annals of Oxford, and those annals go back some distance; in fact, two centuries before Columbus stumbled on the land from which so many of the diners came.

For Frank the celebration had clouds that even the Oxford sun could not dissipate. His friend of nearly fifty years, Sir Francis Wylie, had died shortly before the reunion and was sorely missed. The Allens were no longer at Rhodes House; Sir Carleton had been succeeded by E. T. Williams, who brought to the post a brilliant record as a chief aide to Montgomery in the campaign in North Africa. Frank himself had just been succeeded as American Secretary to the Trust by Courtney Smith, who was to carry on his work in distinguished fashion. He had every confidence in the new men, but he was no longer in the inner circle. And above all, Marie was not at his side.

At the reunion in Princeton he had himself been the central figure; at the reunion in Oxford he retreated to the periphery, and the central figure was, as it should be, the shadowy but dominating one of Cecil Rhodes. It is true that Leopold Amery, the senior Rhodes Trustee, went out of his way in his address at the great banquet to remind his hearers of what Frank had done for the Scholarships. "The wonderful work he did for so many years will not soon be forgotten. We are glad to think his lead has been followed successfully in Canada, Australia and South Africa, and that in every nation of the British Commonwealth there are now national associations which link Rhodes Scholars across the years." But Amery, in his far-off South African days, had actually known Rhodes in the flesh, and his main tribute was reserved for the man everyone wished to hear about. Rhodes, as a "slender, fair-haired rather dreamy boy" in a "quiet Hertfordshire vicarage" had "spent a whole night poring over a map of Africa" and then, at seventeen, had taken off for Cape Town. At twenty he was applying from the other side of the world for admission to University College, Oxford, which turned him down. He was accepted, however, at Oriel, which he later saluted with a gift of a hundred thousand pounds. For eight years he commuted back and forth between Africa and England, attracted powerfully both by the vast possibilities in the way of wealth and empire of "the dark continent" and by the magnetism, which he never escaped, of "the city of the dreaming spires." The story is symbolic of him that he enlivened lectures at Oxford by passing round raw diamonds in the classroom. One likes to think of this lad from the mines listening, as he did, to Ruskin's inaugural as Slade Professor of Fine Art. He was no scholar; it took him eight years to get his degree, and he would never have qualified for one of his own scholarships; but Oxford was to the end an ideal for him, the symbol and center of civilized life. When he died at forty-nine in "a squalid little cottage," he left the bulk of his great fortune to disseminate the influence of Oxford throughout the English-speaking world.

There was a special convocation in which five Rhodes Scholars were given honorary doctorates by the university—one each for Australia, South Africa, Canada, and the United States, and a further one for the States and Canada jointly. This last distinction went to Wilder Penfield (New Jersey and Merton, '14), who had already won the Order of Merit for his pioneer work at Montreal in the surgery of the brain. Canada was honored through F. C. J. M. Barbeau (Quebec and Oriel, '07), Anthropologist to the Dominion; Australia through Lieut. Gen. Sir Edmund Herring (Victoria and New College, '12); South Africa through the Chancellor of the University of Cape Town, the Hon. A. van de Sandt Centlivres (South Africa and New College, '07); and the United States through Senator J. W. Fulbright (Arkansas and Pembroke, '25), who was honored for founding the Fulbright Scholarships "in the direct Rhodes tradition." These candidates were all presented in impeccable Latin by the University Orator, who supplied English translations for the audience, explaining in a brave move to save face for the Scholars that it was done in response to the "overpowering entreaties" of their wives.[5]

Knight of the British Empire

Frank Aydelotte had already received the Oxonian doctorate and, of course, could not receive it a second time. But he was singled out later in that year of 1953 for a very particular kind of recognition, which was given him not so much for his academic work as for his public service in strengthening the ties between Britain and America. He was summoned to Buckingham Palace to receive the honorary K.B.E. (Knight of the British Empire) from the hands of the Queen. He crossed the sea again for the acceptance ceremony and drove to the Palace accompanied by his son. When the Queen offered him the royal hand, he smilingly shook it with his own left hand, explaining to her surprise and amusement that he had injured his right arm, which was now reserved for golf. Since he was not a British subject and the knighthood therefore was honorary, he did not kneel and receive an accolade on the shoulder from the royal sword. The ceremony was simpler; the two sat and chatted informally for fifteen or twenty minutes, and the Queen then handed over to him the insignia of the order. He was now a genuine knight, entitled at least technically to be addressed as "Sir Frank Aydelotte," though long custom has decreed that in such cases the honor is to be acknowledged by letters after the name rather than by a "Sir" before it. Frank was naturally much touched and pleased by this recognition of his half-century of effort to bring the two countries closer together. When he came home, he had many inquiries about the incident at the Palace, but to the despair of his women friends, he never could remember what Her Majesty had been wearing.

Without these women friends, in Princeton, to help him take care of himself and the house, it would have been almost intolerable to come back to 88 Battle Road, where memories of Marie were everywhere. His sister Nell came and lived with him in the big house. His Rhodes secretary, Elsa Jenkins, who was used to converting with equanimity the almost impenetrable script of his first drafts into fair copy, was still with him for half of each week and reported his ups and downs to his son in Iowa. Two Swarthmore students who had been his secretaries at the Institute, Jane Richardson and Kathleen Kehoe, were ready with prompt help in case of need. Perhaps most important of all for maintaining his familiar way of life, Margaret Morton, his housekeeper, who with her husband had long been in the family's employ and knew all his habits and preferences, was still there to run the household, both at Waterford, where he continued to go in the summer, and at Battle Road.

Failing Strength

In May, 1953, Elsa Jenkins sounded an ominous note in a letter to Bill in Iowa. "Thursday night we went to the Nassau Club for dinner, and he seemed perfectly well until after we had descended the steps to go home. He then took my arm, became quite dizzy, and before we knew it he had fallen (taking me with him). His head seemed clear the whole time. We got up, he became dizzier, and down again we went." He did not want to go to a hospital, and Elsa got him into a car and drove him home. These spells were to recur. His blood pressure was slowly rising, and it was difficult for a man of his energy and strenuous habits to keep his activity within the limits that his condition required. During his last years he had the expert advice of his friend Dr. DeWitt Hendee Smith, a Princeton specialist and a former Rhodes Scholar-at-Large at Balliol, whose counsel no doubt prolonged his life. But the loss of elasticity in the small arteries of the brain which comes with advancing years is not reversible, and the vagueness noted on his two last visits to Oxford steadily increased. He had heard that liquor served to relax these arteries, and though he had neither drunk it himself nor served it to others during the whole of his time at Swarthmore, he now felt free to drop the restrictions if he wished. He had a strong relish for sherry and was somewhat ashamed of the number of bottles of it that he could and did dispatch. Sometimes he wanted to forget. To the outer world he maintained the same sunny and equable appearance as ever. But things had not gone as triumphantly at Princeton as they had at Swarthmore; Marie was no longer present to give him support; and he could not count on the inexhaustible physical resilience of earlier years to bring him bouncing back to form again. There were times when he could only sit and brood, with a sad sense of frustration and loneliness.

One event of 1956, which proved to be his last year, cheered him greatly. His son William, now professor of history at the University of Iowa, was married in the summer to Miss Myrtle Kitchell, Dean of the School of Nursing at the same university. Frank took much satisfaction in this marriage and a strong and immediate liking for his new daughter-in-law; indeed, as Alfred Brooks wrote to William later that year, "He glowed with pleasure whenever your names were mentioned." Early in December, the new Mrs. Aydelotte had professional meetings that took her to the east, and she seized the opportunity to spend a week with him at Princeton, commuting daily on business to New York. Before she left she broke the news to him that the Aydelotte line of succession was to go on; he was to become a grandfather. He fairly crowed with delight.

He never saw the coming grandchild. The practiced eye of his daughter-in-law recognized that his life was now hanging by a fragile thread. The end came sooner than anyone at the time anticipated. She had scarcely reached home in Iowa City when she and Bill were called back by word that their father had suffered a massive stroke. He was transferred to a hospital in Princeton where he received solicitous care, but he had fallen at once into a deep unconsciousness—too deep for recognition, apprehension, or pain. For eight days he lingered in this state before the end came quietly on Monday evening, December 17, 1956.

Hail and Farewell

On the following Saturday a memorial service was held in the Quaker Meeting House in Princeton. Patrick Malin, then head of the Civil Liberties Union, and soon to become President of Robert College, Constantinople, came down from New York and spoke movingly about his former chief. The next day another memorial service was held in the Meeting House on the Swarthmore campus. Both of Frank's successors in the presidency of the college, John W. Nason and Courtney Smith, and the long-time Dean of the College, Everett Hunt, were there to pay grateful tribute to him; and the meeting was closed by his son, who spoke of the central part that Swarthmore had played in his affection and his life.

The name of Aydelotte had not been much in the public press of late, but the news of his death brought it into prominence again. The New York *Times* published a full account of his work and appraised it editorially; *The Times* of London added to its long obituary a number of appreciations written by various hands. An avalanche of letters and telegrams descended on the house in Battle Road. Many were from former students and Rhodes Scholars whom he had helped over stiles in unforgotten ways. Many were from college and university Presidents who had sat with him on committees or studied his educational policies with an eye to their own institutions. "He was a joy to work with," wrote former President Dodds of Princeton. President Virgil Hancher of the University of Iowa spoke for Rhodes men generally when he wrote: "He was loved and admired by every generation of Rhodes scholars." "He was a great educational statesman," telegraphed President Wells of Indiana, "of whom his Alma Mater was very proud."

Not the least prized of these appreciations came from overseas. The Vice-Chancellor of Oxford sent a message of sorrow and esteem. Brasenose College reported that it was arranging a memorial service in its own chapel, which was held on January 31. Sir David Keir, Master of Balliol, after writing of Frank's friendship for Britain, added: "More special to me and to Balliol was the link that bound us through the Eastman Chair, for which he did so much, and which has been so conspicuous a success. As we look back on the long and illustrious line of American scholars who have become Fellows of Balliol, we remember also the care Frank took that we should get the flower of the American learned world here." Sir Carleton Allen, who spoke with full knowledge, wrote: "What your father and mother did for the Rhodes Scholarships in the U.S.A. can never be overestimated. They and the Wylies between them really made the whole system into the shape which it was to assume in perpetuity." Englishmen are not commonly tempted to excess of praise for middle-western Americans, so the following two sentences about this particular middle-westerner, both from members of the House of Lords, are significant: "My own thoughts today are of the departure of a kind and steadfast friend, never so happy as when he could advance the happiness of others." And from another member of that austere House, who had known him more intimately: "All the trumpets will surely be sounded for him on the other side, and there will be many to 'rise up and call him blessed.' "

Estimates and eulogies of his work, deliberately drawn up, came in from the faculties of the Princeton Institute and the University of Indiana, from the Board of Managers of Swarthmore, and from other institutions that he had served. These have been preserved in the family archives. They will not be reproduced here, partly because they would contain nothing new to those who have read the preceding pages, partly because the atmosphere of eulogy for a friend recently lost and that of objective appraisal go ill together. *De mortuis nil nisi bonum.*

The Unity of a Life

We are already at some distance from the events of that December. We are at a better point of vantage than the critics who wrote in his lifetime or the friends who wrote in grief at his death for seeing what he stood for and what his true stature was. Some readers may have gained the impression of a man with endless irons in the fire, too distracted by the business of the hour and by his multiple interests to go very far along any one line. Nothing could be further from the truth. One can see in looking back that his life had a remarkable unity and singleness of purpose.

Nor is it difficult to see where that unity lay. For his last forty-five years he was dominated by one great idea: he wanted to introduce into this country the sort of education that would "reprieve democracy from mediocrity." His distinction was that he saw clearly and attempted to meet the central difficulty of American education: we are trying to do two things at once which tend to cancel each other out: to achieve quantity and also quality, mass education and also educational excellence. Frank Aydelotte believed in the validity of both these ends; he saw how they militate against each other; and he developed a plan to harmonize them. It will pay us to look for a moment at these two aims.

Frank was sometimes suspected of being an aristocrat who had too little belief in democracy. There seems to be no good evidence for this. He had himself come up through the ranks from a small-town public school; he believed fervently in the state university system of which he was a product; his educational ideal was that *everyone* should go as far and as fast as his abilities permitted. A democracy without an educated citizenry seemed to him a danger to itself and to the world. He detested discrimination on the basis of race or creed or national origin; he was a defender of the rights of minorities; he worked for the repeal of the McCarran Act; he was a liberal in his practical politics.

On the other hand, he saw all around him the results of an educational confusion, of a facile and fallacious passage from a sound view of democracy to an unsound travesty of it. Democracy means equality in the sense of equal consideration; it means that no one's interest is to be ignored; no one is to be arbitrarily passed over in the distribution of public privilege. But it does not mean equality in values, which is absurd; it does not mean equality in abilities, which is contrary to fact; and it does not mean equality of subject matter, for some subjects are as educationally central as others are plainly peripheral. His major effort was to counter the forces in democracy that tended to make it self-defeating. Our colleges and universities were being overwhelmed with students; excellent. But we must consider whether, if our colleges admit everybody, they will not end by educating nobody, whether the dead weight of numbers will not drag the standards down, instead of the yeast of education leveling the masses up. Mass education makes for conformity, the ironing out of idiosyncrasy, and it almost inevitably gives more attention to helping lame dogs limp along than to coaching the fleet of foot to their fastest pace. This is not good enough. Democracy needs leaders, and this is no way to produce them. To treat a person of great ability as if he were merely an average man is to act a falsehood and under the guise of nondiscrimination to discriminate against him.

Once he had seen this clearly, Aydelotte had an ideal in life. The insight he undoubtedly owed to Oxford. His roots were in the Middle West, and he always remained there in the sense that its moral idealism and simplicity, its outgoing neighborliness, its assumption, inherited from the pioneers, that "a man's a man for a' that," were part of his temperamental equipment. But his meeting with Oxford was a case of love at first sight, from which he never recovered. The effect of that old enchantress is perhaps not the same on any two Rhodes Scholars. A few she has repelled as a moldy, medieval relic. Some have been so swept away by her that they have come back to their own country aliens in outlook as well as in accent. Frank belonged to the fortunate group whose Americanism was unalterable, but who were open in all their pores to that indescribable spell. "Adorable dreamer . . . who hast given theyself so prodigally . . . only never to the Philistines!" The American from the plains, who would have admitted that he was something of a Philistine, found himself in the college of Walter Pater, looking out on St. Mary's where Newman had preached; and when he stepped out of his front door it was into the High Street, whose pavements had been worn by the feet of Addison and Johnson, Gibbon and Froude, Shelley and Arnold and Swinburne. These people were not dead classics—not in Oxford, not when Frank's tutor, Walter Raleigh, talked about them with laughter and affection, as if they were old acquaintances.

The students, too, were like none he had known; indeed, they were not like each other; they were already markedly individual in their interests and enthusiasms. The most popular study among them was Greek and Latin literature, read *in extenso* in the original with a facility that only a Ph.D. at home could command. If this literature was alive for them, if their discussion of philosophical and political issues had a surprising ease and point, that was not an accident. These were picked men, the winnowed best from the public and private schools of Britain. Still, their attainments and their privileges were bought with a price. Britain was not attempting the higher education of the many. She looked with scarcely concealed contempt on the hundreds of American institutions that scattered their thousands of B.A.'s annually. She had put her educational eggs in two antique, gorgeous baskets, Oxford and Cambridge, which received the best students, the best scholars, the best teachers, and the most money. Quantitatively the American ideal was the more generous and equitable. Qualitatively the British product was incomparable.

Now the endeavor of Frank Aydelotte's life, to put it roundly, was to synthesize the Middle West where he came from with the Oxford of his admiration. The ideal of educating everybody he never gave up, but he said comparatively little about it, because it was already virtually part of the American religion. But the insistence on quality was not, and here was occasion for a crusade. He turned his life into such a crusade. He gave himself to the discovery and endowment of the best brains he could find, and he did this at four distinguishable levels.

His first effort was with undergraduates. Taking Swarthmore as his experiment station, he sought to prove that, even in a small college, one could separate out for special treatment those who could respond to it, without injustice or discouragement to the rest.

His second effort was made at a higher level, with the Rhodes Scholars. He soon saw, after becoming American Secretary to the Rhodes Trust, that the system proposed by Rhodes was not getting the best men. A candidate who would have ranked fifth or sixth in Pennsylvania or California might come out first and get the appointment in a less populous neighboring state like Delaware or Nevada. By proposing a Parliamentary change in Rhodes's will, which broke the country into six-state blocks and selected the best from each of them, he permanently raised the quality of American Rhodes Scholars.

His third effort was at the next level, that of the young professional who was beginning to find himself. As one of the organizers of the Guggenheim plan and long-time chairman of its selection committee, he combed the country for the most promising young scholars and scientists, artists and musicians, with a view to giving them freedom to think, write, and create. In many cases they were started on distinguished careers.

The fourth effort was at the level of already acquired distinction. His aim at the Institute of Advanced Studies was to search out the ablest scholars he could find of any age and provide them with the conditions for research on the frontiers of knowledge. From his induction at Swarthmore in 1921 to his retirement at Princeton in 1947, he was thus pursuing, with great variation of means, a single end: raising the level of American life by the discovery and encouragement of talent. The best guarantee of a democracy of rights was an aristocracy of brains and character. He would have agreed with Henry Allen Moe, his ally in the sedulous search for American talent:

> Without an aristocracy, we should be lost; having it, we surely shall be saved. That is, indeed, what our manifest destiny is, our cultural, non-territorial manifest destiny: to have the greatest aristocracy of brains and character the world has ever known. Having that aristocracy is the only way to the Great Society: there is no other way.[6]

The Quality of the Man

It was for this lifelong campaign to liberate American talent that he should be remembered. But for those who knew him, there is something else he will be remembered for, which is harder to convey to anyone who did not know him. This was the unique personal quality of the man. It did not come through at once to those who met him casually, nor perhaps at all to those who knew him only in the years of his failing strength. First impressions were in his case more than usually deceptive. He was not prepossessing physically. The egglike baldness, the oddly shaped head, curiously flat on top, the eyes small and too close together, the outsize ears, the somewhat awkward toed-in gait, the offer of a left hand to shake—these did not add up to a captivating first impression. But the second impression quickly erased the first. It was the sense of a temperamental *joie de vivre*. He enjoyed meeting you; he enjoyed listening to you, not, it was clear, out of policy, but out of pleased and eager expectancy. We have heard Richard Crossman's impression that he was like Happy in *Snow White*. He carried into all companies an irrepressible tendency to chuckle with pleasure over the things and people around him. His colleagues were extraordinary exhibits of ability and reasonableness. His students were bursting with a promise that might justly be crowed over. His Board of Trustees? How lucky he was to be surrounded by such a Stonehenge of solid sense and judgment. The alumni? Some of them, to be sure, were questioning what was going on, but that showed the depth of their attachment; they were all fine fellows.

If this sunniness of temperament had been a matter of principle, it would have been shaken by untoward fact. But it sprang from deeper than intellectual strata in his nature; it was a sort of instinctive euphoria which, like that of Emerson, dwelt by native preference on the blues and golds of the world rather than the grays and the browns. And it was highly contagious. Even the Cassandras tended to forget what they had to croak about in this cheerful and confident presence. If cheer had been a professional manner put on to soothe opposition, they would soon have sensed its vulnerability. But it was not. He genuinely felt that way. He would come into his office of a morning exulting in the prospect of dealing with the day's problems and driving them all, like the Gadarene swine, down the slopes and into the sea. You would come in to see him with some brooding worry, and soon he would be throwing back his head in contented laughter about nothing much except that you were you, and he was he, and what a thing it was to be alive. Of course, that solved nothing. But it was extraordinary how difficulties dwindled as the fog of anxiety lifted.

It would be idle to say that such a temperament had no drawbacks. People who habitually take geese for swans are likely to go further at times and include ugly ducklings. It has been reported that college chairmen, seeking advice about young philosophers from the Harvard department, slowly learned that William James's famous "whoops of blessing," so widely and generously bestowed, were less to be relied on than the cooler appraisals of George Herbert Palmer. Frank Aydelotte, like James, was apt to see auras about people's heads that were hardly visible to others. He made some howlers in his appointments, as he would certainly have admitted. He was always valuable on a committee where his prolific and impulsive ideas could be submitted to check, or where candidates were to be chosen on the basis of written evidence. Professor Wallace Notestein says: "For nine years he and I worked together on the Guggenheim. . . . He was all kindness and consideration for every possible candidate, and yet, when it came to the point, he stood for high standards all along the line." At times, however, committees left him to interview candidates and make appointments on his own, and then the "intuition" on which he confessedly relied was too mixed with the milk of human kindness to be wholly reliable. Some of his swans came home to roost as birds of a very different feather.

Mere sunniness of temper is not courage, but it may be closely allied to this. Courage is of different types. There is the courage of the man who hates strife, but forces himself to face it from a sheer sense of duty: the kind of courage Kant admired. That was not Aydelotte's type. There is again the courage that loves a fight for its own exciting sake, the courage of the celebrated Irishman who, seeing a brawl in progress, inquired whether this was a private fight or anyone could get in. Then there is the courage, still temperamental, but at a higher level, of the man who is intelligent enough to see the difficulties, but revels nevertheless in taking responsibilities and making decisions. This was Aydelotte's type. It is the kind of temperament that turns some wartime leaders into idols—Montgomery, Eisenhower, the Admiral Beatty of the order at Jutland: "Captain, the ships are behaving badly today; turn two points nearer the enemy." The man to whom difficulties are a challenge and an exhilaration may be no wiser in his decisions than the man on whom responsibility lies like a blanket soaked in worry, but he will lighten his burdens by his attitude, and those of the persons around him by his mere presence. There was a touch in Frank Aydelotte of his own Elizabethan seamen, and as he walked his Swarthmore quarterdeck, one could sense the delight he felt in turning his little craft into the teeth of the wind and sailing out on a high adventure.

That this self-confidence survived unscathed after Frank's experience of Oxford is itself evidence of its depth. The Rhodes experience in the early days could be a trying one. The Scholars had been marked successes on their campuses at home. If they elected an honors school at Oxford, as most of them did, they had to start over again, near the bottom, in a place where no one had heard of them, where the academic methods were novel, the standards taxing, the manners subtly different, their fellow students seemingly unresponsive, their very speech something of a reproach to them. Since 1905 the positions of Britain and America in the world have been roughly reversed, and the American in Europe is no longer set down automatically as a provincial or a frontiersman. But the hurdles then were high. For some of the early Rhodes men they were too high; their self-confidence was eroded by the experience; they came back neither good Englishmen nor wholehearted Americans. It was a testimony to Frank's vitality that he could subject himself completely to the English methods and, instead of being intimidated by them or rendered diffident or self-distrustful, should take them over, re-tailor them to American needs, and then go crusading back to England for changes in the Rhodes administration itself and in the Oxford professorial staff. Emerson's *Self-Reliance* was a favorite of his, and he clearly had wells of that sort of water to draw upon. Oxford did, to be sure, make him over; but it never paralyzed or inhibited him, never made him into anything but himself, never turned him into anything that was not unmistakably American.

Though a man of action, he was a dreamer. He brooded over a great many more eggs than he ever hatched. He was not a nine-to-four executive; he would mull over his work on the golf course, on his cross-country trips by train, while shaving in the morning or lying awake at night. And because of his confidence and optimism, his dreams were apt to blow themselves up to grandiose proportions like those of Cecil Rhodes himself. Who else would have thought of inviting the League of Nations, or a division of it, to the Institute at Princeton? He used to muse on the possibility of mobilizing the Rhodes Scholars of the world to found a new college in Oxford. When consulted by a philanthropist about possible scholarships he was ready with a plan, far-reaching and detailed, which had clearly arisen earlier out of his independent musing. His colleagues were made uneasy at times by a drive and sweep of conception that were uncomfortably Napoleonic and made them feel too much like hesitant pygmies. Lord Elton writes: "When my wife and I saw him last at Princeton, just about a year before he died, he had begun to evolve a Cyclopean but still inchoate project for a vast, and still vague, new foundation which should accumulate Rhodesiana of many kinds, and in particular the biographies, the writings and even the correspondence of American Rhodes Scholars."[7] Given time, he would have put this through. It is unlikely that anyone else will have the energy and persuasiveness to do so.

Lady Wylie, a shrewd observer, once remarked that he "had something of the despot in his make-up." One has to stop and reflect to see that this was true. No one in the little Swarthmore kingdom that he ruled with so strong a hand would have described him in this way. If he was an absolute ruler, at least his subjects never felt as if they were exploited or trampled on. Still, one can see in looking back that he dominated the college and held it in the hollow of his hand. He put through reforms that were daring enough to have provoked revolt in many a college and to have swept the President out on a wave of protest. He did have his troubles, as we have seen, but on the whole he had his way. It would be absurd, nevertheless, to suggest that he was an academic Castro or Franco. It was not in his nature to draw a line between "I" and "thou" or to set his chin grimly and force an enemy to back down. He was that more baffling kind of despot who disarmed his enemies before they clearly knew what was happening—by seeking them out for consultation and advice. A critic might say that this was a cynical substitution of craft for coercion. But this would be wrong again. Aydelotte would have read *How to Win Friends and Influence People* with strong distaste; he would have agreed that honesty is the best policy, but would have regarded that as a sorry reason for adopting the policy. What made him so disarming to opponents was no calculated strategy at all, but something harder to foil: an unsuspicious, deep-seated good will; an assumption that his opponent was a reasonable man, acting from motives as disinterested as his own; a readiness, therefore, to take him into his confidence and treat him with a kind of bubbling affection as a comrade in the joint and glorious war against the dark; and all this combined, of course, with an overwhelming, transparent belief in the rightness of his cause. Opponents were at an odd disadvantage in dealing with such a man. To demand a showdown with him seemed a bit silly, even to themselves. For the most part, like old soldiers, they merely faded away.

Frank Aydelotte was a happy man, but his happiness was not that of the philosopher or the saint or the epicure; nor was it that of the humorist, for though there was much laughter in his house, his sense of humor hardly rose above the average. His happiness was that of natural zest and we must add—if somewhat dangerously—of "positive thinking." He refused to hedge it about with negative thought about his fellows. The singular comment was once made about Mirabeau that when the time came for him to take revenge on the people who had wronged him, he did not take it because he had forgotten all about them. Frank had something of this same blessed obliviousness. Not that he was immune to resentment; he felt it keenly if a colleague let him down by double-dealing or disloyalty, and he was known to have marked such a person for quiet elimination. But he did not allow his resentments to turn into cankers or poison his bloodstream with bile. There are many whose "disinterested" comments about their colleagues betray a rancorous envy, and those whose continued return, like crows to carrion, to others' misfortunes discloses nothing as clearly as their own malice and insecurity. Frank was exceptionally free from this sickness of mind. He knew that anyone who looked for it could find what was stupid or worse in the people around him, but he preferred not to look for it and was apt to fall silent or go off on another tack if others began retailing juicy discoveries. This was less from priggishness or principle than from the feeling that where there was so much to be done and enjoyed, it was a bore to spend more time than necessary on the depth or breadth of human fatuousness. If you could do something about it, that was different, and you could get his ear quickly enough. If you couldn't, why dwell on it? To rub one's hands, as Kierkegaard did, over men's tendency to fall on their noses in the mud seemed to him pointless and morbid.

The most memorable things about Frank Aydelotte, we have suggested, are his achievement as an administrator and his quality as a man. As a college administrator he was probably the most vigorous and successful exponent we have had of the selection and support of excellence at all levels. Here his initiative has been potent; it helped to set a style that is now common in this country; it was taken up by many colleges, foundations, and institutes that are today searching out and supporting prospective leaders. As for the quality of the man, that unhappily is more evanescent. But it, too, has a kind of "corporate immortality." In his mobile and gregarious life, Frank Aydelotte touched thousands of others and by his unique combination of energy and gaiety, generosity and courage, infused into them something of his own strength. He preferred lighting candles to railing against the dark. He worked hard—incredibly hard—and drank delight from it to the full. He lived, even when his ships were behaving badly, with a gusto and joy of battle that set up reverberations of confidence in all around him. The reverberations still go on.

NOTES

CHAPTER ONE Indiana Boyhood

Unpublished sources: Frank Aydelotte's sketch, "Sullivan, Indiana 1880–1896," 5¾ typed pages. Many talks with Frank Aydelotte, his sister Nell Aydelotte Rice, and a host of relatives and friends in Sullivan, which the writer had the good fortune to visit with Mrs. Rice.

1. *Publications of the Huguenot Society of London,* London: Spottiswoode et al., IX (1911), 179, 187, 199, 208, 219; XIII (1929), 78, 99, 110, 224, 262; XVIII, 69.

2. *The History of the Aydelott Family in the United States* (privately printed), pp. 60–61, 64, 66–67, 79.

3. *History of Greene and Sullivan Counties* (Chicago: Goodspeed Bros. & Co., 1884), pp. 711, 628, 611, 613, and *passim.*

4. Thomas Woody, *A History of Women's Education in the United States* (New York and Lancaster, Pa.: The Science Press, 1929), II, 456–457.

5. John Andrew Rice, *I Came Out of the Eighteenth Century* (New York: Harper, 1942) pp. 266–268.

6. Theodore Dreiser, *A Hoosier Holiday* (New York: John Lane, 1916), pp. 413, 17; *Dawn* (New York: Horace Liveright, 1931), p. 44.

7. Will Hays, *The Memoirs of Will H. Hays* (Garden City, N.Y.: Doubleday, 1955).

8. Meredith Nicholson, *The Hoosiers* (New York: Macmillan, 1900), p. 219.

9. James Albert Woodburn, *History of Indiana University, 1820–1902* (Bloomington: Indiana University Press, 1940), I, 69.

10. Nicholson, *op. cit.,* Chapter IV, "An Experiment in Socialism"; *Dictionary of American Biography,* "Robert Dale Owen."

11. Woodburn, *op. cit.,* pp. 349–350.

12. William Douglas, ed., *The American Book of Days* (New York: H. W. Wilson Co., 1948), p. 530. Columbus Day was celebrated in 1892 on October 21, the date corrected in accordance with a change in the calendar since 1492. Since then, it has been celebrated on October 12, the date on Columbus' calendar.

13. Harry Thurston Peck, *Twenty Years of the Republic, 1885–1905* (New York: Dodd, Mead, 1913), p. 353.

14. Henry Steele Commager, *The American Mind* (New Haven: Yale University Press, 1959—paperback), pp. 394–397.

15. Peck, *op. cit.,* p. 352.

16. Hays, *op. cit.,* p. 39 (quoted from a local newspaper).

CHAPTER TWO   Student at Bloomington

Unpublished sources: Frank Aydelotte's sketch, "Bloomington, Indiana 1896–1900," 4⅙ typed pages. Scrapbook of copies of letters about F.A., submitted to support his application for a Rhodes Scholarship (1905). Letters to F.B. from F.A.'s contemporaries at Indiana. Notes on talks during two visits to the university with various persons who remembered F.A. as a student.

1. James Albert Woodburn, "Higher Education in Indiana," In Herbert B. Adams, ed., *Contributions to American Educational History* (Washington: Government Printing Office, 1891), Chapter X.

2. James Albert Woodburn. *History of Indiana University, 1820–1902* (Bloomington: Indiana University Press, 1940), I, 371.

3. David Starr Jordan, *The Days of a Man* (Yonkers on Hudson: World Book, 1922), I, 186, ff., 293.

4. Charles F. Thwing, *A History of Higher Education in America* (New York: Appleton, 1906), pp. 312–313, 436.

5. Woodburn, *History*, I, 385.

6. *Indiana University Catalogue* for 1896–1897.

7. F.A.'s sketch.

8. Official transcript for F.A. from Indiana, dated July 2, 1957.

9. Letter to F.B. from Mrs. C. S. Sembower, an undergraduate with F.A., later wife of a colleague in the English department (August 29, 1959).

10. Letter to F.B. from Mrs. Cecilia H. Hendricks, who had been a student of F.A.'s and also his colleague in teaching a course in freshman English (June 20, 1959).

11. Woodburn, *History*, I, 424.

12. Scrapbook. Letter from J. C. Hubbard, April 1, 1905.

13. Woodburn, *History*, I, 429.

14. F.A.'s sketch.

15. Letter from Mrs. Hendricks.

16. Letter from Mrs. Sembower.

17. Letter from Mrs. Hendricks.

18. Scrapbook.

19. F.A.'s sketch.

20. Burton Dorr Myers, *History of Indiana University, 1902–1937* (Bloomington: Indiana University Press, 1940), II, 393.

21. *Daily Student*, December 14, 1898, p. 1.

22. *Ibid.*, January 30, 1899.

23. F.A.'s sketch.

24. Fred K. Gale, *Indiana Teacher.*

25. *The Arbutus* (Bloomington: Senior Class, Indiana University, 1900). Dedicated to David Starr Jordan. F.A.'s name or photograph appears on pp. 18, 19, 58, 59, 82, 96, 97, 104, 105, 120, 121, 236, 237; his story, p. 126.

CHAPTER THREE   Time of Testing

Unpublished sources: Frank Aydelotte's letter to F.B., August 10, 1955. Scrapbook of copies of letters about F.A., submitted to support his application for a Rhodes Scholarship (1905). Talks with F.A. and Alfred Brooks.

1. Scrapbook. Letter from Theo B. Noss (March 18, 1905, California, Pa.) refers to Professor Bryan's recommendation.

2. William S. Taylor, *The Development of the Professional Education of Teachers in Pennsylvania* (Philadelphia: Lippincott, 1924), Chapter V.

3. F.A.'s account.

4. Henry S. Cauthorn, *A History of the City of Vincennes, Indiana, 1702–1901* (Terre Haute: Moore and Langer, 1902).

5. *Ibid.*, pp. 61–62.

6. Letter of September 27, 1900, Indiana University Archives.

7. Scrapbook.

8. Cecil Rhodes's Will, quoted in full: *The Times* (London), April 5, 1902, pp. 14a, b, c.

9. *Ibid.*, p. 11b.

10. F. C. S. Schiller, "Cosmopolitan Oxford," *Fortnightly* (London), LXXVII (May, 1902), 814–820.

11. *The Times* (London), April 5, 1902, p. 11b; October 13, 1904, p. 6a.

12. *'Varsity*, May 31, 1906, p. 353. "The Rhodes Scholars," No. VI in a series, "Lost Causes."

13. American comments quoted: *The Times* (London), April 7, 1902, p. 7b.

14. For impressions of Harvard personalities, I am indebted to J. Donald Adams, *Copey of Harvard* (Boston: Houghton Mifflin, 1960); Rollo Walter Brown, *Dean Briggs* (New York and London: Harper, 1926) and *Harvard in the Golden Age* (New York: Current Books, 1948); M. A. DeWolfe Howe, *Barrett Wendell and His Letters* (Boston: Atlantic Monthly Press, 1924); S. E. Morison, *The Development of Harvard University, 1869–1929* (Cambridge: Harvard University Press, 1930).

15. Story from Alfred Brooks.

16. C. T. Copeland and H. M. Rideout, *Freshman English and Theme-Correcting in Harvard College* (New York: Silver, Burdett, 1901).

17. F.A.'s account.

18. Scrapbook. Copies of letters from C. T. Copeland and L. R. Briggs.

19. Letter of January 14, 1903, Indiana University Archives.

20. *Neighborhood House, 1896–1946* (Louisville, Ky. privately printed). Sent F.B. by a Swarthmore alumna, Louise Yerkes Kain.

21. F.A.'s account.

22. Sam Adkins and M. R. Holtzman, *The First Hundred Years—The Story of Louisville Male High School—1856–1956*, p. 118.

23. Abraham Flexner, *I Remember* (New York: Simon and Schuster, 1940), pp. 54–55, 322.

24. Scrapbook.

25. Letters of March 17 and May 11, 1905.

26. This item and the one in note 22 sent to F.B. by the principal of Louisville Male High School, W. S. Milburn.

CHAPTER FOUR Rhodes Scholar: First Year

Unpublished sources: Fifty-one letters home from Frank Aydelotte, September 29, 1905—October 2, 1906, quoted without footnote references; F.A.'s sketch, "Oxford 1905–1907," 5½ pages. F.A.'s letter to F.B., from Waterford, August 10, 1955. Marie Osgood's diary, October, 1905, January, 1906. Impressions of F.A. at Oxford, from: Lady Wylie; Rhodes Scholars R. P. Brooks, Julius Brown, C. W.

Bush, L. Cronkhite, P. Kieffer; Englishmen at B.N.C., Messrs. Icely, Iredell, and Trotter.

1. Frank Aydelotte, *The American Rhodes Scholarships* (Princeton: Princeton University Press, 1946), pp. 2–5.

2. John Corbin, *An American at Oxford* (Boston and New York: Houghton Mifflin, 1902).

3. *Oxford Magazine*, February 21, 1906, p. 232.

4. John Buchan, *Brasenose College* (London: F. E. Robinson, 1898), p. 143.

5. *The Times* (London), May 9, 1902, p. 10c.

6. Robert H. Stephen, "The Rhodes Bequest," *Oxford Point of View* (Oxford), I, No. 1 (May, 1902), 16–20.

7. Percy Gardner, *Oxford at the Cross Roads* (London: Adam and Charles Black, 1903), pp. 3, 18, and *passim*.

8. F. C. S. Schiller, "Cosmopolitan Oxford," *Fortnightly* (London), LXXVII (May, 1902), 814–820.

9. *'Varsity*, October 20, 1904, pp. 386, 389.

10. L. E. Jones, *An Edwardian Youth*, (London: Macmillan, 1956), pp. 66–67.

11. Sidney Ball, "Oxford's Opinions of the Rhodes Scholars," *American Oxonian* (Bloomington, Ind.), I, No. 1 (April, 1914), 3–20.,

12. *Oxford Magazine*, XXIV (October 18, 1905), p. 5.

13. "Busselliana," *Brazen Nose*, IX, No. 3 (May, 1959), 100–102.

14. *Oxford Magazine*, XXIV (October 18, 1905), p. 3.

15. Robert Preston Brooks, *Under Seven Flags—An Autobiographical Sketch* (Athens, Ga.: privately printed, 1957), pp. 15–17.

16. *'Varsity*, May 17, 1906, p. 315; June 7, 1906, p. 370.

17. C. H. Firth, *The School of English Language and Literature* (Oxford: B. H. Blackwell; London: Simpkin, Marshall, 1909), pp. 10, 16, 31, 34, 38, 53.

18. H. W. Garrod, *The Profession of Poetry and Other Lectures* (Oxford: Clarendon Press, 1929), "Walter Raleigh," pp. 266–270.

19. Elizabeth Mary Wright, *The Story of Joseph Wright, Man and Scholar* (London: Humphrey Milford, Oxford University Press, 1934).

20. See Sir Francis Wylie's delightful account of his years in office in *The First Fifty Years of the Rhodes Trust and the Rhodes Scholarships 1903–1953* (Oxford: Basil Blackwell, 1955), Chapter 2, "The Rhodes Scholars and Oxford 1902–31."

21. *Ibid.*, pp. 5–9, 61–62.

22. Brooks, *op. cit.*

23. R. P. Brooks's diary, unpublished. October 15, November 1, 7, 1905.

24. Brooks, *Under Seven Flags*.

25. *Oxford Magazine*, November 8, 1905, p. 54.

26. *Ibid.*, November 29, 1905.

27. *Ibid.*, p. 108.

28. Marie Osgood's diary; entries for October 16, 1905, January 7–17, 1906. Kept by her son, William Osgood Aydelotte, in Iowa City, Iowa.

29. Eben Putnam, ed., *A History of the Families of John, Christopher and William Osgood* (Salem, Mass: Salem Press, 1894), pp. 246–247.

30. Walter Raymond Spalding, *Music at Harvard* (New York: Coward McCann, 1935), pp. 196–197.

31. Information from Dr. Hamilton Osgood's granddaughter, Rachel Warren Barton (Mrs. Robert Barton) of Glendalough House, Annamoe, County Wicklow, Ireland.

32. Unpublished accounts by Rachel Warren Barton and Margaret Deneke of Oxford.

33. Articles on George Grey Barnard: "Barnard's Mighty Sculptures for the Pennsylvania Capitol," *Current Literature*, XLIX, No. 2 (August, 1910) 207–209; "Barnard's Medieval Cloisters in New York City," New York *Times*, December 6, 1914, Section VI, p. 11; Obituary, New York *Times*, April 25, 1938, pp. 1 and 3; Editorial, New York *Times*, April 26, 1938, p. 20.

CHAPTER FIVE Rhodes Scholar: Second Year

Unpublished sources: Forty-nine letters home from Frank Aydelotte, October 12, 1906—December 19, 1907, quoted without footnote references. F.A.'s sketch, "Oxford 1905–1907," 5½ pages. F.A.'s letter to F.B., from Waterford, August 10, 1955.

1. Subject of paper given in *Oxford Magazine*, February 13, 1907, p. 209.

2. Strictly, his rank when he went to Bloomington was "Acting Associate Professor," according to the *Indiana Daily Student* of January 11, 1908; changed to "Associate Professor" after his first semester, according to the issue of June 24, 1908.

3. Frank Aydelotte, *Elizabethan Rogues and Vagabonds* (Oxford: Clarendon Press, 1913), Preface.

4. In the Irish Civil War, Erskine Childers was executed by the Free State on November 24, 1922.

5. Letter from Marie Osgood to Rosamond Kimball, February 14, 1907, from "Moret-sur-Loing." Kindly brought to my attention by Miss Kimball.

6. *Oxford Magazine*, June 19, 1907, pp. 416, 421.

7. F.A. did not edit this.

8. F.A.'s letter to F.B., August 10, 1955.

9. Clippings saved by F.A.'s mother with his letters.

10. F.A.'s letter to F.B., August 10, 1955.

CHAPTER SIX Teaching English at Indiana

Unpublished sources: Files of Frank Aydelotte's correspondence and other papers kept in William O. Aydelotte's house, Waterford, Conn. F.A.'s letter to F.B. from Waterford, September 17, 1954. Letters to F.B. from Mrs. Cecilia Hennel Hendricks, Professor Frank Davidson, and Miss Louise Dillman. Impressions of F.A. from conversations with friends and acquaintances in Bloomington, including Miss Lillian Berry, Alfred Mansfield Brooks, William Lowe Bryan, Professor Frank Davidson, Mrs. Cecilia H. Hendricks, Mrs. Hedwig Leser.

1. *Indiana University Bulletin*, 1908.

2. Information about courses F.A. took as an undergraduate and taught at Indiana, from the Office of Records and Admissions, compiled by Miss Louise Dillman.

3. Letter to F.B. from Mrs. C. H. Hendricks, March 6, 1958.

4. Letter to F.B. from Professor Frank Davidson, July 22, 1957.

5. F.A.'s unpublished essay, "On Not Doing One's Duty," among the Waterford papers.

6. Regulations for the D.Litt. and D.Sc. degrees published in the *Oxford Register*, 1905, p. 82.

7. Letters from Norman Foerster to F.A., October 28, 1912, and February 5, 1913, in the Waterford files.

8. Letter from Roosevelt P. Walker, December 14, 1913, in the Waterford files.

9. Frank Aydelotte, ed. *Materials for the Study of English Literature and Composition* (New York: Oxford University Press, 1914).

10. C. S. Sembower's letter to F.A. in the Waterford files; Professor Davidson's Letter to F.B., July 22, 1957.

11. *American Oxonian*, I, No. 1 (April, 1914), 48.

12. *Ibid.*, I, No. 2 (October, 1914), 105–106.

13. *Ibid.*, I, No. 1 (April, 1914), 3–20.

14. *Ibid.*, I, No. 2 (October, 1914), 63–83, 86–101.

15. Henry Greenleaf Pearson, *Richard Cockburn Maclaurin* (New York: Macmillan, 1937), p. 91; *Technology Review*, X (1909), 331.

16. Letter from Riborg Mann in the Waterford files.

CHAPTER SEVEN   Teaching at M.I.T. (Part One)

1. Letter from Rachel Barton to F.B., September 16 (no year).

2. Letter from Rosamond Kimball to F.B., January 25, 1959.

3. May Sarton, "I Knew a Phoenix in My Youth . . . ," *New Yorker*, April 3, 1954, pp. 29–33.

4. Letter from William Ernest Hocking to F.B., June 8, 1962.

5. Letter from Henry Latimer Seaver to F.B., June 20, 1962.

6. *Ibid.*

7. Frank Aydelotte, ed., *English and Engineering*, 2d. ed. (New York: McGraw-Hill, 1923). Quotations in the three preceding paragraphs from the Introduction, pp. xiv, xv, xx.

8. Letter from F.A. to Riborg Mann, May 24, 1918.

9. Letter from Perry Molstad of A. T. and T. to F.B., July 3, 1962.

10. Letter from A. C. Vinal to F.A., September 26, 1919.

11. Letter from F.A. to C.R.M., see note 8.

12. Frank Aydelotte, *Final Report of the War Issues Course of the Students' Army Training Corps* (Washington: War Department, May, 1919), pp. 7 ff.

13. Letter from Colonel John H. Wigmore to F.A., February 14, 1919.

14. Letter from F.A. to C.R.M., May 21, 1918.

15. *Final Report*, pp. 15–17.

16. *Ibid.*, pp. 10–11, through passage by Dean Woodbridge.

17. Letter from F.A. to Professor Morris Tilley, University of Michigan, April 22, 1921.

18. *American Oxonian*, III (1916), No. 1, 31–34; No. 2, 67–72, 73–78; No. 3, 99–102; No. 4, 147–152.

19. Letters from F.A. to Theodore Roosevelt and Herbert Hoover, April 18, 1917; Hoover's reply: *American Oxonian*, IV (1917) No. 3, 111-112.

20. Letter from F.A. to Mr. Clulow, of the Oxford University Press, about *The Oxford Stamp*, May 18, 1917.

21. *Technology Review*, XX (1918), *The Oxford Stamp* reviewed by R.E.R., pp. 97–98.

22. *American Oxonian*, V, No. 1 (January, 1918), 40–41.

23. Letter from John St. Loe Strachey to F.A., May 21, 1918.

CHAPTER EIGHT   Teaching at M.I.T. (Part Two)

1. Letter from F.A. to John Nason to help him write an article on F.A. for the *American Oxonian*, February 26, 1948.

2. "Results of the British Universities' Mission," *American Oxonian*, VI (1919), No. 1.

3. Letter from F.A. to Frank Parker Day, January 20, 1919.

4. Letter from F.A. to L. W. Cronkhite, February 28, 1919.

5. Letter from F. W. Wylie to the Rhodes Trustees.

6. Letter from F.A. to Warner Fite, July 15, 1920.

7. Letter from C.R.M. to F.A., April 19, 1918.

8. Letter from F.A. to the architect, Horace Mann (brother of Riborg), February 3, 1919.

9. Nicholas Murray Butler's offer of a position at Columbia, letter to F.A. of January 8, 1920; F.A.'s reply to John Coss, January 12, 1920.

10. Offers and inquiries in a folder in F.A.'s files: "Presidency Offers and Inquiries."

11. Letter from F.A. to Warner Fite, September 23, 1920; to Joseph Swain, October 27, 1920.

12. Letter from George Herbert Palmer to F.A., October 24, 1920.

13. *American Oxonian*, VIII (1921), No. 1.

14. Letter from F.A. to Mrs. Paul Poynter, February 10, 1921.

15. Letter from F.A. to Max Farrand, April 24, 1920; to Angell and Capen, February 4, 1921; to Angell, June 23, 1921. For Fellowships founded for British holders, see Chapter 13.

16. F.A.'s account.

17. Exchange of letters between F.A. and Warner Fite: February 23, 25, 28, 1921, quoted in the following two paragraphs and part of the third.

18. F.A.'s account.

19. Letter from F.A. to M.O.A., June 29, 1921.

20. *American Oxonian*, VIII, No. 2 (April, 1921).

21. Laurence A. Crosby and Frank Aydelotte, eds., *Oxford of Today* (New York: Oxford University Press, 1923).

22. *American Oxonian*, VIII, No. 2 (April, 1921).

23. *Phoenix*, March 8, 1921. p. 1.

CHAPTER NINE   Fortunate Place and Time

1. "Sorority" was often used by outsiders, but seldom within the college.

2. "Spectators and Sports," in Frank Aydelotte, *The Oxford Stamp* (New York: Oxford University Press, 1917).

3. Edward Magill, *Sixty-Five Years in the Life of a Teacher* (Boston and New York: Houghton Mifflin, 1907), p. 223.

4. Included in the *Swarthmore College Catalogue* statement on Engineering for many years: in 1921 (Vol. XIX, No. 2.) p. 87.

5. Homer Babbidge, "*Swarthmore College in the Nineteenth Century*," typescript of unpublished doctoral dissertation, Yale Library, p. 247.

6. Magill, *op. cit.*, p. 225 and *passim*.

7. *Ibid.*, pp. 265–266.

8. *Ibid.*, p. 242.

9. George William Pierson, *Yale: College and University*, 1871–1937 (New Haven: Yale University Press, 1952). Vol. I, Chapter 17, "Honors Work at Yale." President Hadley's interest, p. 329.

10. *Ibid.*, p. 319.

11. *Ibid.*, p. 338.

12. *Ibid.*, Between 1910 and 1920 the population had increased by 15 per cent, college enrollment by 60 per cent, members of college faculties by 33.26 per cent ("college" including undergraduate departments of universities). *Historical Statistics of the United States, Colonial Times to 1957*, Prepared by the Bureau of the Census with the Cooperation of the Social Science Research Council: Table A 1–16; Table H 316–326.

13. Pierson, *op. cit.*, II, 61.

14. John Dewey, *Democracy and Education* (New York: Macmillan, 1917), pp. 105, 115, and *passim*. (The biographer's interpretation of Dewey depends partly on courses and seminars with him during two years in the Columbia Graduate School.)

15. *The Inauguration of Frank Aydelotte as President of Swarthmore College*, Supplement to Catalogue Number, *Swarthmore College Bulletin*, XIX, No. 2. (Twelfth Month, 1921), 18–19.

16. *Ibid.* "Inaugural Address," pp. 19–25. Quotation from the Address used in *Swarthmore College Catalogue*, pp. 23–24. Cf. *Catalogue*, 1922–1923, pp. 45–46; *ibid.*, 1939–1940, p. 51.

17. "New College Presidents," New York *Evening Post*, October 22, 1921 (article quoted in *School and Society*, November 5, 1921). The Presidents were John M. Thomas, State College, Penna. (October 14, 1921); Livingston Farrand, Cornell (October 19, 1921); Dr. J. A. C. Chandler, William and Mary (October 19, 1921); Frank Pierrepont Graves, University of New York at Albany (October 20, 1921); Frank Aydelotte, Swarthmore (October 22, 1921).

CHAPTER TEN   Portrait of a Man of Action

1. *Time*, June 5, 1933, p. 47.

2. Comments in interviews.

3. *An Adventure in Education: Swarthmore College under Frank Aydelotte*, by the Faculty (New York: Macmillan, 1941), p. 211.

4. *Ibid.*, Preface, written by Brand Blanshard.

5. *Report of the President*, 1921–1922, p. 8.

6. *Ibid.*, 1939, p. 16.

7. *Swarthmore Remembered*, published by the College in 1964: "Chance Encounter," pp. 124–125.

8. *Phoenix*, February 9, 1926, p. 4.

9. *Ibid.*, September 22, 1921, p. 1, "Intensity"; October 4, 1921, p. 2, "Intellectual Curiosity"; October 17, 1922, p. 2, "Serious Athletics."

10. *Ibid.*, June 12, 1922, p. 3.

11. *Ibid.*

12. Marion Hall Holland to Everett Hunt.

13. *Phoenix*, February 22, 1922, pp. 1, 2.

14. *Swarthmore College Bulletin*, Alumni Issue (February, 1957), pp. 3, 28. Laurence Lafore, at that time associate professor of history.

15. Typescript in the Aydelotte files.

16. *Phoenix*, June 13, 1921, p. 4.

17. *Ibid.*, May 23, 1922, p. 6.

CHAPTER ELEVEN   The Start at Swarthmore

1. *Phoenix*, March 7, 1922, Editorial, p. 2.

2. *Catalogue of Swarthmore College*, 1922–1923, pp. 45–46; 1923–1924, pp. 45–49.

3. *Bulletin of the National Research Council*, VII, Part 2, No. 40 (January, 1924), 1–57.

4. *Ibid.*, X, Part 2, No. 52 (April, 1925), 1–96.

5. Conference in March, 1925, at the University of Iowa.

6. *Report of the President*, 1923–1924, pp. 7–9.

7. *Catalogue*, 1923–1924, pp. 27–34.

8. *Report of the President*, 1923–1924, pp. 10–12.

9. *Ibid.*, 1922–1923, pp. 9, 10.

10. *Phoenix*, September 25, 1923, pp. 1, 3.

11. *Report of the President*, 1924–1925, p. 17.

12. *Ibid.*, 1923–1924, pp. 13–14.

13. *Ibid.*, 1921–1922, pp. 18–19.

14. *Phoenix*, October 17, 1922, p. 2.

15. Philadelphia *Evening Bulletin*, October 12, 1922; New York *Evening Journal*, April 9, 1923.

16. At Alumni Banquet, February 24, 1923; reported in the *Phoenix*, February 27, 1923, p. 4.

17. *Report of the President*, 1922–1923, pp. 22, 27; *ibid.*, 1924–1925, p. 23.

18. *Ibid.*, 1921–1922, p. 12.

19. *Phoenix*, November 22, 1921, pp. 2, 6.

20. *Ibid.*, December 6, 1921, p. 1.

21. Prom held on March 30, 1922; reported in the *Phoenix*, April 18, 1922, p. 3.

22. *Report of the President*, 1922–1923, p. 13; reference includes quotations in the next paragraph.

23. Supplement to *Friends Intelligencer*, Proceedings of Friends General Conference, 1922, pp. 25–27.

24. *Report of the President*, 1923–1924, pp. 12–13.

25. *Ibid.*, 1924–1925, pp. 6–10.

26. See Chapter 12.

27. Philadephia *Evening Bulletin*, February 5, 1923.

28. *Ibid.*, February 15, 1924.

29. *Ibid.*, April 15, 1924.

30. F.A. to M.O.A., January 19, 1922.

31. *Phoenix*, January 8, 1924, p. 2; Mrs. Aydelotte spoke on the radio to announce the formation of the Women's City Club, with 1,250 Charter Members.

32. F.A. to M.O.A., from Cleveland, March 13, 1925.

33. F.A. to R. S. Ellison, Casper, Wyoming, October 8, 1923.

34. F.A. to F.B., September 24, 1954.

35. "Thirty Years of Florida Vacations," typescript by F.A., no date.

36. *Frank Aydelotte*—In Memoriam. Ozone Annual Meeting, December 6, 1957.

37. *Report of the President*, 1924–1925, p. 11.

38. Abraham Flexner, *I Remember* (New York: Simon and Schuster, 1940), pp. 322–332.

39. Frank Aydelotte, *Breaking the Academic Lockstep* (New York: Harper, 1944), pp. 35–36. F.A.'s memory, after fifteen years, has here deceived him. The "much needed financial assistance" was not at stake in this meeting, but had been granted in

February. The meeting was held on May 13, and the visitor was Dr. Wickliffe Rose, President of the General Education Board (*Phoenix*, May 19, 1925).

40. *Phoenix*, March 3, 1925; President's speech of February 28, 1925, reported on p. 1.

41. *Phoenix*, March 31, 1925, p. 6.

42. *Report of the President*, 1924–1925, pp. 19, 21–22.

43. Abraham Flexner, *An Autobiography* (New York: Simon and Schuster, 1960), p. 45.

CHAPTER TWELVE   On His Mettle

1. Appointments to the faculty, 1925–31 (* = Stayed until retirement; R.S. Rhodes Scholar): *Chemistry:* *Edward H. Cox, *Duncan Graham Foster; *Civil Engineering:* *Scott B. Lilly; *Economics:* *Herbert F. Fraser, Patrick Malin, *Clair Wilcox; *Education:* Frances Burlingame; *English:* (R.S.) Frank Parker Day, *Everett L. Hunt, (R.S.) Alan Valentine, *Elizabeth Cox Wright; *French:* Louis Cons, *Edith Philips, Margaret Pitkin; *German:* *Lydia Baer; *Greek:* *(R.S.) L. R. Shero; *History:* *Mary Albertson, (R.S.) Troyer Steele Anderson, *Frederick J. Manning; *Mathematics:* *Arnold Dresden, *Michael Kovalenko; *Music:* *Alfred J. Swan; *Philosophy:* (R.S.) Brand Blanshard, (R.S.) George Thomas; *Physics:* *(R.S.) Milan W. Garrett; *Political Science:* *J. Roland Pennock; *Zoology:* Detlev Bronk, *Walter J. Scott; *Librarian:* *Charles B. Shaw.

2. *Phoenix*, March 2, 1926, p. 3.

3. *World's Work*, May 1929, p. 52.

4. *Ibid.*

5. *Ibid.*, p. 53.

6. *Ibid.*, pp. 53–54.

7. *Ibid.*, p. 56.

8. *Ibid.*

9. *Report of the President*, 1926–1927, pp. 8–9.

10. *English Journal*, April, 1933, pp. 310–319.

11. *Minutes of the Board of Managers*, IX (December 6, 1927), pp. 308–309.

12. F.A. to Charles F. Jenkins, December 27, 1927.

13. Caroline Worth to Frank and Marie Aydelotte; steamer letter, undated, addressed to the S.S. *Aquitania*, sailing January 27, 1928.

14. *Minutes of the Board of Managers*, IX (March 6, 1928), 386. Favorable report on honors work presented and approved.

15. Robert C. Brooks, *Reading for Honors at Swarthmore* (New York: Oxford University Press, 1927), Introduction, pp. v–vii.

16. *Catalogue*, 1922–1923, pp. 45–46.

17. *Ibid.*, 1930–1931, pp. 43–44

18. *Ibid.*, pp. 46, 47–53.

19. *Report of the President*, 1930–1931, pp. 38–39; 1921–1939, pp. 51–52.

20. See note 14.

21. *Catalogue*, 1927–1928, p. 49. First seniors in courses to take comprehensives, Class of 1928.

22. Alexander Dunlop Lindsay, *The Essentials of Democracy* (London: Oxford University Press, 1929).

23. *New York Times Book Review* on *The Problem of Unemployment*, June 28, 1931.

24. *Report of the President*, 1927–1928, pp. 8–9.

25. *Ibid.*, 1929–1930, pp. 17–18; pamphlet written by Kenneth Meiklejohn and Peter Nehemkis.

26. Edward Martin Biological Laboratory first in use in 1937–1938.

27. *Report of the President*, 1929–1930, pp. 7–11.

28. Subsidy for honors work granted in 1925.

29. *Report of the President*, 1936, p. 5.

30. *Phoenix*, March 4, 1930, p. 4.

31. *Report of the President*, 1921–1939, p. 71.

32. *Ibid.*, 1929–1930, p. 12.

33. Maurice Cramer to F.B., September 12, 1955, p. 1.

34. *Ibid.*, p. 2.

35. *Ibid.*, p. 1.

36. *Ibid.*

37. *Report of the President*, 1930–1931, pp. 7, 8, 9.

38. *Ibid.*, pp. 19, 20.

39. *Ibid.*, pp. 17, 10.

40. *Ibid.*, pp. 11, 12.

41. Typescript of speech.

42. *Phoenix*, September 25, 1928, p. 4.

43. Quoted in the *Phoenix*, February 15, 1927, p. 2.

CHAPTER THIRTEEN   Adventures with Foundations

1. *Christian Science Monitor*, March 14, 1923.

2. Article published in *Scribner's*, June, 1923; summary in *American Oxonian*, July, 1923, pp. 69–72. Quotations in this and the next paragraph are from the summary.

3. Letter from Dr. George Parkin to F.A., September 12, 1918.

4. Letter from Sir Sidney Lee to F.A., March 21, 1923.

5. Memorandum on "Benjamin Franklin Scholarships," May 13, 1923, included in a letter of that date from F.A. to Beardsley Ruml.

6. Conferences in England, July–August, 1923, with: (A. E. Morgan, Professor of English, University College, Exeter, New York, July 13); C. H. Sampson, Principal B.N.C., Oxford, July 23; A. L. Smith, Master of Balliol, Oxford, July 24; Reverend Hudson Shaw, Oxford, July 25; Joseph Wells, Warden of Wadham, Oxford, July 25; W. S. Adams, Professor at All Souls, Oxford, July 25; Miss Penrose, Principal of Somerville, Oxford, July 25; E. S. Craig, Assistant Registrar, Oxford, July 26; Sir Charles Firth, Regius Professor of History, Oxford, July 26; Sir Herbert Warren, President of Magdalen, Oxford, July 26; Buchanan Riddell, Principal of Hertford, London, July 27; J. St. Loe Strachey, Editor of the *Spectator*, London, July 27; Albert Mansbridge, Secretary of the Workers Education Association, London, July 27; Sir Frank Heath, Secretary to the Department of Scientific and Industrial Research, London, July 27; G. Dawson, Editor of *The Times*, London, July 27, and August 3; Sir Michael Sadler, Principal of University College, Oxford, July 28; Sir Henry Miers, Vice-Chancellor of University of Manchester, July 28; Ernest Barker, Principal of King's College, London, Dulwich, July 29; Sir Walter Fletcher, Secretary of the Medical Research Council, London, July 30; Sir Arthur Shipley, Master of Christ's College, Cambridge, July 30; Peter Giles, Master of Emmanuel College, Cambridge, July 30; Dr. Pearce, Master of Corpus Christi,

Cambridge, Vice-Chancellor, July 31; Arthur Goodhart, Fellow of Corpus Christi, Cambridge, and in charge of Davisson Scholarships, July 31; Sir Hugh Anderson, Master of Caius College, Cambridge, V.C.-Elect, July 31; Professor Gilbert Murray, Oxford University, London, August 1; Dr. Alexander Hill, Secretary, Universities' Bureau of British Empire, August 2; Miss Caroline Spurgeon, Professor of English Literature, Bedford, College, London, August 3; Captain Beeman, Sir Henry Babington-Smith, T. B. Hohler, London, August 3; Lionel Curtis, Irish Office, London, August 3 and 13; Dr. Farnell, Vice-Chancellor, Oxford, August 4; Lord Charnwood, London, August 7; Lord Milner, Rhodes Trust, August 8; Mr. Barnard, Assistant to Lloyd and in active charge of administration of maintenance grants for scientific research, August 10; Sir Gregory Foster, Principal of University College London, August 12; Dublin Conference, August 16: Professor John Joly, Trinity College; Professor A. W. Conway, F.R.S., University College, President D. J. Coffey, University College; N. S. Loughnane, English Civil Service, on duty at Vice Regal Lodge, Dublin; The Governor-General of Ireland, Vice Regal Lodge, Dublin, August 16–17.

7. Letter from F.A. to Dean Woodbridge of Columbia, September 1, 1923.

8. Letter from F.A. to R. H. Simpson, January 24, 1924.

9. Beardsley Ruml to F.A., April 23, 1924.

10. Letter from F.A. to Dr. Max Farrand, April 24, 1920.

11. Article giving account of Prince's interest, his meeting Mr. Harkness, etc.: Oscar N. Solbert, "Continuing the Rhodes Scholar Idea," *World's Work*. July, 1926, pp. 344–346.

12. Edward S. Harkness to F.A., March 11, 1925.

13. Max Farrand "The Commonwealth Fund Fellowships," *Educational Record*, July, 1925, pp. 260–263.

14. Max Farrand to F.A., February 25, 1925.

15. From memorial to Senator Guggenheim read at Trustees' Meeting on March 20, 1942; Printed in *Reports* for 1941 and 1942, p. 9.

16. Carroll Wilson to F.A., February 25, 1924.

17. Wilson to Senator Guggenheim, April 10, 1924.

18. Wilson to F.A., May 5, 1924.

19. Wilson to F.A., "Sunday"; in F.A.'s writing, "before May 22, 1924."

20. Wilson to Senator Guggenheim, May 9, 1924.

21. Senator Guggenheim to F.A., June 30, 1924.

22. F.A. to Wilson, August 19, 1924.

23. Unpublished typescript by Aydelotte on Endowments for Foreign Study, Sec. VII, p. 22.

24. Henry Moe, in report of September 18, 1924, to F.A., refers to "your memorandum of August 19 to Mr. Wilson," p. 1, with four suggestions noted. Copy of memorandum in F.A.'s files.

25. Moe to F.A., September 18, 1924 (dated in F.A.'s writing), p. 1.

26. *Ibid.*, pp. 7–9; interview with Dean Ford, September 17, 1924.

27. Second report, pp. 7–9, dated by F.A. "Sept., 1924." Interview with President Vinson on September 25.

28. *Ibid.*, pp. 10–13.

29. *Ibid.*, p. 1.

30. F.A. to Wilson, October 16, 1924.

31. Printed "Outline of Purposes," without date or numbered pages, but refers to the first awards to be made for 1926–1927; this quotation from p. 4 (supplied).

32. *American Oxonian*, April, 1925, p. 33.

CHAPTER FOURTEEN   Swarthmore: 1931–1940

1. *Report of the President*, 1931–1932, p. 6.

2. *Ibid.*, 1939, reviewing the period 1921–1939; Report of the Comptroller, pp. 72–73.

3. *Ibid.*, 1933, p. 10: F.A. to Clair Wilcox, Secretary of the Faculty, May 18, 1833.

4. *Ibid.*, Charles F. Jenkins to Clair Wilcox, July 10, 1933.

5. *Ibid.*, 1934, p. 7.

6. F.A. to his brother Will, June 18, 1933.

7. *Phoenix*, October 11, 1932.

8. *Catalogue*, 1927–1928, pp. 44, 49.

9. *Ibid.*, 1934–1935, p. 39.

10. Conference held at Cornell University, November, 1935. Frank Aydelotte's paper was published in the *Journal of Proceedings and Addresses of the Association of American Universities*, November, 1935, pp. 102–114.

11. *Ibid.*, p. 110.

12. *Ibid.*, p. 111.

13. *Ibid.*, p. 112.

14. *Ibid.*, p. 114.

15. *Phoenix*, November 24, 1931, p. 3.

16. Delta Zeta.

17. *Phoenix*, November 17, 1931, p. 4.

18. *Ibid.*

19. *Ibid.*

20. *Ibid.*, January 12, 1932, p. 1.

21. *Ibid.*, December 15, 1931, p. 4.

22. *Ibid.*, March 1, 1932, p. 1. These figures represent a plurality for sophomore bidding, but not the necessary two-thirds majority. The question was given to a committee to settle, including the Dean of Women, alumnae, and students, who decided in favor of a year's moratorium.

23. *Ibid.*, October 18, 1932; Social Reconstruction Program described.

24. Phoenix, December 13, 1933, p. 1.

25. Cf. Everett L. Hunt, *The Revolt of the College Intellectual* (New York: Human Relations Aids, 1963), pp. 58–67. The author, Dean and professor of English at Swarthmore for many years, knew students well.

26. *Swarthmore Remembered*, published by the College in 1964, p. 113.

27. *Ibid.*

28. *Ibid.*, pp. 114–115.

29. *Phoenix*, February 26, 1965, p. 1; report of dinner on February 23. Hunt, *op. cit.*, pp. 54–56.

30. Mimeographed memorandum to the Board of Managers from William Tomlinson.

31. Mimeographed memorandum from Charles F. Jenkins to the Board of Managers.

32. *Report of the President*, 1935 pp. 5–6.

33. *Architectural Record*. LXXIX (May, 1936), 368–373; *Garnet Letter*, May, 1936, pp. 3, 8; *Report of the President*, 1935, pp. 10–11.

34. *Ibid.*, 1936, p. 5.

35. *Garnet Letter*, May 1936, pp. 3–4.

36. *Ibid.*, December, 1936, pp. 3–4.

37. *Report of the President*, 1938, p. 15.

38. Robert S. Woodworth, *Contemporary Schools of Psychology* (New York: Ronald, 1931), p. 93.

39. *Ibid.*, p. 116.

40. F.A. to Fred M. Kirby, May 22, 1929.

41. This did not happen. The citation is from the *Phoenix*, April 29, 1930.

42. F.A. to Fred M. Kirby, June 11, 1934.

43. *Garnet Letter*, January, 1938, p. 2.

44. *Phoenix*, October 5, 1937, p. 1.

45. *Report of the President*, 1938, pp. 17–18.

46. *Ibid.*, 1937, pp. 10–11.

47. Maurice Cramer to F.B., September 12, 1955.

48. Walter J. Greenleaf, *College Salaries 1936*, Department of the Interior, Bulletin 1937, No. 9 (Washington: Government Printing Office), p. 23.

49. Conference plan developed at Rollins: students spent six hours per working day in three two-hour conferences.

50. John A. Rice, *I Came Out of the Eighteenth Century* (New York: Harper, 1942), p. 311.

51. *Bulletin of the American Association of University Professors*, XIX, No. 7 (November, 1933), 416–438.

52. Rice, *op. cit.*, pp. 309, 312, 318, 327–329.

53. *Harper's Magazine*, April, 1936, pp. 516–530.

54. Rice, *op. cit.*, pp. 338–340.

55. M.O.A. to Maurice Cramer, April 3, 1932.

56. Published in the University's Monthly Review, *Revista Mensuel*, IV, No. 19 (May, 1932), 16–18.

57. F.A.'s sketch for a proposed autobiography.

58. F.A. to Abraham Flexner, undated (January–February, 1938).

59. *American Historical Review*, XLVIII, No. 1 (October, 1942), 1–19. Mr. G. R. C. Conway is described here as one who "has performed the miracle of making himself at the same time a successful business man, a sound scholar, and a book collector who knows the books which he collects," p. 1.

60. The Very Reverend Sir George Adam Smith of Aberdeen and Lady Smith; Dr. Robert Sangster Rait of Glasgow, late Historiographer-Royal for Scotland, and Mrs. Rait (soon to be Sir Robert and Lady Rait); the distinguished chemist Sir James Irvine of St. Andrews and Lady Irvine; and the Canadian-born geologist Sir Thomas Holland of Edinburgh and Lady Holland. Maurice Cramer's typescript, "A Cat May Look . . . ," p. 3.

61. *Ibid.*, pp. 3, 5–6.

62. Abraham Flexner, *An Autobiography* (New York: Simon and Schuster, 1960), p. 252.

63. *The Times*, June 24, 1937, p. 11.

64. Barbara Ballou to her parents, October 15 and 22, 1939.

65. *Phoenix*, October 17, 1939. "The President's Message," p. 4.

66. *Ibid.*

CHAPTER FIFTEEN   The Institute for Advanced Study

1. *I.A.S. Bulletin* No. 1 (December, 1930), p. 8.

2. Flexner to F.A., February 23, 1939.

3. Abraham Flexner, *I Remember* (New York: Simon and Schuster, 1940), p. 355.

4. Abraham Flexner, *Universities: American, English, German* (New York: Oxford University Press, 1930), p. 45.

5. *Ibid.*, p. 23.

6. *Ibid.*, pp. 217–218.

7. Flexner, *I Remember*, p. 52. See also *I.A.S. Bulletin*, No. 1, pp. 10–11.

8. Flexner, *Universities*, p. 218.

9. Flexner, *I Remember*, pp. 358, 359, 361.

10. Abraham Flexner, *Daniel Coit Gilman* (New York: Harcourt, Brace, 1946), pp. 53–109.

11. *I.A.S. Bulletin*, No. 1, p. 18.

12. Flexner, *I Remember*, pp. 371–372.

13. Abraham Flexner, *An Autobiography* (New York: Simon and Schuster, 1960), pp. 257, 259.

14. *I.A.S. Bulletin* No. 3 (February, 1934), p. 2.

15. *Ibid.*, No. 2 (February, 1933), p. 7.

16. Flexner, *I Remember*, p. 395.

17. Flexner, *Autobiography*, p. 259.

18. Raymond B. Fosdick, *Adventure in Giving* (New York: Harper and Row, 1962), pp. 158–159, 321; *I.A.S. Bulletins*: 1933, p. 3; 1934, p. 2; 1935, p. 2; 1936, p. 2 (adds pledge which is repeated through 1941); 1937, p. 3; 1938, p. 3; 1939, p. 4; 1940, p. 3; 1941, p. 3.

19. Walter J. Greenleaf, *College Salaries 1936*, Department of the Interior, Bulletin 1937, No. 9 (Washington: Government Printing Office), figures for 1930–1931, p. 27.

20. *I.A.S. Bulletin* No. 1, pp. 26, 28.

21. Flexner, *I Remember*, p. 365.

22. *I.A.S. Bulletin*, No. 3, pp. xiii–xiv.

23. *Ibid.*, pp. 5–7.

24. Flexner, *I Remember*, pp. 372–374.

25. *I.A.S. Bulletin*, No. 5, p. 10.

26. *Ibid.*, pp. 11–12.

27. Flexner, *I Remember*, p. 389.

28. *Ibid.*, p. 369.

29. *Ibid.*, pp. 361–363, 393–394.

30. Helen Christine Bennett, Article on Louis Bamberger and Felix Fuld, *American Magazine*, June, 1923, pp. 72–73, 121–122.

31. F.A. to Herbert Maass, March 16, 1946.

32. From a description by Beatrice M. Stern.

33. Flexner, *I Remember*, p. 392.

34. *Ibid.*, p. 366.

35. Flexner, *I Remember*, pp. 287–288.

36. Recorded by Mrs. Stern.

37. Flexner, *I Remember*, pp. 389–390.

38. *Ibid.*, pp. 396–397.

39. Copy in F.A.'s files.

40. Einstein to F.A., March 26, 1939.

41. Flexner to Louis Bamberger, August 1, 1933.

42. F.A.'s trip to Mexico in 1939 is discussed in Chapter 14.

43. Flexner to F.A., August 28, 1939.
44. Flexner, *I Remember*, p. 393.
45. *Ibid.*, p. 394.
46. New York *Times*, October 17, 1939.
47. Flexner, *I Remember*, p. 395.
48. *Ibid.*, p. 392.
49. One draft in F.A.'s files.
50. Flexner to F.A., November 15, 1939.
51. Compare *I.A.S. Bulletin* No. 3, pp. xi, xiii; No. 9, pp. viii, ix, xi–xiii.
52. Members of the Department of the League of Nations: Alexander Loveday, Great Britain; John H. Chapman, New Zealand; Paul Deperon, Belgium; Folke Hilgerdt, Sweden; Martin Hill, Eire; Mrs. P. W. van Ittersum, Netherlands; Miroslav Kriz, Czechoslovakia; John Lindberg, Sweden; Constantine F. MacGuire, Eire; Ragnar Nurske, Estonia; Jacques J. Polak, Netherlands; J. Ansgar E. Rosenborg, Sweden; Percy G. Watterson, Great Britain. *I.A.S. Bulletin*, No. 10, p. xviii.
53. Letter from Carl J. Hambro.
54. F.A. to Louis Bamberger, November 18, 1940.
55. Appendix to Minutes of Trustees' Meeting, May 19, 1941, Report of the Director, p. 11.
56. Houghton to F.A., May 20, 1941.
57. Appendix to Minutes of Trustees' Meeting, May 18, 1942, Report of the Director.
58. *Ibid.*, October 15, 1942, Report of the Director.
59. *I.A.S. Bulletin*, No. 12 (October, 1946), "Report of the Director."
60. *Ibid.*, No. 10. (October, 1941), p. 3 (most recent statement of full-time principle).
61. *Ibid.*, No. 12, p. 10.
62. Appendix to Minutes of Trustees' Meeting, January 25, 1943, Report of the Director.
63. *I.A.S. Bulletin*, No. 11 (March, 1945), p. 5.
64. Appendix to the Minutes of Trustees' Meeting, January 25, 1943, Report of the Director, pp. 2.
65. Flexner to F.A., May 7, 11, 27, 1943.
66. Lowe's title, continued: *A Paleographical Guide to Latin Manuscripts Prior to the Ninth Century*, all published by the Clarendon Press, Oxford.
67. *Damascus: Studies in Architecture;* after Herzfeld retired he brought out Vol. III, 1946, and Vol. IV, 1947.
68. This quotation and the two following are from F.A. to Flexner, December 22, 1942.
69. Flexner to F.A., January 17, 1944.
70. Appendix to Trustees' Minutes, April 18, 1944, Report of the Director, pp. 3–8.
71. Quoted by Herbert Maass in the report of the Committee on Institute Policy, in the Trustees' Minutes, January 19, 1945.
72. Faculty luncheon held on November 6, 1944; faculty held a special meeting on November 20, 1944, to pass the resolution quoted in the text, also reported in Trustees' Minutes, January 19, 1945.
73. Minutes of Special Meeting of the Trustees, March 2, 1945, pp. 1–9 (from longer version of Minutes, not in shorter version; both in F.A.'s files).
74. Minutes of the Corporation, April 20, 1945, p. 3.

75. Cf. Flexner, *I Remember*, pp. 58, 208, 322–323, 346, 393, with *Autobiography*, p. 256.

76. F.A. to F.B., July 28, 1955, p. 2.

77. Notes of F.A. on interview with a Trustee, dated November 20, 1944; from Mrs. Stern.

78. Minutes of special meeting of the faculty, November 20, 1944.

79. Appendix to Trustees' Minutes, April 18, 1944, Report of the Director, p. 8.

80. Appendix to Trustees' Minutes, April 20, 1945, Report of the Director, pp. 4–6.

81. Minutes of the Faculty Meeting, May 22, 1945, pp. 1–7.

82. Appendix to Trustees' Minutes, April 18, 1947, Report of the Director, p. 6.

83. Obituary of John von Neumann: New York *Times*, February 9, 1957, p. 19.

84. *Ibid.*

85. Marston Morse to the Hon. Herman Erikson, Minister of Sweden, January 18, 1946.

86. Appendix I to Trustees' Minutes, April 18, 1947, Report of the Director, pp. 1–6.

87. *Ibid.*, pp. 13–14.

88. New York *Times*, October 16, 1947, p. 29.

CHAPTER SIXTEEN   The Commission on Palestine

1. Bartley C. Crum, *Behind the Silken Curtain*, (New York: Simon & Schuster, 1947), p. 10.

2. *Ibid.*, p. 11.

3. R. H. S. Crossman, *Palestine Mission* (London: 1947), p. 21.

4. *Ibid*, p. 30.

5. Crum, *op. cit.*, p. 7.

6. *Ibid.*, pp. 21–22.

7. *Ibid.*, p. 28.

8. Frank Aydelotte, "Palestine Diary." This is an unpublished journal in which Frank wrote daily entries on the commission's tour, beginning with the departure from New York. It was written in a succession of notebooks, each of which, when completed, was despatched to Marie at home. In typed form it runs to 101 pages.

9. The story has been told by Rebecca West in *The Meaning of Treason*, (London, 1948), Chapter 2.

10. Crossman, *op. cit.*, p. 118.

11. *Ibid.*, p. 128.

12. *Ibid.*, p. 144.

13. Crossman, *op. cit.*, p. 173.

14. Department of State, *Report of Anglo-American Committee of Inquiry* (Washington: Government Printing Office, 1946), p. 2. Hereafter cited as *Report*.

15. Norman Bentwich, *Israel*, (London: Benn, 1952) p. 36.

16. Crum, *op. cit.*, p. 85.

17. London *Times*, November 19, 1945.

18. *Report*, p. 19.

19. *Ibid*, p. 37.

20. Crum, *op. cit.*, p. 150.

21. Crossman, *op. cit.*, pp. 102–103.

22. Quoted by N. Bentwich, *Fulfilment in the Promised Land,* (London: Soncino Press, 1938) p. 22.

23. *Report,* p. 25.

24. Quoted by N. Bentwich, *Israel,* p. 66.

25. *Report,* p. 40.

26. London *Times,* November 19, 1945.

27. Bentwich, *Israel,* p. 142.

28. *Ibid.*

29. Figures reported in *Information Please Yearbook* for 1967.

30. *Report,* pp. 42–43.

31. Crossman, *op. cit.*, p. 131.

32. *Ibid.*, p. 167.

33. *Fortnightly Review*, CLXV, June, 1946, p. 384.

34. *Time,* May 13, 1946.

CHAPTER SEVENTEEN   The Quiet Years

1. *American Oxonian,* XXXIV, October, 1947, p. 202.

2. *Ibid.*, p. 205.

3. *Ibid.*, p. 208.

4. *Ibid.*, p. 206.

5. *Ibid.* XL, October, 1953, p. 168. Joseph Sagmaster (Ohio and Lincoln, '25) was the reporter for the *American Oxonian* of both the Princeton and the Oxford reunions. I am at several points indebted to his excellent articles, (October, 1947, and October, 1953).

6. *Ibid.*, LII, October, 1965, p. 284.

7. *Ibid.* XLIV, April, 1957, p. 60.

INDEX

Abbett, Emma, 172, 177, 255
Acheson, Dean, 347
Adamic, Louis, 287
Adams, J. D., 407
Albertson, M., 414
Allen, C. K., 352, 354, 388, 390, 395
Alumnae: in fraternity crisis, 270
Alumni: criticism of Swarthmore, 272; pride in college, 276; executive secretary, 278
American Oxonian: founding of, 114; the M.I.T. period, 128; F.A.'s withdrawal, 148
American Philosophical Society, xxii, 204
Amery, L.C.M.S., 353, 391
Anderson, T. S., 414
Angell, J. R., 145, 237, 283
Arabs: case for in Palestine, 366; their intransigence, 350, 356, 377
Arnold, M., 112, 209
Athletics at Swarthmore, 196
Attlee, C. R., 343–344, 376
Aydelotte, Frank: birth, 8; boyhood, 9 ff; in high school, 15; at Indiana University, 20 ff; interest in football, 25, 30, 32, 48, 50, 52; at Normal School, 34; at Harvard, 40 ff; at Louisville High School, 46 ff; competes for Rhodes Scholarship, 48–51; first days at Oxford, 58 ff; visit to Paris, 71; to Germany, 81 ff; marriage, 94; takes B. Litt. degree, 100; returns to Indiana, 102; methods of teaching, 104, 181; year's leave in Oxford, 108 ff; founds *American Oxonian*, 114; moves to M.I.T., 118; American Secretary for Rhodes Trustees, 133; invited to

Swarthmore, 146; inaugural at Swarthmore, 160; relations with faculty, 163 ff, 172; as administrator, 168; delegating responsibility, 173; as a colleague, 173 ff; as a conserver of time, 177; relations with students, 178, 202; relations with Managers, 184 ff, 218 ff; relations with alumni, 186; choosing new faculty, 210; the Honors program, 147, 160, 188 ff, 212 ff, 221 ff; as fund raiser, 229; vacations, 232; educational theory, 224 and *passim;* work on British fellowships, 241 ff; on Guggenheim fellowships, 244–254; personal finances, 284; in Mexico, 288; D.C.L., Oxford, 291; resignation at Swarthmore, 292; takes reins at Institute, 320; defense of humanities, 325; the war years, 326 ff; Institute business, 330; retirement problems, 335; two years of grace, 339; contribution to I.A.S., 341; on Palestine Commission, 343 ff; London and a collapse, 351; in Cairo, 355; in Palestine, 357 ff; in Lausanne, 360 ff; Princeton reunion, 382; routine of later years, 385; loss of Marie, 387; Oxford reunion, 390; knighthood, 392; death, 394; the unity of his life, 396; his educational ideal, 398; personal quality, 399; a happy man, 403
Aydelotte, Marie: 57, 61, 74–76, 79, 80, 82, 85, 88–89, 90; marriage, 94 ff; collaboration with F.A., 99; accident in harbor, 100; an operation, 140; interest in Vedanta, 148; President's wife, 166, 176, 203 ff; PresidentWomen's City Club, 204; on vacation, 233; at Oxford, 291; at Olden Manor,